Tell All I'm Not That Way Anymore

Dr. Bennie T. Davis, Sr

Copyright © 2022 Dr. Bennie T. Davis. All rights reserved.
Empowerment Publishing & Multi-Media
ISBN: 9798865365990

Note: Some of the names in this book have been changed to protect the privacy of the people involved.

DEDICATION

This book is dedicated to my mother, Bobbie Jean Davis, and my grandchildren Ja'Niyah Davis, Kehlani Fletcher and Messiah Davis.

Table of Contents

INTRODUCTION v
1. PLAY THE HAND GOD DEALT YOU 1
2. WHERE DO I GO FROM HERE? 18
3. THE LIFE OF CRIME 37
4. ACCOMPLISHING THE IMPOSSIBLE 55
5. DEATH KNOCKING AT THE DOOR 74
6. A PRAYING MOTHER 99
7. OVERCOMING PUBLIC OPINION 115
8. ON THE ROAD TO RECOVERY 138
9. WHAT HAPPENED 152
10. DARKNESS SHATTERED MY LIFE 177
11. HE WILL NEVER QUIT 199
12. UNQUALIFIED 230
13. NEVER GIVE UP 264
14. AFTER 294
15. FEAR OR WORRY WILL NEVER STOP ME 315
16. THE STORY BEHIND MY LAUGH 344
17. TOMORROW 382
18. SURVIVING THE THREE H'S BECAUSE OF THE FORTH ("H: HATERS, HINDERER, HELLRAISER... HELPER-JESUS!") 413

ABOUT THE AUTHOR 483

INTRODUCTION

I, Bennie T. Davis, grew up in a small town called Marion, South Carolina. I am the oldest of three children. As an infant, my destiny was already chosen for me. My mother was told I would not live for more than a week. The school system failed me because they felt I would never be anything and that my mother should give up on me. They wanted her to send me to a facility that could better help me due to my disability of being autistic and having epilepsy. I was a young man who went from special education to regular classes and excelled in getting my doctorate. Throughout my education, some supportive teachers helped me along the way.

The streets tried to consume me because I made a lot of money selling drugs while in college and was able to live a lavish life and become a business owner. I later learned that was not life for me. There were too many people that wanted to harm me, see me do bad and spend the rest of my life behind bars because of envy and greed. A so-called friend set me up, and I was shot and left for dead. A young man that I loved so dearly, as a brother, allowed his own anger to falsify statements against me and my mother, stating that we physically abused him.

With all my troubles came strength, and God had a plan for me. I became a mentor and even coached sports since I could no longer play a sport I loved. People I thought were on my side tried to set me up for the ultimate decline. People in the community did not want to see me be a great church pastor or a leader for the city of Marion.

At every turn, someone was trying to knock me down. In my quest to do what the Lord called me to do, I faced other Christians who wanted to see me fail for their own selfish reasons. They didn't want to see me prosper. They did not want this Godly man to lead the people and succeed. They were consumed by my past and hearsay. Through all of my transgressions, I did not allow my past to haunt me. Although they did not want me to succeed, God still prevailed. I have a praying mother, prayer warriors and an awesome God and angels who protected me through it all.

God is almighty. He is greater than any man, woman, judge, attorney, law enforcement, disability, or schoolteacher. He will make a way out of no way. When people give up on you, slander your name and accuse you of the unthinkable, always know that there is a higher power that is so great that he will bring you through the storm. God will not put you through any more than you can bear.

When you think you are at the end, and all you can see is a roadblock, God will remove all those barriers and clear the pathway. Trouble doesn't always last, although sometimes it seems that way. You can do anything through Christ who strengthens you. Don't give up. He will never fail you, for Joshua 21:45 says, "There failed not ought of any good thing which the Lord has spoken unto the house of Israel, all came to pass." This means his good promises to you will come to pass. God never fails. Trust in the Lord with all your heart; he will make light in your darkest days.

He will see you through it in his own time. I was hard like a coffee bean in hot boiling water, but instead of the heat changing me, I changed it and the environment around me. My disability and what others viewed of me did not overcome me; I overcame it. I made it, and so can you. Never let anyone make you feel that you are less than them. Anything in life is possible.

You always have choices in life. Sometimes you choose wrong, but it's never too late to change the path that life leads you.

The devil did not want Bennie T. Davis to exist. He did everything he could to stop my existence. The Devil wanted me dead or in prison, for some crimes I did not commit. The Devil didn't want me to be Mayor or a pastor. He tried to stop me from helping the youth with pretrial intervention. The devil tried to intervene by having a young man falsely accuse me of beating him. He even tried to constantly stop me from volunteering with the youth on the basketball team and at the recreational center. He did everything that he could do to stop someone from being delivered. He did not want me to live a comfortable, productive life. But, through it all, look at what was accomplished. Through all of my trials and tribulations… Look at God. The battle was not mine to fight. God won the fight.

This book encourages everyone that it's not over till God says it's over. "When thou passest through the waters. I will be with thee; and through the rivers, they shall not overflow thee; when thou walkest through the fire, thou shalt not be burned; neither shall the flame kindle upon thee, for I am the Lord thy God." Isaiah 43:2

Some of the names in this book have been changed to protect the privacy of the people involved.

1. PLAY THE HAND GOD DEALT YOU

Rachel was the younger daughter and was exceptionally beautiful. She had it going on. Jacob worked for seven years for Rachel, his wife-to-be. Leah was the daughter who was always overlooked. The family members passed over Leah to get to her sister Rachel. If any of them had walked away, it should have been Leah.

Leah was not just ugly, but she was also crossed-eyed. Jacob fell in love with Rachel the first time he laid his eyes on her. Jacob hated Leah, like everyone else, only because she was ugly. Regardless, Leah played the hand that God dealt her, and because of Leah's actions, she became Jacob's first wife.

Leah was hated; God was with her. In the end, Leah played her hand correctly and overcame it. This summary may be read in its entirety in the Bible Genesis 29:16-35. Leah's story reminds me of how my life started, but I always played my hand and overcame in life. From the start of my life, I had many ugly problems. Somehow God has always turned that ugly situation around for my good because I always played my hand, and God was always with me.

There had been no children in this small neighborhood in Marion, South Carolina, for over ten years. This Sunday afternoon, the temperature was about 67 degrees, and the wind blew. The sun was slowly going down, and darkness started covering this small-town community in the city of Marion. A young woman named Bobbie Jean Davis was having a normal day. Not long after dinner, as she was lying down relaxing from a long day, the unborn baby in her stomach began kicking and moving like no other time in her pregnancy.

Since this was her first baby, she did not know what was occurring and that these were indicators that she was going into labor. During this time in history, midwives (typically a woman) trained to assist women in childbirth came to the house to deliver the babies. The news got out so fast around the community. Everyone was so happy because the wait was now over. The joys of children will soon be in our neighborhood. Here comes a baby boy or girl.

Two young teenage women named Mabel Davis and Debra Dorsey were peeping through the curtains' crack outside the bedroom window. They knew something was happening because they saw the midwife going to Mabel's sister's (mother's house). Mabel said to Debra, "The baby is coming tonight, and we will get to see this baby come into this world."

Sometime between 6:45 - 8:00 PM on November 12, 1967, Bobbie Jean Davis gave birth to a 10-and-a-half-pound baby boy. He was named Bennie Tyrone Davis. The neighborhood was full of joy because it was a boy. Bennie's aunt Olentha Shaw named him. The neighbors and friends started coming to the house, and others called the mother to get all the updates about baby Bennie. They were happy.

Sadness and stress came to the Davis family and neighborhood a few days later. The new baby, Bennie, started having 'cluster seizures' (one after the other). My mother and those who were visiting at that time tried everything to stop the seizures, but nothing they did was helping, and for Baby Bennie, things continued to worsen.

The doctor told the mother, "Your son has epilepsy, a neurological disorder in which nerve cell activity in the brain is disturbed, causing seizures. Epilepsy may occur due to a genetic disorder and/or acquired brain injuries such as brain trauma or stroke. Bennie had the worst kind, identified as Grand Mal seizures (tonic-chronic seizures)."

The doctor continued talking, disclosing the prognosis that her son had only one week to live due to the seizures. He continued, "because of the seizures, the test indicates that your son's brain is not functioning enough to allow him to suck a bottle." That gravely was causing him to have major weight loss. The doctor thoughtfully said, "If your son dies like I believe he will, I will not put the cause of death as a tumor on his brain, which caused epilepsy, so the insurance can pay it off. I hope that this will be a help to the family."

I surprisingly made it through the first week and remained hospitalized for more than four weeks. I even sustained surgery on my head during that time. The neighborhood people would visit Baby Bennie and his mother. The neighborhood came together as a family to help by donating diapers, milk, clothes, and money.

The frequency and intensity of the seizures caused my eyes to become crossed. The doctors did three surgeries on my eyes, hoping to get them straight. That failed because I continued to have seizures. The doctor said this baby would always have seizures. I was given one year to live by the doctor. He also advised my mother and the family to always have someone with baby Bennie since a seizure could happen at any time. Over a year had passed, and I was still alive, having seizures, sometimes 2 to 3 times a week.

My aunts and uncle gave us unconditional care and support. One day Mother was working, and she hired a young lady to keep me. During those years, houses in much of this area were heated by wood-burning heaters. Mother doesn't know what happened, but the babysitter was responsible for endangering my life. We realize now that the babysitter either was not paying attention to me or she dropped me on to the heater. When my mother arrived home from work that day, all she heard was loud and distressful cries coming from frail me.

Mother ran and saw what could be best described as the right side of my face melting. (My mother could not afford a house phone back then) Frantically, mother ran with me in her arms to the house next door and pleaded for someone to take us to the hospital right now! Holding me tightly and crying, we arrived at the hospital. We ran into the emergency room, where I was immediately seen by the doctor.

Ointment and gauze were wrapped around me, and needless to say, I just kept screaming from the pain, agony and discomfort. I returned home that day with explicit directions on how I should be delicately cared for. As for the babysitter, I never really heard what transpired, but I know that any furious, angry, enraged mother is a force to be reckoned with! Today the whereabouts of the babysitter are unknown. I am sure she never had the opportunity to babysit me again.

The years passed, and I continued to defy the doctor's prediction. I lived, and I even was blessed with a little sister who I adored dearly. A few years later, my brother Chris was born. Our neighborhood was growing with children.

On Christmas, my paternal grandmother would always bring Christmas presents for my sister and me. Then one Christmas, I was looking for my grandmother to come, but she never showed up. Not only for Christmas, she never came or said another word to either of us. The pain continues to exist and will not go away because we never did anything but have a love for her.

My uncle Sandy and his wife Lorine moved next door to us with their children. The couple had a three-year-old son named Timothy Hemingway. All of the neighborhood children were bigger than Timothy. One day Timothy was at home jumping on the bed. He fell and broke his arm, but that never stopped him from playing because he believed he was just as big as everyone else.

A few years passed, and I started a neighborhood football team named the IGA Posse. We would go all over the city of Marion, playing different teams.

The love of coaching has continued with me all these years. I even now love helping children to believe and to better themselves. Looking into a young man's eyes and seeing the athlete's excitement and pride in his parents is why the job of coaching is worth it all.

Every summer, my mother would allow us to go to that city so nice that it was named the same twice. (New York, NY.) While visiting New York, I met a girl named Erica, and we were in a relationship. From that day until now, we have remained friends. One summer, while vacationing in New York, I started having seizures. One was so severe I had to be hospitalized for a few days.

I asked my family not to tell my mother because she may not let me come the distance to NY for more summer vacations. I wanted to believe it was my fault that I was having seizures. My aunt Mildred would not let me believe it, and she let me know that God would heal me from this sickness. It was almost time for school to begin. Aunt Mildred, Aunt Mabel, Aunt Doll, and Aunt Marshal put money together. Aunt Mildred took Alethea (my sister), Chris (my brother), and me shopping for school clothes. The new school term was one of the few times I would have new clothes. The first school day's excitement and anticipation were thrilling, like the night before my birthday. I looked forward to putting on my new clothes for the first time.

Not long after the school term had begun, I suffered an extremely bad seizure. When I got to the point where I could talk, I requested that my mother contact Elder Park. I just knew that if he prayed for me, everything would be alright, and God would heal me. The seizures started coming back-to-back. Someone contacted Elder Park, who visited the hospital, to see about me. I had slipped into a coma since I had been unconscious for several hours, and the only positive thing was that I was still alive. Elder Eugene Park held both my hands and started praying for a while. My mother witnessed that her son's eyes came open at the end of the prayer, and I was conscious of everything happening around me. Someone asked, "Bennie do you know who I am?" My response "Elder Park, the dancing man for Christ." As I moved my eyes, I saw tears rolling down their faces. My mother said my son is not just alive, but he is aware and able to identify the people around him. After a few days, I was released from the hospital and went home.

On Saturday, we had a neighborhood football game. I ensured I was on the best team because I was not running that football. Sometime during the game, I stood up. Our team was waiting for the ball to come to us. All I could see was the ground coming at me. I started having a seizure. All the players ran to me, asking what was wrong. Someone ran and got my mother. People started coming outside, and some came over to where I was lying on the ground. Someone picked me up and laid me down in the back seat of a car.

When I regained consciousness, I was in the emergency room at the hospital. My mother was working and was not there with me. My brother Chris was able to locate our mother, who immediately left the job to come to check on me. I am unsure who went to pick up my mother. Still, by the time they had gotten to mother, she had already walked or run a significant distance toward the hospital. I did not remain in the hospital; I was soon discharged to go home.

One day my mother had some friends over at our house, and some of them had their children with them. The adults were in the house, and the children were outside playing. I was on the porch sitting on the banister, acting like I had it going on. I said something to one of the girls, and before I knew anything, she pushed me off the banister, and I hit my head on one of the bricks lying around the flower bed. My head busted open on contact, and blood came down my face.

Someone called for my mother, saying that her son was bleeding and he was having a seizure. My mother was coming out of the house so fast she was almost running. One of mom's friends took us to the hospital. They gave me stitches to stop the bleeding, closed the hole in my head then discharged me.

A letter came in the mail requesting that she bring her son to the Board Meeting on the following Friday. The letter read: The School Board would like to offer Bennie T. Davis options for his and his parent's lives. My mother and her family were in church on that Thursday night. Elder Park had a prayer line, and my mother got in the prayer line to ask God to give her favor with her son's future.

My mother told me the day of the meeting came so fast, but she and I were on time for the meeting. The meeting was with the school board and the treating physician. We walked in, and it was the doctor, school officials, and representatives from the Disabilities and Special Needs Agency. After introducing themselves to my mother and I, the meeting began. The doctor said, "This sickness that your son has called epilepsy is not going to get better, but worse. As your son gets older, he will get bigger and stronger, and you will be older and weaker. Bennie will never be a normal child because of this; it will be great if you put him into a group home. He will have around-the-clock help. The way things look, if he lived to see 15, that would be a wonderful option." He said, "I believe he will pass away before eight years old, and I know you love your son, but give him up because there isn't anything else to help him from getting sick."

My mother's mind was made up to play her hand and let God work it out. My mother told them, "I will be keeping my son Bennie Davis at all times with God on my side." Someone said Ms. Bobbie Davis, you still have time because it will be another year and a half before he starts school. My mother responded, "Don't wait for that call to come because my son and I will be together till the end of time.

Thank you for meeting with me today, but Bennie will remain with me."

As my mother and I walked out the door, I told her, "God would work it out because one day, I would be president." When we got to the other side of those four walls, tears started coming down my mother's face as she got into the car. The lady taking us home told mama everything would work out for her son.

It was the summer before I was to start school. My sister, brother, and I went to the Seven-Eleven store. We walked in with our empty soda bottles, and each got a soda. After we had opened them, we went to the cashier to pay for them with our empty bottles, not knowing we still had to pay with some money. The cashier said not to leave the store, for we would be stealing. I let the lady know my grandmother lived across the street and allowed me to go to ask her for the money. The cashier let me go to my grandmother's. I rang the doorbell and explained what was happening at the store when she came to the door. I told her that all I needed was $3 and would bring her change back. She looked at me and said, "at this time, I don't have any money to give to you to help you pay for those sodas." I walked from her house, knowing now that she had no love for me, my sister, or my baby brother.

As I walked back to the store, I wondered what I was to do now that I couldn't get help from my grandmother. For an hour, I walked around Marion searching for someone to help, and there was no familiar person I knew. If Mama found this out, all of us would be in BIG trouble. When I returned to the store, Alethea and Chris still stood there. One of our mother's friends had paid our bill, and our mother learned about the soda situation.

By the time I made it home, Mama was at the house. As I walked in the yard, I asked myself if there was anywhere or any place I could go for the rest of my life. I didn't want to go into that house because

I knew Mama was mad at what we did, but it was all because of me. As I walked into the house, I stepped in the doorway while my mother helped me into the house faster. I told her I saw people give an empty bottle of soda, and then they would get a soda and open it. I never saw them pay, but I guess they did pay the difference. Mama said you will never return empty bottles to any store from that day to this day; that never happened again.

I had two weeks left before I started school. I was so excited about going to school for the first time. It felt like a dream, but my eyes were still open. Days before I started school, the School Board met with my mother for the second time because they learned I had epilepsy and autism. Autism is a developmental disorder of variable severity characterized by difficulty in social interaction and communication and restricted or repetitive patterns of thought and behavior.

This meant that I could not attend traditional public school and would be enrolled in special education classes. My mother was told that I would never receive a high school diploma. They told her I would still get a paper/certificate saying I attended school for 12 years. They said there would be no need for "Bennie to learn how to read, write or do mathematics."

I am now finally attending school with other children. The students who attended Special Education Schools all had challenges of some kind. I remember sitting in the classroom, and my classmates were just looking up at the lights, and they would make a noise because they were nonverbal. Because of my autism, I would drool. It was hard for me to talk, and I would look up at the lights like my other classmates. That lets you know if nine people are doing something negative, you will be the tenth.

The teachers let us draw pictures, sleep, play kickball and talk to our friends. I knew how to print my name. I was in that school for six years; the teacher never gave the class homework. The Board continued advising my mother to send me home when I graduated from school with the certificate.

These people should have been helping my mother, but they told her that her son would never amount to anything. What does a mother do when the people she trusts advise her because of autism and epilepsy? Her son should be put away because she was a single parent and could not handle me and send me home?

After six years in special education, a test was administered to all the students. Only six students could attend public school, and I was one of the six. What excited me and surprised me was that I passed the test and was placed in 6th grade. My first day of public school was August of 1981. It was my first time on a school bus. The first school that I attended was for fifth and sixth graders only.

I had never seen so many children in one place before. I said, "Wow." Every person I saw looked like they had on new clothes and sneakers. Five other kids had been tested like me and entered simultaneously. I mainly hung around and stayed close to them. One of the kids started bragging about his new clothes and telling him how much his mother paid for them. He made me feel that he believed that he was better than me. He even asked me where my new clothes and shoes were? And I told him that I had on my new clothes and shoes.

I remember my mother saying, "Do not forget your purpose, and the only purpose you have is to receive your High School Diploma." "Clothes get old, but your diploma will always have its value as the world's foundation. With a high school diploma, you have choices. Without a diploma, you do not have choices because your choices have already been made for you."

My mother was a housekeeper. It was not about how much money she made but what she did with what she made. Our new clothes came from the flea market. She got my first pair of leather sneakers for a dollar. She washed them and polished the shoes when she got them to the house. My mother would not allow her children to go outside on Christmas day. I always wondered why, and one year I asked her. "Son, I do not have money like our neighbors to buy bicycles, games, and new clothes and still pay the bills. But as God blesses me throughout the year, I will get you all the things I can afford and buy all the different things you need."

Our mother was protecting us. She did not want our feelings hurt or want us to feel like we were less than any other child. She told us there were some things she could not buy for us, but there was nothing she would not do for us.

That Monday, I wore my new clothes and loved her for always getting me the best she could afford. On my first day of school, I was in regular classes, the bell rang, and I walked into the building. I had to ask where my class was located. When I walked into the classroom, my heart felt like it had stopped and started back because I was in a classroom with normal students for the first time. The class was homeroom, and my very first class was history. Now here I am, a teenager, and I only know how to print my name and a few more words. I was on a first-grade reading level. The history teacher said, "Christopher Columbus sailed around the world." I could not spell Christopher Columbus, but my brother's name was Chris. Then I drew a bus, circled it, and drew a boat. When I looked at the picture, I interpreted it as Christopher Columbus sailing worldwide.

This was the method for my future. I went to each of my teachers, explained that I had a reading problem, and asked them if they would come to me and read the test, and I would verbally give them the answers. Each teacher willingly helped and allowed me to have specific accommodations.

I met new friends, and yes, people would talk about me. They would pick at the way I looked. "You see how he looks. His eyes are crossed, his hair is red, and he has freckles." That was enough to bring a person's self-esteem down. It did not because I was only focused on staying in school. I knew I was not going back to special education. One day I went home, and my mother said, "Do you have homework? Let me see your work." I showed it to her. She was so proud of me and believed I could make it.

I could not do the homework one day, so I told my mother. She told me when I go to school the next day, to ask my teachers for help. I did as she said. I later found out that because my mother did not finish school, she did not understand how to help me do the work.

I passed to the next grade and made it to junior high school. I enjoyed two great years in Junior High School. I was never on academic probation. I was a manager for the football team. I received an award for math in the 7th and 8th grades, and I went to prom both years. At my 7th grade prom, my mother even brought me a suit to attend. Everything was looking up for me. The teachers were working with me, the coaches were working with me, and I had a new set of friends. Then one day, in the 8th grade. I asked to go to the bathroom, but soon as I left the bathroom to go back to class, I had a seizure, and someone found me.

I do not know how long I was in the hallway shaking. When I realized what had happened, I started crying. I pleaded, please do not send me back to special education. I will not have any more seizures; just help me. I want to graduate and get my high school diploma. The doctor discharged me out of school for a few days. While home, I begged my mother not to let them put me back in Special Education. I promised her that I would not get sick again. "It will all work out" was all she said.

I returned to school. I was scared that the students would make fun of me and did not want to be around me anymore. I did not know if the teachers decided to put me back in special education. Still, when I returned to school, I went into my homeroom class, and the students made me feel like I was a part of this great class. The teachers made me feel necessary for the first time in my life. I did not feel like a unique student. They treated me like an average person. Tears began to roll down my face, but those were tears of joy because I was accepted into the school family. They let me stay in public school.

I am now at the end of my third year of junior high school. I passed to the next grade and would be promoted to 9th in just a few weeks. I would be in my first year of High School. Amazingly, I would be listed as a high school freshman. I had a desire to play football. The school sent out a letter to the students that junior varsity summer football practice starts in August. I believe I am the only student from then to the present who came out openly and told them I was an epileptic and an autistic student who played football. I practiced just as hard as anyone else. I had a great football season.

I was not a starter, but I did play in every game. August of 1983 was my first year of high school. Bennie T. Davis is a first-year student at Marion High School. Being in a big school with all these different people was amazing. I was able to meet new people and have new friends and teachers. I went to my homeroom class, and Mr. Jerry Coleman was the teacher and my football coach. Because I started public school in the 6th grade, I could not take college prep classes and was put into basic classes. My first year was wonderful. I played football, and I ran track. I was never on academic probation things were looking great for me. I was promoted to the 10th grade as a sophomore. We were at the end of the school year, and now it was time to enjoy the summer. I had about two weeks remaining in this term.

It was a beautiful spring afternoon. I was returning home after playing basketball on Strawberry Street. On my way home, I passed Mt. Pisgah Missionary Baptist Church. I took a short cut by turning onto the one-way street as I approached my grandparents' house. I was on the other side of the street with no warning; everything started spinning faster and faster than I saw the street approaching my face. I hit the ground face-first.

Blood was coming from my head. I had an uncontrollable shake because I was having a seizure. I could not stop. I do not know how long I was there, but so much blood came from me. When my eyes opened, I remembered looking over at my grandparents' house; the door was visible. My grandmother Georgia Thomas was standing at the door. She hated that her son had children with my mother so badly that she would not call for help and would not come and help me. I could have died, but my grandmother looked out of her door, saw me in my blood, and she shut the door. She made me feel like, 'let that bastard boy die; he is better dead than alive.'

A young man was walking by and saw me. He was the son of the young lady who pushed me off the banister when we were younger. He allowed me to put my arms around his shoulders and slowly walked me to my Aunt Grace's house, where I was then taken to the hospital. I stayed overnight in the hospital. The doctor said I would be out of school for a few days. When this happened, I was happy about not being in school at the time because I did not have to tell anybody I had a seizure (I did not want to return to special education). After the doctor released me, I went to school and finished my first High School year.

Summer try-outs for the varsity football team for Marion High School were my big opportunity to make the team. I was in the 10th grade but would have to hit some big young men. I was looking forward to hitting against a student named Tootsie. My first day of football practice with the varsity was amazing. I was looking forward to tomorrow's practice because then I could hit against

Tootsie, one of the most prominent players on the football team and the biggest and best on the team. At the end of practice, we all went into the locker room, and everybody was getting dressed to go home. I got dressed and then started walking home through the fox field.

There was a train track right by the football field. When I began walking across the Railroad tracks, the world started spinning and spinning. I started shaking, and then I started having a seizure again. I did not know how long I was on the tracks, but I was on it for a while. Someone found me lying on the tracks. There were no cell phones during this time, so someone would have to find help or try to help. Someone called for an ambulance to come to administer help to me. I was bleeding when the EMT came to help me. Before they put me in the ambulance, they asked me, did I know my name, and I said, "Bennie T. Davis." They asked me, "Where are you going?" I told them I was going home, leaving from football practice, and will play against Tootsie tomorrow.

I did not know that my tomorrow would never happen and that today had been my last football practice due to the seizures. The doctor told me that playing football was too dangerous for me. I so desperately wanted to play football. When I returned to school, Coach Rankin confirmed that I would no longer play football for Marion High School. He emphasized that I might get hit, have a seizure, and die.

I was horrified that this could be the cause of my being placed back in special education. The Coach said, Bennie, you can be a manager for the varsity football team. I was elated. Coach Rankin said that I would not be allowed to manage basketball and I would not be running track.

Now, what will I do about all this free time? I was doing well in my classes, even though my classes were basic. The classes were very demanding of me, yet I was passing. I knew I could improve my grades, but I needed extra help. I learned that there was a resource class every day for one hour. I decided to drop the study hall class. I immediately went to my guidance counselor to request that I be placed in the resource class since I needed extra help with my work. The counselor told me that I did not qualify because my grades were too high to attend. I went to the principal, and the guidance counselor, and I fought until they put me in the resource class.

That was one of my greatest decisions, as it helped me in so many ways in school. Every day I was able to go to tutoring, and they worked along with all my teachers. I was able to complete my homework and my tests. One day after lunch, everything was going nicely, and I had just passed a big test. I was writing down my notes and asking questions in my English class. Suddenly, the classroom started spinning, and it got faster and faster. The next thing, I was having violent muscle contractions (hitting the desk repeatedly). I hit the floor and had a loss of consciousness. Unlike past seizures, I was in the classroom around my classmates this time. The ambulance was called, and I was taken to the hospital.

Dr. Bennie T. Davis Sr was a below-average student but did above-average things.

TELL ALL I AM NOT THAT WAY ANYMORE

2. WHERE DO I GO FROM HERE?

I felt so good about my life and that the most incredible days of my life were in front of me. I accomplished something man had said I would never accomplish. I received my High School Diploma. My high school guidance counselor told me I did not qualify for college.

She reminded me that I was only at a second-grade reading level. I did not take any college prep classes or any regular classes. I just took the required courses to graduate. She suggested I attend a trade school or allow my mother to put me in an adult home facility. Just thinking about what she told me in my junior year of high school made me upset with her, but I realized that she was only telling me about the statistics and the certifications required to attend college.

Now I am at a point where I must decide about my future. Where do I go from here? I have some negative experiences attached to my name. My ethnicity was unfavorable, and having been reared in a single-parent home was not the norm. I only had six years of public schooling and had a low reading level, and had only been enrolled in basic classes. I was the only student with epilepsy and autism to attend college in Marion High School history. But despite my educational background, Mr. Norman Jameson told me he would still give me a scholarship for running track for Voorhees College. I am going to college against my high school guidance counselor's recommendation, statistics, family members, and friends.

Determined in Fall 1987, I enrolled at Voorhees College, Denmark, South Carolina. During the summer of 1987, Voorhees had a weekend visitation for all incoming freshmen. I was so excited about spending the weekend on campus. I had to inform Mr. Norman

Jameson that I did not have transportation to get to the campus and would not be able to participate in the freshmen orientation for the weekend. I was convinced that Voorhees was the college for me. After speaking with Mr. Jameson, he said, do not worry about transportation. I will pick you up so you will not miss the freshmen orientation.

As the days went by leading up to the time to go to the campus for the weekend, Mr. Jameson called and confirmed that he would pick me up. My mother began to get my clothes together the day before I left; she ensured everything was clean, starched, and ironed. I was so excited about going to Voorhees College. On Friday morning at about 8:00 a.m., Mr. Jameson came and picked me up. I had never been out of Marion County.

Everything was a first for me, especially going alone without my family. I was so excited about going to Voorhees that this felt like the most extended trip of my life. It felt like I was never going to arrive. After watching cars pass by and looking out my window at the different buildings, restaurants, and houses, I finally reached my destination, Denmark, South Carolina. There were three red lights in the town, but a sign read Voorhees College at the last red light. I was looking for a big building, but only small old buildings existed. My hometown Marion, South Carolina, was more progressive than Denmark, South Carolina.

In 1897, Voorhees College was founded by a young Black woman, Elizabeth Evelyn Wright. She was a former student of Booker T. Washington. Ms. Wright, at 23, dreamed of a school for African American youth in Denmark, South Carolina.

The college campus was not large, but it was the biggest I had ever been to, and I loved it from the beginning. This man, Mr. Jameson, had allowed me to attend college and earn a college degree. While looking around the campus with excitement all over my face, Mr. Jameson pointed out that Denmark Technical College was across the street. I was still looking for significant buildings on campus, but there were only small ones. The college campus only had four dormitories, two for the males and two for the females, which held about a thousand students in total. There were more females than males that attended. Looking at the dorms, I noticed that some of the windows were up, and most had fans. As I continued to observe the dorms and the buildings in the academic circle and throughout the campus, I thought they were old and run down; some buildings were abandoned and unusable.

Despite all that I saw, I was still excited about attending Voorhees College. All the upcoming freshmen met each other at Mass Hall; It was there that I received the key to my dorm room. I was escorted to my dorm room to learn how and where to go. It would have been the broken air conditioner in my window if anything could have made me return home. The walls needed painting because beige paint was peeling off the block walls. The mattress was old and covered with plastic, which a good cleaning could have helped make it look a little better, and it was also sunken in from the use of the previous students. I could not hang my clothes in the closet because the bar I was supposed to hang my clothes on was missing. There was a dresser in the room, but some of the drawers were missing from it. What irritated me was that there was no mirror in my room. While in my room, I could hear some of the other students visiting the college saying that they would not come back to this college.

I had already had my mind made up. The only purpose that I am coming to Voorhees College is to get my Bachelor of Science degree. I will work my way through the heat. I will work my way through the cold; I will make it. I am not going to let anything stop me. I had a full day of different activities on campus. After dinner, I had to meet my chaperone, who told me there would be a party in the gymnasium that night and invited me to come.

There was no gymnasium on campus; the party was held at an old elementary school gymnasium behind the boys' dorm. This gym was called the matchbox. I was so excited about going to the college party. So that night, I put on a pair of my freshly creased blue jeans and a wrinkle-free button-down shirt (thanks to my mom) and my leather sneakers. Even though I did not have a mirror in my room, I knew I looked good. I had the biggest grin as I walked into the gym at about 9:00 p.m.

I had a wonderful time that night. I danced with anybody who wanted to dance and anyone who asked me to dance. I danced from the time I got there until it was time for the party to end at midnight. Everyone was sweating. I found out that that was why they called the gym the matchbox. The gym was so small it was like ants on top of each other. I left the party and went back to my room. Once there, all that I could do was crawl into my bed. What an exciting time I had at the party.

The next morning, I missed breakfast because I did not get up until 9:00 am. All the visiting students had to meet at 11:00 for a Q&A concerning the college. I ate lunch at 12:30 p.m. I was really hungry since I had missed breakfast. That day around 2 p.m., Mr. Jameson came by the college to drive me home. He drove me home; All I could think about was a great time. I thanked Mr. Jameson for the opportunity of a lifetime. For some reason, the ride back home felt shorter than when I was going. I could have been so full of joy and excitement that I overlooked time.

Once I made it home, I was excited about telling my family and friends about my college experience. I am looking forward to attending Voorhees College in the fall of 1987. My sister had graduated from Freeport High School in New York, and because of the excitement that I had about Voorhees College, she decided that she would attend Voorhees College as well. She would be getting a scholarship to play softball. The future was starting to look great.

As the summer faded away and the time grew near for me to go to college, I had to talk with my mother. It was about two weeks before I had to leave home and attend college. I had some news that crushed my heart and would be heavy on her heart. I was sitting on the front porch with my mother when I shared that a young lady told me she was pregnant. A few days ago, my mother told her friends that her 19-year-old son was about to attend Voorhees College and was also a virgin. During my high school time, the young ladies I dealt with told me that if I told anyone that, they would never speak to me anymore, and the relationship would end. Because of my disabilities, the young ladies did not want anyone to know they were dealing with me. I was not about to open my mouth because I was experiencing something that I loved.

While waiting for my mother to respond to the news, I shared that the young lady was pregnant. My heart felt like it was going to beat out of my chest. Sweat was running down my face like someone had thrown a glass of water in my face. The big grin that I always had on my face was gone. My mother started thinking about herself because I told her the young lady was still in high school.
Mother looked at me with tears running down her face and said, "Son, this will not stop you from going to college. If I must keep the baby, I will do so until she finishes high school. I will look after the baby throughout the week."

The only thing going through my mind was that I had a child on the way and wanted to be a part of my child's life. How could I take care of my child and attend college simultaneously? I decided I must enlist in the army to take care of my child. I contacted an army recruiter and spoke with him about joining the military. The week before leaving for college, I met with the recruiter. I did not let anyone know that college was not worth it for me; I was on my way to the army to be able to take care of my child.

When I met with the recruiter, he shared the benefits I would receive if accepted into the military. My child would receive a check for benefits such as a college education paid in full. It sounded beautiful to me, so I took the test to enlist in the army, and the recruiter told me to go ahead and attend college. He told me that he would contact me when the test results came back, and we would go from there.

I eventually received his call two days before leaving for college. I was on the phone with the recruiter, my heart was beating fast as I had just run a five-mile marathon nonstop, and sweat was running from the crown of my head to the soles of my feet. I had a big grin that Ajax could not take it off. Then the recruiter told me he was sorry that I could not enlist in the military because I did not pass the test. He said some other stuff, but everything else went blank after I heard that I did not pass the test. My smile slowly began to leave my face, and my heart felt like it had just stopped for a few seconds.

So, I had to stick to my original plan: to go to Voorhees College. It was the 3rd Sunday in August 1987 when the first-year students had to report to college for the freshman orientation. One week before college started, my sister Alethea came home to South Carolina from New York. She was overly excited about going to Voorhees College.

My mother did not have a driver's license or a vehicle, so she contacted Bill Hughes and Cleveland Rollins about taking my sister and me to college. They told my mother they would have us at

Voorhees College on time.

The night before my sister and I left for college, it was finally here. I could not sleep because it felt like Christmas was the next day, and everything I wanted would be in one big gift. Yes, the opportunity to go to college and my sister was going too. I felt that she was only going because she wanted me to have a real opportunity to achieve a college degree.

My sister could have gone to any college she desired because she took college prep courses in high school to prepare for the SATs and college. With her coming to Voorhees with me, I felt I had her support. We both got up at 4 a.m. to go to college; we had to start the trip by 6 a.m. Our transportation was at my mother's house around 5:30 that morning. We started loading up the truck and the car and packed everything we needed for college. It took about three ½ hours or more because neither driver drove fast.

When we finally arrived at Voorhees College, many people and cars flooded the small campus. My sister and I had to go to the Mass Hall to get our assigned room and pay our entry fee. My room was in the Halmi Hall dormitory, and my sister was at the Battle Hall. After we settled in our rooms, everyone had to meet in the chapel. Now it was time to say goodbye to our mother and brother and thank Mr. Bill and Cleveland for ensuring we arrived here safely.

Knowing that she was about to leave us, my mother gave us all the money she had earned in the last two weeks for us to have the things we might need to purchase. Mother had taken out two loans to pay for our registration and room deposits. Lastly, she surprised us with $50 each to spend wisely. It was getting late in the evening we all hugged and said our goodbyes. As we walked to the car, tears started falling from our eyes. My mother had tears of joy and tears of a proud mother seeing not one but two of her children attend college.

My mother said that she may have to drink water, eat sandwiches, and miss a meal so my baby brother could eat, and she would give my sister and me all that she could for us to 'make it.' My brother Chris, Mr. Bill, and Mr. Cleveland started crying too. As my sister and I watched the car with my mother and brother disappear down the road, we stood on the sidewalk with more tears still running down our faces.

I started wiping the tears from my eyes, and I looked back down the road and saw the car returning. Mother wanted us to know that she would return in two weeks with goodies and to see how we were doing. As the car drove away, my sister and I walked towards the road, watching the vehicle until it completely disappeared.

We began walking to the chapel while drying the tears from our eyes. My sister and I had to get together because we now had to get on the job and work to get what we came for, a Bachelor of Science degree. When we walked into the chapel, we finally stopped crying. We sat down and went through our orientation, and what a wonderful time I had. I started meeting new friends. Everyone had to introduce themselves and share their tentative goals. I was able to meet people who were from all parts of the United States and a few from other countries. I was so excited about my new friends and classmates. At the end of the orientation, there would be a black and white dinner with the college president at 6 p.m. that evening, and it would be over by 8:00 p.m. We should be in bed by 9:30 p.m. that night. Going to bed at 9:30 was a little early for me, which I thought until I was overtaken by sleep when I got into that bed.

On a Monday, the registrar had scheduled all freshmen for the required entrance exam. This test was designed to let the college see if students could start taking their classes. If a student did not pass the test, he would begin with developmental or excel courses, which would help him to begin his college classes. After I received the instructor's information about the entrance exam, I only had enough time to prepare for the black-and-white dinner. For the first time in my life, I was being treated fairly despite my disabilities. In the past, I would always deal with inequality. My incapacities were relatively inconspicuous here because no one knew I had epilepsy or autism.

I rushed to my room and started getting my clothes out, not realizing I had a beautiful black and white outfit that my mother had packed for me. The tears began again at the thought of the sacrifice of my mother providing for my needs. I still have that outfit to this day. I cannot wear it because I was 171 pounds then (now I am over three hundred pounds). I got dressed and believed I was the best-dressed young man on campus. It was time for me to leave and allow the Voorhees campus to see Bennie T Davis. I had a wonderful time meeting the college president, the faculty, the instructors, and some of the staff. The college president let the entire student body know that we were all part of the Voorhees College family, and whatever they could do to make it better for us, school administrators would try to do it.

At the end of the black-and-white dinner, all the attendees were encouraged to return to their rooms and get a good night's sleep to do great on their entrance exams the next morning. We all left dinner to go back to our rooms. I walked my sister to her dorm to ensure she got there safely; then, I walked across the campus to my dorm. When I entered my room, my roommate was there, and I met him for the first time. We had the dorm room door open, and several young men congregated in our room. I believed the young men liked me because I kept them laughing. Some of the young men played basketball and baseball, and some did not play any sports. I was the only one who ran track out of the group. Around 9 p.m., the young men went to their rooms to be prepared for the test in the morning.

I made sure that I told the young men I would not miss breakfast because that was the most important meal of the day, especially before taking a test. At 6:45 a.m. the next morning, I was up and dressed by 7:30 a.m. I left my room and began walking downstairs to the cafeteria (which was in my dorm) to get breakfast.

While in the cafe, I interacted with the young men who had introduced themselves to me the night before. We all sat together at the table and ate our breakfast. After we all finished eating, I saw my sister in the cafeteria with her newfound friends, and I introduced my sister to the young men. We all left together and walked across the campus to the St. James' building, where test coordinators administered the exam. I was in the building for about 20 minutes before the coordinator gave the test. The test was up to three hours long. Before we began, the instructor told the class that this test would determine if we would begin college courses for our major or begin with developmental or excel studies. The test was essential and significant. I realized that anybody with a high school diploma could attend Voorhees College. The only requirement was to take the entrance exam to be evaluated, and proper classes would be assigned.

The auditorium was filled with young people sitting at their desks anxiously awaiting the entrance exam. When the test started, I looked, and there were some words I had never seen before. I was not familiar with anything on the test, but I did not leave any questions unanswered. I took my time taking the test and occasionally asked the instructor for assistance. He would read aloud a few questions and explain some things I did not understand. As it was almost time for the test to end, the instructor announced that at 3 p.m., everyone must report to the Mass Hall for registration and to get their entrance exam results. After the test, I turned in my exam and headed straight to the cafeteria. It was lunchtime, and there would be a break before going to registration and test results.

While in the cafeteria, I had time to enjoy my new friends and find out how my sister was doing. The time flew by so fast that my sister had to remind me that it was time to go to the Mass Hall to register for my classes. The lines were exceptionally long, but getting our classes did not take long. My sister passed the test, so she could start her college courses. I discovered I did not pass the entrance exam and would have all excel courses. I only had two credits toward graduation in my first semester of college.

College courses were two or three days a week, but excel courses were four days a week. I had my sister make my class schedule. I would ask her not to schedule my classes from 12:30-4:00 p.m., but if she had to, let it be at 2 or 3 p.m. I requested a schedule to watch my favorite soap operas, The Young and the Restless, The Bold and the Beautiful, As the World Turns, and The Guiding Light. If I had to miss any soaps, it would have to be, As the World Turns. In my first semester, I could watch soap operas because I had early morning classes.

During my first semester of college, I made sure that I received two or three hours of tutoring daily. I would go to my instructors and explain my problems; they worked with me as much as possible. I had my tape recorder during my classes because I was not skilled in taking notes. After all, I was not a good speller, and the instructors talked too fast for me to remember what to write. I believed that if a person could listen to a rap song on the radio repeatedly and repeat the rap, I could listen and learn what the instructors said via my tape recorder. I frequently would listen to the tape recorder until I hypnotized myself to pass my tests.

As I began to settle into my new college life, my mother visited my sister and me just as she said she would. She brought my sister and me things for our dorm rooms that we desperately needed. I decided to do something that I used to do in my high school days: sell Snickers and Butterfinger candy bars. Selling these goodies allowed my sister and I to have some money in our pockets. I felt this would have taken some of the load off my mother.

As the weeks passed, Labor Day was approaching and time for us to go home. It would be our first time since we had been at Voorhees. When we arrived home, the people in my childhood neighborhood were excited. Some of the neighbors asked if I was enjoying Voorhees College. I told them that everything was excellent. And I didn't hesitate to Thank God I had no seizures up to this point. That by itself made things wonderful. Labor Day weekend went by so fast. That Monday afternoon, our ride came by my mother's house to pick my sister and me up to take us back to Voorhees College.

The next time that we came home was for Thanksgiving. The college semester was ending about a week before Christmas. It was an honor for me to finish my first semester of college would be out of Voorhees for two ½ weeks for the Christmas break, and again the time went by so fast. I knew that once I got back to Voorhees, it would be time for track and field season, so I started training early, which was about the first week of December. I would run for miles so that I could get myself in shape. My track coach at Voorhees had told me before I left for the holidays that when I returned to Voorhees, that in January that practice would begin on the first day of classes. At the end of the semester, I had Physical Education and orientation toward graduation. I tested out of excel math class but failed the reading and English classes. God blessed me to not have one seizure during my first semester in college. Thank you, Lord.

It was time to buckle back down and focus on the spring semester. Once again, I had my sister schedule all my classes around soap opera times.

When I first started at Voorhees College, I wanted to pursue a degree in mathematics, but I quickly realized that was out of the question. This semester, I had to take Algebra. That was a subject that I had never taken before in my life until now.

During my first track practice, I discovered that Voorhees did not provide the track team cleats. I received the track uniform, and I had to use one pair of sneakers for the track, which made caused me to wear my dress shoes for my everyday wear. My mother could not afford to buy me a pair of cleats because they were too expensive. After finishing track practice, I would run down the streets of Denmark with my shirt off. One day after my run, I was back on the Voorhees campus when one of my friends said, "Bennie runs like a cave man." From that time on, I was nicknamed Caveman. I was called Caveman by everyone on campus.

I used to go to my sister's dorm room window while standing outside, and I would yell my sister's name real loudly, Alethea! It would be so loud that not only did my sister know that I was outside her window, but the young ladies on the second and third floors would also come to their window. All the young ladies would come to their windows and start chanting Cave; you look so fine, Cave; Cave, you could blow our mind. I became the most popular young man on campus. No one could come to Voorhees College without knowing or wanting to meet Caveman.

The matchbox was the place to be every Friday and Saturday night from 9 p.m. to 1 a.m. if you wanted to party. Most of my friends with whom I spent time enjoyed drinking and getting high, but that was never an interest of mine. I had my natural high; I did not need to smoke, consume, or use drugs. I was always devoted to doing my homework and going to my classes. Regardless of all I did, I put my time in for tutoring five days a week.

I remember going to my sister's dorm room to get her for class. She had just had an enjoyable time that night before at the party at the matchbox. And was not going to class that day. I told her not to forget the purpose of coming here. (To attain that Bachelor of Science Degree.) After that talk, she never missed another class. Having an enjoyable time with her friends was not the purpose of Voorhees.

Now that I am in my second semester of college, I continue to have some excel classes, developmental classes, and college classes. Track season began in March, and I was in reasonably decent shape by the time I ran my first track meet. Voorhees held the track meet at Francis Marion University in Florence, South Carolina, which was only thirty minutes from my hometown, and I looked forward to my mother coming to see me run track for the Vorhees College team.

I imagine that my mother always kept it tucked in her mind. This was her son, who was ignored by his father, abandoned by his paternal grandparents, and rejected by all his paternal relatives. The son, with epilepsy and autism, and probably would not graduate from high school, is now in college and running track at Francis Marion University.

Determined to see me on the day of the track meet, my mother had the lady she worked for bring her to see me run. I came in second place in the mile run. I ran my best time in the mile run, coming in at four minutes and thirty-seven seconds. In the two-mile run, I came in third place. As I was crossing the finish line, I could hear my mother shouting at the top of her lungs, "that's my son," which made me feel so good to hear her voice and see her at my track meet. I received the MVP award for track during my first year of running track.

Now that track season was over, basketball season was also over. The college campus had intramural basketball for the students who attended Voorhees. The young men I hung out with on campus made up a basketball team named 'New Breed.' The group asked me to be their coach, which made me feel good and honored. I told my friends yes; I would love to be the coach for the New Breed basketball team. Whenever New Breed had a basketball game, the gym would be full.

When I, BKA (better known as) Caveman, walked into the gym with the New Breed basketball team, I would always have on a suit, and the audience would stand up and give me a standing ovation. After winning many of our games, New Breed finally made it to the Championship game. I was overly excited because I was allowed to coach a basketball team that had made it to the Championship.

It was a remarkably close and intense game from beginning to end during the Championship game, but as the last quarter clock counted down to the very last second, New Breed lost two points. The New Breed basketball team became a popular name on campus. I wanted to make New Breed a social club on campus. I could not make New Breed a social club, but I worked hard to make it happen, thinking about how wonderful it would have been to have a New Breed social club on campus.

On March 13, 1988, everything was going great in my life. I was walking to my dorm room, and that was when someone ran up to me to tell me that I had a phone call. As I answered the phone, I had all kinds of thoughts running through my mind about who was on the other line calling me. I knew it had to be an important call. I picked up the telephone receiver to say hello and heard an unfamiliar voice on the other end. It was a female on the phone who said that her name was identified herself as Tammy.

She addressed me as Caveman and began to tell me that Carolina (my soon-to-be baby mama) was in labor and was on her way to the hospital. I did not have a vehicle to drive, so I asked different people to take me to the Marion, South Carolina hospital. I did my best to get to the hospital to see my baby enter this world. I had a challenging time finding someone to take me to the hospital when finally, there was a willing person that drove me to the hospital at 10:15 p.m. that night.

I was unable to see my baby when I arrived at the hospital. I let the nurse know that I had rushed from college all the way from Denmark, SC.in a sincere effort to see this baby. The nurse informed me that Caroline had a boy and did allow me to see my son for the first time. I started repeating to myself I am a daddy; I am a daddy.

I was so excited and knew that it was love at first sight. I was genuinely concerned, wondering if my son would have epilepsy. The nurse in the hospital nursery shared with me that my son had five fingers and a thumb and that the doctor removed the extra finger, but everything else was normal. I could only thank God for looking out for my son.

I noticed that his name was Bennie Tyrone Davis, Jr. on the card taped to the foot of the nursery bed where he lay. I stayed there at the hospital with my son for forty-five minutes. The young man driving me to the hospital suggested we head back to Voorhees because it was getting late. After seeing my son, it made me even more determined to graduate from college to be able to provide for him. The driver and I returned to Voorhees at three in the morning.

I did not miss breakfast or any of my classes that day. When I went to my studies, I told everyone I had a son, and one of the young men said he was my son's uncle. Everyone congratulated me on my new baby boy's arrival. As time passed, I was now at the end of the semester. I am a proud father of Bennie Tyrone Davis, Jr., and I knew that I had to make excellent grades and graduate to take care of my son. I passed all my college classes and avoided academic probation.

I registered for summer classes. I finished my second semester and attended my last freshman class meeting, where we voted for our officers for Voorhees 1988-89 school year. I decided that I was going to run for class president during my sophomore year. While I was patiently waiting for all the voting outcomes after my classmate placed their votes.

The college President finally announced that I was my upcoming sophomore class president. When I heard the fantastic news, I started jumping up and down like I was on a trampoline because I was in college and my classmates voted me as sophomore class president. My classmates believed in me, so I knew I had to do important things as their sophomore class president. As of this day, I was the first and only student who attended Voorhees that held the class president's position having epilepsy and autism. All the accomplishments I achieved in my first year of college were mind-boggling. The excitement was over now; it was time to return to business.

It was time for my summer classes to begin, and I would be by myself because my sister went back to New York for the summer to work to have money to buy her clothes and necessities for the upcoming college year. When it was time to register for my summer classes, I found someone else to help me schedule them. Classes were Monday through Thursday, with no classes on Friday. I took three courses for a total of nine hours and successfully passed all of them. Now, I felt the excitement of returning because of my sophomore year, and I would be starting as Bennie T. Davis Sr., class president.

I had so many ideas that I wanted to do. I wanted to make this sophomore class the most momentous experience in Voorhees' history. I went home after my summer classes and spent time with my family and friends. The summer had ended, and it was time for my sister and I to return to Voorhees. Mr. Bill Hughes once again transported the two of us back to campus. My confidence level was up; I believed in myself, that I was qualified to be at Voorhees. When things were rough for me, I learned how to encourage myself.

It was on and popping being back on campus. I was excited about my classes and being a sophomore and extra excited about attending my first meeting as the class President. This class meeting was for me and my sophomore classmates.

The purpose of the meeting was to vote on who would represent our class as the Sophomore Queen. Three young ladies ran for Sophomore Queen, and one of them was my sister. My sister did not win, but she was an attendant to Ms. Sophomore.

At my first sophomore meeting, a large group was in attendance, and they supported me and the things I wanted to do for our class. They were receptive to my ideas about how we would make money by doing fundraisers. My first fundraiser was a Friday night dance. I named the dance the "Lockdown," meaning the doors did not unlock until the last song played. If anyone chose to leave the party before the party ended, they would have to pay to exit it. I can say that my sophomore class made more money than any of the Voorhees classes.

With all the activities, I could still keep a decent GPA (Grade Point Average) fall semester by passing my classes and getting tutoring. Once November arrived, I ran to get in shape for track and field. I wanted to do better than I had done in my freshman year. The spring semester had finally begun, and I was in shape and ready for the track competition. Sadly, it was a short track season because it rained a lot, and the weather prevented the meets. I also had some track meet cancellations because mechanical problems with the Voorhees College bus made it impossible to attend.

I must admit that this college journey was not comfortable by any means. I was the most successful class president than any other class president that year. I worked hard at it. This semester was ending. It was time to vote for the upcoming junior president, and I decided to run for Junior class president.

What surprised me was I had a contender. I became disqualified (I did not have the adequate required number of credits). Therefore, I was ineligible to run for that position. Most of my upcoming junior classmates were unhappy about me not running for class president. My classmates knew I had done an excellent job as Sophomore class president and knew I would do it again. The young man who found out I was ineligible found himself in the same situation I was in, causing him to be disqualified too. The student body selected a female as junior class president.

3. THE LIFE OF CRIME

My summer classes only lasted eight weeks, so I was able to go home for the rest of my summer break to be with my mother and my son. I had about three weeks before returning to Voorhees College, starting my third year of college and my third year of summer classes. I still did not have enough credits toward graduation to be classified as a Junior. Voorhees Administration thought that I would quit college, and this would be the time to do so because there was no way that I could graduate with the classes I was taking.

Yes, I know that Voorhees College allowed everyone to attend their college, but they knew everyone would not graduate. (They gave anyone who wanted it a chance) It was difficult for someone who had not taken any college prep courses and only had taken basic classes while in high school to complete any college.

I had determination! I was determined not to leave this college until I received my Bachelor of Science degree. No matter what it took to succeed, I did it because graduation day was approaching. I wanted to be one of Voorhees' many students to walk across that graduation stage and receive my degree. This time when I went home, my son was four months old, and I would always keep him until it was time for me to return to college. I spent as much time as possible with my son because I wanted to be a part of his life.

As my summer break ended, my sister returned home from New York so we could leave for college. This time I could drive my sister and me back to college. My mother purchased a car for one hundred dollars from her next-door neighbor, Uncle Cleve Dorsey. From the time I could remember up until now, all I ever called him was Uncle Cleve, even though we were not related. So, my sister and I returned to Voorhees to start our third year. By this time, I was the most popular person on campus; even the Voorhees instructors called me Caveman.

My sister and I did not go home often because we were living off campus. We were renting a two-bedroom house for eighty-five dollars a month. My landlord was Dr. Cleveland Sellers from Denmark, SC. I used to see Dr. Sellers with his young son, not knowing that his son would grow up employed by CNN as a Political Analyst and a former representative from SC.

The fall semester had started, and as usual, I was excited about my third year in college. Each semester I had at least one excel class or a developmental class. I knew that I had to begin taking some college classes. I failed my English proficiency exam and could not take any literature classes. I signed up for a literature class anyway and boldly began attending classes. My instructor informed me in Tuesday's class that I had to read one-hundred-plus pages of my literature book before returning to class on Thursday.

I had a reading problem, and the assignment would be impossible for me to read a hundred-plus page and take notes on what I read. I would be unable to understand what I read, so I couldn't discuss it in class on that upcoming Thursday. I searched the campus for someone who could help me, and it did not make a difference whether it was a male or female, provided they could read. I especially looked for someone that enjoyed drinking beer or alcoholic beverages.

My sister advised me to go to the library and pick up the head plot for each story I needed to read. The master plots only had fifteen to twenty pages. This would be ideal since I knew that my reader would not read a hundred-plus pages out of my literature book. I found a guy who wanted the job. He did as I instructed, and I paid him with a case of beer and some alcoholic beverages for reading the primary plots and recording them on my tape recorder. The day before my literature class, I listened to the master plot repeatedly the entire day to familiarize myself with the assignment.

Thursday came for me to attend my literature class. I walked into my classroom with nothing but confidence. If I did not have confidence in myself, I knew I would not be able to stay in this literature class. The instructor checked the attendance of the class. I had a big smile, patiently waiting for my turn to talk about what I had read. Finally, I heard my instructor call my name, Caveman. Are you ready to brief the class with the stories you have read for this class?

I talked so much about the stories my instructor and classmates thought I had read my literature book. I talked and explained so much about the stories that my instructor had to stop me because I was running over the time limit. With me talking about the characters in the story, I could pass the test when it was given. I was passing my classes with B's and C's. I received a C in those classes because the instructor, president and vice president knew I had a reading problem. Getting an A in those classes was impossible for me with my reading level.

One day I was walking on campus, minding my own business, when I heard someone call out to me. I turned around to see who was calling me. I saw a young man waving his hand for me to come to where he was sitting. I walked over to the middle of the campus where he was sitting, and we began to talk. I introduced myself to the young man, and Joey introduced himself.

I did not know the young man named Joey, but he knew me as Caveman. Joey told me that he has been watching me sell candy, soda, and chips on campus and noticed my commitment to hustling. Joey said I was a hustler and wanted to know if I would like to make some fast money. I was grinning with excitement when I heard the words fast money. I told the young man I would love to make fast money. Joey said that I could make a couple of hundred dollars a day.

When he told me that, I did not think my grin could get any bigger, but it did. I was grinning so hard that you could see all thirty-two of my teeth. I wondered to myself, what kind of job is that making that kind of money in the world?

Joey went on to explain to me what he wanted me to do. He told me that he would give me some weed (marijuana) on my face, which meant that I did not have to have any money upfront. Joey told me I would get my money off the top, meaning I would get paid first and then pay him. Then he told me he would get back to me in a few days.

I had a roommate named Curtis living with me off campus, and he was also my roommate when I was living on campus. Sadly, he was dismissed from Voorhees College because the college found out he did not have a high school diploma. I allowed Curtis to continue to be my roommate while he worked at a local gas station in Bamberg, South Carolina. Curtis would always have good money in his pockets. I did not have money like Curtis had.

I remember one time when he and I were hungry, and all we had in the house to eat was some neckbones, canned goods and rice. I fried the neckbones and added barbecue sauce to some of them. Those fried neckbones tasted better than fried chicken to me. One day Curtis asked me to go out to eat, knowing I did not have money. I took a young lady with us when we went to the restaurant.

Since Curtis asked me to go out to eat and had money, I assumed he would take care of my bill. He ordered his food and asked me to buy him something to eat. Curtis was trying to embarrass me in front of my young lady friend. (That experience taught me that some people enjoy seeing you stay beneath them).

Joey asked me to sell weed for him as the days went by. Joey contacted me, we met, and I told him I was ready. Joey gave me twenty-five dime bags of weed (a dime bag sold for ten dollars). Joey told me I would keep fifty dollars and pay him two hundred dollars.

This was when I realized that I did not have to tell anyone what I was doing because he patronized my business after I sold the first dime bag to Drake. After all, the weed was good for him. Drake told people to see Caveman if they wanted some good weed.

Caveman had what they needed, it was the bomb, and a person would get good and high off a dime bag. Within twenty-four hours, I had made over two hundred dollars for myself. I was looking at the money I made that day, grinning hard while recounting it to myself repeatedly.

It was time to re-up (which meant getting more weed), so I contacted my supplier, Joey, who came by the house to pick me up. Joey asked me to drive his car. He gave step-by-step directions on where to go. I pulled the car over to the side of the road, and Joey got out, instructing me to drive down the road and then come back. Joey did not say how far to go, so I drove down the block and turned around to go back. When I returned to where I had dropped him off, I realized I must have gotten back too soon because I caught Joey with all the weed. Joey could not put away some for himself, so he gave me all since I saw him with it.

When I sold the weed, I had this time and made much more money off the top. I decided to get a few young men to sell the weed for me. I found a few young men I trusted who did not mind hustling. Once these young men were selling the weed for me, I took my product to a little area called "The Strip." I began selling my weed on campus and The Strip. I did not want to be just a peddler; I wanted to be the Man.

I had to have the best weed and keep my buyers on The Strip and campus happy. This was when I, Caveman, really blew up and became big. I had some people constantly ask me whether I had some crack, powder (cocaine) as well some weed. I did not know much about crack and powder, but I knew I had to learn more about it. After doing some research on crack and powder, I discovered that I could make more money selling it.

I discovered that I could sell a slab of crack for one hundred dollars, half of a slab sold for fifty dollars, twenties sold for twenty dollars and dimes sold for ten dollars. I had to find a supplier to get some crack and some powder. My mind was made up that those streets would belong to Caveman. I continued to sell drugs and attend classes, which I never missed. I continued to be available for tutoring throughout the week. I made Caveman's name popular in the drug game.

I was making some good money, but there was more money in selling crack and powder, better known as 'white girl.' Within six months, I was the biggest kingpin selling weed. I had the city of Denmark, Voorhees College, and Denmark Technical College all on lockdown. When anyone wanted weed, Caveman was the only name called.

One hot Thursday night, I was on the strip, making money selling my weed, and a young man came up to me and told me that the kingpin wanted to see me. This kingpin (Trell) was Denmark's biggest crack and powder supplier. Trell wanted to meet me because my name was in the streets and how I worked the streets. I followed the young man to Trell's location, and we greeted each other.

He began to tell me that he wanted me on his team. I agreed to be part of his team because I knew I would be making big money with his products. Trell fronted me an ounce of crack and an ounce of powder. I was selling forties for twenty dollars, a fifty-pound slab, and two slabs for one hundred. I started to crush my competition because no one was doing it like me. I was setting a standard for selling drugs.

I started moving so many drugs and selling to so many people that I decided to only sell weight. I made more money selling weight, and I dealt with fewer people. When I started selling weight, I did not care if someone smoked, sniffed, or shot up drugs. I gave them what they wanted; whether it was a half-ounce, one ounce, or a quarter, they would get it for the same price as everyone else I sold to.

One day I decided to see some friends after finishing my classes. I was having a great day. As I was getting in my car to leave off campus and closing my car door, I heard someone say Caveman, so I looked up, and it was a Voorhees College Chief of Security.

The Security officer told me, "As of this day, you are no longer allowed to be on this campus or go to any of the dorms on campus. He told me that the only thing that I could do on campus was to attend my classes." He also told me that I would be arrested if I came on campus for any other reason than attending my classes.

This security officer was also employed at the Denmark Police Department. The security officer knew me because the word around Denmark was that Caveman was the man that had the City of Denmark, Denmark Tech, and Voorhees on lockdown. If there was any weed smoking, the supply came from the Caveman. Caveman also had the best cocaine and crack cocaine. At that time, the cocaine was raw, no cutting was done, and if anyone sniffed it raw, blood would start running out their nose.

A night did not go by that I was not on the strip with the young people working for me. I would leave the strip at about midnight on weekdays, but my crew and I did not leave on Fridays and Saturdays until sunrise.

I continued to get tutored, and I never forgot my purpose. I failed my English class for the second time. I had to pass an English proficiency exam of 50% of my final grade to pass my English class. An English proficiency exam tests English language abilities given by the college board. The exam results would show if a student had the necessary English skills to understand academic writing, produce scholarly writing and communicate effectively. I had already failed my exam once, and if I failed it again, I would receive an incomplete so that it would not interfere with my GPA. Since I was restricted from coming on campus unless I attended my classes, I had my buyers meet at a certain time to get their drugs.

The semester was finally ending, and I had average grades, but I still had to pass my English exam. My English instructor let the class know who would be able to take the test, and once again, my name was called. I only had a few days before I had to take the exam.

I knew I needed to pass this exam to graduate from Voorhees College. It did not matter if a person had passed all their classes and did not pass the English proficiency exam; that person would not be able to graduate. My English instructor knew it would be impossible for me to pass this English proficiency exam because of my reading level.

I knew that God specialized in doing the impossible, so I went to tutoring that day, trying to get and retain all the information in my mind that I needed. The night before it was time for me to take the English proficiency exam, I could not sleep because I knew this was it for me. This would be a particularly good excuse for quitting college if I did not pass my exam.

On the exam day, I ensured I was in the auditorium twenty minutes before the exam started. I was given three topics on the exam and had to choose one to write about. This report must include a three-body paragraph, an introduction, a thesis statement, and a conclusion. Before the exam started, my instructor told the class we could use a dictionary. I did not own a dictionary because I did not know how to read the words in the dictionary.

I took my time doing my exam and made sure each sentence was a group of words expressing a complete thought. I used simple everyday words that a second-grader would be able to understand. When I reached the end of my report, I could not spell "conclusion." That was when I had to start encouraging and reminding myself that my father had graduated from college and my mother worked hard to send me to college. "God, I do not believe You brought me this far to let me down now." For a few moments, not one thing would come to me, then out of nowhere (I realize now it came from God), these letters came to my mind.
"T-H-E-R-E-F-O-R-E," and I restated my thesis statement. The exam lasted two hours, and I used every minute of it. After everyone had finished their exam, it was graded by five English instructors who would read everyone's exam. To pass the exam, three out of the five English instructors had to give a passing grade.

I patiently waited for the results of my exam to be posted. When the results came in that I passed my English proficiency exam, the news that Caveman passed the exam spread around the college campus like wildfire. This was when I realized that I was not going to get the grade I earned because fifty percent of my final grade was from the English proficiency exam. To take the English proficiency exam, I had to have at least an eighty in my English class, and I had an eighty-five.

With me passing the English proficiency exam, my English Instructor only gave me a C for the class, which should have been an "A" or a "B" instead of a C. Only one thing could stop me from graduating now, and that would be myself. In my third year of college, I decided not to run track anymore. I decided to get help with my tuition by using financial aid only and not get the scholarship money for running track because I was still just focusing on my purpose for coming to Voorhees. I aim to graduate with a Bachelor of Science in criminal justice.

It was time to celebrate now that I passed my English proficiency exam. Word had gotten around that on that Friday night, and a party was going to be sponsored by Caveman. This was the biggest house party in Denmark. I invited people from Voorhees College, Denmark Technical College and all of Denmark was invited to my party.

I even invited the young men I had recruited to sell my products, but I told them they could not stay at the party long because money still had to be made, and I had to have all of it, not some of it.

At the party, I had over one hundred blunts ready to be smoked, cocaine ready to be sniffed and all the beer and liquor they could drink. I also had food. I planned to start the party at 10 pm that night, but the people started showing up around nine. By the time 10 o'clock came, the house party was packed with people. Cars were parked on both sides of the street. By 11 o'clock that night, people were standing all around the house, outside and down the sidewalk.

Every Friday and Saturday night, Voorhees College and Denmark Technical College would have a party on their campus, but on this Friday night, both campus parties were shut down because everybody was at the Caveman house party. The sun was beginning to rise, and the party was still going on. Some people stayed all night without any sleep, helping me celebrate passing my English proficiency exam.

Graduating was now the only thing in my sight. As my house party was ending, the Denmark Police drug unit came into my house with warrants looking for drugs. The police looked all over my house, in and outside, trying to find drugs. After hours, the search was over, and no drugs were found. The drugs not smoked or used were back on the streets being sold.

I had a few days left before the spring semester started, so I went home to spend time with my mother and son. When I got home, I could tell that the people in my neighborhood were still excited about me growing up and attending college. I could share with them that I passed a test many people could not pass and would end up quitting school.

I was full of determination that I was not going to quit and that I would graduate. The only thing in my heart was that I wanted to be the first and the only person to graduate from Voorhees College with epilepsy and autism. But most of all, the son that my father and his family called a bastard child would never amount to anything good.

My sister was excited because she was on the right track of graduating in four years. I was proud of my sister because she stayed focused, went to all her classes, and stayed on campus when I moved off campus. We saw each other daily because she would come to my house.

I was doing well in college, but the news returned to my hometown that I, Caveman, sold the best weed and crack, also known as butter. Most of the parents who sent their child or children to Voorhees College or Denmark Technical College from my hometown knew that their child or children had some involvement with Caveman.

The parents blamed Caveman for their child selling or using drugs. Each person decided individually to sell or use drugs, not me. Some were already selling or smoking drugs before college, and some started selling and using after. The young men from my hometown had more freedom than when they were with their guardians and were doing whatever they desired. The parents never looked at their children for wrongdoing; all the blame fell on me (Caveman). Over ninety percent of the people from my hometown who started selling or buying drugs got the drugs from me between 1988-1996.

Since my drug business was increasing, I had to find more peddlers to distribute my drug on the streets. I knew that I had the best drugs, the best weight, and most of all, I had the best prices. I always ensured that all peddlers would make some money when they got any package from Caveman. So now it was time to go back to Denmark to get ready for my spring semester.

I decided to have one of the young men who sold drugs for me stay in my hometown to see how much of my product could be sold on the street. Within two days, he returned to Denmark for a re-up because everything he had was sold. As I returned to the small city of Denmark, I decided to ride through the strip to see how things were going.

The drug traffic was moving fluently, so I decided I was coming back because money had to be made. As soon I was spotted riding through the strip, the word got out that Caveman was back with that raw cocaine, Chocolate Thai and Parkay/ butter.

I loaded my bags with the drugs and then went back and dropped the bags off to my sellers. The strip was back on lockdown with my drugs. Since I could not go on campus, I drove past the campus so the students could see me. Once they saw me, they knew how to contact me to get whatever they needed. I did not sleep at night because I sold drugs all night long.

This was the weekend before it was time to register for college, so I went on campus that Wednesday to register. I knew I had to focus more than ever because this would be my first semester with all college courses, and I had to pass them well. I was ready for the challenge because I was now in the position to graduate, and the drug game was going strong. Then to my surprise, as I registered for my classes, I noticed that my World Literature class was being taught by the right hand to the vice president of Voorhees College.

To this day, the right hand to the Vice President of Voorhees College read my English proficiency exam because when I registered for World Literature, she was assigned as the instructor for my class. The Voorhees College administration was trying to put a stop to social passing. Now I know that without a shadow of a doubt, I had to focus harder than ever. Now I had to start trusting the people more that sold drugs for me. I had to give them more responsibilities. I had to believe in them because I knew that the only thing I wanted to do was graduate.

The decision was made; I had to trust the people around me. I could get my classes and be free from 12:30 to 3 pm on Tuesdays and Thursdays. I was free from 1 to 4 pm on Mondays, Wednesdays, and Fridays to watch the soaps. I still made time for tutoring, and all the instructors were willing to work with me. I explained my situation to my instructors and let them know that I had to bring a tape recorder to class.

It was approaching the end of the month, and it was time for me to re-up my drugs. The first of the month is when I make most of my money. So, I went to three different drug dealers that would give me drugs on my face (on credit). I owed them a little over fifteen thousand dollars with the three combined. I hid whatever drugs that were not on the streets in the woods. I put a lot of faith in the young men working for me. When I hid the drugs, I always took one of my sellers with me. I knew not to keep drugs at home. The precaution was a must just in case the drug unit decided to raid my house; if they did, they would not find any drugs.

All the drugs that I had on the streets were sold. I had one of my boys drive me to the woods. He dropped me off. I went to my hiding spot in the woods to recover my drugs. I could not find any of the drugs. When my driver returned to pick me up, I asked him to help me look for my drugs. When I could not find them, I realized that the young man who had come with me to hide the drugs had doubled back and taken my drugs.

He had a smoke out and sold the rest of the drugs. I could not go to the police because what I did was illegal. My only money was from the drugs already sold, and I had a few dollars of my own money. It was not enough to pay off the three big-time drug dealers.

The only thing I realized is if I had him killed or killed him, I would go to prison for life. I was not able to take a life, and I was not able to give a life. I did know that I would need to find a way to come up with the money to pay back the drug dealers. I remembered that one of the drug dealers liked my sister.

So, I had her call him and act like someone wanted to buy drugs. He gave her 3 ounces and $300 in her pocket. When he left my sister, she called me to come pick up the drugs. I got the drugs, cut them up and put them on the streets. I ran out of drugs before 6:00 PM. I was not able to get in touch with anybody that had the drugs that I needed.

Then, someone said let's go to Orangeburg because I know where some good drugs are and at a great price. This was an older man named Henry that I dealt with because he was teaching me all the ropes. So, I believed him, and we went to Orangeburg. We had to get there before nightfall. I was in an area of Orangeburg called the bottom, and it was something like the strip in Denmark. I was looking around as I had never been in this neighborhood before. We drove up, I was asked what I wanted, and I said I am looking for an ounce of crack.

Someone said I have one for you and I asked to see the drugs. I saw the crack was too small and did not want it. When I said that, I saw a 20-pound weight coming out of someone's hand. It hit me on the side of my head, and blood started coming down my face from my head. My head and face were covered with blood. Henry, the man that drove me to Orangeburg, drove us away as fast as he could. I told him to take me to the hospital.

While on the way to the hospital, the blood was still coming down. I was holding pressure on the wound on my head and doing everything I could to stop the bleeding, but nothing worked. We got to the hospital, and I went straight into the bathroom. I put my head down under the faucet and started running water on my head. As the water was running on my head, the blood eventually stopped. The area my head was busted open started coming back together. I decided not to be seen by anyone in the hospital and told the car's driver, "Let's go back to Denmark. I cannot deal over here anymore."

When I made it home, I told my sister, brother and everyone at the house what had happened to me. Just a little blood still trickled down, but I was so happy to still have my life. I knew things could not get any worse, but my brother said tonight he had been held at gunpoint by some boys in Orangeburg. My brother went to

Orangeburg to buy drugs too, but some boys robbed him and took his money, his jewelry, and my high school ring that my brother was wearing.

Now, as I think back, what would have happened if my sister had called my mother and told her that her sons were killed on the same night (while out buying drugs)? That would have been too much on my mother. God put a hedge of protection around her sons. God said to the streets do what you want to do to them, but you cannot have their life.

Despite that, I still got up and went to my classes. Within two weeks, I paid off all the drug dealers I owed. Things were looking great for me. I was passing my classes and making money. In my world literature class, my instructor was impressed by my performance. My instructor informed the Vice President of Voorhees College that Bennie Davis does his work and that the other instructors are not just passing him because he completes all his assignments. She also told him I had passed all the tests she had given me. She knew I could not receive an A in the class.

I was looking for my sister to tell her what was happening in my life. The sky is not the limit for me because there is something higher than the sky, and that is where I am looking to end up. My sister was happy for me. As my sister and I talked, a person approached her, notifying her that she needed to call home. My sister called our mother, and she finished talking. She put the phone down and informed me that our father had passed away.

When I heard the news for a moment, my heart stopped because I knew I could never talk with him. I would never be able to know why he lied to me. My sister would never be able to hear his voice and never see him alive. Where do we go from here? Now, my sister and I had a decision to make about our father. Will we go to the funeral, will we buy flowers, or will we send a card? What do children that love their fathers do? In our father's and his family's eyesight, we were bastard children he did not want anything to do with or our mother. Whatever we decided to do, Mother would stand by our decision. She is with us.

My mother never said anything evil about our father and encouraged us to love him. We decided not to buy any flowers, a card or attend the funeral, but we would go and view his body at the funeral home.

A few days passed, and I got a phone call from my mother to let us know when the viewing was of our father's body. My sister and I had a school event that day, but as soon as we finished, my sister and I drove to our hometown funeral home to view our father's body.

When we were on the road, I kept looking over at my sister the ride home felt longer than usual. I wanted to see my father. This would be my sister's first and only time ever seeing her father, as a dead man in a casket.

My sister and I made it to the funeral home. We walked down the sidewalk leading to the funeral home's entrance. No one was there except my sister, my father (in the casket) and me. My grandparent's put him away in a beautiful casket. My sister and I looked down at our father laying in the casket. My sister was looking at a man that she never knew anything about. I was looking at a man that lied to me.

My eyes got full of water, and tears started flowing down my face. I looked over at my sister to make sure that she was okay. She stared at a man who decided to walk away from her because he did not want to be a part of her life. I wanted to grab him and pull him out of the casket. I wanted to shake him. I just wanted him to wake up.

Then I realized this man was dead, but for my sister and I, he had been dead our entire lives.

I was ready for us to go. Tears were coming down my sister's and my faces. We got back in the car and went straight back to Denmark. We did not go to our mother's house or see anyone that day.

4. ACCOMPLISHING THE IMPOSSIBLE

As my sister and I were leaving the funeral home, we did not say anything to each other. I began thinking to myself how I would never see my father again. I would never know why he abandoned my sister and me. I would never get to tell him I love him and am happy to be his son. I would never be able to say because of you being my father is the reason why I have the drive to go to college. One day, I will graduate because you graduated from college. When I got on Interstate 95, tears were still coming down my face. I looked over at my sister; she had her seat laid back, and I could see she was crying, too. We did not say anything to each other.

I never really knew my father because he walked out of our lives. His parents informed him that he was superior to her because my mother didn't graduate from high school. He was too good of a man to be with her, and those children would never be a part of their family. My father, Daniel Thomas Jr., and his family never claimed us to be part of their family.

I saw my father twice, once at a funeral and the second time he was dead. My sister had never seen him alive or heard his voice; she only saw him once, and he was dead, lying in his casket. I remember someone pointed my father out to me while I was at a gravesite attending a funeral. I was at the funeral, looking around for my father. All I wanted to do was meet my father for the first time. I knew he was at the funeral, and I just wanted to tell him to forget whatever happened and let us start from now on and have a father-and-son relationship. When I walked up to him, I said, I love you, daddy, do not go back to New York. Let me meet with you first. My father said let us get up tomorrow. Call me at 11:00 a.m., and you can come over and talk.

I was so excited for the first time I laid eyes on him. I told him that I loved him. That night felt like a night I never thought would happen, but it was something I always wanted. It was the greatest day of my life. I was about to get the one thing I had waited a lifetime.

I could not sleep that night. I called his mother's house the next day, and she answered the phone. When I asked to speak with him, she said your father is on his way home to New York. He knew that he was not going to be there. That day went from the greatest day of my life to the saddest day. The only thing my dad did to me was lie. My father's death was something personal.

I was feeling one way, and she was feeling another way. We made it back to Denmark. I asked Alethea if she would stay with me or go on campus. She told me to take her back to her dorm, but as I drove her back, she told me to take her to my house.

Alethea said she did not want to see anyone and just wanted to be alone. I then drove to my house. When I got home, I went straight to my room and closed my bedroom door. No one said anything to my sister or me because the people in the house knew our father had just passed, and we were just returning from seeing him. The next day, I just stayed in bed all day. I did not want to do anything.

I will never know why he was ashamed of my sister and me. I'll never be able to tell him that he was a grandfather and that my second child will be here before the end of the summer.

That night, my boys were calling and coming for drugs. I had to get myself together and get back out on the streets. I knew I would be out all night working the streets on Saturday night. I had to get with my boys and re-up my drugs. I had to return to normal because a person could not be on the streets and not focus on their job. The young men buying drugs from me knew my father had passed away. They showed me much love, and my friends on campus also did. That Sunday, a young man called me from my hometown about getting drugs. So, I met him with drugs and got paid.

On that Monday, I was back in class at Voorhees. I enrolled at Denmark Technical College. I was majoring in auto mechanics. I still made time for tutoring, and at the end of the semester, I made all A's and B's. In one of my classes, the professor had me teaching the course; he left me in charge. There were about three weeks left before summer classes started, so I decided to go home to visit my mother and see my son. I was looking forward to my second child being born. I finished another semester and was not on academic probation. My GPA was decent.

I left Denmark for a few days to spend some time in Marion. I knew my baby's momma's due date was sometime in June. I knew I needed to talk with her when I got to my mother's house. I need to tell her that a young lady was pregnant by me.

When I told my mother the news, the first thing that came out of her mouth was that you went to college to get an education and not get some young lady pregnant. She then asked me why I went to school and got some young lady in college pregnant. She then asked me what if that would have been my sister and some man got her pregnant in college. She told me I should not have done that because I already have a son.

I told my mom that the young lady was just a few weeks away from giving birth to the baby and that this would be her second child. I explained to her that the young lady was not in college, but she was from Marion and was the same one who had my first child. For a few minutes, my mother would not say anything; then, she walked away with tears coming down her face. I walked out of my mother's house and said to myself somehow, I would do for my children. I will not leave them. I will be part of their lives.

I checked the streets to see how my drugs were moving. I came up with a great reason why I had to sell many drugs. I have a son and a child in a few weeks. Since then, I have learned that you do not do things because of your children, husband, or wife, but you do things because that is what you want to do.

Whatever you are doing, you do it for yourself and stop passing the blame to someone else. The young men out on the streets working for me were doing their thing. When the other drug dealers saw that Caveman was back, different drug dealers started coming up wanting to buy the Bombazi, Chocolate Thai, Parkay/Butter, and that raw white girl. I put some drugs on the streets and then supplied the need for other drug dealers. I made time to see my son and see how the young lady was doing because she was about three weeks away from giving birth to my second child.

Seems like time has passed by so fast; now it is time for me to prepare to go back to Denmark because summer classes start in a few days. I decided that I was going to leave that night. I was not telling anyone when I would get on the road. I said goodbye to my mother. It was about 8:00 p.m., my sister, brother, and I left like we were returning to school.

We knew there would be a big party at the club. I knew I could sell some drugs before getting on the road. I did not want to take any drugs back to Denmark. I tried to sell all the drugs that I had in Marion. The money I got from the drug sale in Marion was free for me to do whatever I wanted.

I had a good time at the party; they consumed all my drugs. I got on the road at about 3:00 a.m. and returned to Denmark at about 5:45 a.m. I stayed in bed all day and didn't get up until 7:00 p.m. I went to the strip to see what was going on in Denmark. I spent the rest of the evening in the game room at about 11:00 p.m.. I went to the club. When I entered the club, the DJ was on the stage saying Caveman was in the house.

While I was in the club, people would come to me for drugs, and I pointed them to my boys. After leaving the club, I got home at about 2:30 a.m., along with about twenty tenderoni's. They had a smoke out. I let them smoke until they could not smoke anymore.

The table was spread with Bombazi, Chocolate Thai, and blunts after blunts. The tenderoni's loved doing shotguns back-to-back. The next morning, the girls were in my room when my eyes came open. As I walked through the house, girls were all over my place, laid out. I had to get them out of my house because their time was up with Caveman.

When I got everyone out of my house, I had to find someone to come clean my house. There were beer cans, liquor bottles, and blunt papers everywhere. I had to clean my house before my Jamaican Queen came over; she stayed on campus.

It was only about a week away before classes started for the summer. I decided to get some rest and get my mind right. It seems like these days have passed by so fast. It is time to go and register for a class. Now, I am ready for my summer classes, and one of the courses I had to retake was religion because I did not pass it on the first go-around.

My new classes started on a Monday, so I decided I needed to make some money that weekend because my second child was expected to be born sometime in June. I have been getting tutored every year that I had summer classes, but I had to sign up for it this summer because there were no tutors, as there was the previous summer semester.

Somehow, I was able to get into my tutoring classes. I was so happy about that because, without tutoring, I could not pass my summer classes. About two weeks passed, and I did not have a chance to go to Marion because my instructors were putting a workload on me.

On one hot day in Denmark, I walked through the academic circle and headed to my car. Someone ran up to me saying, "Tammy from Marion is trying to get in touch with you."

So, I went to the pay phone to call home. When I called home, Tammy told me that Carolina was in labor. Out of all days, I received this news on the first day of summer. June 21st changed my life. About 3 hours later, I called to find out how everything was going with the young lady in labor. To my surprise, I discovered I was a father to a little girl.

I was so excited. After my classes were over, I drove to the hospital in Marion. When I got to the hospital maternity ward and looked down at my baby girl, I saw the most beautiful little girl I had ever seen. Her name is Ashley Shaquana Davis.

As I looked down at her, tears began to roll down my face and met under my chin. I realized then that I did not have the most beautiful little girl in the world but in The Universe.

I stayed in Marion for a couple of hours. I rode around in the drug areas to find out if anyone needed any drugs while I was there. Shortly after that, I went to see my mother. Then, I got back on the road and headed back to Denmark. The next day, I told my friends that I was a father to a little girl named Ashley. My friends started congratulating me on the birth of my daughter. Then, I went back to the drawing board, making money. Once again, I passed all my classes for the summer semester.

I celebrated passing my studies and put together a 4th of July cookout for anyone at Voorhees, Denmark Technical College, in the neighborhood and the people from the strip. I had food, alcohol, beer, 100 blunts, Chocolate Thai, Bombazi, Parkay/butter, and the raw white girl.

One of the former Miss Vorhees was in town and stopped by the party to have a good time with Caveman. People at the cookout had blood running out of their noses caused of sniffing uncut raw butter. The party lasted for 24 hours. People were coming and going because everything was free.

The people were smoking so many blunts at once until it was so much smoke that someone high came and told me to call the fire station and report a fire at the house because it was cloudy. I had to get people to help open the house's windows and doors. The house was packed, but then I made an announcement.

Tonight, we have female strippers and only one male stripper. This is the surprise; his name is Speed Bump. All of the lights went out. As the female strippers came out, everyone started screaming.

Then, they saved the best for last. The first time on stage was Speed Bump. Speed Bump came out of all his clothing, and the woman started screaming, "Speed Bump and what a bump that is, Caveman."

They started singing Cave, Cave, you look so fine, you blow my mind, but you look greater as Speed Bump." The former Miss

Vorhees snuck out of the party when the lights came on. The next morning, we were together at the hotel in Denmark.

I finished the last two weeks of school. It was a successful summer; I passed all my classes. The only thing on my mind now was I must go home and see my two stars, Bennie and Ashley. I informed my mom and told her that I would be home for about a week. I wanted to spend some time with them, so I went to Marion on the last day of my summer class. I spent about a week and a half enjoying myself with my children.

Despite all that was happening in my life, I still ensured that drugs were on the streets in Marion. I also made sure that my boys stayed in supply in Denmark. Some young drug dealers saw me coming into town. Those drug dealers knew whatever the appetite called for; I had it for the streets.

One day, this young man asked me to take him to a small city near Marion called Mullins. I drove to Mullins and pulled up to a house full of tenderoni. Once I entered the house, I introduced myself as Caveman, and they forgot all about the young man I brought there.

I saw this one tenderoni, and I started giving her eye contact. She smiled at me, and I slipped a note saying I would return to her town. She gave me her phone number, and it was on then. Caveman was in the house. The next time I went to Mullins, I took my brother so if anybody tried to jump on me, he would fight for me. I told my brother I had a girl for him, so the next night, my brother and I returned to the Mullins' house. What a great time we had that night!

It was time for me to start getting ready to return to college. It was the beginning of my 4th year, and my sister's last year of college was upon us. My sister qualified to be a Senior. I was in my 4th year also but still a Junior.

When a person goes to college, it can only mean one or two things will happen. You will either make it, or you are going to fail. If I considered quitting, this would be a perfect time because my sister is a senior and will soon graduate from Voorhees, and I won't. What would happen when my sister graduated started going through my mind. Who will be here to help me? I was not able to read and have an understanding. My sister was always there, and she did all my paperwork.

It was time to register for college, and my sister had to take her senior pictures. I could only take 12 credits, so I decided to take classes I made a D before. I registered to retake those classes to bring up my GPA. Math and science were my most challenging classes. I had a great working relationship with my professors, and I never forgot about taking the time to go to tutoring. I was juggling between the drug life and college life.

One day, my mother decided to come to Denmark for a few days. My mom did not know that her son was one of the biggest drug dealers in Denmark. Once my mother arrived, I had to ensure no one came to the house for drugs. I went to pick up my mom, and I brought her back to my house. I had to hire a drug user to stay down the street all night to ensure nobody came to my house. I gave him a slab of crack cocaine for his services.

No one came to my house that night, so I gave him a bonus and a half of slab when I saw him the next day. The hired man told me he would be there early that night and that no one would come to my house for drugs. I told the tenderoni that they could not come to the house because my mother was there visiting for a few days. My mother had a wonderful time. I focused on schoolwork, so my mother observed me going to class and returning home.

When I was out, I would supply the streets with drugs. I let the people know they could not come to my house, so they had to get what they needed now. A few young men from Marion came to my house to buy some chocolate Thai. My mother had a conversation with them. She told them they needed to do good in school and that she knew their parents. She encouraged them to do all their work to pass their grade.

She didn't realize that school was the furthest from their minds. Those young men wanted to smoke that Chocolate Thai. None of the young men that came from Marion graduated from college. They all dropped out. The unfortunate part was that their parents did not know, and it was not my fault because I stayed in school. The young men loved the streets and getting high more than staying in school.

My mother went back home and went to New York to see her mother. The word got out that Caveman's mother had left and that he was having a party on that Friday night. Nose bleeding was the talk of Denmark from sniffing that Raw at a Caveman party. I went to class that week and passed out a flyer concerning the party I was having that Friday night.

The matchbox is not the place to be, but you only need to be at Caveman's house. That Friday came so fast, but everything was organized. I made sure I supplied them with drugs. Caveman enjoyed the party as always. The tables were spread with all-you-can-eat, drink, smoke, and sniff. I invited people from the surrounding cities, the strip, Barnwell, Blackville, Allendale, Bamberg, Orangeburg., Columbia and Augusta, Georgia.

The people started arriving at my house at about 10:00 p.m. They knew the party would not end until the sun came up or when the last person left. One of the young men who worked the streets for me was getting high at the party, and he brought a young tenderoni with him. She enjoyed smoking that butter and knew the young man worked for me.

They entered another room, and she got a pipe because she knew it was time to get high. She told the young man to give her the butter, not knowing the young man loved butter. The young man told her to pass him the pipe then he started smoking the crack. When he finished with the pipe, he gave the pipe back to her. The young lady was upset because of nothing he had left in the pipe.

She came looking for me. She told me that my boy was smoking crack, just like her and that he was a crackhead. I had someone to go and find him and let him know I needed to see him. When he came to me, I advised him not to let anyone know he smoked. He said, "Caveman, I could not allow her to smoke all that butter."

I started laughing because he rubbed the floor like he had dropped something. The people were drinking, smoking, and dancing. It was just a fantastic time all night long. It was about 6:00 a.m. when the last few people left the party. About 20 people lay on the floor in my house. Some people could not make it out the door, and some were in their cars because they were too high to even drive their cars. I stayed in the house all day and did not leave. I had my boys come to me to get their drugs. That night, I went down to the strip, the game room, and the club. Mostly everyone who saw me started shouting, "Caveman, Caveman, you had the party of the decade."

I made sure that there were some drugs on the strip, and I went back home and got into bed. I had a rough time because the party lasted all night. I had to get some rest because I knew classes started on Monday. That Sunday, I just laid around and looked at the NFL games. I made sure that I had all of my work for my classes. I had a wonderful week in my classes.

That semester went so fast. I worked hard, and so did my sister. We passed all our classes. My sister is just one semester from graduating with her Bachelor of Science degree in criminal justice. I was so proud of her. I decided to go home for Christmas shortly after the semester ended. The semester ended about a week before Christmas.

I went to Marion to spend some time with my two children. My daughter was just a few months old, and my son was going on three years old. The time just passed by so quickly. When I got to the big city of Marion, I told my sister that before we went to our mother's house, I had a stop to make. I had to ride through the streets and ensure everything was great with the drugs.

I had to do this first because I knew she would not let me back out once I got to my mother's house. I ensured the drug dealers who loved buying drugs from me were okay. Then, I supplied them with the drugs that they needed. After I finished handling things, I went to my mother's house, knowing I would be in the house for the remainder of the night.

I had an outstanding Christmas. I stayed in Marion for the New Year's Eve service because I believed in being in church when the old year went out and the new year came in. I wanted my new year to be blessed. I would always give a seed offering to whatever church I attended for the New Year's Eve services because I knew God would bless me.

I learned the principles of giving. After the church service was over, I went to the club. I had a wonderful time. I supplied the needed drugs. Then, I got on the road to head back to Denmark. My mother assumed my sister, and I had to return to Denmark immediately. I made it back to Denmark at about 5:00 a.m. A week later, it was time to register for classes.

This was my sister's last semester in school. I was so happy about what she would achieve in her life. When my classes started, I accepted that I would not graduate with my sister, but I would be able to graduate a year later.

Once again, I ensured my afternoons were free between 12:30 p.m. and 4:00 p.m. I enjoyed watching The Young and The Restless, The Bold and the Beautiful, As the World Turns and The Guiding Light. That was an afternoon made in heaven for me. This semester, I had tutoring at 3:00 p.m. and a class at 4:00 p.m. During the morning time, I would go to tutoring from 11:00 a.m. to 12:00 p.m. What a great semester this was for me.

One afternoon, someone informed me that someone on the strip wanted to start selling drugs and needed some crack. So, I had someone take me to the strip to find out what he wanted. I had a few slabs on me, and as we left the strip, I had two slabs left. A police officer saw me enter the car, so the police drove behind the car.

The blue lights came on before we could get out of the city limits. I had two slabs on me, and knowing that the police were going to search the car, I only knew to get rid of the two slabs of crack. I would have to throw it out the car window. It was not dark yet, so if I threw it out the window, the police would have seen the drugs go out. The young man pulled over, and I had no place to hide the crack. I had no choice but to eat the two crack slabs or go to jail, which was not an option.

I had swallowed the drugs when the police got to the car. The officer asked the young man driving for his driver's license. Then he asked if he could search the car and called for backup. The officer said, "Caveman is in the car."

The driver told the police that they could not search his car. Then, the officer said he had probable cause because we were in a drug area. By this time, the other police officers arrived on the scene. The police officers searched the car and could not find any drugs. About an hour later, the police officer had to let us go.

By this time, everything in me started getting numb. I knew that that butter was working in me. I could not sleep; I was hot and scared because I did not want to die. During this time, I could have sex with the tenderoni all night long, non-stop. They had me wanting to live and not die. I drank milk and did all kinds of things to get the drugs out of my system. Despite my wrongdoing, I had to deal with it; God would not allow death to take me out. My mother kept her children in prayer. Because of that, a hedge was around me. God protected me.

As soon as we got back, I let my boys know that the people had to pay for this dope since I had to eat some. The people must pay more for the dope. Prices went up on all drugs because there was a shortage of drugs. There were no drugs in Florida, and because of that, Denmark couldn't get any. So, Caveman had the last of drugs. I was the man during this time. I could have any tenderoni I wanted because I was the man with the money and the drugs. Caveman had the power, but I did not let it blow my mind. I never got out of control. I always treated people with respect, even if they smoked drugs; I respected them. Now, this was the last weekend before classes started. My friends were still stealing my drugs when I would go put the drugs up.

On February 16, 1991, my life changed in a way I didn't even know. A few days later, someone came and gave me a note that said, "Caveman, call this number." I called the number, and the person on the other line said you must come home.

I said, "Why do I need to come home?" The person on the other end of the phone told me that I was the father of a little girl named Antoinette Davis. My heart felt like it had just stopped for a moment. I said that I would be home on the weekend. I went home that weekend.

I did not tell anyone why I was going to Mullins. When I got to the young lady's house in Mullins, I walked in. Someone said, "Come and see your little daughter." When I entered the room, I looked down at the little girl and knew then that she was my little girl.

She was so pretty; she and Ashley looked just like twins. I said I am the father of two of the most beautiful girls, not just in the world but in The Universe. Someone in the house told me to pick her up, and I said, "no, she is too small. I do not want to drop her." I stayed with my daughter for a few hours.

I had to get back on the road to head to Denmark. When I returned to Denmark, I told my sister and brother they had a new niece. Then my brother laughed at me and said, now I see why you were riding that bicycle to Mullins. Antoinette was only one month in her mother's womb when Ashley was born. Ashley and Antoinette are the same age. One's birthday is February 16th, and the other is June 21st. I was taken advantage of by Ashley's and Antoinette's mothers.

This spring semester, I only had to do 12 credits, and my sister took the rest of the classes to graduate with her class. This semester passed by so fast. I passed all my classes with good grades. My sister was so excited because she had also passed her classes and was informed that she had met her Bachelor of Science degree requirements.

This graduation was so wonderful because it was on Mother's Day. My sister gave my mother something to let her know that what she did for her and letting her stay with our aunt in New York had paid off. My aunt Mabel Davis, grandmother Rosie Belle Davis, and other family members and friends came to the graduation.

The graduation was outside, and the sun was out. It was hot that day. My mother, brother, grandmother, and aunts rejoiced when they called my sister's name as she walked up and got her degree. She was the first to receive a college degree in the Davis family.

When my sister could say something to me, she said, "Caveman, I did not forget my purpose." After graduation was over, my family and I went out to dinner. Then we went to Marion. It was a great celebration of my sister's graduation. The first grandchild, my mother's first child, to graduate from college.

This is a big accomplishment for our family. My mother was a single parent, who did not finish school but had a doctorate in raising her children. All three of her children graduated from high school. One just graduated from college, and the other is on his way to graduation. The Davis family has something wonderful to celebrate. My sister returned to New York to enjoy her vacation for a few weeks. She returned home to Myrtle Beach and worked while applying for jobs in her major.

I knew I only had a few weeks left before starting summer classes. My sister graduated from college. I have no choice but to graduate from college because it is in my blood. I am not letting anything stop me from graduating from college. So, I returned to school and worked hard in my summer classes. I passed all my classes for that summer.

Caveman's drug crew was still selling drugs on the streets of Denmark. The young men from Marion would not come to Marion because the only thing they wanted to do was stay on the streets of

Denmark and sell drugs. I am only three semesters from graduating from Voorhees college.

Man said it could not happen. A below-average student is about to get an above-average degree. My mother prayed for me, and prayer does change the situation. Something is going to happen when a person prays. After my summer classes were over, I decided to go to Marion for a few days to spend some time with my children and put some drugs on the streets of Marion.

I had to re-up the young men in Denmark with drugs before I went to Marion. While in Marion, I made some money in Denmark and Marion simultaneously.

When I got to Marion, I went to my mother's house. I went to Mullins to see my daughter Antoinette Davis. Her mother asked me when my family was going to meet my daughter. Do not worry about that because I have it under control. I believed that I could keep that secret and not tell my mother. I knew I would not tell my first two children's mother because Ashley and Antoinette were only nine months apart.

I was not able to go through that right now. The only thing that Antionette's mother said to me was that she would be so happy when I could come and get my daughter for the weekend. While sitting in the chair, someone put my daughter in my arms. I held my baby for the first time. Her mother said she looks like your mother and your sister and has sandy red hair like you. I did not take my sister or brother to see my little girl. I told them, "We must keep this from Mama. Antoinette's birth is my secret."

After visiting with my daughter, I returned to Denmark to prepare for my fall classes. My sister returned to Denmark with me because she could not find a job. I told her not to worry about anything and that everything would be alright. Things were going great with me at school. Thanksgiving was coming up, so I decided to go home this year. I came home that Tuesday night and went to see my children. I saw my daughter in Mullins while I was home.

I told my daughter's mother I would be home until that Sunday. She asked if I was coming to get my daughter to meet my family. I said, "Do not worry about it. I got it. They will meet her soon."

Thanksgiving dinner with the family was wonderful. That Friday night after Thanksgiving Day, at about 10:00 p.m., someone knocked at my mother's door. I walked to the door and asked who it was, and the person on the other side called out their name while opening the door.

She called out her name loud and clear. When I looked at the person, it was Antoinette's mother. My crossed eyes got straight; my heart felt like it stopped. My mother, sister, and brother were walking up from behind me. There was nowhere for me to go. She said, "Caveman, it is time for your mother to meet her granddaughter."

As soon as my mother approached the door, the young lady walked to her with Antoinette. She was using profanity and stated, "That is Caveman's baby. Look at her. She looks just like you, his sister, and has hair like your son." I looked at that young lady, and I said, "Who are you? I have never seen you before, and who sent you to my Mama's house?"

She had that liquor in her, and she started cussing up something in my Mama's house. I said, "Let's help her back to the car waiting for her." I wanted her to leave, as I expressed. I hope she can get some help. The next day, I went to the young lady's house, and when I walked into the house, she went off, cursing me out.

I said to myself, I better get out of this house now because my mother thought I was returning to Denmark, and I did not want to get in trouble. When I got in the car, I went straight back to Denmark.

The spring semester was great for me. I earned excellent grades. I passed all my final exams, and as always, I made sure I went to free tutoring from 12:30 p.m. to 4:00 p.m. so that I could look at my stories.

I am now only one summer session away from becoming an alumnus of Voorhees college. There were about two weeks left before the summer session started. I went to Marion to spend some time with my family. I was so happy to inform the people in my hometown and neighborhood, some classmates, and most of all, the naysayers that I would graduate at the end of the summer session. I would have met all my Bachelor of Science degree in Criminal Justice requirements. The people were in disbelief because I should have quit college before graduating, but God.

I went back to Denmark with the mindset that I must graduate. Graduation must happen for me. Graduation is a day that man said would never happen, but I am eight weeks away from obtaining a Bachelor of Science in Criminal Justice. Those eight weeks went by so fast. At the end of my summer classes, I received a letter from Voorhees college informing me that I had completed all requirements to obtain my Bachelor of Science degree.

Mr. Bennie T. Davis Sr. will be a Graduate of the Commencement Ceremony at Voorhees's College in May 1993. Just the thought of knowing that a below-average Bennie made an above-average accomplishment was the greatest news and the greatest letter that I have ever received in my life.

5. DEATH KNOCKING AT THE DOOR

I was excited to know that at the next graduation held at Voorhees College, Bennie Tyrone Davis would be an alumnus of Voorhees college. I knew that I was going to Marion to tell everybody I met that in May 1993, I would be graduating. Voorhees did give me my degree, but I work hard each day, each week, each month, and each year.

The day I found out that I was graduating was the same night Caveman had a smoke out for his personal friends. My brother said to me, "Caveman will you pull one blunt or let me give you a shotgun." He asked me to drink some liquor, drink some beer, so I decided to drink a wine cooler. The next afternoon, I left Denmark and went to Marion.

Everybody I encountered: classmates, teachers, and naysayers, I made sure that I informed them that I had completed all the requirements at Voorhees college. I would be graduating in May 1993. When I told them, they looked so surprised, and most of them did not even believe that I would be graduating.

They did not think that I would be graduating in the summer. Someone said, "How could that be since so many young men and young women quit college, some were on academic probation, and while others were sent home from college, how did you make it only being in school only six years in a low reading level"?

This got me when a young man said, "Are you sure because I was in High School with you, and you were below average?" I let him know that greatness was inside of me. I reminded myself I could do all the things I wanted to do if I just kept believing in myself.

Then, one afternoon, I made sure I was in the streets to find out if anyone needed any drugs. My boys knew that I had some great medicines for them. I only brought a certain number of drugs to run out before I went back to Denmark. This was the first time I ever went to Denmark and did not have to register for college.

I had all this free time to concentrate on selling drugs and having a good time. I could start getting more drugs because now I am out of school. My drug supplier said he could make some great drug deals. I let him know that I needed a lot of Chocolate Thai and that Bombazi I had two people who wanted to buy a couple of pounds of weed from Caveman.

I told my drug supplier that I needed 10 pounds. I had 6 pounds to supply to other drug dealers, and I kept 4 pounds to provide for my boys. I told him to give me 24 hours and I would pay him all his money.

Summer classes had ended, and it was about three weeks before the fall classes were to start. One day, I saw an empty restaurant building. I found out who the restaurant's landlord was and let him know that I would like to rent the restaurant. The landlord leased me the restaurant, and I named it after my son Bennie Jr. BJ's place.

I had a few weeks before Voorhees College, and Denmark Technical College started classes for the fall. The restaurant was ready to open, so BJ's place was up and cooking the most incredible food in all of Denmark when school started. I had my Jamaican Queen. She was able to cook all types of food. She was a cook, also another young man and me.

When the fall semester started, the students at Voorhees College,

Denmark Technical College, and the young people in the community of Denmark had flyers about the grand opening of BJ's place and that Caveman was the owner of this new restaurant. I had Jamaican food, short orders, and sweet potato pies made from scratch.

Now, I can have drugs in the streets and at my new place to get their food and medicines. The police knew I was setting myself up for prison because the police were looking for me to be careless.

Caveman believed he was untouchable, but I knew I had to protect myself. I knew I could not just forget that the police wanted Caveman in prison or become a snitch or an informer to get the big kingpins. People from Voorhees College, Denmark Technical College, and the community of Denmark supported the restaurant.

The people enjoyed the short orders, the Jamaican dishes, the homemade sweet potato pies, and they loved the Caveman burgers. BJ's place cut money off from Hardee's restaurant before BJ's location Hardee's was Denmark's restaurant.

People who attended the surrounding Colleges were able to walk to BJ's place because it was located right behind the college. I had a young man outside the restaurant, and when someone came for drugs, he was able to take care of them while they were waiting for their food to get ready.

My Jamaican Queen was going to Voorhees college, and when she got out of her classes, she would come to the restaurant. The Jamaican Queen was fascinated with being with Caveman. She put school on the back burner. She stopped going to her classes, and she would never go to her hometown in Connecticut.

I would open my restaurant every day and Sunday afternoon to give the students a chance to get out. I had benches on the outside of the restaurant for dining outside the restaurant. When I closed the restaurant at night, I would go to the strip, but if someone needed any drugs before I closed, I would get in touch with one of my boys, and I would get the drugs for him and all the young men who were working for me.

The fall semester was going along fine. It was time for Voorhees homecoming. During this time, the alumni and people who just went to Voorhees started coming to the homecoming week. The whole week was hot and popping. This homecoming, Caveman had a restaurant, and it was open when the party was over at Voorhees.

I was looking for the increase in people coming to get food but did not realize that the Denmark police force had a new police chief. He had no friends and no bribes with any of the drug dealers or police officers. The new chief was not from Denmark. The Mayor and City Council went out of Denmark to get this young man from Charleston, SC.

The only thing this man wanted to do was get rid of the drug dealers and the drugs off Denmark's streets. Not realizing that Caveman would have to yield. So that Friday night of homecoming, at about 9:00 PM, people came by the restaurant to buy food. I got a call from one of my boys saying he needed a couple of slabs because he was out of dope.

I told the young man that I could not come to the strip, so come to BJ's. I left out of BJ's and went to get the slabs. I got back to the restaurant, had the slabs in my hand, and out of nowhere, blue lights had my place surrounded. There was so much light around the restaurant that it looked like it was daylight outside. The police cars were shining bright lights on me and in the restaurant.

The police kicked in the door of the restaurant, and they came in looking for me. I had to do something, and that was too much to eat. So, I dumped all the drugs and weed in the hot oil in the deep fryer. The police searched the restaurant and were not able to find any drugs. The new chief of police walked up to me as I was outside and said, "Caveman, I had you, but our informant told me that Caveman had been too good to him, and he would rather go to court before doing this to Caveman. He said that Caveman treated him like a person and not like a drug head."

Then the chief asked me, "What are you doing for these people to love you that way?" I said to the chief, "I am not a drug man, and I do not know what you are talking about." and he had to leave because he found no drugs. By the time the police left, all the people who were there to buy food were also gone.

Some people who witnessed what was going on at the restaurant knew Caveman was going to jail that night. People were coming from Voorhees, Denmark Technical College, and all over the city to see me get in the police car but, I was still a free man. People visited for homecoming, so I cleaned up and closed down after the police left the restaurant.

After I left the restaurant, I went to a party that was going on off-campus. When I got up the next morning, I went over to one of my friends, house to tell him about what had happened Friday night and to find out more about this new chief of police. When I got to his house, I found out that he was in jail, and most of everyone who was selling drugs got picked up about 5:00 AM from their homes.

It was only a few that were not in prison, and I was one of those few. Not one of my boys was arrested for drugs. I went back to my house and got my brother and sister, and I told them what was going on in Denmark. I said I got to find someplace to move to by Monday, if not today.

My sister left my house, and she went to the store, but she told me that she had to leave Denmark when she got back. I asked her why and she said to me that the chief of police informed her that, "Caveman, my brother, is going to jail for drugs and if I am with him, I am also going to jail."

My sister said I am moving back to Marion. I decided I had to get out of Denmark right then. The next week, I moved to Blackville, SC, and my sister moved back to Marion. For a few weeks, she stayed with a friend of the family. Something had happened, and my sister had to move into our family house, and she did not have any lights for a few days. She was working at that time so that she could get everything paid from that point on.

I found a trailer in Blackville, and I moved that day. I ran into a friend who had just gotten out of jail, and he said, "Caveman, I do not know what is going on. Someone was setting everyone up involved with drugs." The money that the police had to spend to purchase the drugs from Caveman. They said no because the law did not want to spend that much money on the setup.

So, now it was time for the fall semester to start, and that semester took so long because this was my year to walk across that stage to receive my Bachelor of Science degree in criminal justice. I spent my first Christmas in Blackville.
All I was excited about was New Year's coming in because it would be the first semester away from the biggest day of my life. The Colleges and schools were out for the Christmas break, and that night, I had a wonderful time.

The strip was not closed down yet, so I went to the strip to check on my boys to see how things were going. I drove to the strip and saw a police car. Right then, I said I would not stop, but I did, and I went into the game room for about 30 minutes. I got back in my car, pulled off, and saw the blue lights out of nowhere. I had $200 in my pocket when I left the strip. I pulled the car over and then got out of the vehicle. The police told me to get back in the car. I did as the officer told me.

Three more police cars came up to my car. The chief and police searched my car and could not find any drugs. Then they searched me and found no drugs on me, but they found $200 on me. The police took the money from me. I said to myself they could not keep my money, so the next day, I went to the Police Department with my receipts from the restaurant, and it was more than $2000 in receipts.

The police gave me my money back. I knew then that this police chief would not stop until the drug dealers quit selling or go to prison. His only job was to clean up the city of Denmark. I decided the only thing I needed to do in Denmark was to open my restaurant and sell my food. My boys came to Blackville to get their dope from me and ensure I did not go to jail for drugs. I had to separate myself from the strip and all the drug dealers in Denmark. I focused on making the restaurant a success.

One afternoon, my Jamaican Queen prepared dinner for both of us. While we were eating our dinner, she started crying and said, "I need to have a conversation with you. It's about our future. Caveman, I am pregnant, but I do not want any children." I told her, "Let's give the baby to my mother and let her raise the child." She said, "I do not want to have a baby. I am having an abortion because I'm not going to keep our baby, and at this time, I'm not ready for this responsibility." We left our dishes on the table, and I called it a night.

Before I went to sleep, I told her whatever she wanted to do that, I would support her. She stated again I want to have an abortion. A few days later, she made an appointment to go to a doctor's office in Columbia, SC. After she had the abortion, she told me that they were twin boys, and both of us started crying, but for days, I cried because I loved those boys.

The fall semester got started. I was so excited because Voorhees College and Denmark Technical College had opened back up. I put flyers out on both campuses about BJ's place and had a big back-to-college week. I stopped going to the strip and started meeting drug dealers in different places, giving them drugs. I did not let any drugs stay around me.

Now, it was time for the spring semester to start. I was so happy because this is the year that I have been waiting for five years and four summer school sessions. I had to take senior pictures and order my graduation things.

Now, I was only a few weeks from the second most significant thing in my life: my college graduation. What made this day so great was that graduation was on Mother's Day. The class of 1993 was going to be the first class to graduate in the new gym. Now, the day of graduation came, and I could not sleep the night before the big day.

I rented a limousine to take me to graduation. During graduation, I had the driver go and trade that limousine and get another limousine. I was sitting in the gym, and I just started looking around at all the people in the gym.

Graduation was a day. The man said it would never happen, but look at God. What a time it was when the row that I was sitting on stood. I walked towards the stage, and as I stood in line waiting for my name to be called, I said, in my mind, I was able to accomplish something that a lot of the above-average students could not accomplish. Still, God took a below-average student and allowed me to achieve the impossible.

When the president of Voorhees called my name, Bennie Tyrone Davis, I heard that name, a wonderful sound. I walked across the stage, and it felt like my heart stopped. The president put my degree in my hand; I started screaming in my mind that I had accomplished my dreams and my goals.

My hands went in the air after I shook the president of Voorhees college hand. I went back to my seat and opened my degree; then I saw my name. All I can say is that somehow, I made it. The tears of joy started coming down my face. When graduation was over, my class walked outside.

Family members came out of the gym, and they started going around hugging the class of 1993. When I saw my mother, she was walking to me crying, and I ran to her. She put her arms out, and all I could do was fall into her arms. My mom said, my son, "Through Christ Jesus, you made it." My mom was crying along with my sister, brother, other family members, and friends.

This was just a fantastic time that I would never forget. Graduation was an accomplishment because I was hungry for that degree. I thirsted for that degree, and I was not going to stop until I got that degree. I had a party, but it was not a big one. I had a little get-together with a few of my close friends. The table was spread with the usual. Whatever they desired, it was on the table. The get-together was a wonderful celebration of what Caveman has accomplished, and as of this day, he is an alumnus of Voorhees college.

The summer had come, and school was out. I was able to be in

Denmark, running the restaurant while living in Blackville. The 4th of July was coming up, and people started looking for Caveman to have a big party at the restaurant or his house.

A few days before the 4th of July, my brother got into a fight with some young man, and he beat this man up pretty badly. I told my brother that he had to get out of Blackville now. I got him out of Blackville, and I had someone to take him to Marion. I said to my brother. You will not be coming back this way because the police will put you in jail for that man you beat up.

I am now in Blackville by myself, just me and my Jamaican Queen. Now that I am out of school, I could not go to the Voorhees college campus at any time. A few weeks passed. Things were going well. My brother was not in jail. BJ's place was making money, and I was making money on the streets of Denmark, but not as much because of the chief of police.

I had some drugs on the streets of Marion as well. One night, my Jamaican Queen and I were at the house lying across the bed. I was holding my lady close to my heart in my arms. We talked about the things that we would like to do in our lives, and she told me, "Caveman, I am pregnant, and you will be a father, and I am having this baby."

I stopped smoking that Bombazi, and I stopped drinking. The Queen took care of herself, went to the doctors' appointments, took her medication, and ate right. She was about four or five months pregnant and was very spoiled because she had Caveman by her side. She would get her hair done every two weeks with all kinds of designs. Sometimes, her hairdo would be over $300.

The only thing I wanted to do was make her happy and comfortable because we both wanted this baby or babies. After all, last time, she was pregnant with twins. She was looking forward to becoming a mother. She came to my house one day, and she started hurting, and I had someone to take her to the hospital.

The doctor and nurses did everything they could to stop the pain, and then she went into labor. The doctor could not stop the labor, so they had to take the baby, and when the baby was born, he was still born. She came back home the next day when the doctor released her, and when she saw me, tears were coming down her face.

I believe she was crying for a long time. I started crying when I saw her crying and then she showed me the picture that was given to her at the hospital. More tears started coming down my face, meeting under my chin. I just started wondering how I would have loved my three boys. For a long time, my heart was so heavy. My Jamaican Queen could not take it because she was also hurting. A few weeks later, she told me that she was going home to her family and that she needed to just getaway, so she went home.

Anytime I would go to Denmark, the police would pull my car or any car that the police saw me riding in, hoping to find drugs. I decided to close BJ's place and move back to Marion before I found myself in prison. I packed my stuff up, and I moved back to Marion. I was on the down-low because I had to find out how the drugs were getting around in Marion.

I had to come up with new ideas and how to get my drugs on the streets. I found a trailer house out in the woods. I had to get out of the city limits of Marion. I called my place 'Out West'. It had 3 bedrooms, but one of the rooms was called 'The Get High' room. Marion did not have a place where drug dealers could sell drugs like the strip in Denmark.
The drug spots were at different houses and in fields, so when the police came, the drug dealers would see the police before they saw

them. Sometimes, I had to ride around Marion and find people that were looking for drugs. I found out that I had to go to the club on Thursday, Friday, and Saturday nights to sell most of my drugs. I knew I would have the best Parkay/Butter, Bombazi, Chocolate Thai, and that raw-powder-no-cut, 'Nose Bleed'.

I started selling my drugs in Marion. Now, Marion is Caveman headquarters. I recruited the young men that I wanted to be drug dealers. I supplied the drug dealers, but no one was allowed to come to my house. For a long time, people did not know that I was in Marion. I built a powerful name in Marion. Caveman was back and was giving up more weight than any other drug dealer.

I was quickly introduced to the people who helped me and let me know when the drug task unit was coming to do a drug bust. There was a police officer that I paid, and when he would get drugs from other people, he would put the drugs back on the streets. The officer would get half, and I kept the other half. I remember one time this city police officer ran up on some drug dealers in a field, and one of my boys was there, and the police let my boy go, but the others went to jail. Before that night was over, I had all the drugs back on the streets of Marion.

After several months, I decided I needed to do something else to make money so it would not be all about drugs. I needed another source of income. I would have loved to open a BJ's in Marion, but there was no restaurant for lease or rent around Marion.

One day I talked to a young man about starting a business. He said, "A club would be a great business for the type of work you are doing; I have a club in Gresham that I would like to lease." I went to see the club, and it was one of the most beautiful clubs around Marion.

This club was about 25 miles out of the city limits of Marion in a place called Gresham, South Carolina. I let the man know that I would like to lease the club. So, he let me lease the club. When I opened the club, I named the club 'Stitches.'

I had the grand opening, and I thought many people would come out to my club because of my name. To my surprise, the grand opening was a big bust. I closed the club at about 1:00 AM and went to Marion to see what was happening with the other clubs.

There was one club packed with people, and I told myself I must find out what I needed to do to get these people out of Marion and get them to 'Stitches.' I opened two weekends in a row and could not get the crowd to come. I went to the club in Marion that was located on Mill Street. The club was jumping, it was popping, and it was the hottest club going on in Marion.

I found out what they were doing to get the people. I found out that all it was the best DJ in Marion, DJ Red Rock. There were so many people at the club and many people standing outside. I knew then that I must get DJ Red Rock to 'Stitches.'

I stayed outside the club until they closed. I spoked with DJ Red Rock when he came out to go home. I asked him how much he was getting paid for playing at this club. He told me how much he got paid for DJing at the club, and I offered to pay him much more than what he was getting. He agreed to DJ at 'Stitches,' starting the 4th of July weekend.

I said let me have a re-grand opening on the weekend of the 4th of July. I have Flyers made, but I had to do things that no other club was doing. I decided to have at the re-grand opening all the gin and juice, all the Brown liquor, and all the beer a person could drink. I had male and female strippers; all of this was only $5 to come into the club, and I had a VIP 100 Chocolate Thai, Bombazi, better known as blunts.

This was called a Caveman production. I got over 1000 Flyers made up. I put Flyers out in Marion, Mullins, Nichols, Florence, Friendship, Gresham, Britton's Neck, Johnsonville, Hemingway, Hamer, Dillon, and other surrounding cities. It was showtime at 'Stitches'. It was the biggest re-grand opening in club history. I also added all the chicken bog a person could eat.

Outside of the club, I hired two Sheriffs to ensure that no one would be loitering around the club. I had them so that no other Officers could come into 'Stitches.' That 4th of July night was called 'Lockdown.' If a person walked out of the club, that person must go home. The doors were unlocked at 6:00 AM when the sunrise the next morning.

People came from all over. 'Stitches' parking lot and the 'Paradise' parking lot were packed with cars on both sides of the highway. DJ Red Rock had the house on fire all night long. There were people on top of people. This was the start of 'Caveman Productions.' The talk around Marion was 'Stitches' and 'Caveman Productions.' Just about every place I went, someone would ask me if I would be open that night. I would tell them that the doors opened at 11:45 PM, and it was going to be a repeat from the night before.

I would be open all week with a party each night. On my way to 'Stitches,' I had to pass a place called 'Sugar Shack,' when the people at 'Sugar Shack' saw me pass by about 11:30 PM, they would get in their cars and follow me to the club. A young man came and told me that he had left 'Stitches' one night and that he was so drunk when he came to a stop sign that he stayed there until the next morning. He said that he woke up at about 8:00 AM, and then he went home.

The young man came back the next night because of the great time he had friends with him. The 4th of July was in the middle of the week, and Stitches was jam-packed. It was the only club that could open seven nights a week, and people were on top of each other. One Sunday night, I had a 2-dollar night. There was all you could drink and all you could eat until it was all gone. Stitches quickly became the number-one club in all of Marion County.

It was on the local radio station in Marion, and every day from 2 to 5 pm, there were commercials about what was going on. 'Stitches' was another Caveman production. At the end of July, I had a car show, and people came from far and near to be in the biggest car show of the summer of 1994. People were dancing on the outside and drinking on the inside. I also had Chocolate Thai, Bombazi and over 100 blunts.

My boys walked the ground, and they had that Parkay/Butter, better known as Crack and that White Girl, better known as powder. There were many people at the Stitches car show, but most of them left the show and went into Stitches. The party started all over again all-night DJ Red Rock put on a show like never before. From that day to now, there has not been a club like Stitches in Marion County. I only kept a limited number of drugs at the club because I wanted the club to be successful. The only drugs that were outside were the 100 blunts.

It was about time for school to start, so I had a Back-to-School jam every weekend in August. I put on a comedy show one night and had an Arsenio Hall look-alike comedy show. Some people came from all over. It was the weekend before Labor Day weekend. I had an R&B group come down to do a concert. The name of the R&B group was New Beginning, and the lead singer was Usher Raymond IV, better known as Usher. Today, he is one of the number-one R&B

singers in the USA.

Two weeks before my birthday party, my brother was at a friend's house and sitting in the yard drinking beer. A police officer drove by and saw the young men drinking. The police drove upon them. The young men had opened containers, and one of the young men was my brother. When I returned to Marion, I discovered my brother was arrested for an open container.

I went to the police station and saw an officer standing in the courtroom. I went to him, and I asked about my brother. The officer told me that my brother Chris had paid his fine, was released, and never went to jail. So, I said to the officer, thanks, now get you something to eat. Then I walked out of the police station thinking that everything was fine. I got with my brother, and he told me he would not be drinking any more outside. I never said anything else about what had happened to my brother.

Coming up to the Labor Day weekend, I was advertising that the party would start that Friday night and last until after Labor Day. I had people that were coming from everywhere. This was another Caveman production. It was better than any other one that I had in the past.

I opened that Sunday night at my usual time, about 12:00 AM, and we partied until the sun was coming up. I opened on Labor Day at about 1:00 PM. I had a few bar-b-que grills outside and the usual on the inside. People came and partied with the Caveman all day long. The party ended at 2:00 AM. It was time to get the drugs out because it was a holiday weekend. My boys were selling drugs like never before because Marion was on lockdown. It was just a few weeks away from Caveman's birthday.

I had a Halloween party in between. I gave away door prizes, and some people got into the party for free. Now, I started working on the next biggest party at Stitches. Happy Birthday, Caveman. I put flyers out about this party. I had more strippers than I ever had before, male and female, and more free liquor than ever had before. I had so much Bombazi, Chocolate Thai, and that raw powder.

I opened the doors at 10:00 PM, and more people came to the 'Happy Birthday Caveman' party. I was not able to let anyone into the party. I had to turn people around at the door as the party was going on. I told this young lady, "Tonight, you will be my birthday gift, and I will unwrap you tonight at Out West, my place."

A few minutes later, before the party ended, another young lady came to me and said, 'I am spending your birthday with you.' I told her that I had a lady going home with me, and that is when she promised me not this night. She said, "I am the only lady going home with you.' I said, 'So you say.' Yes, she did go home with Caveman. I had a young man take the other lady home. I told her I was not going home that night because I had to get some drugs.

The Shriners Ball was coming up the following weekend, and that Saturday, there was going to be a Shriner's parade, but I was hiring my Shriners at Stitches that Friday, Saturday, and Sunday night. I had the flyers out that Friday night. I wanted to party until the sunrise. By this time, I had a new DJ named Miami Cave Ice.

I had a store that kept my kegs of beer. The store's name was Gooch. So, I would pick up my kegs of beer at about 5:00 PM and then take them to Stitches and put them on ice. On this Friday, as I drove up to the Gooch like I always do. I went inside the store to get my beer kegs and carried them to my Jeep. I put the kegs of beer in the back of the Jeep. As I walked around the jeep and got in, I shut the door, cranked up and drove off.

Out of nowhere, the police cars and blue lights were surrounding the vehicle that I was driving. They jumped out of their cars, and I could not open my vehicle door. The Chief of Police, Captain, and Lieutenant were there because tonight, the police knew that Caveman was going to jail and then prison.

The police opened the vehicle door and had a warrant for my arrest in his hand. The police officer read the warrant and informed me that they had me for bribing a police officer. Then, they began to search my vehicle for drugs and found none. Before the police put the handcuffs on me, they searched, and no drugs were found.

I told my friend, who was already at the store when I arrived, to open the club because people were coming to have a great time. The police were more concerned with finding drugs than putting me in jail for their warrant on me. That was the only way they could search for me, but the embarrassment was mostly on them. I believe the police had the local TV news people on standby waiting for the phone call to see if any drugs would have been found. It would have been the headline on the local news and the Marion Star, the local newspaper.

Then I experienced something I had never experienced before when the police put the handcuffs on me. I realized I was going to jail. I told the officer I did not do anything and was put in the police car. Then, what felt like the longest moment of my life. I never felt so much pain and disappointment as they took me to the jailhouse. I just started looking around the jailhouse while the police took me through the process. The officer said that I was going to be in jail for a long time.

Then, I was given an orange uniform and taken to a cell. That was when I realized that jail was real. During that night, tears began to come down my eyes and met under my chin. This young man was in the cell with me, looking at me crying, and he said Caveman is a crybaby and a punk. When we got together, I told him, "I am not a crybaby, and I am not a punk, but my mother did not teach me how to live like an animal. This is not the life that I wanted to live."

I knew that I would be in jail for the weekend because there was no bond hearing until that Monday. Not knowing how much my bond was going to be, I continued to cry. That Saturday, while I was in jail, I could hear the starting of the Shriner's parade. The jailhouse was located within walking distance of the main street where the parade was held. I could hear the music that started playing at the parade. I was wondering did anyone opened the club. I hope so because some money would have been made. That money could help pay my bond.

I felt like time had just stopped and was not going anywhere. The biggest news in Marion that weekend was that Caveman was in jail and that prison would be his home. This was the longest weekend of my life, but Monday did come. It was time for me to go to my bond hearing. A police officer came at me and took me to the police station, and then he put me in the courtroom to wait for the court to start.

I was just put in a box with the other inmates. While waiting for the judge to come, a police officer came to me and took me to an office. As I was walking into the office, I saw Dr. Henry McGill Jr. and other police officers, along with members of the drug task unit, walking in the office beside the one that I was walking in.

The officers were sitting telling Dr. Henry McGill Jr. why he should not get Caveman out of jail. They stated to him that this is one of the biggest dealers in Marion County.

"We got Caveman; do not stand for his bond; he will get an

exceedingly high one and then stay in jail."

Dr. Henry McGill Jr. replied, "No matter what his bond is, I am standing for it because he is not spending another night in jail."

Then, as the police took me back to the courtroom, I saw my mother and sister going into the courtroom. I was sent back to the box again. Then Judge Brown walked into the courtroom, everyone stood up, and the court started.

Finally, my name was called, and by that time, Dr. Henry McGill Jr. was also in the courtroom. The police told the Judge what had happened and why I was in jail. Before he gave me my bond, they told him that Dr. Henry McGill Jr. was standing for whatever bond was set. Then, when the bond was set, Dr. Henry McGill Jr. signed the bond, and I was released.

I believe that some people can see greatness in you before you see it in yourself. Dr. Henry McGill Jr. did not just stand for the bond, but his reputation was on the line. He was a pastor of one of the biggest Baptist churches in Marion. The chief of police was a member of his church. He was the owner of the greatest and biggest funeral home in Marion County. He was the first black on the City Council board, and people respected him highly.

When I got out of jail, I made sure I went to Dr. H. McGill Jr. and told him thanks for what he had done for me. I got in touch with my brother, and I asked him if he opened the club. He told me, 'No, the club was closed all weekend." I knew then that I had to get some flyers made up to get them out to the people about what would happen all that weekend at Stitches.

I put in a rush order for some flyers to be made that week. I got a phone call that this plant wanted to rent the club for the Christmas party. Someone from Blumenthal Mills called me about having their Christmas party at Stitches. Blumenthal Mills was one of the most significant plants in Marion County.

I catered the Blumenthal party; for anyone to come in at the door, it was $45 per person and $30 in advance. I had to get the Thanksgiving party right for Stitches because Stitches was hot, and Caveman was hot. I never had anyone to get shot, and there was no fighting because I had no loitering. When a person walked out, they were going home.

I always had a patty wagon from the Sheriff's Department, so if any trouble started, they would be going to jail. The Thanksgiving party started on Thanksgiving night to that Sunday. I had some Pastors from Marion County come before the club opened, and they would have some strippers and a private party in the club's backroom. The pastors that were there also loved Caveman's drugs. Today, they are still pastoring at a few churches.

I had a friendly crowd, but it was not as many people as it once was because I went to jail that weekend. I went over to my mother's house, and she had a letter for me. The letter informed me of the date that I had to be in court for my preliminary hearing. The hearing was right before Christmas. I went to court, and I had a Public Defender. The public defender and I made it there about the same time. The lawyer and I were waiting to be called. When I was called, we walked into the courtroom together and sat at a table. Then, a police officer read the warrant, informing the judge of the reason for my arrest.

Judge Brown listened to everything that Officer Craig Hopkins had to say, and then the judge explained, "How could Bennie bribe you when his brother paid his ticket?"

The judge went on to say that sometimes people would come to court, and their charges were dropped. Some of those people would give him money to buy himself some lunch as thanks for a job well done. The judge went on to say that this was not a bribe, and he looked at me and said the charges were dropped. The lawyer and I did not have to say anything. Then, my $40.00 was returned to me.

The week before Christmas, Blumenthal had their big party at Stitches. The people did come out and had a great time. Some people said it was the best Christmas party ever since they were working at Blumenthal. I opened the club for Christmas, but many people did not come out. The New Year's Eve was the same way; few people came out. I decided I had to give up Stitches. That big bounce-back that I was looking for did not happen. I decided that I would give up on the club and sell drugs full-time, and that is what I did. I started dealing with a lot of young ladies. I remember one of my so-called friends came to Marion, and I got her to come Out West, and she stayed with me for a few days. Someone told this lady that Caveman sent her home, and someone else was at his house.

The next night, I went home after the young lady returned home. I went to my room to get in bed and pulled the covers back, and my bedsheets, bedspread, and pillowcases were cut up like spaghetti. The one thing I know is that this person took their time doing this. I remember once this guy talked about how faithful his wife was, and another young man was telling him how faithful his girl was to him. I told myself that both of those young ladies loved coming Out West. I learned a long time ago not to tell everyone who you are dealing with. Only three people will not tell; that is me, myself, and I.

One day, the young man's wife came over to my house, and when she was walking to her car, one of my boys came up and saw her. I believe he went and told her husband because he started acting funny towards me, and to this day, he does not care for me.

It was coming up to the 4th of July, and I ran out of dope, and there were no drugs in Marion. I had to get some so. Now it is the 4th of July 1995. I called a few of my friends and said, "I need to make a run to get some drugs." The young man I had in the car said, "Let's go!" Then we got out of Marion. I did not give anyone time to go home, and there were no cell phones.

I had to go back to my old stomping grounds in Denmark. I did not let anyone know that I was there. I sneaked into town. Even though I was doing wrong, my mother was praying for me. I was supposed to have gotten a couple of pounds of weed. I knew this man who kept great weed but not the greatest weed. My boys were out of town, so I got the Chocolate Thai and Bombazi.

Something went wrong, and I could not get a couple of pounds of weed, but I could get the crack and powder. I wanted more crack, but my boys would not call me back. So, I said, let's get out of here. The young man driving had some dirty clothes in the trunk of his car, so I wrapped the drugs up real neatly in his dirty clothes. Then, we were on our way back to Marion. I said there is no Chocolate Thai, but I have that Parkay/Butter. Then we jumped on the Interstate and hit I-95 north. When we crossed the Santee bridge, I looked up and saw blue lights. There was a roadblock on the bridge. I asked the young man if he had a registration, driver's license, and proof of insurance, and he said yes, he had all of that. When the police saw four young black men in the car out of all the other cars, the police said to pull over in the other lane.

When I looked around, to my surprise, I saw canine dogs coming to sniff out some drugs, but as I stated earlier, my mother was praying for me. They searched the car and went in the trunk. The dogs and the police were in the car's trunk, and they picked up the clothes and the dog did not sniff out any drugs. The dogs could not smell anything because there was no cut in the drugs.

I looked down in the water and said that I might have to jump if they found anything. I am not going to jail, and I am not going to prison. Then I thought about what I would say if the dope were found, "Who's drugs are those?" "It is not mine!" "I don't know anything about any drugs." Then a police officer came and said we could return to our cars and have a great 4th of July. I said the drug price would increase, and everyone would pay for these drugs in Marion.

I knew I had to devise a better way of getting drugs into Marion. People started mailing drugs, and whoever got the drug mail to their house would get paid some good money. I also started paying someone to drive to get the drugs, and I would follow them in another car. One time, the police got a tip that I was out of town and what day I would be returning. On the day of my return to Marion, the police set up a roadblock because the police knew I was coming that way. I decided to come into Marion the other way so the person who had the drugs could get through the roadblock without any problems. When I pulled up in my yard, someone notified the police and told them that Caveman was in his yard now and I was looking at him. The police, not knowing my drugs, went through the roadblock.

Things were looking up for Caveman in the drug game. I knew people were jealous of Caveman, but I did not realize the extent of their jealousy. On September 8, 1995, on a Friday night at about 7:00 PM, Labor Day weekend, I was at the game room shooting pool. There was a shortage of drugs in Marion. One of my friends or one of my so-called friends set up a drug deal for me to buy some drugs. When the young man walked into the game room, my friend said to me that he was the man with the drugs. The young man and I were walking out the door. I asked my friend to go with me. He said everything was good because he was also my boy.

I believed what he said to me, and I walked out of the game room and to the car. A young lady was driving the vehicle. I got in the back seat of the car, and I went to the tennis court behind Fox Field. They were having a home game, so when she drove up, the young man then looked around, and he said no, it is too much light, then I said OKAY. As we left, I could hear the fans hollering at the game. We drove down 501, going towards Latta, South Carolina.

I had her pull over to one of my friend's houses then I got out of the car. The young man went to the front door with me, and then I knocked on the door, but no one came to the door. Then I said to the young man, let's go to the back door, and I walked around the house. I went up to the porch and knocked, but no one came to the door. Then I walked off the porch and down the steps, and I did not know that the man had gone back to his car. He ran back to me. Then he said, "I hate MFs like you." He reached into the front of his pants and pulled out a gun, a 9-millimeter, and pointed it at my head and told me to give him the money. I gave him the money. It was $2500. Then he said you must die this night.

6. A PRAYING MOTHER

Looking down the barrel of a 9-millimeter gun as it pointed at my head was not an everyday occurrence. I was now at the point of death, knowing that the bullet would come out when the trigger was released, and my life would be over, ended at once. I started asking myself, why me? Why would my friend do this to me? Now I understood what happened to Jesus when Judas came and kissed Jesus, and then Jesus called him a friend. I could not believe that a friend did this to me. Someone who stayed at my house when I ate, he ate. He stole drugs from me, but I still look out for him. All I could do was say, save me, Lord, do not let me die. The attack kept running through my mind. Why did he do this to me? I would have done anything for him. He didn't have to put me in this position.

I believe God dispatched an angel. The gun got heavy in the gunman's hand, and then he pointed the gun at my chest, and the only thing that was going through my mind was if he pulled the trigger, I knew I would never see my children and my family anymore. I told the young man, "You must not kill me. You have the money. Please don't take my life."

Then he pointed the gun down to my legs and began shooting me. The young man pulled the trigger four times, and I saw the fire come out from the gun each time as the bullets entered my legs one at a time. So, much pain went through my whole body. I felt a burning sensation. It felt as if my legs were literally on fire. The first bullet entered my right leg and came out the other side of my right leg. The second bullet nipped my right and left leg, the third bullet entered my left leg, and the 4th bullet missed my legs.

After the young man shot me, he ran back towards his car and hit the gun twice as he ran. He left me in the backyard to die in my blood. I could smell the scent of burning flesh from the gunshot wounds to my legs. I looked at the gunshot wounds in my legs and saw the blood gushing out like a waterfall.

I could see the inside flesh of my leg through the bullet holes. I then put my fingers on each bullet hole wound in my legs, hoping to stop the bleeding, but nothing I was doing helped me. The pain was like no other pain that I had ever felt in my life. I started walking because I had to get to Hwy 501 so someone could find me. My legs got so heavy I could not pick them up, not even for one more step, and then I collapsed and fell to the ground. I lay on the ground.

I believe that the same Holy Ghost anointing that called Lazarus from the dead and carried him out of the tomb, God released that same anointing, moving me to the other side of Hwy 501.

The attack was Labor Day weekend, and the traffic was bumper to bumper, but somehow, I got across the road to the other side. If I had stayed in the backyard, I would have been found dead, but God. When my eyes came open, I was lying on the side of the 501 highway. I saw an 18-wheeler coming down the road. Every place each bullet went in my legs, it was burning. I was hurting so bad the blood continued to flow, and I couldn't stop the pain. I just started screaming and hollering for help, somebody, anybody, help me, and there was no one there to hear me because I was all alone.

As the truck got closer to me, I said to myself. I will roll myself in front of the 18-wheeler so that the truck could run over me to die then I won't have to go through any more pain. As I prepared to roll myself on the highway, I collapsed, and my eyelids came together. A white man was on his way home and saw me lying on the side of the highway. He pulled over and saw me lying in my pool of blood in the grass, bleeding to death, unconscious, and unresponsive.

There were no cell phones during this time. So, the white man left to call for an ambulance to come and see me. As he went to get help, another man called my name, "Bennie, Bennie!" I could barely open my eyes, and he said, "Do you know who I am?" I responded and said, "Uncle Sam." Then he said to me, hold on, I'm going to call for help, then he left. Ricky Jackson and his wife were on their way home. Ricky said to his wife that he looked like a big deer on the side of the road. Let me pull over and get that deer.

When he walked across the street, to his surprise, when he looked down to get the deer, he looked down and said, this is a human being. When he looked a little closer, he said, "Bennie, Bennie!" his wife got out of the car and ran across the road. My eyes were opened just a little; it felt like I was taking my last breath. Then I said, "Ricky, let your wife blow breath in me because my air is running out. Please do not let me die." They never left my side, and she continued to breathe in my mouth.

Shortly after that, I saw blue and red lights flashing from the ambulance and the Sheriff's cars. As soon as the paramedics got to me, they put an oxygen mask on me. The paramedics said to each other as they put me in the ambulance, "It does not look good because he lost a lot of blood. I hope he can make it to the hospital."

Uncle Sam and the white man did make it back as they put me in the ambulance. I heard one of the paramedics say that this man was lucky the bullet did not hit the central vein in his leg because he would have died instantly. I am now in the ambulance, rushing to the hospital, and once I got there, I was taken right to the operating room because I was in bad shape.

Uncle Sam went to tell my mother what happened to her son. Uncle

Sam went to the door and called my mother, "Becka, Becka, this is Sam."

As he was walking into the house, my mother said, "Sam, here I am; how are you doing?"

Uncle Sam said, "Rebecka, come with me. Bennie is in the emergency room."

She said, "Bennie had a seizure?"

Uncle Sam said, "No, Bennie was shot, and it doesn't look good for him."

My mother just walked out of the house with what she had on. Uncle Sam got her to the hospital, and when my mother walked into the emergency room, crying and asking, "Can I see my son."

A nurse had told my mother that she could not see me because of preparation for surgery and that they were doing all they could to save her son's life.

About 30 minutes later, someone came out into the waiting room and said that his mother could see him before Bennie died because he wouldn't make it through the night. My mother walked into the operating room, crying and praying, thanking God for letting her son live and not die.

Then she walked up to the bed; she called my name twice, then I opened my eyes and said, "Mom, I love you so much. Stop crying because I will be alright. Mom, if God allowed me to live, I said I wouldn't be in the streets like I used to be and do what I was doing."

Shortly after that, my mother started praying then I started having seizures back-to-back, for the first time in years that I had episodes. The nurses got my mother out of the room, and I heard the doctor say that if the gunshot wounds didn't take him out, the seizures would kill him because of the blood he had lost when my mother walked back into the waiting. My Mom's Prayer Warriors were waiting on her, and they made a spiritual prayer closet in the waiting room and then closed the waiting room door. They started praying, telling God what they needed God to do for them. They knew prayer changed the situation, which continued until God wrote a prescription. Out of everybody in that hospital, the doctor prescribed medication for Bennie Tyrone Davis, Sr. It says Bennie shall live and not die because I specialize in doing the impossible.

During this time, the only thing on Marion's streets was the gunman who had snuffed out Caveman's life. Many people believed he was found dead, and some said he passed during surgery because he lost too much blood. Caveman was and was still in surgery. He lost a lot of blood, and then his oxygen got low.

The doctor knew that I was at the point of death, and he told one of the nurses to let the family know there was nothing else I could do to save this young man. Caveman just stopped breathing, and he flat-lined. Someone put a white sheet over his head. Someone went to let the family know that he passed away. Then, a nurse looked down at Caveman and saw that Caveman was breathing. Debra Fling was standing at the window when my mother gave birth to me, and she was one of the nurses in the operating room who found Caveman breathing. She went to the waiting room and told my mother, family, and friends that Bennie would make it and that things were getting better for him. He will survive in the next 24 hours if everything stays as it is. Then she entered back into the operation room. The doctor stopped the bleeding but left one bullet lodged in my left leg that the doctor decided not to remove at that time because it may cause more bleeding. The right leg, where the shot went all the way through, had split a vein, which caused the doctor to have to tie up the vein in my right leg. I would have bled to death if the doctor had not done that. I stayed in ICU for less than 48 hours and was placed in a regular room.

My mother never left my bedside. She stayed in the ICU just as long as I did, then she went to the common room and stayed with me. My mother was right there, always in my presence to ensure I would make it. After a week had passed, and I was still so heavily sedated, I was doing so much better. The doctors said I would go home in a few days, and I was so happy.

When a doctor walked into my room, I was so excited because I just knew he was coming to tell me the good news that I'd be going home within a couple of days, but the first thing the doctor said to me, "Mr. Davis, you are lucky to be alive. Most people died from gunshot wounds and loss of blood."

Then he told me the shocking news: I was going to lose my right leg. When he started explaining about the artificial leg, my eyes got full of water. I thought about my three children. I would never have an opportunity to play any sports with my children. I want to show my son the techniques for playing football, show my daughter how to play basketball and show them how to run track. My life has been taken away from me because of my decisions. The only good news I could see was my children's father is still alive. I looked over at my mother, and tears were rolling down her face, but at the same time, she was telling me we're going to make it because this too shall pass. My Mom saw that I was disappointed about the doctor's news about what was about to happen to me.

Then the doctor said that this surgery must happen as quickly as possible and that this procedure would be scheduled for in the morning, and the doctor walked out of the room. Everything that could have been said, I never thought the doctor would give me the news that bad. Mama looked at me crying and said, "Son, it will be alright because God did not bring you this far to leave you. Even with an artificial leg, God is still good because you are still alive. I would rather have a son alive with an artificial leg than have a dead son with two legs because you are still my son. I still love you with two legs or without, and then she said I thank God for allowing my son to still be alive."

Shortly after that, the doctor left, and Mr. Page walked into the room and my mother told him what the doctor had just said. Then Mr. Page said, "Let's join hands," then he started praying, and Mama started crying. My life felt like it was over, not realizing how good God had been to me. I said to myself, go ahead and get that artificial leg because I am still alive. Mr. Page prayed, saying God, thank you because you specialize in doing the impossible, but the one thing I remember during that prayer was weeping may endure for a night, but joy cometh in the morning. Mr. Page continued praying, and he said I do not know how you are going to do it, but God, this is family, and You can make a way right now for this young man. Then he began to say thank you, God. My mother began thanking God, and tears were coming out of her eyes. I found myself just saying, "Yes Lord! Yes Lord! I believe You will work it out for me," and then Mr. Page began to say thank you, Lord, for doing it for your son. Amen.

As Mr. Page was leaving my room, Sister Ella Shannon entered my room. Every day I was in the hospital, she would come by after she got off work and sit with my mother and me for a few hours. My mother shared this day with her the doctor's report about my right leg's amputation. Sister Shannon reminded my mother that prayer changes situations. She told my mother that she would be praying that God work a miracle in her son's life before he had to go to surgery. I asked my mother not to let anyone else come into my room except my family. People came to my room to see how bad I look and then went back into the streets and told people that they saw Caveman and he didn't look good. The only thing that was going through my mind was after the surgery, I would only have one leg. I was praying that God gave me the strength and understanding to cope with one leg, and I thanked the Lord for sparing my life. God, if it is anyway possible, don't allow my leg to be amputated. My sister and brother came to visit me, and I told them about the surgery that would take place the next day. I was crying because I wanted to keep my leg, but then my brother and sister told me they loved me and were so happy that I was still alive. When they left the room, no one else came to see me that night. I had my mom turn the television and lights off, and I just laid my head on my pillow and then cried myself to sleep.

I started dreaming about the surgery, then I woke up and started staring at the ceiling. This night was the strangest night of my life because it was so long but went so fast before I knew it. My mother had me up and was washing me the day of my surgery then she started praying for me. My mother kept me clean the whole time I was in the hospital every day. I could not get out of bed to go to the bathroom, but my mother would make sure I could use the bedpan when I did have to go. What would a mother not do for their child? I thank God for blessing me with a loving mother.

The orderlies came to get me to get prepped for surgery. My Mom had me ready to go to surgery. When I was on my way to surgery, my mother, sister, and brother were in my room. They told me they would be waiting for me when I returned from surgery. The last words that I heard on my way out of the room were from my mother. She said it would be alright because you would not allow this surgery to defeat you and that she loved me. When I saw my family, they were crying, making me cry. As I went down the hallway, I said to myself, is this a dream because I need to wake up? I realized it was not a dream, but I'm in this predicament because of my decision. I said to myself, 'Lord, it is in your hands.'

The orderly took me to the operating room, and one of the nurses started asking me questions about myself. She asked me what is my name? When is your birthday? What is your mother's name? I answered the questions then she said I'm going to put this over your nose and mouth, then I need you to breathe in deep breaths in and out. I obeyed, and shortly after that, my eyelids started coming together, but the last thing I heard from the doctor was before amputating his leg.

"Let's see if the gangrene has entered his blood."

The doctor checked my thigh and was not able to find any gangrene. Then they checked my knee and were not able to find any gangrene. Then the doctor checked under my knee to the ankle and found gangrene. He went to my ankle, and the doctor found gangrene. The doctor cut all the gangrene out of my right leg from under my knee to my ankle. My leg was left open now after the doctor removed the gangrene. The day before, the gangrene had covered my right leg. I looked to God because only He can stop the gangrene.

After surgery, I was placed in ICU. When I woke up, I still had two legs. All I could say was thank you, Lord, for specializing in doing the impossible. I did not know how long I was in ICU. I did have another seizure. I heard my mother calling my name, then my eyes came open, and I said, "Mom, I love you." Sometime later, someone rolled me back to my room, and by this time, my sister, brother, Sister Ella Shannon and my mother were also back in the room, and they started thanking God when they saw my two legs. The removal of the gangrene left a scar under my knee to my ankle. The doctor cut out all the gangrene. Today, the scar is just a reminder to me to see where The Lord has brought me.

My right leg was bandaged up and stuffed with gauze. After returning to my room, I was given lunch because I could not eat anything before surgery. I was so excited about eating some food. While I was eating, my Pastor and some of the church family and friends came to see me. Now that the street people came by to see and talk about how Caveman looked. The church folks were coming by to see how Caveman was looking so that they could have something to talk about during devotional service. I had some visitors that came by that lived in the neighborhood that I grew up in. Seeing them gave me so much joy. One of the hospital chaplains came to my room and asked if he could pray for me. I told him yes, so everyone that was in the room came together.

The chaplain prayed that God continued to strengthen me. The days were going by so fast, and later that afternoon, the pain medicine started wearing off, and the pain started coming in. My leg was stinging and hurting so badly that I started crying. A nurse came to my room after I pressed the button to alarm the nurse. I told her that I was in so much pain, and the nurse gave me a shot for the pain. Not long after that, the pain left me, and I stopped crying. I began talking to my family. I was not able to feel anything because I was extremely high.

Everyone in my room left at about the same time because my mother let them know that I must get some sleep. My Mom and I were in my room alone when the nurse came in to check my temperature and blood pressure. When she walked into my room, I started hallucinating. I shouted to my mother, "Duck, Mama duck, call the army! People coming in here to kill us." I pulled the covers over my head so I could hide from the army.

Then I asked my mom, "Are you alright? Are you alright?" I did not have any control over myself. I was given the medication so I would not be hurting, but the medication made me lose my mind. To ensure that I did nothing to myself, the nurse called for help, so the nurses tied my hands up to the bed because I had an IV, and they did not want me to pull it out. I don't know when I went to sleep, but I was hurting so bad the next morning when my eyes came open.

A doctor and nurse came into my room at about 11:00 AM that morning. The doctor asked me, "How are you feeling? What is your pain level from one to 10?" I responded to the doctor, "Do you have a higher number than ten because ten is too low." That's when he explained that he would give me something that would take away the pain. He said this may be the last time I would get this, and then I'd be taking pills. The doctor said I don't want you to get addicted to the shots we give you.

Then, before I got the shot, the doctor unwrapped my leg. He explained that it was to get the gangrene out of the lower part of my leg when my leg was cut. Then he went on to say that he kept it open, and the nerves are raw, and there's nothing there. He let me know it was going to hurt badly. The doctor had the nurse take the wrappings off my leg then she pulled the gauze out of the hole in my leg. And out of nowhere, the pain started going throughout my body. I was not able to do anything but holler, scream, and cry. I was able to feel the nerves moving, and I said to my doctor, "This is too much pain. Give me a shot, give me a shot so that I don't feel this pain anymore." I told the doctor, "Please help me." Then I started calling my mom. "Help me, Mom, help me, Mom," and she started crying because she had never seen her son in that much pain.

When the doctor and the nurse calmed me down, he had my mother, and I looked at the cut in my leg. I was able to see the bone, blood, and nerves jumping. I could still feel the pain. Then I just laid back down, looking at the ceiling. The nurse repacked my leg and then wrapped it up. The only visitors that I had that day were family and Sister Shannon. As time passed, it started getting late, and the pain came back like never before. I had my mother press the nurse call button to contact a nurse. I said to my mother, "Mom, I can't take this pain. I need something now to help me." I started crying. The nurse came into the room, and I asked her if there was anything she had for pain that I could take because the pain was coming back, and I couldn't bear it. She said the doctor had ordered one more shot, with this being my last shot. After the nurse gave me the shot, she said that she had to repack my leg.

While the nurse repacked my leg, there was some pain, but the shot took a lot of that pain away because I was so high from the shot. As the nurse was almost done rewrapping my leg, to my surprise, Debra Fling walked into my room. I was so happy to see her. My mother was also happy because she was able to ask her questions about what I was going through and how long her son would be hurting like this. After all, this is a lot of pain he is experiencing.

Every day and every night, my mother and I were in the room alone. I started hallucinating again. I told my mother, "Some people are on the other side of the door, killing people." I said, "Look at all the blood coming in here. We are next to be killed. Let's get out of here because we have just a little bit of time. Mama, I got to get you out of here now because the blood is all over the floor. I will help you get out of the window, and then I will come behind you, but let's go now because all of those killers will knock the door down, and we will be killed." When the door opened, I started screaming as loud as I could. "Help, help somebody help my mother and me; these people came to kill us."

It was Debra Fling that opened the door. She called for help, and then she pressed the button for help. A few men and women came in the room running then I started hollering, "They are coming with guns, they're shooting, somebody just got shot and killed now they're about to kill me along with my mother." Then I felt the nurses who came in tie me down again so I would not hurt myself, my mother, or someone else who may have been in my room.

As the days passed, the nurses started weaning me off the shots. My leg still had to be changed each day, and tears still came from my eyes. Two weeks passed, and the doctor came in and informed my mother and me that I had to have another surgery. This surgery was to draft skin from my thigh to cover the hole in my right leg. The doctor asked me which leg I would like the skin to be drafted from, but the doctor said, "I recommend that you draft the skin of the same leg from which the gangrene was cut out." I agreed with the doctor. He then said the surgery would take place in the morning.

It was about two hours before visiting hours ended when my door came open, and my friend Brains was walking into my room. She came in cursing, "What the hell happened with them MF's? They got to be handled!" She went on to say, "Those who did this shit to you…" Then she saw my mother and said, "I'm sorry, Miss Pocahontas." I met Brains when I wanted to start selling drugs in Mullins, and she let me know who had the money to buy the drugs, and she told me all the rats in Mullins so I wouldn't deal with any of them. She set me up with a few of her girlfriends. This friend was my dog. To this day, we're still friends. Brains got her life together after she made the 6:00 news on television. I loved saying to her, "That is all you ever wanted to do was make the headlines." She stayed for about an hour and kept me laughing, and my mind got off of the surgery I was having the next morning.

The whole time I was in the hospital, that night was the most fun I had with my friend. The morning came so fast, and my mother got me up so I could be ready. Then, the hospital orderlies came for me to go to the operating room. The surgery lasted about two hours and was a success.

When I returned to my room, my mother, brother, sister, pastor, church members, and friends were waiting for me to return. They said a prayer over me that God continued to heal me. A social worker came to my room and told me that if I were not out of the hospital within 30 days, my SSI check would be cut off. I was in the hospital for only 30 days. A few days before it, I was released from the hospital.

Dr. Henry McGill Jr. visited me, and that was the same day that OJ Simpson was found not guilty. He prayed for me before he left the room. The whole time that I was in the hospital, not one person from the Marion County Sheriff's Department or the Marion Police Department came to get a report about the shooting. They never investigated it and never asked about my friend who set everything up to have me killed. They never went to the game room to ask questions. The entire Law Enforcement Dept. of Marion preferred that I was dead because my life was not worth anything since I was a drug dealer. They never looked for the man who attempted to murder me, and, in a sense, they were thanking him and my friend for what they did to Caveman.

Two weeks later, I got home and found myself in church. I could not drive, so Billy Hughes would come and take me to church on Sunday mornings, Sunday evenings, and Bible study nights. One time, Billy Hughes came to pick me up for the church and was late. I was in my wheelchair waiting for him to come, and when I saw him pull up in the yard, I was so happy. I stood up, and then I started walking. I never stopped walking. I didn't even have a cane, a walker, or a brace. When I walked into the church, everyone who knew my story started praising God because the church family knew it was nothing but a miracle. I remember telling my mother I would not be in the streets like I used to be, but I knew I did not say I would be saved.

Shortly after that, I started back selling drugs. I was selling drugs most of my time, and a small part of my time, I was a church-going man. I started driving back. My Pastor went to Indiana, Maryland, to do a revival, and he asked me to go with him to help him drive. I said, "Yes, I would love to go with you." When I was up there, he shared with the church family what had happened to me.
The next night, I was asked to share my testimony, and when I gave my testimony, the people started praising God all over the church. I said to myself, 'It's time for me to give my life to the Lord.' I said, "God, it's time for you to come into my life because you have been good to me," and I said to myself, when I get to church on Sunday, I'm going to ask God to save me.

Not knowing what was going on in Marion when I was about to get back on the road, I called my mother to share my good time and how the people were blessed while I was there. My pastor and I got on the road to come back to Marion. When I got home, I did not know what was going on, but my Pastor came into the house. He helped bring my bags into the house. Then, my mother hugged me and told me that my sister had been falsely arrested for the distribution of crack cocaine, and the drug task unit had a warrant for my arrest for the distribution of crack cocaine. She told me I had to go turn myself into the police.

I got upset and said, "Why did you tell me this? Because I would have rather lived on the streets of Indiana, Maryland than come back to Marion to go to jail and make time in prison!"

The Police Department and Sheriff's Department that's over the drug task unit served me with a warrant for the distribution of crack cocaine. They did not investigate or ask any questions. They did not even make any attempts to find the person who attempted to murder me. They never asked my friend anything about what had happened.

DR. BENNIE T. DAVIS

7. OVERCOMING PUBLIC OPINION

Public opinion has stopped a multitude of people from going forward in life. For a person to defeat public opinion, the first thing that must be done is to overcome it. To overcome public opinion, a person must overcome three statements and three types of people. The statements remind me of when I was in school. I loved saying sticks and stones may break my bones, but words would never hurt me. I found out that there are no sticks, stones, or broken bones that I ever experienced worse than the words that people said to and about me.

Broken bones come back together again, but the words people say will never leave, and anytime you see that person, whatever words are said will replay in your heart. If you can ever overcome those three statements and those three types of people, you will overcome public opinion. They say they tell me, and I heard those three statements that have caused more people to be killed, more people in jail, in prison, destroyed marriages, friendships and church families.

The three types of people that will always be a part of your life no matter what your age bracket is. What blows my mind about it is that in the Bible, Jesus chose His disciples, but today, we choose these types of people in our lives. All the names start with the letter H, which is hell raisers, haters and hinders. That is why if we overcome public opinion, success comes to our lives.

Overcoming public opinion is not a one-time thing, but it is a lifetime. People will continuously have to overcome what they say, they tell me; I heard hell raisers, haters and hinders. The reason why I know about overcoming public opinion is because it happened to me, and it is still happening in my life today. A person will be reminded of their past for the rest of their life.

I knew once I returned home from the revival, I would need to turn myself into the Marion Police Department. I'm sure my mother informed the police when I would be returning home from the revival. I did not want to get my mother into any trouble by not turning myself in. I did not have any money, and I could not run away because I would have been on the run for the rest of my life. I had no choice, so I got something to eat, and then I turned myself in.

When I walked into the police station, it was like they were more excited about arresting me for distribution of crack cocaine, but those same people were not excited about finding the person or persons that were involved in getting me shot. A young man attempted murder in my life that was not important, but arresting me for drugs was more important. It reminded me of when I had that seizure in front of my grandparents' house, and my grandmother looked out of her front door and shut the door, saying let that bastard die. Now, the Marion police are saying the bastard did not die when he was shot, but he will die in prison because, at the end of the day, Caveman will not walk on the streets of Marion anymore.

Shortly after I entered the police station, an officer came to me and asked me, are you Bennie Tyrone Davis, I responded yes, and that was when the officer read the warrant and proceeded to arrest me for distribution of crack cocaine. Then the police took me through booking, and I felt like my hands were tied and my heart was crying. I was given a personal recognizance bond because I was not a flight risk. On my mind was the wonderful revival that I had just been in a few nights ago. I had an opportunity to share my testimony and was able to see what God had done for me and how it impacted other people's lives.

At this time, my mind was made up that I had to go ahead and give my life to God. Out of all that, I came back to Marion, SC, and now look at me facing time in prison being arrested. Now look at Satan telling me, "Bennie, you need not be saved because now you must get a lawyer, and that is going to take money." I said, "I might as well stay in the streets selling drugs." I should turn it over to Jesus, but I said, "Caveman can handle this." So, I walked out of the police station, not saying anything to anyone, knowing that in order for me not to go back to jail, I had to pay a lawyer. The best lawyer that I found during this time for drugs was Attorney Jack Lawson.

A few days passed, and my mother said to me and my sister, "I would like for you all to go and get prayer from one of my friends." We both said, "Mom, that would be fine," because we need all the help we can get because we cannot make any prison time. The next day, we went to Prophetess Mary Williams's house for her to pray for us. After she prayed, she began to talk to my sister and me. She said I am going to draw what God is showing me. She drew a picture of a tree, a house, and a car then she said, "When you come in the yard, a man walked out to the car. I kept saying I do not remember going to anyone's house. The warrant said that this drug sale took place on McMillan Street in Marion, SC.

When I got back to Marion, we looked for McMillan Street, and sure enough, McMillan Street was found. As soon as my sister went down McMillian Street, I saw the tree and the house. This is where the informer resides. I said, "Let's wait until we go to court because I know that this man never had to buy any drugs from me because he was my friend. I always looked out for him because he would fix my car and keep it clean."

Jack Lawson was our attorney, and he set up a meeting at the police station. When we went to the police station, we found out that two of the police officers did the recording out of the tree that was in the yard at this time. I knew that it was the informant. He did set my sister and me up for selling drugs to him. I never let the informant know that I knew that he was the informant that set us up.

When I was out there on the streets, I learned that if a person is out to kill you, don't let them know that you know that they are out to kill you because then they would protect themselves. I had to pay my attorney, so I had to sell drugs. I informed him that we had the down payment and would pay every other week. What I did not understand was I was arrested the first part of the year, and the next month, I was in general session court.

My sister and I were put on the top of the drug list to be tried in court. I was hoping that they were going to give us more time before going before the judge, but on the third day, our attorney let my sister and I know that we were going before the Judge during this court term. I informed our attorney that we wanted a jury trial because I believed that we could beat this case they had against us. Then, the attorney told us it was a 95% chance we could win, but it was a 5% chance that we could lose.

Now, the solicitor's office was giving us a deal: if we pleaded to the charges, they would drop the distribution of crack cocaine and give us possession of crack cocaine, and our sentence would be probation. Only one would get probation, and the other would get off free with no charges. My sister said she would take the charges and plead guilty. Our attorney went to the solicitor's office to let him know that Alethea would plead guilty to the charges. Immediately, the solicitor told my attorney that only one can plead guilty, and that should be Caveman.

The school zone and all the other charges were dropped that was on my sister. I said let us have a jury trial because we can win this case. My lawyer said, "Mr. Davis, win or lose, I am going to walk out that door and go home to my family. If the verdict comes back guilty, you and your sister will not be able to go home. You would have to sit in that box with the guilty people, and you both would go to prison for a long time."

Then he said, "You can walk out that door with me today, but the only way that can happen is that you must plead guilty."

My lawyer went on to say that the solicitor will recommend probation, and your sister will go free.

"Mr. Davis, you can jump this hurdle and never look back again."

He said to me, "Mr. Davis, you can have a wonderful life. Let me know what you are going to do after lunch, and let your family know what you are going to do."

During our lunch break, I got a call from my doctor's office, and they informed me that I had to come back in for surgery to remove the bullet from my right leg. I was so happy I said now it looks like I will not be going to court this time. I returned to the court and informed my lawyer that I was going to have surgery the next day. I had to leave court to go and get a letter from the doctor stating that I was going to have surgery the next day. After I got the letter, I took it back to court with me and gave the letter to my lawyer, and he said to me that I was released from court the next day. I had to report back to the courtroom within 24 hours after surgery. I went to the doctor the next day, and he did the procedure in his office. After the bullet was removed, the doctor showed me the bullet that came out of my leg.

I returned to court and was presented before the judge, but what I did not understand was why the solicitor wanted me to go before the judge so badly. After I stood the judge, I was told not to plead guilty, but then, at the same the solicitor was recommending probation. When my records were pulled, it showed a guilty plea. This is the way that the system gets young men to believe that they are pleading not guilty and getting probation, but at the same time, on our records, they got a guilty plea. The system is not fair towards black people.

When I appeared before the judge, he stated to me, "Before anyone comes before me regarding any type of drugs, I'd rather for that Sheriff that is standing at the door to pull his gun out and shoot me." My heart felt like it had stopped beating. This judge wanted to send me to prison. What am I going to do? I remember fasting, praying and using the principles of the Bible. I believe that God is going to work the impossible whether I plead guilty or have a jury trial. The judge said, "You do not have to accept what the solicitor recommends." I told him that I understood, and I was given 2 years' probation.

At the end of the day, my sister's charges were dropped, and now I had two years' probation along with restitution. I had to pay money back, and the solicitor knew that I was disabled and was not able to work. What got me was that just a few months ago, when I was shot and left for dead, not one officer of the Marion County Police Department took the time to find the person who attempted murder on my life. Now, the law wants to see me in prison that is why I got this sentence. This will surely send me to prison because it is impossible to pay fines without a job.

Yes, it is a setup for me and so many other young people imprisoned today because it is impossible for them not to fail. Therefore, I believe that the law is created against anyone who has committed a crime, especially Blacks. I made up my mind; I was determined not to allow a judge to have my life in their hands again. I had 24 hours to report to my probation officer so I could get started with my probation when I walked out of the courtroom with my lawyer.

He looked at me and said, "Mr. Davis, you jump the hurdles and never look back because your wonderful future is before you and not behind you. It is all up to you now, so do the right thing for yourself."

The whole time my lawyer was talking, I was thinking about how I could sell drugs, and no one knew about me being back out in the streets. This is the only way I can pay my probation and restitution. By this time in my drug life, most of the majority drug dealers who fronted me drugs were either in prison or dead. Everything that I have been through, I still had a desire and a love to sell drugs because I was put in a predicament where I had to pay money with no means of income.

The next day reported to my probation officer, and I had the opportunity to meet Mr. Kevin Grant, my probation officer. He let me know that if my probation was revoked, I would have to go back before the judge, and I would make time in prison. He also informed me that I would be taking random drug tests and that I needed to test negative on any drug tests that I submitted. He explained to me about the money that I must pay each month for probation in restitution, and if it is not paid, my probation would be revoked.

I was nervous because the only thing I could think about as he was saying this to me was how I came up with this money so that I wouldn't go to prison when I didn't have a job. I asked him how many other people that is on probation or parole today are sentenced to what would force them back on the streets to sell drugs so they would not go back to prison. I left knowing I had to get on the ball with finding new people who would front me some drugs.

I got in touch with my girl Brains because I knew she would find me someone who had a lot of drugs and could work with me. She got right on the job and found me someone who was able to help me reach my goal. Mr. Kevin Grant said if I do not get in trouble and do not have any violations, he would recommend that I get off probation early. Now, I had to have the restitution also paid in full. I was able to get in touch with one of my boys who was in the drug game with me in Denmark. The young man was able to help me out a great deal, so I was making that come back a little stronger.

I was still in church three to four times a week. I put time into church and used the principles of the Bible so I could be blessed. Yes, I was going to gain the whole world and lose my soul. I had an illusion of making the police believe that I was committed to the church so they would not pay attention to me selling drugs. I knew I was not going to lie to my mother. I said to her when I was on my deathbed, Mama, I will not be in the streets like I used to be. I was simply saying I would be smarter than I was.

I was still attending Power Outreach Cathedral Church. One night, I decided to have a weed party, and people who were invited just came over to smoke weed and have fun. I loved giving people shotguns. I was going around the house giving shotguns all night long. Different ones would get a shot then I would laugh at how they would be coughing and gagging because they could not take all that smoke.

The next day, I had to go see my probation officer, and he said to me today, you must take the drug test. My eyes got big, and my heart stopped because I knew what I was doing the night before I came to see him. He told me that the test would take place after our meeting that day. I already paid my restitution and probation. During the meeting, something happened because someone came for Mr. Kevin Grant, and he left his office, and then he came back into the office and said to me, "You are dismissed because an emergency came up."

I knew then I was not giving any more shotguns until I got off probation. I was so scared because I knew if the emergency had not happened, I would have failed the drug test, and I would have violated my probation. I knew it had to be the Lord looking out for me when the emergency came up, and Mr. Kevin Grant had to go and attend to whatever was going on. I am not going to take any more chances with my freedom, and I am going to finish my probation.

Caveman was still on the streets selling drugs, but I made my probation appointment each month. I was paying my restitution and my probation, and then I stopped paying my restitution because I wanted to be violated so that I could go back to court. I realized that a lot of people get violated, and the reason why they can't beat it is because when it's time to talk to the judge, our young people don't have anything to say but, 'wats up, yo man,' use profanity, and call the young ladies out of their names. When it's time to be intelligent and hold a decent conversation, they don't know how to talk to the judge.

I was willing to take my chances, so I went with my probation officer, Mr. Kevin Grant, and he said, "Because you have not been paying your restitution, Mr. Davis, I'm going to take you before the judge for violation of probation. I just want you to know that you will be making time because you are guilty, and there is nothing else I can do for you because I must do my job." I said, "Do what you have to do." Then he said, "I will see you in court because, as of now, you are on the docket for the next general session court in Marion."

Now, I had to go before the judge in just a few weeks. So, what I did was add up the money that I had to pay so I would not go to prison. When it was time to go to court, I worked the streets selling drugs and made the money that would have to be paid if the judge wanted the money. If the judge does not take the money, I am going to make time in prison for violation of probation.

I went to court with the money in my pocket to pay the restitution for backup, but I believed that I could say enough to this judge that this restitution would be dropped. This was just too much money I had to pay, and I did not have a job. I refused to allow the system to put me in prison for a long time. I was determined prison would not be my home.

Within six months, I was back in court. I was still selling drugs because I was in love with selling drugs and the power. The last week of the court was on that Friday. My name was called for violation of probation. My probation officer told the judge why he had to violate me. The judge asked me if there was anything I would like to say to the court, and I responded yes, I would love to address the court. I explained to the court what happened to me on September 8th, 1995, how I was shot several times and robbed because of drugs.

No one from the Marion County Police Department ever attempted to find the person who attempted to take my life. I also told the court what happened to me in school, and the judge stopped me and said, "Since you have been through so much, Mr. Bennie Davis, today we have a class from Marion High School that is in the courtroom. Turn around and tell them something to encourage them to fight for their education and to never want to come to this courtroom."

I turned around, and I began to tell the class, along with everyone else who was in the courtroom, what had happened to me in school. I told them about me selling drugs and how I got shot and robbed. The people started crying and praising God in the courtroom. I then showed them the leg that was cut open, and then some people started speaking in tongues; when I turned around and looked at the judge, tears were coming down his face. The judge said to me that within the next three months, I must go to 10 different churches and organizations and tell them the great things that God did in my life, and the restitution would be dismissed.

After court, the three statements came up; it was stated to me they say this judge finds everybody guilty that violates probation. They tell me the last person who came before this judge was given the maximum time, and I heard that they made it mandatory that they serve each and every day with no early release, but all I know is I must overcome public opinion. Yes, they say, they tell me, and I heard, but out of all that, I had God on my side.

I got in touch with Uncle Cleve Dorsey and told him what the judge told me, that I must go to ten churches or organizations and tell them my testimony. He told me that he would talk to his wife and ask if she would put me on her Sunrise Jubilees Anniversary program on the fourth Sunday in September, which was held at Mount Pisgah Missionary Baptist Church. Then, a few days passed, and Uncle Cleve came to my house and said, "Bennie, you will be on the program."

I was still selling drugs and having weed parties. I told my Pastor, Dr. William Young Jr., that I had to go to 10 churches or organizations and give my testimony, and he allowed me to give my testimony at church one Sunday morning. I loved being a Caveman, but I was not buying as many drugs as before; I had to cool down a lot.

One day, I was at the store with my mom, and she said hello to Bishop Mack Davis. My Mom introduced me to Bishop Mack Davis, and I began to tell him about my situation about going to ten different churches and organizations and giving my testimony. Bishop said that he had a program coming up the following Sunday, and he asked me to come and give my testimony. I was so happy because things were falling into place for me. The fourth Sunday of September approached so fast. The Sunrise Jubilee's Anniversary has finally gotten here, and I was so excited.

Earlier that day, a young man got in touch with me because he needed some drugs. I told him that I had to be in church at 4:00 pm, and he had to make this thing happen before 3:15 pm because I had to get ready and be at the church by 4:00 pm. The young man and I did get up with each other at about 3:15 pm. The drug deal happened while I was on my way to church. When I was approaching the church, there were so many cars in the parking lot and a lot of people walking into the church.

When I walked into the church, there were so many people seated, and some were standing up, waiting to get a seat. When I came in, an usher came to me and escorted me to my seat. Everyone was having a great time in The Lord listening, singing and enjoying the gospel groups that were singing. A group was called up named the Heavenly Voices, and when Ervin Kinney started to sing, the people in the church went up in praise. I had drugs on me while I was sitting in church, and I said to myself I am going to sell the rest of these drugs after I get out of church.

Halfway through the program, the Master of Ceremony announced that today we have Brother Bennie Davis, and he is going to give his testimony. At the end of the service, there was still a crowd of people. The Master of ceremony introduced me to the people; he said once again that Brother Bennie Davis was going to share his testimony, and I hoped someone would be encouraged and believe that you can overcome whatever man said that you can't accomplish. He then instructed the people to stand to their feet and make some noise as Brother Bennie came to the front. When I walked to the front of the church, I began to speak, and the people started screaming and hollering. I told the people that I once was out of place, but now I am in place. I told them what happened to me and some of the people started jumping, shouting and speaking in an unknown tongue.

I felt the presence of God like never before, and something came upon me, and I knew for a fact that something was happening to me, and it was the spirit of the Lord. My mind was renewed, and my heart was changed. When everything was over, the Master of Ceremony had a preacher to come dismiss the service. After the service, people came to me and shook my hand, and Pastor Fogan came to me and said that he wanted me to come to Sandy Grove Holiness Church and speak. That was the first church that I was invited to give my testimony. After the program was over, I took my mother home, and I told her that I would be back later.

I went back on the streets to get rid of the rest of the drugs that I had on me. As I was out on the streets, this young man walked up to me, and he looked me up and down, and then he said, "Caveman, you do not look like that hustler anymore. Therefore, I say people see greatness in you when you do not see greatness in yourself. Something happened, you look totally different." I had some drugs that I had to sell. I said to myself when I sell these drugs, and it will be over; no more selling drugs. Then I said to myself, why wait and try to sell all these drugs and take the risk of being set up again? I sold the young man the drugs for less than the price. The hunger that I had to sell drugs was no longer there, and it was gone. I knew that was something that only God could take away from me. God took that desire from me to sell drugs because I asked Him to do it. I believe and trust in God.

From that day until today, I have not sold any more crack, powder, Bombazi or chocolate Thai. I was not just delivered, but God came into my life and saved me because I also asked Him to do that for me. I was saved from my life of sin right there on the streets on that fourth Sunday. God delivered me, saved me, brought me out of sin, and I was forgiven for all my sins. When I got home, I was able to tell my mother and my family that I was saved and that my sins were forgiven. I told my mother that I was not just in the church, but I was saved now, and heaven was my home.

Tears began to come down my face, and I said there were no more drugs, and prison would not be my home. Because of the judge, I was drawn to Jesus due to his sentencing me to go to ten churches or organizations and give my testimony. For the first time in my life, I knew that I was free because my sins were forgiven and that the Lord saved me because I had the faith to believe. During the time of telling my testimony, I found forgiveness from the Lord for myself. I was able to successfully complete the sentence that the judge gave me. I turned my paper over to my probation officer, showing that I did go to the churches, and he doesn't know the guy that lives with me. Mr. Kevin Grant said to me, "Mr. Davis, you did a wonderful job, and the people heard your testimony and were blessed." He said that I needed to get in some of the schools around Marion or any other place to tell my testimony because my testimony would encourage our children.

I had to take a drug test, and Mr. Kevin Grant had someone to go with me. On the way back to Mr. Kevin Grant's office, I heard some probation officers having a conversation about Caveman. They were saying this thing about Caveman being saved. It will be over as soon as his probation is over. Now, he is playing the law, and there is no God in him; the only thing he is good for is selling drugs and making time in prison because they have a cell for him. I walked past the door like I did not hear a thing, and I asked had anyone seen Mr. Kevin Grant. I said to myself you all do not know the God that is on the inside working on the outside. God delivered me. I was doing so well with my probation officer; he said to me I am going to find out if I can go ahead and release you and get the rest of your probation dropped. I am never looking back because I have a future before me. I was looking forward to the next time I had to meet Mr. Kevin Grant because I was looking forward to hearing some great news that my probation was over. I was at the probation office waiting for Mr. Kevin Grant to come and get me. Mr. Kevin Grant came and got me, and we walked into his office, and he told me to have a seat. I was so happy. He then told me that he spoke to someone about me getting off probation, but he was told that Caveman was going to do all his two years.

God was still opening doors for me, and I was just walking into the doors, giving God the praise. I received a letter in the mail letting me know that my driver's license was going to be suspended for a year because of my plea for the possession of crack cocaine. I was wondering to myself how in the world I would be able to get around and go to church for a whole year. I would have to get someone to take me to church and any other places that I would have to go. I must get something done about this situation. I got in touch with a young lady that I knew, and I had her take my mother and me to Columbia, SC, so that I could apply for a provisional driver's license.

A provisional driver's license allows a person to drive to and from work or school so that they would be able to work or attend school. God opened doors for me to get my license so no matter where I was going, I would be driving to work for the Lord. One day, I was driving, and the police stopped me. I told the police officer that I was working for the Lord, and I was never stopped by the police again. During this time, Marion was infested with drugs in different places like the Honey Hole, The Bluff, Rosewood and Black Cat Alley. I went to Mayor Bobby Gerald's office, and I had a talk with him about going into the drug areas and telling our young men and ladies the danger of drug distribution and possession. I am the one person who could tell them that they could take the shoes of failure off and put on the shoes of success because I have done it myself. Drugs only do one or two things, and that is prison or death; there is no in-between.

The Mayor said to me that there should be no preaching and that I could only tell my testimony in the different drug areas in the city of Marion. I invited the Chief of Police to come to my event, which was going to take place that Saturday. The first place that I went to was the Honey Hole. Gene Fling paid for tents, and my mother cooked some chicken bog. I had the event announced on the local radio station, and people came from far and near, young and old. The people who came were blessed. The police were at my event to see if I was going to follow the instructions that were given to me by the Mayor. Of course, I did what I was asked to do. After a few times telling my testimony, the drugs stopped in the Honey Hole.

Prayer changes situations. I finished my probation successfully. I started looking into getting a pardon from the state of South Carolina. One of the requirements for getting a pardon was I had to get a list of the good things that I was doing in Marion County.

I started looking for a building, but I was not able to find one. I talked to my Pastor and told him that I was called into the ministry to tell the good news. When my Pastor would preach, I would look at him and say this is how I would look, bringing the word of God. Bishop Mack Davis's mother had an afternoon program at Morningstar in the Weeping Willow Community. She invited me to come to the program and give my testimony. That afternoon, the guest speaker did not show up for the program. I was asked to bring forth the word. What a great time we had in the Lord. This was my first sermon. I preached without a minister's license. The Lord's presence filled the sanctuary. At the end of the service, some of the people were coming to me, telling me that I sounded like I had been preaching for years.

One day, I was at a gas station getting some gas. As I was walking back to my car after paying for the gas, I saw Mr. Norman Pee, and he was the general manager at 94.3 FM radio station. He told me about a gospel show Jack Woodberry hosted Monday-Friday from 3 a.m. to 6 a.m. Mr. Pee asked me if I would be interested in being a part of the radio staff and working with Jack Woodberry. I told him that I would love to do it. During this time, some people still believed that I was selling drugs and was not saved and living for the Lord. So, when the opportunity came, I knew that God was working through Mr. Pee. I was going through a time of being rejected not from the outside of the church but in the church.

I was asked to come to a church for a black history program, and I was the guest speaker. This was going to be the start of something great. The day had come for me to preach on the black history program. I arrived at the church, and as I entered the sanctuary, I started walking up to the pulpit, and I was stopped by one of the deacons of the church. The deacon told me that the pastor did not welcome me in the pulpit and for me to sit with the other deacons. I was told when it was time for me to preach that, I had to stand at the podium where the church secretary does the announcements.

He then went on to tell me that the pastor did not want to be in the same pulpit that I am in because I was not qualified. This is a black history program, and here it is: a black man putting his knee on my neck, but I would not stop breathing, and I would not stop going forward. When I finished speaking, the Pastor of the church got up and preached a sermon. The subject was "An Uncle Tom". The members of the church just put their heads down. After service, some of the members came up to me and told me that church could have been dismissed after I sat down because I had already brought forth the word of the Lord. The tears started coming down my face, and yes, my pride was hurt.

DR. BENNIE T. DAVIS

These are the warrants that were served to Dr. Bennie T. Davis Sr.

INCIDENT REPORT

Date: 04/21/2015 10:57 SHERIFF DEPARTMENT
MARION COUNTY SHERIFF OFFICE
Agency I.D.: SC0340000
Report #: 201 -1000004

Incident Type: 11A - RAPE - FORCIBLE (ATTEMPTED)
Completed: YES
Forced Entry: NO
Premise Type: 03 20
Units Entered: 1
Type Victim: Individual

Incident Location: LIPSCOMB ROAD (UNKNOWN NUMERICS), MULLINS SC
Zip: 29574
Weapon Type: 40

Incident Date: 09/30/2014 1900
Date Reported: 10/01/2014 1320
Dispatch: 10/01/2014 1319
Time Arrived: 1332
Time Departed: 1340
Location No.: 02

Complainant: ALLEN, ANGELA DENISE
Resident: Y Race: B Sex: F Age: 28 Eth: N
Daytime Phone: (843) 423-9019
Evening Phone: (843) 319-6650

Address: 2918 PARK DR, FLORENCE, SC 29574
Location No.: 01

Victim: ALLEN, ANGELA DENISE
Relationship to Subject: AQ
Resident: Y Race: B Sex: F Age: 28 Eth: N
Daytime Phone: (843) 423-5019

Height: 5-7 Weight: 150 Hair: BLK Eyes: BRO

Address: 2918 PARK DR, FLORENCE, SC 29574
Location No.: 01

Visible Injury: NO
Victim Using Alcohol: NO
Drugs: NO
Two-Man Veh: NO One-Man Veh: NO Detective/Plainclothes: NO Other: Alone Assisted: J - This Jurisdiction

Suspect: DAVIS, BENNIE TYRONE
Race: B Sex: M Age: 46 Eth: N
DOB: 5-10 Weight: 295 Hair: BLK Eyes: BRO

Address: [redacted], MARION, SC 29571
Location No.:

Subject Using Alcohol: NO Drugs: NO Unk
Arrested Near Offense Scene: NO
Total # Arrested: 1
Date/Time of Offense: 09/30/2014 1900
Date/Time of Arrest: 1045

Offenses: RAPE - FORCIBLE (ATTEMPTED)

Narrative:
ON THE ABOVE DATE AND TIME, I MET WITH COMPLAINANT AT THE CORNER OF DUDLEY ROAD AND OLD EBENEZER (CHURCH), IN REFERENCE TO ATTEMPTED CRIMINAL SEXUAL ASSAULT. UPON ARRIVAL, I SPOKE WITH MS. ANGELA ALLAN, WHO REPORTED THAT LAST NIGHT, SHE WAS AT KEITH CROSS'S CLUB HOUSE AT THE ABOVE LOCATION, WHEN MR. BENNIE DAVIS ATTEMPTED TO RAPE HER. MS. ALLAN REPORTED THAT SHE WAS SITTING IN A CHAIR, WHEN MR. DAVIS CAME UP TO HER AND HELD HER DOWN IN THE CHAIR. MS. ALLAN REPORTED THAT SHE TRIED TO FORCE MR. DAVIS OFF OF HER, BUT HE CONTINUED TO HOLD HER DOWN AND TRY TO REMOVE HER CLOTHS. MS. ALLAN REPORTED THAT SHE SCREAMED AND MR. CROSS CAME INTO THE ROOM AND ASKED MR. DAVIS WHAT WAS HE DOING. MS. ALLAN REPORTED THAT MR. DAVIS THEN GOT OFF OF HER AND THEY WENT OUTSIDE AND BEGAN TO ARGUE. MS. ALLAN REPORTED THAT SHE THEN LEFT THE RESIDENCE, WITHOUT FURTHER INCIDENT. MS. ALLAN REPORTED THAT THE REASON SHE DIDN'T REPORT THE INCIDENT LAST NIGHT, IS BECAUSE SHE WAS SCARRED. MS. ASHLEY ALLEN WAS WITH MS. ANGELA ALLAN WHEN THE INCIDENT OCCURRED. MS. ASHLEY ALLEN COMPLETED A VOLUNTARY STATEMENT, IN REGARDS TO THE INCIDENT. MS ANGELA ALLAN, COMPLETED A VOLUNTARY STATEMENT AS WELL. I ADVISED MS. ALLAN AN INCIDENT REPORT WOULD BE COMPLETED THIS CALL WAS THEN CLEARED.

Subject Identified: YES
Subject Located: YES

Reporting Officer: SGT DANIEL CRIBB Date: 10/01/2014
Approving Officer: SGT DANIEL CRIBB Date: 10/01/2014
Follow-Up Investigation Officer: DETECTIVE SAMANTHA JACKSON 10/02/2014

TELL ALL I AM NOT THAT WAY ANYMORE

throughout the life of the book.

Marion Police Department
1024 South Main St.   P.O. Box 1190
Marion, South Carolina 29571
Phone (843) 423-8616   Fax (843) 423-8604

Dewayne K. Tennie
Chief

MUNICIPAL – POLICE RECORD CHECK
FOR THE CITY LIMITS OF MARION ONLY, THIS IS NOT A SLED CHECK

DATE: 3-20-2017   D.O.B: 11-12-1967   SOCIAL SECURITY #: ~~~~~

NAME: Dennis

CIRCLE ONE: 5 YEAR CHECK   10 YEAR CHECK   20 YEAR CHECK   FULL CHECK

HAS / HAS NO   POLICE CRIMINAL RECORD IN OUR JURIDICTION.
(CIRCLE ONE)

DATE: 5-30-2014   CHARGE: Breach of Peace
DISPOSITION: 30 days suspended upon $1087.50

DATE: 2-19-1996   CHARGE: Conspiracy to Dist Crack Cocaine
DISPOSITION: Pled to Crack Cocaine 5yrs + $5000 payment $500 + Cst + Ass Bal suspended w/ Probation 2yrs

DATE: 2-19-1996   CHARGE: Dist of Controlled Substance Prox to School
DISPOSITION: See above

DATE: 2-19-1996   CHARGE: Distribution of Crack Cocaine
DISPOSITION: See above

DATE: 11-18-1994   CHARGE: Offering Bribe to Officer
DISPOSITION: Nol Pros

DATE: 6-6-1990   CHARGE: Disorderly Conduct
DISPOSITION: 30 days suspended up $25=

DATE: _____   CHARGE: _____
DISPOSITION: _____

DATE: _____   CHARGE: _____
DISPOSITION: _____

DATE: _____   CHARGE: _____
DISPOSITION: _____

MARION POLICE DEPARTMENT

RECEPTIONIST / SECRETARY

DR. BENNIE T. DAVIS

Warrant No: 2014A3310100671

STATE OF SOUTH CAROLINA
County: X — Marion

THE STATE against Bennie Tyrone Davis — 2014-100054

Address: Marion, SC 29571-

Sex: M Race: B

Prosecuting Agency: Marion County Sheriff
Agency ORI #: SC0340000
Prosecuting Officer: Samantha Jackson - 0147

Offense: Sex / Assault with intent to commit criminal sexual conduct - First degree
Offense Code: 0253
Code/Ordinance Sec: 16-03-0656, 0652

This warrant is CERTIFIED FOR SERVICE in the County/Municipality. The accused is to be arrested and brought before me to be dealt with according to the law.

RETURN

A copy of this arrest warrant was delivered to defendant: Bennie Tyrone Davis on 1/22/2015

RETURN WARRANT TO:
General Sessions LOGGED 10/28/14 BOOK 20 PAGE 1379
103 N. Main Street
PO Box 295
Marion, SC 29571

AFFIDAVIT

County: X — Marion

Personally appeared before me the affiant **Samantha Jackson** who being duly sworn deposes and says that defendant **Bennie Tyrone Davis** did within this county and state on or about **9/30/2014** violate the criminal laws of the State of South Carolina (or ordinance of County: X — Marion) in the following particulars:

DESCRIPTION OF OFFENSE: Sex / Assault with intent to commit criminal sexual conduct - First degree

I further state that there is probable cause to believe that the defendant named above did commit the crime set forth and that probable cause is based on the following facts:

On September 30, 2014 at approximately 2200 (10pm) at the Outback on Lipscomb Road, Mullins, SC in the County of Marion, one Bennie Davis did touch the victim on her chest and attempted to take her clothes off. Therefore one Bennie Davis is charged with assault with intent to commit Criminal Sexual Conduct, this being a violation of SC Code of Laws 16-03-0656

STATE OF SOUTH CAROLINA
County: X — Marion

Affiant's Address: 2715 E Highway 76 Suite C, Mullins, SC 29574-
Affiant's Telephone: (843) 423-8216

ARREST WARRANT

TO ANY LAW ENFORCEMENT OFFICER OF THIS STATE OR MUNICIPALITY OR ANY CONSTABLE OF THIS COUNTY:

It appearing from the above affidavit that there are reasonable grounds to believe that on or about **9/30/2014** defendant **Bennie Tyrone Davis** did violate the criminal laws of the State of South Carolina (or ordinance of County: X — Marion) as set forth below:

DESCRIPTION OF OFFENSE: Sex / Assault with intent to commit criminal sexual conduct - First degree

Having found probable cause on the above affiant having sworn before me, you are empowered and directed to arrest the said defendant and bring him or her before me forthwith to be dealt with according to law; A copy of this Arrest Warrant shall be delivered to the defendant at the time of its execution, or as soon thereafter as is practicable.

Judge's Address: 2715 East Highway 76, Suite B, Mullins, SC 29574-

Mackin Darril Hayes
Judge Code: 7016

Issuing Court: X Magistrate   ☐ Municipal   ☐ Circuit

TELL ALL I AM NOT THAT WAY ANYMORE

ARREST WARRANT
E-563468
STATE OF SOUTH CAROLINA
☐ County / ☒ Municipality of Marion

THE STATE
against

BENNIE DAVIS
Address: ▓▓▓▓▓
MARION, S.C. 29571
Phone: _____ SSN: ▓▓▓▓▓
Sex: M   Race: B   Height: 509   Weight: 250
State: ___ DL #: ___
DOB: 11-12-67   Agency ORI #: 0340100
Prosecuting Agency: Marion PD (MCCDU)
Prosecuting Officer: H. Hendley
Offense: DIST. OF CONTROLLED SUBSTANCE IN PROX. TO SCHOOL   Offense Code: ___
Code/Ordinance Sec.: 44-53-445

This warrant is CERTIFIED FOR SERVICE in the ☐ County / ☐ Municipality of _____. The accused is to be arrested and brought before me to be dealt with according to law.

_____ (L.S.)
Signature of Judge

RETURN
A copy of this arrest warrant was delivered to defendant BENNIE DAVIS on 2-19-96
Cindy R. Chany
Signature of Constable/Law Enforcement Officer

RETURN WARRANT TO:

STATE OF SOUTH CAROLINA
☐ County / ☒ Municipality of Marion

AFFIDAVIT

Personally appeared before me the affiant **Hayvern Hendley**, who being duly sworn deposes and says that defendant **Bennie Davis** did within this county and state on **8-15-95** violate the criminal laws of the State of South Carolina (or ordinance of ☐ County / ☒ Municipality of **Marion**) in the following particulars:

DESCRIPTION OF OFFENSE: Distribution of Controlled Substance in Proximity to a School

I further state that there is probable cause to believe that the defendant named above did commit the crime set forth and that probable cause is based on the following facts:

That on or about 8-15-95, one Bennie Davis did unlawfully distribute a quantity of crack cocaine, a controlled substance, within one half mile of Johnakin Jr. Hi, in Marion to an undercover police officer; this being in violation of section 44-53-445 SC Code of Laws, 1976, as amended.

Sworn to and subscribed before me on 2-14-96
_____ (L.S.)
Signature of Issuing Judge

Signature of Affiant: _Hayvern Hendley_
Affiant's Address: P O BOX 1193, Mullins
Affiant's Telephone: 464-7528

STATE OF SOUTH CAROLINA
☐ County / ☒ Municipality of Marion

ARREST WARRANT

TO ANY LAW ENFORCEMENT OFFICER OF THIS STATE OR MUNICIPALITY OR ANY CONSTABLE OF THIS COUNTY:

It appearing from the above affidavit that there are reasonable grounds to believe that on **8-15-95** defendant **Bennie Davis** did violate the criminal laws of the State of South Carolina (or ordinance of ☐ County / ☒ Municipality of **Marion**) as set forth below:

DESCRIPTION OF OFFENSE: DISTRIBUTION OF CONTROLLED SUBSTANCE IN PROX. TO A SCHOOL

Now, therefore, you are empowered and directed to arrest the said defendant and bring him or her before me forthwith to be dealt with according to law. A copy of this Arrest Warrant shall be delivered to the defendant at the time of its execution, or as soon thereafter as is practicable.

_____ (L.S.)
Signature of Issuing Judge
Judge Code: 077

Judge's Address: _____
Judge's Telephone: _____
Issuing Court: ☐ Magistrate ☒ Municipal ☐ Circuit

ORIGINAL

DR. BENNIE T. DAVIS

ARREST WARRANT
2014A3320100142

STATE OF SOUTH CAROLINA
☐ County/ ☒ Municipality of
MARION

THE STATE
against

BENNIE TYRONE DAVIS
Address: [redacted]
MARION SC 29571
Phone: _____ SSN: _____
Sex: M Race: B Height: 5-9 Weight: 250
DL State: ___ DL#: ___
DOB: 11/12/1967 Agency ORI#: SC0340100
Prosecuting Agency: CITY OF MARION POLICE
Prosecuting Officer: LT TONY FLOWERS
Offense: SELL OF COUNTERFEIT ITEM, VALUE MORE THAN $10,000 Offense Code: 3309
Code/Ordinance Sec. 39-15-1190(B)(1)

This warrant is CERTIFIED FOR SERVICE in the
☐ County/ ☐ Municipality of
_____. The accused is to be arrested and brought before me to be dealt with according to law.

_____ (L.S.)
Signature of Judge
Date: _____

RETURN
A copy of this arrest warrant was delivered to defendant BENNIE TYRONE DAVIS
on 5-30-80A
_____
Signature of Constable/Law Enforcement Officer

RETURN WARRANT TO:

STATE OF SOUTH CAROLINA
☐ County/ ☒ Municipality of
MARION

AFFIDAVIT

Form Approved by S.C. Attorney General April 13, 2005 SCCA 518

Personally appeared before me the affiant LT. TONY FLOWERS who being duly sworn deposes and says that defendant BENNIE TYRONE DAVIS did within this county and state on 04/29/2014 violate the criminal laws of the State of South Carolina (or ordinance of) ☐ County/ ☒ Municipality of MARION in the following particulars:

DESCRIPTION OF OFFENSE: 39-15-1190(B)(1) / SELL OF COUNTERFEIT ITEM, VALUE MORE THAN $10,000

I further state that there is probable cause to believe that the defendant named above did commit the crime set forth and that probable cause is based on the following facts:

ON APRIL 29, 2014 ONE BENNIE TYRONE DAVIS DID KNOWINGLY AND WILLFULLY HAVE IN HIS POSSESSION 129 ITEMS THAT WERE IDENTIFIED AS COUNTERFEIT WITH A RETAIL VALUE OF $28,925 IN A 2000 LINCOLN TOWN CAR (VIN 1LNHM83WXYY770821) BEARING SOUTH CAROLINA LICENSE TAG KAE 307 WHILE PARKED IN FRONT OF 801 SOUTH MAIN ST. THIS INCIDENT OCCURRING WITHIN THE CITY LIMITS OF MARION AND CONSTITUTING THE CRIME OF TRANSPORT, TRANSFER, DISTRIBUTE OR SELL A COUNTERFEIT ITEM, WITH VALUE OF MORE THAN $10,000 BUT LESS THAN $50,000.

_____
Signature of Affiant
Affiant's Address 1024 S MAIN ST
MARION SC 29571
Affiant's Telephone 843-423-8642

STATE OF SOUTH CAROLINA
☐ County/ ☒ Municipality of
MARION

ARREST WARRANT
TO ANY LAW ENFORCEMENT OFFICER IN THIS STATE OR MUNICIPALITY OR ANY CONSTABLE OF THIS COUNTY:
It appearing from the above affidavit that there are reasonable grounds to believe that on 04/29/2014 defendant BENNIE TYRONE DAVIS did violate the criminal laws of the State of South Carolina (or ordinance of)
☐ County/ ☒ Municipality of MARION) as set forth below:
DESCRIPTION OF OFFENSE: TRADEMARKS / TRANSPORT, TRANSFER, DISTRIBUTE OR SELL A COUNTERFEIT ITEM, WITH A VALUE OF AT LEAST $10000, BUT LESS THAN $50000, 1ST OFFENSE

Having found probable cause and the above affiant having sworn before me, you are empowered and directed to arrest the said defendant and bring him or her before me forthwith to be dealt with according to law. A copy of this Arrest Warrant shall be delivered to the defendant at the time of its execution, or as soon thereafter as is practicable.

Sworn to and subscribed before me
on 05/07/2014
_____ (L.S.)
SAMUEL R DROSE
Judge's Address 2715 E HIGHWAY 76, SUITE B
MULLINS SC 29574
Judge's Telephone 8434238208
Judge Code: 7215 Issuing Court: ☐ Magistrate ☒ Municipal ☐ Circuit

ORIGINAL Case: 14-0574

TELL ALL I AM NOT THAT WAY ANYMORE

DR. BENNIE T. DAVIS

ARREST WARRANT
2014A3310100671

STATE OF SOUTH CAROLINA
[X] County [ ] Municipality of
Marion

THE STATE
against
2014-100004

Bennie Tyrone Davis

Address: [redacted]
Marion, SC 29571-

Phone: ___ SSN: [redacted]
Sex: M Race: B Height: ___ Weight: ___
DL State: ___ OL #: ___
DOB: 11/12/1967 Agency ORI #: SC0340000
Prosecuting Agency: Marion County Sheriff
Prosecuting Officer: Samantha Jackson - 0147
Offense: Sex / Assault with intent to commit criminal sexual conduct - First degree
Offense Code: 0253
Code/Ordinance Sec: 16-03-0656, 0652

This warrant is CERTIFIED FOR SERVICE in the
[ ] County [ ] Municipality of ___
The accused is to be arrested and brought before me to be dealt with according to the law.

_____(L.S.)
Signature of Judge

Date: ___

RETURN
A copy of this arrest warrant was delivered to defendant Bennie Tyrone Davis on 1/22/2015

_____
Signature of Constable/Law Enforcement Officer

RETURN WARRANT TO:
General Sessions
103 N. Main Street
PO Box 295
Marion, SC 29571

ORIGINAL ORIGINAL

STATE OF SOUTH CAROLINA
[X] County [ ] Municipality of
Marion

AFFIDAVIT ORIGINAL

Personally appeared before me the affiant Samantha Jackson who being duly sworn deposes and says that defendant Bennie Tyrone Davis did within this county and state on or about 9/30/2014 violate the criminal laws of the State of South Carolina (or ordinance of [X] County [ ] Municipality of Marion) in the following particulars:

DESCRIPTION OF OFFENSE: Sex / Assault with intent to commit criminal sexual conduct - First degree

I further state that there is probable cause to believe that the defendant named above did commit the crime set forth and that probable cause is based on the following facts:

On September 30, 2014 at approximately 2200 (10pm) at the Outback on Lipscomb Road, Mullins, SC in the County of Marion, one Bennie Davis did touch the victim on her chest and attempted to take her clothes off. Therefore one Bennie Davis is charged with assault with intent to Commit Criminal Sexual Conduct, this being a violation of SC Code of Laws 16-03-0656

_____
Signature of Affiant

STATE OF SOUTH CAROLINA
[X] County [ ] Municipality of
Marion

Affiant's Address: 2715 E Highway 76 Suite C
Mullins, SC 29574-
Affiant's Telephone: (843)423-8216

ARREST WARRANT

TO ANY LAW ENFORCEMENT OFFICER OF THIS STATE OR MUNICIPALITY OR ANY CONSTABLE OF THIS COUNTY:

It appearing from the above affidavit that there are reasonable grounds to believe on or about 9/30/2014 defendant Bennie Tyrone Davis did violate the criminal laws of the State of South Carolina (or ordinance of [X] County [ ] Municipality of Marion) as set forth below.

DESCRIPTION OF OFFENSE: Sex / Assault with intent to commit criminal sexual conduct - First degree

Having found probable cause and the above affiant having sworn before me, you are empowered and directed to arrest the said defendant and bring him or her before me forthwith to be dealt with according to law. A copy of this Arrest Warrant shall be delivered to the defendant at the time of its execution, or as soon thereafter as is practicable.

Sworn to and subscribed before me on 10/28/2014

_____(L.S.)
Signature of Issuing Judge
Mackie Darrill Hayes
Judge Code: 7016

Judge's Address: 2715 East Highway 76, Suite B
Mullins, SC 29574-
Judge's Telephone: ___

Issuing Court: [X] Magistrate [ ] Municipal [ ] Circuit

ORIGINAL ORIGINAL ORIGINAL ORIGINAL ORIGINAL

TELL ALL I AM NOT THAT WAY ANYMORE

ARREST WARRANT

2013A3310100331

STATE OF SOUTH CAROLINA
[X] County/ [ ] Municipality of
Marion

THE STATE
against
Bennie Davis

2013-0500542

Address: [redacted]
Marion, SC 29571

Phone: (000)000-0000   SSN: [redacted]
Sex: M   Race: B   Height: Weight:
State: SC   DL#: 99999999999
Agency ORI#: SC0340000
Prosecuting Agency: Marion County Sheriff
Prosecuting Officer: Samantha Jackson - 0147
Offense: Assault / Assault & Battery 2nd degree

Offense Code: 3413
Code/Ordinance Sec: 16-03-0600(D)(1)

This warrant is CERTIFIED FOR SERVICE in the
[ ] County/ [ ] Municipality of _____. The accused is to be arrested and brought before me to be dealt with according to law.

(L.S.)
_____
Signature of Judge

Date: _____

RETURN

A copy of this arrest warrant was delivered to defendant **Bennie Davis** on **6/25/13**

_____
Signature of Constable/Law Enforcement Officer

RETURN WARRANT TO: LOGGED 6/6 20 13
General Sessions   BOOK 19   PAGE 2712
103 N. Main Street   SHERIFF OFFICE
PO Box 295   MARION COUNTY, SC
Marion, SC 29571   SW RICHARDS

ORIGINAL   ORIGINAL

STATE OF SOUTH CAROLINA
[X] County/ [ ] Municipality of
Marion

AFFIDAVIT   ORIGINAL

Personally appeared before me the affiant **Samantha Jackson** who being duly sworn deposes and says that defendant **Bennie Davis** did within this county and state on or about **5/28/2013** violate the criminal laws of the State of South Carolina (or ordinance of [X] County/ [ ] Municipality of **Marion**) in the following particulars:

DESCRIPTION OF OFFENSE: Assault / Assault & Battery 2nd degree

I further state that there is probable cause to believe that the defendant named above did commit the crime set forth and that probable cause is based on the following facts:

On May 28, 2013 at 216 Wellington Ct. in the County of Marion, one Bennie Davis did unlawfully injure the victim using a towel and a belt with the apparent present ability to cause moderate bodily injury. Therefore one Bennie Davis is charged with Assault & Battery 2nd Degree, this being a violation of SC Code of Laws 16-03-0600(D)(1)

_____
Signature of Affiant

STATE OF SOUTH CAROLINA
[X] County/ [ ] Municipality of
Marion

Affiant's Address: 2715 E Highway 76 Suite C
Mullins, SC 29574-
Affiant's Telephone: (843)423-8216

ARREST WARRANT

TO ANY LAW ENFORCEMENT OFFICER OF THIS STATE OR MUNICIPALITY OR ANY CONSTABLE OF THIS COUNTY:

It appearing from the above affidavit that there are reasonable grounds to believe that on or about **5/28/2013** defendant **Bennie Davis** did violate the criminal laws of the State of South Carolina (or ordinance of [X] County/ [ ] Municipality of **Marion**) as set forth below:

DESCRIPTION OF OFFENSE: Assault / Assault & Battery 2nd degree

Having found probable cause and the above affiant having sworn before me, you are empowered and directed to arrest the said defendant and bring him or her before me forthwith to be dealt with according to law. A copy of this Arrest Warrant shall be delivered to the defendant at the time of its execution, or as soon thereafter as is practicable.

Sworn to and Subscribed before me
on _____

(L.S.)
_____
Signature of Issuing Judge
Mackie Darrill Hayes

Judge's Address: 2715 East Highway 76, Suite B
Mullins, SC 29574-
Judge's Telephone:
Issuing Court: [X] Magistrate [ ] Municipal [ ] Circuit

Judge Code: 7016

ORIGINAL   ORIGINAL   ORIGINAL   ORIGINAL

8. ON THE ROAD TO RECOVERY

I would not allow what happened to me by that pastor to make me hold my head down. I kept my head up because I knew who I was in the LORD, and I knew that God sent me to tell the "Good News." I was overly excited that Brother Jack Woodberry had contacted me. He told me, "I would love to have you on my show." The following Monday, I began working with him. This was my first time on a radio show. I was also asked to be his radio partner. Brother Jack introduced me to the radio audience with, "God has been good to this young man, and today, whoever hears this testimony will be encouraged. Following the commercial, Brother Bennie will be sharing a part of his testimony."

I was given approximately 5 minutes on the broadcast. That would be just enough time for the listeners to want to hear more. After my testimony, the phones started ringing off the hook. People were calling the radio station asking who is that young man with a testimony like that. They requested to hear more. Brother Jack informed them that I would be completing the testimony later tonight. There was a local GE (General Electric) plant located not many miles away (Florence, SC). There was a group of young ladies who worked there on the Midnight shift that always listened to the show. There was a spokesperson from General Electric by the name of Jeanette Waiters who called the station.

She requested to speak to this brother, Bennie, whose testimony is going to bring people to Christ. "You will be unable to talk to him tonight, but he will be here on my show every morning. Please call back tomorrow, and I will let you speak with him. Tonight, he has a little more of his testimony to tell the audience." That broadcast ended, and on our way home, Brother Jack said, "Tonight, more calls came in than any time that I have been doing this gospel radio show."

He said, "People just could not believe one person went through all that you did and remained in your right mind." I was so pleased to hear how people's lives were being changed. This was a fantastic opportunity for me to be on the radio and to learn how to work inside a radio station. I learned how to use the mixer board and to always have music playing in the background to avoid a space that would prevent interference noise. On this show, I was able to touch the lives of people that I would never see or meet. The audience heard of miracle after miracle that God performed in my life. It was worth it all. The responses were overwhelming.

I was so excited about what Jack Woodberry said about what happened after I told my testimony on the show. I wanted time to pass quickly so that I could get back to the radio station. When I drove home, I went straight into the house to tell my family about the wonderful experience I had at the radio station. There were so many people's lives touched through my testimony and the way I learned how to work the board to do the show. I didn't go to sleep that night because I was too excited, and I was thanking God for the opportunity that was given to me.

I left the house at about 10:00 AM the next morning in search of a building. I drove down a little street named Fairlee Street in Marion, SC, and there was a building for rent. I copied the phone number from the for-rent sign displayed on the door. I called the number and inquired about renting the building. The appointment was set for me to view the building at 1:00 pm. I met the landlord at the building that afternoon; immediately, as I walked into the building, I loved it. Right at that moment, I knew God was working in my favor. I was pleased with the quoted rent amount. I was accepting a price that I could afford.

She said, "Mr. Davis, you have 24 hours to pay me the deposit and rent. If you are unable to pay, I will let I will let someone else see this place." I went home and shared the information with my family. I had the money for the deposit but not for the first month's rent. What happened next was confirmation that God was working in my favor.

One hour later, I was riding through the Honey Hole neighborhood and saw Mr. Edgar Moore and Ms. Carrie Lamar. I stopped and began telling them about the building that I had found. That was when Mr. Edgar Moore said, "Ms. Carrie and I have been collecting money for your ministry and contributing to it because of what you are doing in Marion. You are helping especially those who live in drug-infested communities. We want to give you this money for your program." Here is the miracle: that contribution was enough money to pay the first month's rent.

What an Awesome God I have on my side! It was not 24 hours, but just in a few hours, that God blessed me with all the money I needed. I called the property owner, took her the money, and she gave me the key. As I walked off her front porch, I was giving God all the praise. I picked up my family, and I took them to see the building. They were all very excited about it. I called the electric company and water company to have the lights and water turned on. I made it home early enough to doze before going to the radio station. I had been up and moving fast for more than 16 hours.

That morning, Mr. Jack picked me up at about 2:15 a.m. As we were riding, I shared with him what had happened to me yesterday. He suggested that I would talk about that on the show. He hoped that Bennie Davis would be on the show to tell one more part of his testimony. I presented my testimony about the building and how God had blessed me with the start-up money for the center. (A name for the center had not yet been decided).

Hours into the program, I heard a song with the lyrics, "I am not that way anymore." There was the 'aha moment' that would be the name of the youth and adult center. The lights on the phone started lighting up with people calling from all over. One man called to say that he had to drive his car to the side of the road where he could hear my testimony. He had to tell how that testimony gave him faith to believe that God could save his son, who was using drugs. Just before the end of the show, sister Jeanette called to discuss my new building situation. I had no problem disclosing that it was an empty building. At that point, she promised to get something together and bring it to the center. I was grateful and gave her the directions.

I ended the show by describing the center as A program that will have opportunities for young men and women to find jobs and support anyone who had been in trouble with the law, anyone on drugs or selling drugs. A program that would teach self-sufficiency. I further explained that I would personally go to court with those young people and talk on their behalf.

The following day, I went to the unemployment office to inform them that I had a program to aid youth/adults who had been/are in trouble with the law and those with significant barriers. The program had professional development, employment opportunities, employment training and support services. I gave the invitation to the Unemployment Office to use the youth center by referring their clients to the center. I explained that it was a new program, and I did not have a phone yet. While standing there, the staff called the phone company and started phone services for the program. He added it to his account, causing me to never have to pay for that phone bill. A partnership was just born, and God kept blessing me with miracles.

I left there and went to the center to wait for sister Jeanette. It wasn't long before she arrived with a truck full of different goods, and greatest of all, she had chairs. The tears were beginning to fill my eyes because the only thing I knew was she only heard me on the radio broadcast. This was the first time I had ever seen her, and there was no knowledge of us ever meeting before. She walked in, and Mr. Jack followed and introduced her to Mother and me. Mother started crying as Sis. Jeanette began telling what she had brought. When we unloaded everything, the center looked wonderful. Words were not able to express the joy and happiness that was going through my body.

One day, I saw my Uncle Sam, and I told him that I needed some chairs to start having church. He was leaving for New Jersey for a few days. When he returned to South Carolina, he called and instructed me to meet him at the center. I arrived as he was parking his truck with 50 chairs. With all the chairs combined, it was enough to start having church services within a few weeks.

I was able to pay the rent by having various preachers come and conduct revivals during the month. The first person who preached a revival was Prophetess Mary Williams from Hemingway, South Carolina. People came from all around to the revival. The Center was filled to its capacity each night. Enough money was raised to pay rent for two months in advance.

One day, my mother and I were cleaning the center, and an unfamiliar lady stopped to donate the money for the light bill. God kept blessing and surprising me with his awesomeness. I immediately deposited the money into the center's bank account. All these happenings made me more and more excited about having "been called" to bring the good news (the gospel) and the new ministry into Marion.

Days later, I was relaxing, just driving my car, when I saw a few of my friends standing around on a porch. I parked to tell them that "God had called me into the ministry." I saw my friend, Dr. Henry McGill, Jr., and proudly said to him, "Now I can come to your church and preach" (Mount Pisgah Missionary Baptist Church)." His response crushed my heart. I felt so much pain and disappointment in his words. It was the same hurt I felt months earlier when overhearing the probation officers conversing that "I, Caveman, was just pretending to be saved, and as soon as probation ended, I would be back on the streets where the prison cell would be waiting for me."

Dr. Henry McGill Jr. said, "You are too ignorant to preach at Mount Pisgah Missionary Baptist Church, and for that reason, I will not allow you to preach there." Everyone that was on the porch started laughing at me. What he said may have been the worst, despicable, abhorrent words ever spoken to me in my face. It was years later I learned that those words were among the greatest words that were ever spoken to me. That incident taught me that just because there is a calling in your life does not mean you are prepared. You must study the word of God, and you must have sound doctrine (truth). He continued and made it clear to me that the Bible is the first resource, and anyone (preachers especially) who fails to know the Bible and be able to explain it accordingly is not helping people to find the Lord nor directing them to Jesus and salvation. He did not tell me what I wanted to hear, but he told me what I needed to hear.

It was years later, after I had attended Bible college, received my degree in theology and obtained church knowledge that I was several times invited to preach at Mount Pisgah Missionary Baptist Church by Dr. Henry McGill Jr. As time passed, I began having service on Sunday afternoon, where people started coming, and the congregation started growing. I continued to preach while people told me I did not need to worry about getting a license to preach because God had called me. I listened to them because they had been in church for years.

The Sunday afternoon services made room to have revival once a month. I would invite different preachers of different denominations, males and females. I was often invited to preach at different churches, too. Eventually, church services began to be on Sunday morning. That first Sunday morning, I parked at the front of the church and was about to unlock the church door when I saw Debra Fling. I invited her to come to the morning service, and I let her know how God blessed me with this building and that I have been having service for several months now. I told her that today I am having my first Sunday morning service and that I would like for her to come because God is blessing here at I Am Not That Way Anymore Youth & Adult Center.

Her response was, "I will come and visit one Sunday, but I cannot come today."

I said, "I will be looking forward to seeing you in the service one Sunday."

The following Sunday, during service, guess who walked in the door! It was Debra Fling. When I saw her, my heart began to overflow because this was the same Debra that was looking in the window at the house when I came into the world (a midwife delivered me). This is the same Debra that was in the emergency room when I had gotten shot, and the doctors said, "By morning, I should be dead," this is the same Debra that was at Mount Pisgah

Missionary Baptist Church singing when I gave my life to God. Now, this same Debra was entering into the House of the Lord to hear a word from heaven preached by me. My mother asked her to sing a song. When she sang solo, you could feel the presence of God throughout the entire building.

The whole atmosphere changed. When I stood to bring the word of God, I said to her, "You are going to be my one-voice choir." From that Sunday until she passed away, she was a partner at the church, and I was her Pastor. At the church, Debra was chairperson of the Deacon ministry, Sunday school teacher, and the one-voice choir. She was also attending Cathedral Bible College during this time. Sister Willena Frink was president of the Pastor's Aide. Sister Billie Lou Clark was with me from the beginning of the ministry until she passed away in 2019; she was the church secretary and the Clerk. Debra invited her cousin Penny Nesmith to come to the church service with her, who became a member and the first Deacon with Marylin White. Penny Nesmith was the first member to get a Ministry License and currently is the lead Pastor of Glory Belongs to God Ministry.

I noticed when people get in trouble, one of the first things that the judge asks a person is, have you finished school? That made me decide to visit the Adult Education office to inquire how I could help people receive their GED. I was talking to a young man who worked there and about the center, and he asked me if I would like to be a mentor for the state of South Carolina through the solicitor's office. I let him know that I would love to be a mentor. I took part in a three-day orientation. I had to fill out an application for SCLED (South Carolina Law Enforcement Division). That authorized me to get background checks on each person in my mentor class. Despite my criminal record, I was able to become a mentor for the state of South Carolina through the Solicitor's Office. I was one of the first in Marion County to become a mentor.

This really boosted my confidence. I decided that I must do more to help more people to have a better life. For some time, the church did not have a PA system. I went to a bond court with two young men that the judge had set their bond at $90,000.00, totaling $180,000.00.

I called Gene Fling to stand the bond to get the young men released. Gene was not able to because his bail bondsman license had expired. I went to the judge's office to talk with him, and shortly, the Chief of Police walked into the room. This is the same Chief that would have put Caveman away for life, but God did not let it happen. The Chief recommended that the judge work with me. God is still working things out for me. The judge let me know that he was going to allow me to stand for the bond, and by their court date, I would have had the opportunity to work with them.

The money that I was paid was enough money to buy a new PA system for the Center. I did not have to borrow the money, but God blessed me with more than enough. I was not a bondsman, but I was more than a conqueror. I did not qualify to stand for the bond for the young men, but God qualified me, and God showed me a favor. By the time General Session Court arrived, I had those young men in church every Sunday, and each of them had a job. I had them doing things that would help them get their time reduced or even dismissed.

On court day, I was able to stand with them and address the court. I told the judge of the achievements and goals they completed during the time I have been working with them in the center. These young men were facing 20 to 30 years of incarceration. Due to the center, the requirements, and the accomplishments, one young man was sentenced to only seven years, and the other young man was sentenced to five years.

When the court dismissed that day, men and women began to contact me to arrange to go to court with them. I scheduled different times for each of them to meet me at the center. They came, and I would inform them of the mandated requirements for my services.

They were as follows:
- Must attend church every Sunday,
- Must obtain a high school diploma (if they did not have one)
- Must begin taking courses toward a diploma. I would help

them to attain one.
- Must master job interview techniques
- Must find and secure a job
- Must complete the proper amount of volunteer hours (minimally two days a week).
- Must volunteer once weekly (if employed)

Monthly, there would be a special program for neighborhood young people to come to be empowered and encouraged. The volunteers would explain to young adults and teenagers what their charges were and what they had done to be awaiting sentencing by the court. The goal was to persuade adults and teenagers to make the same mistake to not find themselves in the same predicament.

One day, I received a phone call from a David, that was in trouble, and he had been summoned to General Session court. He asked me if I would go to court with him to speak on his behalf. I agreed and set up a meeting to meet with him at the center. During the meeting, I found out that he did have his High School diploma, and he was not working. I let him know by the court date, he needed to be employed.

My role was to show how his life could become better by working with me. I explained the requirements, rules and expectations. He heard about the "I Am Not That Way Any More Center," and that is the reason he started the program, particularly so that I would go to general session court with him.

One Sunday, it was raining very hard, and he rode a bicycle in the rain not to miss service. He knew that if he did not come to this service, I would not be going to court with him. In order to receive service from the center, there was zero tolerance when it came to missing service or not doing what Mr. Bennie asked to be done. On this Sunday, while he was in service, one of his friends was busted for drugs.

It was the night before General Session court would begin. David came to my house to remind me of the time I needed to be in court.

The next day, I arrived in the courtroom early to walk before the judge with him. He was called, and we walked to the bench together. The solicitor read the charges but accentuated that this was his third offense with drugs. His jail time could be up to 20 years. The judge looked down at both of us and asked who I was.

"I have Pastor Davis with me."

The judge replied, "This is a shame that you have this pastor in this courtroom when he could be doing something else to help someone who needs help."

He continued, "There are so many other people that need help in Marion County for him to be in this courtroom with you who just want to sell drugs."

The judge stared at him and said, "You know that this is your third strike, and the solicitor requests your sentence to be the maximum time."

The judge continued, "I do not have to listen to what the solicitor recommended. I want to hear what the Pastor has to say, and then I am going to give my sentence. The judge continued talking and made sure it was clear how he felt about a person selling drugs and how much time David would be facing in prison for selling drugs. The judge went on to say he hated drugs and drug dealers and routinely sentenced them to the maximum time allowed by law. Finally, the Judge looked at me and said, "Pastor, now I would like to hear from you."

I began to talk, and I said, "Your Honor, I was a former drug dealer, and one day, I stood in this same courtroom. A judge told me those same words, but from that time to now, I have rehabilitated myself. I have started a center named 'I Am Not That Way Anymore Youth & Adult Center.' I handed the judge a letter explaining the program in more detail and that the Mayor, Chief of Police, Sheriff, and Magistrate Judge supported the program. I proceeded to tell the judge, "David has been working faithfully with me. He has been coming to service, volunteering time in the Youth Center, and he has a job."

I went on to tell the judge, "Yes, he sold drugs, but now he is working with someone who is showing him by example how to change. We both know that a drug dealer has no good ending. Drugs only bring one of two things... It brings death, or it brings prison."

The judge was ready to give his sentence. "Young man, I was going to give you seventeen years, but because you brought the Pastor with you and after the Pastor spoke on your behalf, I decreased it to 12 years. When he began to let the court know how he overcame selling drugs, I decreased it to six years. Then he gave me this letter, and I saw that the Mayor, Chief of Police, Sheriff, the Magistrate Judge supported this program. Your sentence is three years with a cap on it, and you will not do any more than three years. If they decide to allow you to get out before the three years on good behavior, that will lessen your stay even more."

He was locked up for one year and a half, then was released from prison. He never got into any more trouble with the law, and he raised his children. Today, he is a respectable young man because he is self-sufficient. He left Marion and never looked back. Every now and then, he will come back home to visit his family.

Thanksgiving was close, and I decided to feed anyone who wanted a Thanksgiving dinner. I invited our local TV News Stations, Channel 13 (WBTW), Channel 15 (WPDE) and our local newspaper, The Marion Star. My mother cooked and prepared all the food. Sister Jeanette, along with other people, donated money, and some came to help serve the food. The Police Department, Fire Department and our local hospital were invited to get a dinner because they had to work on Thanksgiving Day. If anyone was not able to come to the center to get their dinner, I had the dinner delivered to their jobs. God blessed us with more than enough food. There were plenty of leftovers. This was not just for the homeless, but this was for anyone. People came from far and near. Everyone was able to have a wonderful Thanksgiving dinner, and during the time of giving out dinners, we also gave out flyers to let the people know that there would be another dinner served on Christmas.

The news people were there, and the newspaper people were there to interview people who got their food, and they also interviewed me. For Christmas, the center had a Christmas dinner, and we were able to go to ten different homes and give out gift cards. I had a group volunteer to come along with Sister Jeanette and me. This family stayed in the housing complex on Strawberry St. in Marion, South Carolina. This mother did not apply to get help from the Center, but someone turned this family's name into the center. I was so excited about knocking on the door because this family had no idea what was on the other side of the door. Someone asked who is it from behind the door, and I replied, "Pastor Bennie Davis." The door slowly opened. When she looked, her eyes got big, and then her mouth opened wide as she wondered what was happening. I explained that someone had given us her name for her family to have a great Christmas. She allowed us into her home, and she called her children into the room. They got so excited and wondered if these things were theirs as tears were streaming out of their mother's eyes. I will not forget the tears of joy we all shared. The children started opening their gifts. They had gotten some new clothes for school. When they saw those coats that they tried on, the family started crying again because they appreciated it and were filled with joy.

Their mother said, "Today, our family was not getting up early because there would be nothing for my children to see." The joy that this family and the other families experienced was PRICELESS. The family thought that they were forgotten, but God had them on His mind. The spirit of God gave me the vision to give, and God surrounded me with people who gave donations that allowed ten families to have a good Christmas because of it.

Also, we were able to have a Christmas dinner and fed every person that came to get dinner. The food we had leftover was donated to the homeless shelter. Words were unable to express the joy and happiness that I had for the people who helped to make these families feel so much better and so happy. I continue every year to supply the Thanksgiving and Christmas Dinners. I also still bless families with Christmas gifts with the help of Mr. James Wood, Mr. Emerson, and Mr. Kevin Rowell, aka "Crook," as sponsors.

Three weeks before Christmas, I went to Marion Recreation Center and put in an application to become a volunteer coach for the Recreation Center. Because of my criminal record, I was blackballed from being a coach. The position was given to someone else. But God! The week after Christmas, I received a phone call from Mr. Billy Thomas, athletic director for the Marion Recreation Department.

He said, "Mr. Bennie, a coach quit, and we are in desperate need of a coach. Would you like to coach this team?" I said to him that I would love to be this team's coach, and as of this day, I have coached for over 20 years. For three years, I had the best record, and I was named the All-Star team head coach. Every team I coached was named 'New Breed.' I instilled in them that they are champions, and I reminded them of that every day. They had to say before and after basketball practice as a team, "We are champions, we are winners, and we are fighters!"

Years have passed, but when I see a New Breed former player, I ask, "What are you?"

They would answer, "I am a champion, a winner and a fighter!"

At the end of each year of our season, I would have a program at the church, and each player would get a plaque to let them know that they are valuable to the team. I let the young men and women know if it were not for them, it would not be a team because we are champions. One year, we did not win a game, but we battled hard, and the parents supported the team because they saw the improvement in their children.

One day, I was out, and I met this preacher. She said, "I heard the good news that you were called into the ministry, and now you have a new ministry in Marion."

I replied, "Yes, God has called me into the ministry, and yes, I am a pastor."

Then she asked, "Would I be in service tomorrow night? If not, she would like for me to come to a Bible study that she teaches."

She suggested I come to see how I like it. I said, "I would be honored to attend your Bible class because I want to learn more about the Bible."

She told me, "A call to the ministry is a call to preparation."

That night, I went to Bible study at Gilbert Woodbury's Barber Shop. When I was in the hospital, Mr. Gilbert Woodbury would come to the hospital every week to cut my hair at no charge. I answered some biblical questions, and I believed with all my heart that I was doing pretty well. After Bible study was over, I was leaving when Deacon Windom called me. He asked me to read what you said from the Bible. I was not able to find the scripture because I was going on what I had heard and not what the Bible said. He recommended that before you say anything out of the Bible, read it for yourself because tonight, you were in error for what someone else said and not what you read in the Bible.

He opened his Bible, found the scripture, and read what was written. He went on to say, "For you to be a Pastor, you must know the word of God for yourself." From that day to this day, if I do not read the Bible, I do not preach it, I don't say it, and I don't teach it. I thanked Deacon Wisdom for that valuable lesson. I did continue to attend Bible study, and I even answered some questions correctly. I enjoyed myself and continued to go to class.

I finished the semester by completing all the assignments and all the tests. The Instructor of Bible Study informed me that because I graduated from Voorhees College with a Bachelor of Science degree and am now attending Cathedral Bible College, I will be able to combine my credits and I will earn my master's degree in Christian Education. That was the beginning of my going to Bible college.

9. WHAT HAPPENED

My confidence was up because now that I am in Bible College, I am looking to one day obtain a master's degree in Christian education. I applied to become the Chaplain at the Marion County Detention Center. One day, I received a call from the Detention Center to inform me that I would be the first and only Chaplain for the Marion County Detention Center. I was advised that every Saturday at 6:00 pm, I could minister to the women inmates. At 7:00 pm, I would minister to the male inmates. I was so excited about this opportunity to be the new Chaplain for our new Marion County Detention Center. I looked forward to attending the Marion County Detention Center on Saturday evenings.

My first time doing the service, I let the female and male inmates know that they were much greater than the crime they had committed. I let them know that Jesus gave up the ghost for them, Jesus shared His blood for all of them, but it is up to them to want more out of their life. I went on to tell them that their life is greater than being in this jail cell or in prison, but they are the only ones who can turn it around. I also told the young women and young men that they must want it more than anything else. I would always end each service by saying success or failure is like a football field. If you stand on the 50-yard line or if you run the touchdown on the left, you must run 50 yards. If you run to the touchdown on the right, you must run 50 yards. No matter what decision you make to run, to have success on the line, it's going to take 50 yards to fail in life, or it's going to take 50 yards to make the effort for whatever decision you run in. You must make a choice now for your life.

The other ministers and bondsmen got upset because the Detention

Center let them know that Pastor Bennie was over the female and male inmates. Then they started complaining, saying I was ministering to the women and men; then, on Monday, I got them out of jail. One day, after I just ministered to the young men, I was walking to the door to go home. The man who was second in charge of the Detention Center said, "Pastor Davis." Then I turned around and said, "Yes, sir." He said, "Come with me. I need to talk with you."

I followed him into his office, and I sat down. Then he said, "Pastor Davis, you have a choice; you are either going to stop helping these young ladies and men get out of jail, or if you don't stop, I am going to have to relieve you from your chaplain duties. But if you stop, then you can stay the chaplain here at the Detention Center. Pastor Davis, if you continue helping people get their life together and get them out of jail, you cannot be the chaplain anymore."

I responded to him, "Sir, you have already made the decision, but I am going to continue to help young women and young men get out of jail. So, I guess this will be my last night at the Detention Center." I did all I could to hold back the tears because I did not want this man to see me crying. What hurt me was I always looked forward to coming to encourage these young men and women. The tears started coming out of my eyes and rolling down my face, but then I remembered Jeremiah was a weeping Prophet; when a man cries, he has someone to cry to, and his name is Jesus. I stood up, shook the gentleman's hand, and said thank you for the opportunity to be the chaplain at this Detention Center.

When I walked out of the door, I did not allow what happened to me to make me put my head down, but I looked up and believed that better days were coming. I was at the center one day, had just gotten out of a meeting, and was waiting for someone to come by about a job. I heard a knock on the door. I went to the door and opened it, and there stood a young man with his mother. We walked into the center, and I introduced myself to the young man and his mother. They introduced themselves to me; before I could say anything else, the young man said, "Can I do my community service hours at the Youth Center?"

Then he explained to me this is a program through the solicitor's office. The name of it is Pre-trial Intervention, better known as PTI. When a person completes this program, their crime will never go on their criminal record. Then the young man said, for me to be able to do my community hours, you must call the solicitor's office and get an appointment, and then we can go together. I called the next day, and the young man and I went to the solicitor's office.

The meeting was at 10:00 am with a young lady, but before we went into the meeting, I said to the young man, "Look a person in their eyes when you are talking to them or when you are saying something to them."

When we walked into the office, we both introduced ourselves to the lady. She introduced herself to us. The lady asked me why I would want the center to be a place where people could come and do PTI?"

I told the young lady I had a nonprofit organization called "I Am Not That Way Anymore Youth/Adult Center." I began to share with her what happened to me in my life and why I desire to help other young people. By the time I finished talking, her mind was made up, and she said this is the perfect place. God blessed me with this program.

When man put me out of the Detention Center, God opened a bigger door for me. Then, the lady asked me who I preferred to work with, and I told her male or female. I told her that the males would work in people's yards, cutting grass, etc. The females read books on tape, typed, and set up appointments. Then, if some of the ladies would like to work in the yards with the men, I would allow that also. I asked the lady if it would be alright if I put an ad in the local newspaper so that any senior citizens who would like to get their yard done for free could contact Pastor Bennie Davis.

She said to me that would be great. When I made it back to Marion, the lady from the solicitor's office called me to let me know that I had several more people coming to the center to do community service hours. If anyone who was on pre-trial intervention and was unemployed came to me, I would help them find a job by the time they finished their community service. If anyone came to me who did not have a high school diploma, I would help them get back into school so they could graduate. If anyone came to me who desired to get into college, the only college I knew I could help them get into was Voorhees College.

There was a young man who came to me from Lexington, SC, on weekends to do his community service hours. This man did not want his family and friends to know he was in trouble with the law. I worked with black people, white people, rich people, and poor people. I remember one time a young man and a young lady came to the center to start their community service, and both were white.

They shared with me how their people felt about Blacks, and they said to me if our family saw you with us, they would get terribly upset. I told the young man that he had to cut grass. He said to me that he had his own lawn mower. I responded by saying that is great now; let me take you and show you the yards that need to be cut for the next 4 weeks. The young man said, I cannot ride in your car, but I will follow behind you. Then you could show me the yards I need to cut, and then I will return on the weekends and do my job.

The young lady had people who owned many businesses in Marion. She said, "If you come to any of my family's business and see me, please act like you don't know me because if you come up to me and say something, my family is going to know that I have done something to get in trouble."

So, I said to her you are going to read books and record them on tape and do some typing for me. The young lady read the books, called me, and informed me that she would have the work in the mailbox. This is how the young man and young lady did their community service hours. Each of them came and thanked us for working with us and not judging us because of how our family feels about black people.

Everything was going great. I was a pastor of a new ministry and director of a youth center in Bible college to attain my master's degree in Christian education. Now, I have a site for pretrial intervention. I knew that there was greater for me. One day, I was in Bible College, and my instructor was teaching. I was looking at her with amazement.

My instructor was explaining the Word of God. This was when I realized that there was a lot of stuff that I did not know about the Bible. My eyes and my mind were open then, out of nowhere, I started saying to myself I would love for this beautiful young lady to be part of my life. I was thinking about the different things I could accomplish with her. She is a very classy lady, and most of all, she respects herself, and she demands respect from other preachers, pastors, and people.

Many people with ministries do not believe in female preachers, but she still went forth with the Word of God. She is a strong, beautiful young black lady who intrigues me in many ways. The only thing I could think of was that if I could have someone like her in my life, I would be even stronger. After class, I approached her to tell her how much I enjoyed her class.

I said, if I had it my way, you would not just be my lady, but you would be my wife. She did not say no; she laughed and said, "Really." Then, my heart felt like it had stopped beating. This is when I made it up and asked her to go out to dinner with me. She did not say no, and she made me believe that it was some hope that she would go to dinner with me. After class, I told her, "I am going to walk you to your car because it is dark outside and raining." The wind was also blowing badly. When we had made it outside, we saw a puddle of water by the door of her car.

As we stood under the shed, I looked into her eyes and was automatically hypnotized. Still, just wanting to make her happy, I told her, "Give me your car keys so that I can go get your car and drive your car to you because I don't want you walking in that rain or stepping in that puddle of water." Then I said to her, "I do not want my lady's feet to get wet, so I would rather for me to walk in the rain." I walked to her car and drove the car to her. I made sure she got in the car, closed the car door, and said to her, "As soon as you walk into your house, call me so I will know that you made it home safe." She let her car window down a little and said, "I will call you to let you know that I made it home."

I said, 'This young lady will be the perfect lady to be my wife.' She called me to let me know that she made it home safely. While I was on the phone talking to her, I found out that she loved going fishing. I said to her, "Let's go fishing, and when can we go?" She said that she would call and let me know.
I started saying, 'Yes, yes, yes,' in my mind then I said okay to her. I said, "Have a good night's rest, and I look forward to hearing from you soon." Then that beautiful voice came through the phone. She

said, "Now, when I go fishing, it will be early in the morning, and I like to stay all day, if not half of the day."

I responded, "I will be waiting to hear from you, but I know whatever day we go, I do not want that day to ever end." I said, "Your voice is so sweet. I might need to go to the doctor and get checked for diabetes."

It was on a Sunday night at about 7:30 pm; the phone started ringing, and I answered it. On the other end was that outstanding lady. I had been dreaming and hoping she would call me, and now my prayers were answered. She said, "Get up early in the morning; we are going fishing."

I said, "Great, I will wait for you to come."

As soon as I put the phone down, I went and asked my mother if I could use her fish stuff because I was going fishing. When she got to the house the next morning, I waited outside.

She did not have any bait, so I said, "I got you. I have bait for the both of us."

While fishing, I said, "If I catch more than you, can I take you out to dinner?"

She laughed at me and said, "Let's do it because I will have more than you."

I had a wonderful time, but the most important thing is that I never met anyone who wanted me to succeed in ministry and in life. This is a lady who had everything any person would want in their life. I would not let a day go by without calling her because she would always tell me something I needed to do to help me better myself in the ministry.

Valentine's Day was coming up, and I was thinking, what can I do for this lady that would be like no other Valentine's she ever had? I decided I knew what I would do to make her have the greatest Valentine's Day in her life. I was out looking for her on Valentine's Day, so I went by her house, but her car was not in her driveway. I started to ride down different streets, going to different stores where she loves shopping. I was riding down the road and looked across the road into a parking lot, and guess who I saw?

Yes! I saw my future. The greatest opportunity that I would ever have in my life. Then I made a U-turn, and by the time she made it to her car, I made it to her. I saw the most wonderful, beautiful lady that I have ever laid my crossed eyes on. I said to myself, 'I must have her, and when I went to her.' I jumped into the car, rubbing my eyes. She said, "What's wrong, Pastor Davis?"

I said, "Nothing. But three things happened to me today."

She said, "What are the three things that happened to you, Pastor Davis."

"First, I felt like Christopher Columbus when he discovered the USA, and I discovered you. Second, I have been rubbing my eyes because you have been all in my eyes all day, and I have been unable to see anything but you."

The third thing that happened was I got down on my knee in the parking lot; then I asked her if she would be my wife, and she said, "Yes."

At that time, she called me her 'Teddy Bear.' I looked at her, and I called her my Honey. I said, "From this day on, I must fight and protect you from all the bees trying to sting you for the rest of my life." That was the greatest yes I ever heard in my life because the only thing I knew was on Valentine's Day, I became a hunter.

He that has found a wife found a good thing, and I found the best thing that could ever happen to me. I couldn't believe that she said yes and meant it. When we got together that afternoon, she got all her Valentine's gifts from me. I gave her an engagement ring, and I put the ring on her finger, then I reminded her that there was no beginning and there was no ending. This is how my love is for you. My love did start for you, but it will never end. Then I shared with her that this engagement is between you and me because I do not want anyone to come between us.

I wanted this wedding to happen, and we both agreed it was something wonderful. I was going to class looking at my teacher, knowing she would soon be my wife. We never said anything to anyone, but people could see the ring on her finger but never asked her if she was engaged to be married. I invited her to come to church with me as my guest.

On Sunday, the door came open, and she walked into the church with that outstanding smile. The only thing I could say to myself was, 'I am about to have the finest wife, not just in the world but in the universe.' Not one partner in the church knew that one day she would be the First Lady but the only lady.

We were at the end of the church service when my wonderful fiancé came in, and I asked her to sing a song before I ended church services. Billy Lou Clark announced that Pastor Bennie Davis would be the guest speaker that day at Good Hope AME church in Centenary, South Carolina, at 4:00 PM. I asked the young lady if she would come to hear me preach, and for the first time, she accepted my invitation. That afternoon, we had a wonderful time in the spirit of the Lord. My fiancé did come, and she enjoyed herself. At the end of the service, I was walking out of the church door, and my fiancé came to me and she said that I did a wonderful job.

The subject of the sermon that I preached was 'Overcoming Public Opinion.' That Sunday night, I gave her a call, and she told me that she spoke with her pastor about doing our wedding. She let me know the date of our wedding and where it was going to be. I was so happy it was just a few weeks away on a Sunday at 6:00 PM.

We were just going to invite a few people close to our family, like my mother, sister, brother, and Sister Jeanette. I called Deacon Debra Fling as I wanted her to sing, but she did not answer her phone. That was the only reason why she was not there. My future wife had her grandbaby there as well. Dr. A.C. Robinson officiated the wedding, and she made him promise not to tell anyone, and he said he would not. Dr. A.C. Robinson told my wife after the wedding that he would be telling his friends whose wedding he officiated, and she said that would be great.

The wedding was so beautiful everyone was so happy for my wife and me. When the wedding was over, Dr. A.C Robinson called around and told a few of his friends who had just gotten married, and he let them know it was Pastor Bennie Davis and a member of his church. That was the hottest news in the City of Marion. People started calling from all over, texting me, and leaving messages on the answering machine until it was full. The next day, people came up to me and asked if it was true and if I really got married.

I told them, "Yes, I did, and I love being married."

Billie Lou Clark called me and said, "Pastor, is it true? Are you married? That is what the people are saying in Marion, but I said the last time I saw my pastor, he was not married."

I told her, "Yes, I got married yesterday afternoon when I left church."

Then she said, "Pastor Davis, if you are happy, that is all that matters because you could not have found a better wife."

I said, "Thank you so much."

I went to my mother's house, and when I walked into the house, she said, "Pastor, people keep calling and coming by here asking me did my son got married. I told them yes, he did, and I was there, and the wedding was great."

My mother asked me to take her to the store. We were in the store for about thirty minutes. After we left the checkout, I took the bags to the car. On that day, I had on a pair of white shorts, and I was looking as fine as I could look. I got in the car and took my mother home but when I got out of the car my white shorts were black! Someone had poured oil into my car seat. I did not know people were that upset with me!

There were some people who had stopped coming to the church, and some people stopped speaking to me. I did not realize that other ladies were looking at me. I told them all that I was the bear and my wife was my honey. I am not going anywhere but to protect her for the rest of my life.

When I got home, my wife and I were talking at the table. She asked me did I had my minister's license and was ordained. I said no because people said I did not need a license. Then she took her time and explained to me and showed me in the Bible why I had to be licensed and ordained. She told me, "Now, if the only place you want to preach is at your church, you can, but Pastor, if you have any desire to preach at any of these major churches in Marion, you need to be ordained and licensed." I told her I had a minister's license, but it was not from the church I was a member of.

The minister's license I had was one of my pastor's friends who got them for me, but I was not ordained. As we talked, she asked how can you teach the truth but you are not doing the truth. Pastor Davis, for you to do better, you just want to improve your preaching and teaching. After my wife and I finished talking, I had a desire to want to do better; that was when I realized I had to get some help. When I got up from the table, I went into our room and called Dr. AC Robinson, and I scheduled a meeting with him.

He told me that Wednesday at 4:00 pm would be the best day for him to meet with me. I was on time for the meeting. I explained to Dr. AC Robinson that I needed help with my sermon to preach better. I wanted to learn how to put a sermon together and conduct myself when I was on the pulpit. He told me we could meet every Wednesday at 4:00 pm. We can review the sermon you would like to preach on that Sunday.

He would give me pointers and tell me how to do it. One day, he was talking to me, and he said, "Pastor Davis, what I am doing for you today, you will be doing for someone tomorrow." Dr. AC Robinson encouraged me when I needed it the most. I thanked Dr. AC Robinson for what he did for me. I became successful from then on, and I am still learning how to better understand the Word of God.

My preaching and teaching did improve. I was determined to stay at Cathedral Bible College because I was gaining knowledge. People would say, "You do not have to stay in school. It is unnecessary; let the Lord teach you, and when you open your mouth, the Lord will speak for you." I said, "That sounds good, but I realize Jesus taught his disciples for three years, and now I am being taught the Word of

God, so when I open my mouth, I will have the right things to say for the Lord." That same year, I graduated with a master's degree in Christian education.

It was time for Pleasant Grove Missionary Baptist Church's annual revival. I went to the revival and had a great time each night. One night, the evangelist for the week was preaching the Word of God, and I started thinking about the different things Dr. AC Robinson was doing to help me better understand God's Word. He made time for me out of his busy schedule and never tried to influence me to join Pleasant Grove. As I was sitting there, the Spirit of the Lord came upon me. The Spirit of God told me, "This man has been a Pastor to you without you being a part of this church family. Now, how much more will he be able to do if you become a member."

About this time, I heard the Evangelist ask if there was anyone who would like to become a member of this church. I stood up right then and walked up to the altar alone. That night, I became a member of Pleasant Grove Missionary Baptist Church and remained a member of Pleasant Grove Missionary Baptist Church. I was the first and only person to join the church that night. I had a meeting with Dr. AC Robinson, then he explained that I am your Pastor, and you are an associate minister at the church.

He went on to say that now he can license and ordain me. He gave me a date for when all this would take place. I was licensed and ordained at Pleasant Grove Missionary Baptist Church. My wife was so proud of me. She said she saw the love that I had for God in me and the determination in me when I went to get help so I could do better. Dr. AC Robinson never told me not to come on Wednesdays. I stopped alone, but he said his door was still open for me. My wife and I were pastoring together, and the people started visiting the church. Some ladies walked out of the church and never returned to this day when they found out that my marriage was real and that she was part of the church.

Everything was working in my favor. I was married, had a site for pre-trial intervention, working with the youth and adults, helping them find jobs, helping people get off drugs, helping them get out of prison, and I'm going to the court with them. I saw myself making a difference in Marion County and people from far and near. Whoever would come and ask for my help, I would help them. I went to different schools working with students. The only thing required was for their parents or guardians to come and request help from the Center.

I would go to the school and sit in the classroom to see what help the student needed. Then, I would get the student into a tutoring class. Because of the young people doing community service through pre-trial intervention, I could have tutoring at the center. When I go to a classroom concerning a student, the first thing I do is ask the instructor of the class what the student must do to get an A out of this class. I do not believe a student is average or below average but an above-average student. My job is to get the students to believe they are above average.

I remember I was at the center one afternoon, and a mother came to the center about her son. She said someone told her about the work I was doing to help young people who were in school. I said to her, "How can I help your son."

She said, "Before I go any further, how much must I pay? I have a job, but I go to work before my son goes to school, and I am at work when he gets out of school."

I said to her, "There is no charge. I give back to the community by helping young people stay in school."

Then she said, "I did not graduate from school because I dropped out, my brothers dropped out, one of my sisters dropped out, but only one sister graduated from high school."

She said, "I do not want this to happen to my son because his cousins and friends dropped out of school about two weeks ago." Then I asked her to please give me her son's name, the school he attends, his grades, and what kind of help she needed. She told me that her son was cutting school, and he may have missed too many days to be promoted to the next grade.

Then I told her not to tell her son someone was coming to his class. I told her starting tomorrow, I would be in his class. If I do nothing else, my son will pass his grade and graduate from high school because he will not be a statistic of a high school dropout.

The next day, I went to the school's main office to let them know who I was there to see. When I was at the school talking to them, the young man's mother called to let the school know that I was coming to see her son to see if I could help him. She also told the school that I would be going to her son's classes to sit in the classroom with him. I went to each class he had that day. I was in the classroom waiting for him to make it to class.

I did this for a few days; he did not know that I was coming for him, so one day, he did not show up to school. So, I decided to introduce myself to the young man at his house, but I waited until his mother got off work then I went to the house. When I walked into the house, he realized I was at the school for him. The mother, her son, and myself sat in the living room.

I told his mother, "Your son did not attend school today. This must have been one of his cut days."

Then I asked him, "Why did you miss class?"

He said that he missed the bus. Then I let him and his mother know that he won't miss the bus anymore because starting tomorrow, I will be taking him to school, then he won't have the excuse that he missed the bus. I took him to school the next day for a whole week he was at school on time for his classes. As he went to class, I walked in with him.

One day, it was time for lunch, and I was entering the lunchroom with the young man. He stopped walking, and I stopped. He said, "Pastor Davis, will you please go home and don't come to my school anymore? If you do this for me, you won't have to ever come back to this school for me anymore."

I told him, "I am going to show you that I trust that you will do the right thing for yourself, and I will not pick you up tomorrow, and I won't come to school to sit in class with you anymore."

I told him, "You have no choice but to graduate because I know your father graduated, and you can do the same thing as your father. Just because people say your father had high blood pressure, that does not mean that you are going to have high blood pressure. Just because people say that your father had diabetes, you are going to have diabetes, so if you can have all the negative of your father, why can't you do the positive things your father did in his life? I cannot say that he did not cut class anymore, but I can say he did not quit school and was 21 years old when he walked across that stage to obtain his High School diploma. He invited me to come to his graduation, and I was there when his name was called."

I was going to different churches preaching the Word of God, and things were just going wonderful in my life. I chartered a bus, and my church family and friends had a shopping spree in New York for the 4th of July weekend. I had to do a revival at Friendly Church of the Apostolic Faith Incorporated in Jamaica, NY. People were delivered and set free on the last night of the revival. The church that I Pastored was the House of the Lord.

Billy Lou Clark said to me, "Pastor, when you get back to Marion, SC, you better preach just like you did tonight in this house." That Sunday morning, we went to have service at Pastor Donnie McClurkin's church and after the church service was over, I had the opportunity to meet him for the first time. I told him a portion of my testimony. That afternoon, I attended Pastor Donnie McClurkin's service that he held every fourth of July outside called 'Church Without Walls.' He had me come up and give my testimony. As I was giving my testimony, the people started praising God. There were so many people that were there from all over the United States.

That following year, the church, along with myself, went to New York for the Easter Sunday morning service with Pastor Donnie McClurkin, and there were over 10,000 people there. When we got to the church that morning, the church had reserved seating for my church family. Pastor Donnie McClurkin said, "I have a pastor/friend and I would like for him to come up and give his testimony. Can everyone stand to your feet as my friend Pastor Bennie Davis come forth and give his testimony." When I walked on the stage, I stood by Pastor Donnie McClurkin and asked, "how much time do I have?" And he said, "ten minutes."

I looked around the stage, and there were people all around me. I made up my mind that I was going to tell the people what the Lord had done for me. When I opened my mouth and started telling my testimony, the people started screaming and shouting. This is the first time I ever spoke in front of that many people. God blessed each person that was in the building. When I finished giving my testimony, I bent down and lifted my pants leg so that the people could see how my leg was cut and was left with a hole in it. The people went up in praise, thanking God, and you could feel the presence of God all over that building.

Pastor Donnie McClurkin walked back onstage when I finished giving my testimony, and the only thing he could say was, "What a mighty God," and I could see the tears that came from his eyes. When the Easter program was over, people came from all over to see me and to ask for a CD or a book of my testimony. Some came and said I heard testimonies in my life, but I never heard anything like the one you just told today. Out of all that you have been through, you still have your right mind; you are not in jail, you're not dead, you are a survivor. God has you here for a purpose for your life.

This was the greatest Easter program I had ever attended. A mother came to me with tears coming out of her eyes and rolling down her face. She grabbed me and hugged me. She said, "I have a son who has given up on life. He has a sickness that the doctor said is not curable, and he will live with this sickness for the rest of his life." She went on to say he is on drugs, has been in jail, and has spent time in prison. I wish that he could have been here today to hear your testimony. You have encouraged me. I reminded her that a mother's prayers can change situations. Then she said, you are going to touch and change the lives of people that you never met because you are a living testimony. Then she asked, do you have a CD or a book so I can take it to my son so he can hear the true testimony?

I told her that I did not have either a CD or a book. Then I thought to myself I would have loved to have had a CD, and I would love to write a book, but I'm not able to write. I'm not even able to spell. I allowed that negative spirit to enter my mind. That negative spirit came just to remind me what I could not do. It is why a CD or a book will never come to pass. Then I encouraged myself, I can do all things through Christ Jesus, which strengthens me. I said to myself God did not bring me this far to leave me because God specializes in doing the impossible.

There was someone from Pastor McClurkin's staff who came to me and said, follow me to Pastor Donnie McClurkin's office. I took Debra Fling with me so that she could also meet him. When we walked into his office, Pastor Donnie McClurkin said I would like to thank you for the great job that you did, and then I introduced him to Debra Fling. We spent about 20 minutes with him, and then after that, we went to the bus because the church family was waiting for us to come. When we got back on the bus, everyone went to get something to eat.

After our meal, we got on the road to head back to South Carolina. Everyone was talking about the wonderful time that they had and how beautiful the testimony was. Someone on the bus said to me I have never heard you give that testimony the way you did today. I replied, "I was never in front of over 10,000 people before. I may never get another opportunity, so I had to take full advantage of the opportunity that was given to me." Someone said to put the DVD in the church service that was given to you. I put the DVD in, and it started playing. We were looking for the testimony, but it was not on the DVD. It started playing when Pastor Donnie McClurkin was preaching, but the memory was in my heart. I replayed it in my mind repeatedly. We made it back to South Carolina. I was still excited about the things that happened in my life.

One day, my wife and I were talking, and she was telling me that the Youth Center cannot be a church name and to let the Youth Center birth the church. That was when Greater Christ Temple Church of the Harvest was birthed. A few days later, my wife answered the phone, and the person on the other end said something to her. Her eyes got big, then her mouth was open, and she put her hand over her mouth. I was able to see the joy in her eyes.

She hung up the phone, and then she came to me as she was so happy. She hugged me, and she said I have some good news. She told me, "The church I tried out for has voted, and the majority voted for your Honey to be the Pastor. Now, all I must do is accept it, and then I will be named the new pastor of the church."

She said, "Pastor D., I do not know what to do because we are working together with the ministry that God has given to you, and I love working with you."

I said to her, "As long as I am Pastor of Greater Christ Temple, you will always be a part of this ministry. Now, this door has been opened for you. Now, you need to walk in the door and be that great pastor that I know that you will be for that church."

Then she said, "Yes, I will do it!"

Then she called and informed them that she accepted the job as pastor. My wife was the first female Pastor in the Little Pee Dee Association.

I was working on my master's degree during this time. I needed help with my schoolwork. The Lord put a young man in my life, and he helped me by reading my books on tape. One day, I heard a knock on the door, and I went to the door and said, "Who is it?"

He said, "It is me, Pastor D, and from that day to this day, people started calling me Pastor D."

The young man passed away some time ago, but I appreciated all the help that he had given me. The same year, a couple of months later, I walked across the stage, and I received my doctoral degree in Christian Education. Things were still just going my way.

Due to my epilepsy, being shot and losing half of my right leg, I was listed as disabled. I was receiving SSI. I received a letter from SSI stating that I had to meet with them. I had a meeting with them, and I was asked about my marriage. Then I was told that my wife must turn in her income, and if her income is a certain amount, then my SSI benefits would be cut, and I would no longer be able to receive a check. When my wife and I looked at the money she was making, we knew that my check was going to be cut off. I believe when a man decides to have a girlfriend or a wife, they are asking for responsibility. If a man cannot make a woman's life better, then he needs to leave that woman alone. I wanted to do my part as the man. I was thinking if my check was cut off, then I must find a job.

Until I found a job, then, my wife would have to take care of me, and if I got sick or needed any medicine, she would have to pay for it with her money. Then it was said to me the only way I could continue to receive my check was that we would have to get our marriage annulled. When my wife and I went to church that Sunday, we explained to all the partners at the church that we were going to end our marriage, and we did not want them to think that there was any disagreement between my wife and me. We loved each other; if we had it our way, this marriage would not end.

We have love for each other, and it will never end regardless of what the law says for me to keep my SSI benefits. Then I said to the church this Bear will love his Honey until the last breath I take on this earth. Debra Fling got so upset. She said, "This does not make any sense. You two are so happy together; stay with each other because you can and will make it together."

It seemed like yesterday when I had to pack up all my clothes and put them in the van. As I was putting my clothes in the van, I cried the entire time. After I put my last load in the van, I walked back into the house, put my arms around my wife and said, "Your Bear will always be here for you anytime you need me." I went on to say that you can call me day or night; it does not matter about the time. Just know that I am here for you because you brought something great to my life. You did something great to my life that no other women have done for me. You loved me not for what I did for you or was able to give you, but because you instilled so many great things in me, I will never forget the one thing that stands out that you did for me. When you told me the truth after I received my master's degree, you told me this out of love, but I initially thought it was hate that you had for me because of what you said to me. You told me, Bennie, do not go back to college for your doctoral in Christian education just to have a title, and you cannot represent a doctor.

I stayed out of college for two years, working on the different things in the Bible that I was weak in because I was hungry for more knowledge about God's word. I worked so hard those two years to improve myself. I went back to college and obtained my doctorate degree in Christian Education. She gave me the most encouraging words that any wife could have given to their husband, and I love her for being real with me. When I let her go out of my arms, I walked out the door to the van, and the tears started coming down, and I was not able to stop them. I would not look back because everything I loved, I had to walk away from it- from her.

That was the longest walk I ever had to take. When I got to the van, I left the house, and that was a long ride I had because I was alone. A place I believed I would never be any more in my life, but I am back by myself. I had to end a life of love with the lady I waited my whole life for, and now the only reason I had to go was so that I could keep my SSI and Medicaid card. Life is so hard, but if I were not focused on the Lord, I would not have made it because my rib was taken away from me.

It was an election going on for president of the United States, and candidate Barack Obama was coming to Marion. One day, I was getting my haircut at the barber shop, and Emerson Hunt said, "Pastor D, have you ever heard of Barack Obama?"

Then I replied, "No, I never heard of him. This is my first time hearing about him. Is he a Democrat?"

Emerson said, "Candidate Barack Obama is not just coming to Marion, SC, but he is coming right here to my barbershop, and if you want to see him, then be here on time next week." I made sure I was on time to the barbershop. I made it to the barber shop and got myself a good seat. Someone said he would be here in minutes. I was so happy because there was a black man running for President of the United States.

When they drove up, someone ran inside and said, "He is here. He is outside now!" He got out of the SUV, and the Secret Service walked in first; then, shortly after that, the candidate Barack Obama walked in. I was the first person he spoke to. I had on my 3-piece suit and my snakeskin shoes. Candidate Barack Obama said, "Can I have those shoes." I said to him, "You do not want these shoes because they are plastic shoes. If you go out in the sun, they will start to melt off your feet." Then he started laughing about what I said about my shoes. I took a picture with him. What a great opportunity it was to meet him because he was our first black president of the United States.

I was doing a telemarketing business, and I was making money for the church, but I had a vision to put my testimony on CD. I got in touch with a young man that had a studio. He helped people with doing their CDs. He began working on the CD with me. Deacon Debra Fling wrote a song called, 'Battlefield for My Lord' and Jack Woodbury interviewed me on the CD. We were working on the CD in the studio, but I ran out of money, and it looked like the CD was at a standstill. It seemed like the CD was not going to be finished, and my vision would not come to pass. I asked Sister Jeanette for the rest of the money so my vision could come to pass. She invested in the CD, and I asked her if she would like to be my manager; because of her giving me the money, I was able to finish the project. She never asked for money, but I made sure I gave her all of the money back. Sister Jeanette believed in the testimony and that people could be delivered and set free.

During this time, my mother always had a dream of having her own restaurant because she enjoyed cooking various types of food. She got the opportunity to open a restaurant, and it was named after her. It took some time, but her restaurant was the number one soul food restaurant in Marion County called Becca's Place. People would be traveling to Myrtle Beach from all over, and they would stop and get some hog maws.

One Sunday, I had to go to a prison out of Charleston, SC, to minister to a young man who was on death row. I asked Deacon Debra Fling to speak that Sunday morning at the church. The young man had a wonderful time along with Sister Jeanette and me in the service. As Sister Jeanette and I were walking to the car, we were talking about how the young man believed the word of God. I asked Sister Jeanette to drive back to Marion. When we got into the car, I got my phone to check my missed calls and to see if anyone had texted me.

I had some missed calls, but I had more text messages. I said let me look at my text messages first, then I will call the people who called me. I read one text and said people need to stop playing with me by texting lies. Then I said no, no, Jeanette, someone was playing with me on my phone. I said this does not make any sense. I cannot read this because some of the words I cannot read. I said read this to me, Sister Jeanette. Then she read what the text said. "Pastor D, Deacon Debra has passed away!"

I said, "No, no, she is not dead. She spoke at the church today. Give me the phone, and let me call her mother!!" I said, "People need to stop lying because no one could believe things like this. This is not good at all for anyone!"

I called her mother's house, and someone answered the phone. I didn't know who it was, but I said, "How are you doing today?"

The person said, "Pastor Davis, Debra is dead. She was in a wreck, and her car flipped over. She could have died then or on her way to the hospital. I do not know when it happened, but she is dead."

My heart did not just stop, but it felt like it came out and fell in my lap. I was not able to say anything at first, but the tears began to come down my eyes and roll down my face. I said, "Sister Jeanette Deacon Debra is dead."

I hung up the phone, and for about 45 minutes, I did not say a word. I just sat there and cried and said no, no, no, not Deacon Debra; she is the One Voice choir. She is the chairperson of the Deacon ministry. She did not play about her Pastor D. She did not let anyone say anything about her Pastor D. I looked at Sister Jeanette and said what am I to do, and she said, "Pray, pray, pray because prayer changes situations and everything will be all right." When we got on the road, I was still crying. When we got to Marion, we went straight to Deacon Debra's mother's house.

10. DARKNESS SHATTERED MY LIFE

Before the car could come to a complete stop, I opened the car door to get out of the car. I got out of the car and started walking to the door of Deacon Debra's mother's house. I was still crying, but now it was much worse than before. I made it to her mother's house. When I saw the funeral home light in the front yard, a lot of people standing around and sitting on the front porch, I knew that it was real; she was dead. My nose started running as I went up the steps to go on the porch; there were people standing around. They were looking at the tears coming from my eyes and rolling down my face. Everyone was looking at the condition that I was in, and no one said a word to me.

When I made it to the door, someone said go on in the house, and they opened the door for me. I walked into the house and saw her mother, and then I began to cry a little harder. I had to pull myself together. I told her mother to let me know if there was anything that I could do and that I was here to do it. I started discussing how much Deacon Debra meant to me and the church family. Deacon Debra brought joy and happiness to the church family and me. I just kept asking what happened, what happened, they could not do anything to save her.

I suggested to the family if there was anything that I could do, please let me know; I am just a phone call away. I went to her mother, hugged her, and said, I love you so much. Sister Jeanette and I walked out of the house together, and someone said, "Sister Jeanette, you need to drive for Pastor D because he is not in any condition to drive." She responded, "He had been crying all the way from Charleston, and he only said a few words, but most of the time, he just was crying, saying, 'No, no, not Deacon Debra.'"

Sister Jeanette drove me to my mother's house. When we made it to my mother's house, we went inside the house, and I was still crying. When I arrived at the house, Billy Lou Clark walked in behind me. She was saying how excited she was about the late Deacon Debra bringing forth the word that Sunday morning for service. She said, "Pastor, I knew she was going to sing a song or two, then she was going to preach as you preach, Pastor D. All I could say was yes, I know she would have done a great job."

We then started talking about what we had heard about what had happened to the late Deacon Debra. After time had passed, I told everyone I would lie down. I was hoping that this was a dream, and I would wake up, and everything would go back to normal, and the late Deacon Debra would be alive and not dead.

I woke up in the middle of the night and went to my mother's room.

I said, "Mama."

She answered back, "Who is it?"

I said, "Bennie."

Then she asked if I was alright. I said yes but asked if anything happened to Deacon Debra. My mother said, "Yes, she was in a wreck and was killed in the wreck." Right then and there was when I said it was true. Then I went back to my room and got back in the bed. I could not go back to sleep. I stayed awake for the remainder of the night. I saw when the sun came breaking through the sky. I started thinking and said there would be many people at the late Deacon Debra's funeral. I said to myself, I am going to be doing the late Deacon Debra's eulogy, and I got to be right.

That was when I told myself, let me get in touch with my friend Deacon Willie Windon. Sometime that day, between 3:00 pm and 5:00 pm, I returned to the late Deacon Debra's mother's house. When I exited my car, I was walking towards the porch when a family member called me. They said, "Pastor D, I need to tell you something."

I asked him, "How are you doing, young man."

He said, "I need to tell you something."

He said, "You will not be doing the eulogy."

That was when darkness crushed me. I asked him if I was not going to be doing the eulogy and who would do it. He said she always wanted her brother to do her eulogy whenever she died. I did not want to believe it because I only knew that she was not at the church where her brother was pastoring every Sunday morning, but she was at Greater Christ Temple Church of the Harvest.

I had to hold my composure because I felt my eyes tearing up, and I was not going to allow this man to see me cry because the late Deacon Debra meant so much to me and our church family. Then he told me you have five minutes to say something about her before the eulogy. I shook his hand and said good enough, then I walked away and never went in the house. I was so upset with what happened to me that I forgot to go into the house!

Then I remembered I was going to the house to see about the late Deacon Debra's mother and if there was anything I or the church could do for her.

I told myself not to turn around and go back to that house because, by now, everyone in the house knew that I would not do the eulogy. By this time, the tears were coming from my eyes and down my face. I said, what am I to say in those five minutes about someone as great as the late Deacon Debra. What came to me was that five represented Grace (God's favor in the five points of a star). I knew I was going to take full advantage of it. I will be able to let the world know how wonderful and great this woman of God was for the body of Christ.

When I got in my car, I told myself to call Billy Lou Clark, and I told her what happened. Then I said once again I have been overlooked and black balled. I was unable to hold back. I had to pull off the road and start crying because I was hurting badly. I told Billie Lou Clark that people just do not believe I am capable enough to do a home going service, but I was given five minutes. I am going to say what is in my heart. Then I got myself together and went home and told my family what was said to me, and then I went to my room.

The days passed by so fast. The night before the funeral, I was not able to sleep. All night, I kept waking up and going back to sleep. It seemed like the day was never going to come. I went over and over what I was going to say in my heart about the late Deacon Debra. Time had passed, and everyone was ready to go to the church for the funeral. We left the house early so that the family could find a seat. When I got to the church, cars were everywhere, all around the church, and there was not anywhere to park. So, I was dropped off in front of the church, and my sister found a place to park the car.

When I walked into the church, it was standing room only in the sanctuary. The late Deacon Debra was a well-loved person. She made everybody comfortable. Everyone had memories of this wonderful lady. The master of ceremony called me up, and as I walked to the microphone, I was praying that God give me the words to say to the people. I let the people know that Deacon Debra was a good Samaritan. She was not just any type of Christian. She was not a fig tree Christian, but she was a palm tree Christian. A palm tree's leaves are green all year long, and the roots are very deep.

Anytime a storm comes, a palm tree will not and does not break but bows down. While the palm tree is bowing down, a palm tree will praise God, and when the storm is over, a palm tree will raise back up and say, thank you, Lord. The presence of God filled the sanctuary, and the people stood up and started hollering, clapping, crying, and praising God.

After the funeral, a deceased family member shook my hand and said what a wonderful word you said about the late Deacon Debra. She is still greatly missed by our church family, and she will never be replaced. That following Sunday in church was our first Sunday with the late Deacon Debra being gone. It took us some time to adjust because we all cried about her passing. Then, we each said something about what the late Deacon Debra meant to us. Mother Davis did the singing. It reminded the church family how the late Deacon Debra would say Mother Davis would put her own words in the song and change it around. It also reminded the church family that when Mother Davis told the late Deacon Debra, she would lead the song and back her up.

We all started laughing, but it still hurts today as I write this, thinking about how wonderful she was to the church. Then sister Clark said, the late Deacon Debra's memories will always be with us here at Greater Christ Temple, and her memories are still with me.

About a month later, a bad storm came to Marion, and it really damaged the roof of the building where we were having church service. When we went to service that following Sunday, we found holes in the roof, and water was all over the floor. I decided to cancel service immediately, and then we started moving the church furniture from the areas where the roof leaked. I said to the church family it would be impossible for us to have service in the building.

Mother Davis said, "If Pastor Davis and the church family would like to have service in the lobby of my restaurant before I open on Sunday, you are very welcome to do so." The church family, along with myself, agreed to have service in the lobby of the restaurant. The church gave Mother Davis some money each month until the roof was repaired.

Greater Christ Temple did not have a large congregation. Now that we could not have service in the church, there was no afternoon or night service. We could not raise any money, so I prayed and asked God to give me some ideas so that I could raise money for the church. One Saturday, before the restaurant opened, I was running around getting things for my mother to cook. I was riding back to the restaurant and was almost there when I saw a yard sale at the local IGA grocery store.

Someone was selling designer handbags, shoes, and wallets, and people were coming from all over Marion to buy the products. Then, a man drove an SUV with handbags, shoes, wallets, clothes, and hats. The people surrounded him to buy his products. I thought the church could raise money by selling designer handbags, wallets, and shoes because we still had to pay rent for a building in which we could not have service. I got with someone, and they sold me some designer handbags, wallets, and shoes, and the church started getting money.

When school started and during Christmas time, the church would give sneakers away to the children in the community. The center would help the families that were working and buying their own house, renting their house or apartment. Every time the programs came, the same group of people were there. The ones who got government assistance or did not have any rent to pay are always getting help. The ones who were working and paying bills without getting any government assistance were always looked over.

It was time for my annual checkup with my doctor. During my visit, he said that I was doing great, but he advised me to start going to the gym. I started going to Swamp Fox gym in Marion, and I met a few young men, and they worked with me. Shawn Gause, Sharon Foxworth, Semore, Cowboy, and Emerson Hunt worked out with me five days a week. When I returned to the doctor, I lost over 50 pounds. The doctor was so proud of my weight loss because now I could walk so much better, and he encouraged me not to stop whatever I was doing because it was working. Then the doctor said to me, Mr. Davis, continue to have good eating habits because what you eat can put weight on you.

One morning, my sister and I went to the hospital to work out when I heard that the local IGA had caught fire. This grocery store was a part of our neighborhood for many years. The same day of the fire, my daughter Antoinette's grandmother's homegoing service was taking place. My mother had to open the restaurant, so I asked my daughter Ashley to help her until I returned from the funeral. After I left the funeral, I went by the IGA, and I could see the smoke was still coming from the building.

There were so many people standing outside. There were firemen, police, investigators, the news crew, and people from the community. I continued to go to the restaurant, and when I pulled up in the parking lot of the restaurant. I got out of the car and proceeded to go to the door of the restaurant. As I was unlocking the door, a car pulled into a parking lot. A young lady stepped out of the car and said, "Pastor D." I turned around, then she started walking towards me. I said how are you doing then she stopped walking towards me and said, "Come here, Pastor."

I went to see what she wanted, and she asked, "Do you have any more bags?"

I said, "You are my girl. If I do not, I will find you something. Come to the restaurant with me, and let us talk."

I let my mother know that it was me, then the young lady spoke to my mother. We continued our conversation as we sat at the table in the dining area. While we were sitting down talking, two white men came and walked in the door. I said to them we are not open yet. One of the men said can I purchase a soda. I realized that he was Officer Flowers from the Marion City Police Department, and the other man with him was with SLED. As they were walking out, the lady at the table with me stopped the man with the officer and said, "Would you like to purchase a Michael Kors handbag along with a wallet to match your wife or your girlfriend."

Then he replied, "No, I do not care for one," and walked outside. He returned to the door with his badge out, showing the lady that he was a SLED agent. I was walking out of the back door, and I left the restaurant. Currently, he was letting the lady know who he was in law enforcement. The SLED agent told the lady to take me to the handbags in your car. Then she took him outside to her car and opened the car trunk. There were no handbags in her trunk, and the agent asked her, "Where are the damn handbags?!"

He said to her that she or Pastor D was going to jail. Then she said, "It is not my car, but the white car over there belongs to Pastor D!"

The handbags are in the trunk of his car. The SLED agent returned to the restaurant and asked, "Where is Pastor Davis?"

Then my mother said, "He is not here. He left to go to his daughter. Today was his daughter's grandmother's home-going service, and I believe he returned to support his daughter."

The SLED agent asked my mother where the keys to the white car were. She said, "My son has his own keys." By this time, the agent returned to Officer Flowers and said, "Pastor Davis is not in the restaurant." Immediately, Officer Flowers called for backup, and the police surrounded the restaurant, looking for Pastor D.

The City Administrator was across the street at the IGA. He came to the restaurant as the police ran the license tags to my car. It came back that the car belonged to I Am Not That Way Anymore Youth and Adult Center Incorporated. One of the police officers called to get a warrant to search the car, but by this time, my sister and Sister Billie Lou Clark made it to the restaurant before the warrant was made to search the car. Not long after that, they made it to the restaurant. A police officer came with the warrant, and then Sister Billie Lou Clark and my sister permitted them to search the car.

The City Administrator unlocked the door to the car, and the SLED agent and the police officer started searching the car like bees looking for honey. There were sneakers in the back seat of the car. Someone said let's open the trunk because that is where the gold is, the handbags. Someone found the button to release the trunk, and one of the police officers pressed the button; the trunk popped open, and they found handbags, wallets, sandals, boots, and name-brand watches.

The SLED agent said, "Pastor Davis never propositioned me, asked or approached me about buying anything from him. It was the lady that stopped me."

As they started taking the items out of the car trunk, people were passing by the restaurant looking. Some cars pulled over just to see what was happening and what they were taking out of the car. Some people got out of their cars so they could see what was happening. Word spread over Marion County that Pastor Davis, better known as Pastor D, just got busted with drugs, handbags, and shoes. Someone said he is not any Pastor D, but he is the same Caveman he has always been because they also found DVDs of underage children having sex with adults, and this man needs to be in prison for the rest of his life.

SLED busted other stores in Marion for selling handbags before they came to me, but they made a big deal out of busting Becca's Place. People started calling my sister, the church's partners, and family members, gossiping about what was said, but no one had a name.

SLED had my car towed to the Marion County Detention Center pawn yard. By this time, I had already called my lawyer, Thurmond Brooker, and explained everything to him. He told me not to go back to the restaurant. He told me that he would call the Marion Police Department and let them know that he is now representing Pastor Bennie Davis. I knew that I had to get someone who would fight for my freedom. I knew that Attorney Thurmond Brooker was the man for the job because he attended Voorhees College at the same time I was attending. We both fought to graduate, and I knew he would fight for my freedom.

The next morning, I turned myself into the Marion County Detention Center. I got a bond and was released within an hour and a half. The warrant was for $125,000.00 worth of imitation Michael Kors handbags and accessories. Those police officers knew that there was not $125,000.00 worth of handbags, shoes, or anything else in the trunk of my car. Because of this so-called bust at my mother's restaurant, business slowed down.

It was time for the general session court to start, and my lawyer called to tell me that I had to make my first court appearance. I thought I would never be in this predicament again, facing time in prison for a long time. I was still preaching, encouraging people, and was always going to the jail in South Carolina, ministering that God is still able to bring them out, but at the same time, I needed to believe my own preaching. God is still able to do it for them and me.

I was in court, and the solicitor was calling the roll. When he called my name, it felt like everyone in the courtroom started looking towards me. I answered by saying, here, and I stood up so the solicitor could see me. As I was sitting in the courtroom, a young man sitting behind me said, "Pastor D is here? You mean to tell me that the police did not have anything else to do but to arrest a man making a difference in Marion." The young man said, "I know why I am in court, but Pastor D, my brother, just did his PTI (Pre-Trial Intervention) with you."

I remember the day. It was raining hard that day, and the solicitor would not allow anyone to come inside the building. The courtyard was filled with mostly Black young men. As time passed, the court doors opened for the people to enter the courtroom. When I got in the courtroom, I started counting the people in the roll call as they came into the courtroom. I counted 125 people, of which 122 were black and three were white. So, it took 122 Black people to be arrested and only three whites before a general session court could be held. On this day, so many people were in the courtroom, such as family members, friends, and jurors. Due to the courtroom's crowdedness, some people could not stay and left to go home or stand outside. Shortly after that, my attorney, Thurmond Brooker, walked into the courtroom and said, you are on standby, and dismissed from court for the week.

I was still working with PTI for the solicitor's office. But to my surprise, I was the only one arrested for handbags appearing in general session court. Not one person in Marion County was in court but me. When I discovered that I was the only one from Marion County, I started believing it was a setup to bring me down. I did not have any proof yet, but I knew something was wrong here. I was on standby for the remaining time in general session court.

I still had people coming to me doing PTI. Before a person could start PTI with me, we would have a meeting first. One day, someone came to meet with me because they had to start PTI; I asked them what crime they had committed. I was told their arrest was for the distribution of handbags, which occurred the same day that I was busted. Nevertheless, they did their community service with me, and I signed off on the paperwork. I knew for a fact that I should have been able to do PTI for selling those handbags, also. I asked them if anything was taken from them because my car had been confiscated, and they said nothing was taken from them.

My mother did foster care for many years. She loved working with young people. During this time, she was working with this agency for several years. It was a few days before the end of the school term. My mother called me one afternoon and said, "Pastor Davis, I need you to come out to the house and speak to this young man because he will not take his medicine. He will not listen to anything I say to him, but he will listen to you."

I went to my mother's house and spoke to Anthony about what he was doing to our mother (because he was considered our little brother). I told him the importance of taking his medication and how his behavior was out of control because the medicine was out of his system. I told Mama, "I will call law enforcement and have someone come out to the house."

An officer came, and I explained what was happening with my little foster brother. The officer entered the house, walked into the room, and told him why he should do the right thing by taking his medicine. Then he said, "It would help if you listened to your guardians because they are here to help you." The officer's last words were, "Anthony, you should do right so you will not get into any trouble." When the officer left the house, Anthony was angry and said, "I am going to get you and Mother Davis in some trouble!"

The next day was a regular day. My mother got Anthony prepared for school, and they both went outside to wait for the bus. I went to the house at the regular time to pick Mother up to go to the restaurant to have the food prepared and ready before opening at 11:00 a.m. We were still rebuilding the business from the time that SLED came and busted the restaurant. I was still in general session court. It has been about a year since that time.

The day went well until 4:00 pm when the phone started ringing, and Mother answered. After a few minutes, I saw tears fall down her face out of nowhere. Then she said, "No, no, no, that never happened."

I went to my mother, asking what was wrong as she handed me the telephone. I said, "Hello, who is this that has my mother crying?" The person identified herself as a worker from the after-school boys and girls program calling about her son. "Anthony came to me after school. Someone called from the school to inform us that someone needed to call Law Enforcement because someone abused Anthony in his home before coming to school. Department of Social Services (DSS) has been notified, and Samantha Jackson, the investigator from the Sheriff's Department, is here asking Anthony questions about who abused him." I said, "No one in my mother's house did anything to Anthony."

I looked around to see where my mother was. She was sitting down in a chair, crying with her head down. I heard her praying. I knew right then I had to hold back the tears because I had to be strong for my mom. I told Mother, "Do not worry. Put it in the Lord's hands."

Customers started walking into the restaurant, and I asked them to give us 20 minutes, and dinner would be ready. I had to tell my mother that Anthony, whom she loved, would not return home. I advised her that DSS and the agency that you are working with started investigating you and me. My mother said, "When Anthony came to me, he could only stay in school for 3 hours, but now he can stay a full day and pass all his classes. All I wanted to do was see my son graduate from school, become independent, and move into his own house. Now, what am I to do? God give me the strength to go through this."

There was another call announcing someone was coming to take a report and that Anthony would not be coming back home until the completion of the investigation. For some reason, the customers that I told to come back never came back. The rumors began, and word around town was "Pastor D and his mother beat and bruised the foster child. The foster child had to be taken from the after-school program, and how Anthony looked was shameful. They beat up on him. They both need to be in jail and then sent to prison for beating that child." I decided to close the restaurant for the rest of the day.

Then, as we were preparing to leave, Dr. Henry McGill, Jr. walked in, and I told him what was happening. He said, "This does not make any sense. Mother Davis, you love that young man. Do not worry about anything; everything will be alright."
Then, as we were going home, mama burst out crying out of nowhere. She was not crying like when I got shot, as she was with this young man. She has so much love for him she looks at him as her son and sees so much greatness in him. My mother cried all the

way home. She never said anything to me when I got to her house. She just went straight to her room and pulled the door together. I stood at her door and asked her if she was alright. She never said anything, but I could hear her crying. My sister and her son Elijah would go to her bedroom door throughout that night and could hear Mama crying. She cried to sleep, and when she woke up, she still cried. The pain was so severe.

The next morning, at about 6:00 a.m., I went over to my mother's house, and my sister said, "Mama had not been out of her room."

I went to her bedroom door and said, "Mama, do not worry about this. Somehow, we will make it through."

Today, Mama can tell her side along with me, and the truth shall overcome that lie. Later, I heard her get up, then she prayed and said, I will be ready to go in 30 minutes. We went to the restaurant by 11:00 a.m. The restaurant was open, and only three people came to get dinner that day because of what was happening with Anthony. At 3:30 pm, a Child Protective Service Worker came to take a report for the adoption agency. She conducted an interview with Mama first, and then she interviewed me.

After obtaining the information, she said it would be a few days before we would hear back from the agency to decide about Anthony returning to the home. She said, "During the investigation, you are not allowed to contact this young man for any reason or any other agency in South Carolina." Mama started crying when the lady said that to her. I told my Mama, "Do not worry when they review this; they will see that we are not lying, and everything will be all right."

A Sheriff informed us that Detective Samantha Jackson suggested that my mother and I turn ourselves in for Anthony's alleged charges by 10:00 a.m. the next morning. I said we had not done anything.

We were then advised that my mother and I had signed a warrant. I said the warrant must be about beating that child, and I could not believe it.

I said, "No one from the Sheriff's Department came and asked my mother or me; what is going on, man?" Then the Sheriff said, "I recommend you and your mother turn yourself in tomorrow. Pastor Davis, if you do not turn yourselves in, someone will come for you and your mother, so do it this way."

What blew my mind about this was that some people were going around town saying yes, they beat that boy. Both need to be in prison, and they don't even need to be around any more children. I decided to take my mama home because of everything the people said about her and me. As she exited the car, I saw tears rolling down her face. I did all I could, but I could not hold back the tears after seeing my mother crying. I did not go into the house. I asked Alethea to look after Mama tonight, and if anything happened to her, call me because Mama and I must turn ourselves into the Sheriff's Department. I told her it was about that young man Mama had living here.

Alethea went to Mama's bedroom door that night, and Mama was still crying. She checked on her throughout the night, and Mama continuously cried each time she went to the door. I went home and could not eat or sleep the entire night. My eyes stayed open throughout the night as I cried intermittently. I knew the things that Anthony said were far from the truth. I got up the next morning and went to my mom's house. When I got there, I told her that we would not open the restaurant today. My sister asked, "What time must you and Mama turn yourselves in?" I answered, "10:00 a.m." The time seemed like it was quickly approaching. I told my mother, "Let's go to the Sheriff's Department."

When we walked into the Department, I asked for Samantha Jackson. She came to us and read us our Miranda rights, then arrested us and took my mother and me into booking. We were fingerprinted, and they took our mug shots. When they finished processing, my mother and I entered the holding cell. My mother cried, saying, "I've never been to jail. I always told my children to obey the law, but now I am here. I obeyed the law all my life, and now I end up in Marion County Detention Center for something I did not do." The judge was not there, so they had to decide whether to send us to the population or continue in the holding cell. Mama could not stand up, so they put her in the holding area's center, where there was a bench to sit down. I asked if I could stay with my mother because she could not be alone in this jail. But the officer said, "You will be in a holding cell, and if you and your mother cannot pay the bond, then the next thing will be population."

Walking to the holding cell, I stood at the door, looking at my mother. The tears just started coming out of my eyes, but seeing my mother in jail was the worst disappointment in my life. I could believe my brother and I could go to jail together, but not my mother. I could have never imagined anything like this in my weirdest dream. My mother and I were arrested at the same time. Unbelievable! As I continued looking at my mother, I could see her crying, and I heard her praying, "Lord, I am almost 70 years old, and I have never been in trouble or jail, but today, look at where I am now. My oldest son gave his life to God, believing that he could never go to jail anymore but only to minister to the inmates, but today, he is only a few steps away from me in a jail cell." Then I saw her head drop down; she was crying, and I could hear her speaking in unknown tongues.

It was so difficult to watch my mother sitting in jail because of something she did not do. I started thinking about Samantha Jackson. She never came to ask my mother or me one single question concerning this case. About forty minutes to an hour later, my mother and I were still in this holding cell waiting. I could not look at my mother anymore because the hurt was like no other hurt I had ever experienced. I started praying, saying, "Lord, put a hedge around my mother and me. Lord, dry up my mama's tears. God worked through the judge so that we would not go into the population. God, I know victory is coming somehow, someway. Lord, I will go ahead and give you all the praise right now in the name of Jesus, Amen."

I looked at my mother as an inmate. They had the nerve to tell us how much time my mother and I could make if found guilty. We conversed when the officers came out for us to go before the judge for a bond. When we entered the courtroom, our attorney, Thurmond Brooker, was there waiting on us, in addition to our family. I was confident our attorney would get a bond for my mother and me.

If not for our attorney being in the courtroom, Samantha Jackson would have done her absolute best to keep us in jail. She had a point to prove or a quota to meet but not a job to do for the people of Marion County by investigating and finding out the truth. My Mother and I committed no crime. We were just two Black people she would put in the system for statistics, not for the person who committed it.

Out of 125 people in the general session court, it was only three whites because of the quota and statistics. How many of those 122 Black people Samantha Jackson had in court for crimes they did not commit? Many young people were falsely arrested and had no money to afford a lawyer, so they had to plead guilty to a crime they did not commit. The detective appears to be solving crimes, but, in reality, she is only sending innocent people to prison.

All I know is she had my mother and me charged with a crime we did not commit. I know we are not the first and the last accused of a crime they never committed. We were seated beside our lawyer in the courtroom. Shortly after, the judge entered the courtroom, and we all had to stand. Samantha Jackson told the judge our charges, and as she was talking, I looked at my sister. She was crying because she was looking at her mother in a place where she taught her children to do right, and they would never go.

Now, we see that it is not necessarily true. There are more like her on our streets, putting innocent people in jail and prison. The judge listened to what our attorney had to say and our plea of not guilty to the charges. The judge gave us a bond and said that we could not go around Anthony for any reason or would be confined to jail until our court time. My mother and I are in general session court for child abuse charges. I am still in court for imitation handbags. I am destined for prison. After we made the bond, our attorney suggested that he would let us know when to report to the court. He said, "Go home and do not worry because I will fight for your and your mother's freedom."

My mother's business was on a decline because of the handbag arrest at the restaurant. When it finally started to pick back up a little, this happened. We went from the greatest soul food and short-order restaurant in Marion County. Now, people do not want to pass by our restaurant or even come into the restaurant to buy food from us. All of this happened because of one person.

Also, we were still having our church service at the restaurant during this time. New people had begun coming to the services, but then they stopped coming. Obviously, they did not want to be a part of a ministry where the Pastor and his mother were allegedly charged with beating a child. I was at the lowest point of my life. The easy way out was to give up and sell drugs. Most people would have said he has been selling drugs the entire time he has been calling himself

Pastor D. Then some would have said I understand why he gave up because of all he has been through in his life.

I believed that God would do something in my life to let me know there was still an opportunity for me and to hold on a bit longer. God will put people in our pathway to help us when we are at our lowest point in life. One day, I was at the restaurant between 6:00 pm and 10:00 pm when people came to get food. I said, "What are we to do? Should we stay open or walk away? But then I would not have any place to have church service if we close." A call came in on my cell phone, and it was Michael Beaty, aka Petro. He said, "Pastor D, I heard there's a church in Aynor, South Carolina, looking for a Pastor. I know a young man who is a church member; his brother is the chairman of the Deacon ministry, and we work together. If it is okay with you, I will tell him about you because I believe you need this. I will find out about you applying for the position. The church's name is St. Matthews Missionary Baptist Church." Right then, I started smiling. I was so happy. I said, "Yes, yes, go to the man and tell him about me."

Now, I am looking forward to Michael making this happen for me. Right then, I started to believe that I had a great future before me. I need them to accept my application and allow me to preach and teach Bible study and Sunday school. I had never been to the church. I did not care about the congregation or the building. I just wanted my opportunity. Michael said I will let you know what happened when I get off work tonight.

On Michael's lunch break, he called me and said, get your resume together because you got to get it in the mail this week. Right then, my heart felt like it was going to stop or slow down. I believe it did just stop. When I got off the phone, I started jumping, shouting, raising my hands, screaming. This is the opportunity that I have been waiting for. I encouraged myself, and I said in my heart, 'I will be the new pastor at St. Matthews Missionary Baptist Church.'

When I got home, I got my resume and thought when Michael gave me the address, I would put it in the mail tomorrow. That night, at about 11:20 pm, a knock came on the door. I asked who it was, and it was Petro. I opened the door, and he handed me the address. Petro encouraged me to send the resume tomorrow, and then he told me what he said to his friend on the job. He said he told him, "I have another candidate, one more man, and this man is the man you have all been waiting on. He is like no other preacher St. Matthew's had ever heard before." I said, "Petro, I will put my resume in the mail tomorrow." Petro said, "Let me know when you mail it so I can tell my friend that the resume is in the mail."

A week later, I received a phone call. I answered. The caller asked for Dr. Bennie T. Davis Sr. I said, "This is him." He introduced himself as Deacon Timothy Gerald, the chairman of the Deacon ministry at St. Matthews Missionary Baptist Church. "I am calling on behalf of the Church Committee. I want to inform you that we would like you to come in November. Will you be available?"

I responded, "Yes, and I look forward to coming."

Deacon Timothy explained, "It will be the entire month of November, and you will be St. Matthews Missionary Baptist Church's Interim Pastor. Your duties will consist of Sunday school, Morning service, and Bible study on Wednesday night."

I said, "Thank you so much. I will not let myself down, and I will not let you down. I look forward to meeting you, the other deacons, the church committee, and the members. Are there currently any ministers in the church?"

He answered, "We have one amazing minister."

We bid each other a nice day and hung up the phone, and I pulled over on the side of the road so fast. I was extremely happy. I started thanking God, and my confidence level went sky-high. I was so excited I just wanted to continue praising God but decided to go to the restaurant and tell my family about this GREAT opportunity I have in November to become Interim Pastor of Saint Matthews Missionary Baptist Church. Thank you, Lord!

11. HE WILL NEVER QUIT

Tears were in my eyes and started rolling down my face as I was telling my family the great news that happened to me. Of all the times this could have happened to me, this call came at the right time. Now, I am not just sitting at the restaurant thinking about my mother and I going to court. Now, I can focus on preparing myself to preach and teach at Saint Matthew's. I can encourage myself by preaching and teaching to myself, and my faith will be able to grow.

My family was so proud of me. My mother was scared because she said, "Son, you do not think you are putting too much on yourself? This will be your first time with a church family. You have no earthly idea who these people are. I told her, "Mama, God knows them, and because of that, I will be alright." My sister said, "Bennie, do not tell anyone because someone will do something to stop those people from that church from looking at you for becoming their Pastor." I told my family, "Do not worry about it. I am going to do a great job for this church. I will put hours of work in on my sermon and what I will be teaching on Wednesdays."

Each one of my family members that was in the restaurant came to me and hugged me. Each said encouraging words in my ear, and then my mother did something she always does. She started crying and praying. Each family member believes I could become the new pastor at Saint Matthew's Missionary Baptist Church.

A few days later, I called Deacon Timothy and asked him to send me a program outline. He told me I could take a picture of one of our programs and send it to your phone, and I said that would be great. Because I have a reading problem now, I would be able to go over and over the outline of this church service, so I would be able to pronounce the people's names. I do know how to preach and teach the word of the Lord. During November, I will be the acting pastor of St. Matthew Missionary Baptist Church.

It was three weeks before the first Sunday in November, and I knew that I had to fast and pray to God could give me what to tell the people when I preach and do Bible study. Deacon Timothy and the Saint Matthew church family have given me an opportunity that no other church gave me. They made me a candidate to become pastor of St. Matthews Missionary Baptist Church. Because of this opportunity, St. Matthews Missionary Baptist Church would be a part of my life forever. I will have a special place in my heart to the end of my life.

The week before I went to preach at Saint Matthew's Missionary Baptist Church, I had a revival in Charleston, SC. Barbara Jackson set up the revival for me. It was a wonderful time that entire week. My friend Peter Johnson ensured I was at service each night on time. Peter is a friend that I met at Voorhees College in the fall of 1987. Peter contacted some of our alumni friends, Carol J. Powell and her crew. Peter called her and said, "Carol, do you remember Caveman? He is preaching now and doing a revival in Charleston, and it is only two more nights. Can you come out one of those nights?"

She said, "The Caveman from Voorhees? Hell, yes, I got to come see Caveman!"

Peter said, "Yes, Caveman."

Carol and her Voorhees crew walked in that Thursday night. What made me so happy was when they walked in. They knew me when I was Caveman selling drugs, but they put all of that aside to hear me preach. Talking about a wonderful, anointed time we had, and the move of God was in that place.

There were some people that got delivered that night. After church, I met with Carol J. Powell and some of my other alumni friends from

Voorhees. I asked Carol, when we were going outside, "Why did you not come in the prayer line?"

She said, "Pastor Caveman, those people were falling on the floor, so I decided to stay in my seat because I knew I was going down like everyone else because I felt the presence of the Lord."

The next day, the Greater Christ Temple church family came down for that Friday night. We got on the road after church to head back to Marion. I called Deacon Timothy and said this is the Sunday I am with you and the church family. He said, "Yes, we are looking for you on Sunday."

I told him, "I will see you Sunday, Deacon Timothy, and thank you again for this opportunity to be with you all in November."

That Saturday came fast, the day before my interview to become pastor of Saint Matthews Missionary Baptist Church.

I knew they were looking for a pastor, and I only knew I wanted this job as a pastor. Everything I do, the members of that church were going to be interviewing me for the job, so they will ask themselves if this is the man we need as our pastor. During this time, my car was impounded because of the bust from the counterfeit handbags. So Petro was taking me to the church on Sundays. On Wednesday night, my sister said I could use her car.

I went over my sermon that Saturday night, standing in the mirror repeatedly. That night, Petro called me and said, "Pastor, you need to go to bed because I will pick you up early in the morning."

He said Pastor, Sunday school starts at 9:45 AM. We need to be at the church by 9:30 AM; we should be waiting on them and not them waiting on us. Throughout the night, I was waking up excited about the next day.

As I was looking at my suit, I started thanking God because I remembered when I only had one suit and one white shirt. My mother washed it so much it was torn under the sleeve, but then God blessed me, and now I could go to the closet and choose what suit and shirt I would like to wear. As soon as I saw a little sun, I got up and started going over my sermon over and over for that Sunday morning service. I knew I had to do the Sunday school review. I was ready. This is the day I have been waiting on; now, it is the opportunity of my Christian lifetime. Because I fasted and prayed, I knew God was in total control of what would happen in our service today.

My phone started ringing at 6:00 AM when Petro called me, and he said, "Pastor, I could not sleep because I am so happy for you. I believe this church family can help you, and I know you will do everything you can to make them better."

I said to Petro, "I love you for what you said to me. I have been up for some time now because I could not sleep."

Then Petro said, "I will be in your yard at 8:00 AM. We will leave at 8:30 because I must stop and get something to eat."

I told Petro that I had the address to the church. But he said, "Pastor Davis, do not worry about it. I know where the church is. It's on Hwy 319 in Aynor."

I said, "Petro, let me get off this phone so I can go over my sermon and Sunday school lesson again before I start getting ready."

Time just went by super-fast because Mama said, "Bennie, Petro is in the yard."

I said, "Mama, he called me to let me know he would be outside about 8:00 AM, but we would leave at 8:30 because Petro does not want us to be late. If anything, he wants us waiting on them."

I went into my room and pulled the door together, then I started praying, asking God to cover me and give me a fresh anointing word for Saint Matthews Missionary Baptist Church family and guests. I continued to pray to the Lord, "Today, Lord, allow somebody to be delivered and set free from all sickness. Lord, most of all, let someone be saved from sin. Amen."

I got my stuff together and walked out the door. My phone started ringing; it was Alethea. She said, "Pastor, I will be at Sunday school and the morning service to support you, and most of all, I am praying for you."

I said, "Okay, see you then, but I am getting in the truck with Petro now as he is ready to go. I will see you when you get to the church." After I got into the truck, we went to McDonald's so Petro could get something to eat and then hit the road. I was excited and ready to attend the church because this job belonged to me.

I started going over my Sunday school lesson, then looked over my sermon while we went to church. As Petro was driving, it seemed like time just stopped. It felt like he was never going to get to the church. This was the longest drive to Saint Matthew's Missionary Baptist Church. We finally reached Hwy 319, and Petro said, "The church is down this road."

I was so happy. As we were going down the road, every building with a steeple, I was hoping it was Saint Matthews Missionary Baptist Church. I asked Petro if we were there yet and he said almost a few minutes later, Petro put on his signal light and turned into the parking lot. When I looked up, I said, "This is Saint Matthews Missionary Baptist Church?!"

It was like Christmas morning when a child went to sleep knowing his/her parents could not get them anything for Christmas. When he/she woke up, everything they ever asked for was under the Christmas tree. This is how I felt when I realized this was the church.

I could not believe this was happening to me. I said to myself look at what the Lord has done for me. God doesn't judge our future by our past. I do not care what comes or goes. I said, "Lord, give me the words to say today to this church family and guests." Petro said, "I am putting you out at the church door, Pastor, then I am going to open the door for you." I could not believe Petro was doing all this for me. I stood at the door of the church and waited for him. We walked into the church together. As I walked into the sanctuary, it was like no other I had ever been to in my life.

I told myself, Bennie, you can become the pastor of this church, but you must make the members greater than they are right now. Petro and I found a place to sit, and then shortly after that, Sunday school started. At the end of Sunday school, someone said Dr. Bennie Davis, will you do the Sunday school review. I answered and said a few things about the Sunday school lesson during Sunday school. It was at the end of the Sunday school, and I had to give the review. The people in Sunday school were amazed at what I said about the lesson.

The Superintendent of Sunday school did not realize that I was the speaker for that Sunday morning, so he came over to Petro and me and said, "We welcome our two guests."

Deacon Timothy said, "No, that is our pastor for the month."

When Sunday school was over, Deacon Timothy came to me and had me follow him to the office in the back of the church. When we got into the office, he introduced himself to Michael and me because now Michael was acting like he was my armor-bearer, carrying my briefcase. This man never did this for me.

As Michael and I were walking out of the office, three men were coming into the office; the third man shut the door behind him as he walked into the office. Deacon Timothy introduced them to me: Deacon Ralph Van Fore, Deacon Terry Williams, and Deacon Dennis Gerald. These young men make up the deacon's ministry here at St. Matthew Missionary Baptist Church. I told them that my name was Pastor Bennie T. Davis, better known as Pastor D. Each of them shook my hand, making me feel like a King and essential. They were also excited about me being there, which built up my confidence. Deacon Dennis informed me that someone would get me when it was time for me to come to the sanctuary. He said, "This is your office. Get behind your desk because you are the Pastor for November."

The Deacons were older than me but treated me with so much respect. When they all left the office, all I could do was start thanking the Lord for putting such great people around me. I started reviewing the program outline to make sure I could pronounce the people's names. I could say some of their first names and not their last names, and then I could say their last and not their first names. So right then, I said, I got to come up with something. As I was pronouncing and reviewing the names, there was a knock at the door.

I said, "Please enter."

Then the usher walked into the office and said, "Dr. Bennie Davis, it is time for you to come into the sanctuary."

I replied, "I am ready, but could you come here momentarily? I have a question to ask."

The usher came to the desk that I was sitting at, and I asked, "What is your name?"

She said, "Cindy Brown."

I said, "Could you pronounce these names for me," and Cindy pronounced the names.

I said thank you because the people's names from Aynor are unlike those of the big city of Marion. I told her I was now ready to go but give me a minute, and she walked out of the office. Shortly after, I put on my coat and walked out the door. Cindy Brown was standing at the door waiting on me. This never happened to me before, so I had to act like this was not new before she started walking towards the sanctuary. Cindy asked me what I would like to drink, and I told her anything but soda as she led me to the sanctuary. After Cindy ensured I was seated, they ended the devotion service and returned it to me.

Before I started service, I remembered Deacon Timothy saying to me on our phone that there was one minister in the church family. I stood up and went to the pulpit. I asked if we had any pastors or ministers in the sanctuary. Only one young lady stood up, and I invited her to sit with me. When she came up, I greeted her and said anytime I come into the sanctuary and take my seat, I would like you to sit beside me. I asked her to read the morning scripture of her choice, and I asked her what her name was. She said, "Yes, I will read the scripture; my name is Minister Cross." Then she took her seat.

I proceeded with the morning service. My sermon was a question: "Are you fireproof?" There were only a few people in the audience, but I preached like it was a church full of people. I told the congregation, "Take your feet off the breaks and mash the gas because Pastor D. is filled up with an anointing word from heaven for you today, and by the time this service is over, I want to be on empty."

Before I ended the sermon, people cried out, clapped their hands, stomped their feet, and said amen. I called for an altar call, and the people got up and came around the altar like whatever they were looking for would happen from today.

During prayer, the Spirit of the Lord filled that building, and the people's hands went up in the air. Some of the people just started saying thank you, God. When I said amen and everyone was returning to their seat, I told them to tell three people they had already done whatever they asked God to do. We had a wonderful service. I gave the benediction. I walked down from the pulpit and was headed to the office. A few people came and shook my hand. I got to the office door, and someone came and unlocked the door so that I could go into the office.

Shortly after I was in the office, a knock came on the door, and I said to enter, and it was Deacon Timothy. I could not hold back. I was grinning, and I said Deacon, I am in love with the St. Matthew church family. I enjoyed myself today. Deacon Timothy asked me if he could pull the doors together. I said yes, sir. He shut the door and asked me if I would like to try out for Pastor of this church, and my response was, "Yes, I would love to be the Pastor of this church. Not just try out but to BE the Pastor."

Deacon Timothy said, "Dr. Davis, I must get a background check on you, but for me to get this background check. Dr. Davis, you must sign this agreement so the search committee can request your criminal record. There is a fee that we must pay to get this done."

I told Deacon Timothy, "I do not have to sign that agreement, and St. Matthew's does not have to pay that fee because I will tell you my criminal record. Now, I would like you to know that Mayor Bobby Gerald saw that I made a change for the better in my life. He paid my application fee and wrote a letter to help me get my pardon. Let me tell you my criminal record first. I did get my pardon from the state of South Carolina. In 1996, I was found guilty of the distribution of crack cocaine. I received two years' probation.

In 2013, I was charged with counterfeit handbags. In 2014, my mother and I were charged with allegedly beating a child. My mother and I are in general session court for charges we did not do. I know we will beat all those charges that Mother and I have.

Deacon Timothy said, "Dr. Davis, that was then, and this is now. God has come into your life, and I could see today that our church family received the word God put in your heart. Do not worry about the background check. I will tell you about the search committee and church family."

Deacon Timothy said, "Dr. Davis, next month, Reverend Edward Soles will be coming to pastor the church, and at the end of the month, the church family will be voting on the new Pastor for St. Matthew's."

I told Deacon Timothy I do not care who comes after me, but no one is better. "I may not have been your first choice, but I am the right choice. I am not worried about who comes before or after me. No one can mount up to what God put into me. I believe this job belonged to me when you allowed me to come for an interview."

Deacon Timothy said, "Dr. Davis, if you have some free time, I would like to invite you to dinner, and then you can go home afterward."

I said to Deacon Timothy, "Look at my size. I love to eat any time of the day, so yes, I would love to eat, but Michael must come because I am riding with him." He said that would be great.

Deacon Timothy said, "Dr. Davis, let me go so you can clean yourself up for dinner. I will be waiting for you to come out. I will be at Bible study on Wednesday evening."

As I was walking out of the church, Petro saw me, he came to pick me up, and I said to myself, "What is this?" Because this man never did all this for me. He was not able to get to me, so he stopped. I was waiting for Deacon Dennis to walk with me to the truck, and when I got in, he stood at the truck's window.

He said, "Dr. Davis, I enjoyed service today, and I will be in your Bible study on Wednesday night."

Deacon Dennis said, "Dr. Davis, you see that house over there. The people that own the house are moving. When they move, St. Matthew's will get the first offer to buy the house."

I said, "Deacon Dennis, that would be great because that will be my parsonage when I become your pastor."

Deacon Timothy said, "Dr. Davis, follow me to the restaurant."

I said, "Go on, Michael and I are behind you, boss man."

We went to this big restaurant. I had never been to a restaurant called Fatz before. I asked Petro, "If Deacon Timothy was looking at our size because this is a buffet restaurant." When we walked into the restaurant, I looked for the buffet bar, but there was none. Deacon Timothy had the young man playing the guitar with him at the church. Deacon Timothy told us that we had to wait for a waiter so that we could be seated. On our way to our table, I told Petro they do not have a buffet bar, and he said, "Pastor, you have to order your food from a menu, and then started laughing at me." The food was great. I just had to keep ordering food over and over.

Deacon Timothy ordered his wife her favorite chicken sandwich from Fatz. He called his wife to let her know he had ordered her a chicken sandwich, but she told him she had had something to eat. Deacon Timothy asked Michael if he would like this sandwich. He said, "No, sir."

Then he said, "Dr. Davis, do you want the sandwich?"

I said, "Pass it to me."

Michael looked at me and asked me for half of my sandwich, and I told him, "You have not because when asked, you said no. My job is to make you a man to your word, no, because this is my sandwich now, and I am eating it all, Petro."

The young man with Deacon Timothy said, "If Dr. Davis becomes the pastor at St. Matthew, we will need to take out insurance."

When we all finished eating our dinner, Deacon Timothy paid for everyone. The bill was like a mortgage payment because Dr. Davis was eating so much. He said it will be at a buffet restaurant if we go out to dinner. As we walked out to our vehicles, I said, "Deacon Timothy, I hope you do not stop taking me out to eat, but I will see you Wednesday night for Bible study."

On our way home, Petro and I talked about the wonderful service. I said, "What a great church family. I am already in love with this church family."

I asked Petro, "Do you believe Deacon Timothy will take us to eat next Sunday?"

He said, "If he does, I will not say no anymore."

When we returned to Marion, Petro went to my mother's restaurant. He got out of the truck, and I waited for him to come to my door and open it. Petro was walking towards the restaurant, then he stopped and turned around and said, "We are not at Saint Matthew's. You better open your door and get up."

I opened the door, exited the truck, and entered the restaurant. My sister and family said they had an awesome time in service today.

"We will be going back on the 3rd Sunday."

Petro said, "I was in the last pew in the church to see everyone. Pastor D, those people enjoyed the service. They were captivated by what you were saying. I will be getting off work at 6:00 pm on Wednesday because I will be at Bible study."

Dr. Henry McGill came into the restaurant, and I told him how wonderful the service went and how they treated me like a king at St. Matthew's Missionary Baptist Church. I told him, "I love that church family."

He said, "I am immensely proud of what God is doing in your life, Pastor D. I will be praying that you become the new Pastor of St. Matthew's Missionary Baptist Church."

Dr. Henry McGill got something to eat and played checkers until the restaurant closed. People were coming to buy dinners this Sunday, and business started booming. I said to my mother, "Becca's place is back." I closed the restaurant, went home, and started working on my Bible study lesson for Wednesday night. Time passed by fast, but the days passed by even faster.

The night before the biggest night of my life: I had everything together, but I went over and over it then. After that, I felt more confident that St. Matthew's Missionary Baptist Church needed this. Wednesday came as time went by so quickly that it was time for me to get ready. I waited for my sister to come because I had to drive her car. Alethea drove up in the yard. I walked out. It was 6:15 pm, and I got right in the car.

Alethea said, "Pastor D, I am praying tonight will be a great night for you."

As I was on my way to Bible study, I started praying, saying Lord, give me the words to say so that this church family can better understand your word. By the time I ended my prayer, I was somewhere on Hwy 319. It did not take long at all for me to get to the church. I drove up to the parking lot, and there were cars throughout the parking lot. I was smiling. It looked like the church members had invited someone to come with them to Bible study. When I entered the church, someone said, "Dr. Davis, we do not have Bible study in the sanctuary. We have it in the classroom."

I walked into the classroom, found a place to sit, and started reviewing the Bible study. There were more people in Bible study than at church Sunday morning. One of the Deacons started Bible study and said, "Everyone, put your hands together for our teacher, Dr. Bennie T. Davis." I went to the front of the class and introduced myself.

I said, "I would like you all to call me Pastor D, but if you choose Dr. Davis, that is up to you. Pastor D is fine with me. Is that okay with you, St. Matthew's?"

Someone said, "Pastor D, it is good with us."

I started teaching the class. An hour went by so fast, but it was so good everyone got involved with the Bible study. They asked questions, and I gave them answers. I encouraged everyone to give their input because I told them we are all here to learn from each other. Deacon Ralph Van Fore asked a few questions, and then I answered those questions, and then I ended Bible study. As I was getting my things together to leave, Susan Fore came to me and introduced herself and her husband, Deacon Fore.

She said, "Pastor D, my husband, and I enjoyed you on Sunday and Bible study tonight. I am looking forward to next Wednesday's Bible study."

A few people came to me. Some said, "Pastor D, you are the only candidate trying out for St. Matthews that answers Deacon Fore's questions; now you have his respect."

I smiled, and I said, "I enjoy teaching."

Different ones came and said how much they learned and enjoyed Bible study. I said to myself, 'Look at God.'

They said they would be looking forward to next Wednesday. Someone said, "How about Sunday?" Deacon Dennis told them that church service is only the first and third Sunday, and someone said we need Pastor D every Sunday.

I told everyone that I needed them to invite as many people as possible for Bible study next Wednesday night. Petro was there. As soon as we left the parking lot, he said, "Pastor D, I had an awesome time in Bible study tonight."

When we returned to Marion, Petro and I went to the Huddle House to get something to eat. We talked about Bible study, and Petro said, "There were more people in Bible study than in the Sunday morning service."

I said the church family went out and invited people to Bible study. I told them I needed them to do that same thing next week and invite even more people for Wednesday and Sunday morning service on the 3rd Sunday.

I only got one more opportunity to preach and have three more Bible studies. I told Petro I wanted to become the Pastor of St. Matthews Missionary Baptist Church. I know I have a lot for them to overcome, but if they can overcome my past and allow me to become their pastor, I will work hard. I would work hard to make St. Matthews the number one church in Kingston Lake. I have a vision right now for that church, and when I become the Pastor, I will do many great things with the help of that church family. Together with hard work, St. Matthews will go places they have never been before.

I told Petro when I got home tonight, I would start studying for Bible study next Wednesday night. Petro said, "I will be there next week because I have a few more days to get off early."

Next week, I will bring Alethea Davis, Olentha Shaw, and Anisha Shaw as my guest. When I drove in the yard, I could not wait to tell my aunt Olentha how wonderful my first bible study was at St. Matthews Missionary Baptist Church.

As soon as I arrived at the house, I started calling Aunt Olentha, "I have some great news to tell you about my experience at St. Matthews today." I went to her room and told her the church family received me. I told her that I would love for you and Anisha to come with me to Bible study this Wednesday. Olentha said, "I would be more than honored to go with you because I am so happy for you,

Pastor D. I know if they choose you, they will have a Pastor who will make each person better and greater in their walk with the Lord. I might be biased because I am your aunt, but I believe in your work for the Lord."

I went to my room and started preparing myself for Wednesday night. I wanted to captivate them during Bible study. I could not sleep that much that night. All I was doing was dreaming about becoming the pastor of St. Matthews Missionary Baptist Church. I am never going to leave them. I will be right there until the day I take my last breath. That is how much I loved becoming the pastor at St. Matthews Missionary Baptist Church. The days and nights went by so fast. It was already the night before Bible study, and I had that same excitement.

Most of all, I felt the presence of the Lord as I was studying the Bible. I knew I stayed up longer than I slept, going over and over the Bible study lesson for Wednesday night. My sister drove up and called for me to come so she could get on the road to go to St. Matthews. I was so happy because I had five guests besides myself going to Bible study with me. We got on the road to St. Matthews, and on the way, I just prayed that God use me to bless the church family and guests.

My sister got on Hwy 319, and I said to myself, "It's time," and my heart started beating faster. I just closed my eyes and meditated on the word of the Lord. Within minutes, I heard the signal light come on to turn into the church parking lot. Petro was already there waiting for my arrival. When he saw the car, he got out of his truck and walked to the car to help me with my belongings. There were more cars this week than last, so I knew there were more people. We entered the church simultaneously and went into the classroom for Bible study. Since the classroom was occupied with most of the guests, I knew my job was to get them to come back to Bible study and church on Sunday.

Someone from the church opened Bible study, and shortly after that, they turned it over into my hands. One of the first things I did was have all the guests give their names and tell the name of the church they attend. I guessed to let everyone know what church they attended because now I knew who to focus on. For those not going to church or a member of another church, my job was to make them a part of the Saint Matthews Missionary Baptist Church family. I made sure that within that hour, I asked each of our guests a question so they would feel the love of the church family along with Pastor D. Each person in Bible study was made to feel important. I knew I did my job because the whole class was responding. I did this by encouraging them to join Saint Matthews Missionary Baptist Church.

What surprised me was that a few were members of Saint Matthews Missionary Baptist Church. Some of the members at Bible study last Wednesday night invited members of the church who stopped coming to church to come back to Saint Matthew's Missionary Baptist Church for Bible study. They needed to hear Pastor D teach Bible study because he is good. I told everyone at Bible study that the doors at Saint Matthew's Missionary Baptist Church never closed on you. Our doors are always open, waiting for you to return to the church family that will never stop loving you.

To you that do not have a church home. The doors are also open for each of you to come on and be a part of the greatest church family. I invited each of them to come on Sunday and bring people with them because Saint Matthews Missionary Baptist Church has an outstanding speaker who will be here by the name of Dr. Bennie T. Davis. I said if you do not know who Dr. Bennie T. Davis is, it is yours truly. I had them open their bibles, and I began teaching class. That night, there were between 25 and 30 people in this Bible study. The classroom was getting crowded. I told myself I had two more Bible studies, and then I had to get more people to attend Bible study.

I encouraged everybody to invite as many people as possible at the end of the Bible study. Before I had our prayer, I encouraged everyone to come, and please join us on Sunday morning because God has a word for each one of them. I need each of you to invite as many people as possible because, on Sunday, the church needs to be packed. After all, this will be my last church service here before you all vote for the pastor of this church. I went around the classroom asking each person if they had a prayer request and to please give it now because after we finished praying, I would dismiss. I realized that my 60 minutes would be up. A few other members wanted me to keep going, but I said no, I must follow protocol.

As I began to pray, I could feel the presence of God just moving within the classroom. The people began to cry to the Lord, giving God thanks and how good he had been to them. We had an anointing prayer service at the end of Bible study. The people's faith was elevated, and when I dismissed the church, more people approached me that night. One of the members was Susan Fore, the wife of Saint Matthew's oldest deacon, Deacon Van Fore. She said she enjoyed Bible study and was still excited from last Wednesday night. Susan Fore said how much she was looking forward to Sunday morning service; she told me, "Pastor D, I will vote for you to be a pastor because we have never had this many people at Bible study since I have been here at Saint Matthew's Missionary Baptist Church."

I said, "You know what your vote means."

She said, "What does it mean, Pastor D."

I said, "It means to vote out the enemy, so if you get anyone besides me as a pastor, you all will vote in the enemy."

I said, "When I become the pastor at Saint Matthew's Missionary Baptist Church, this will be the hottest church in Kingston Lake."

I spoke with Minister Anderson and reminded her not to forget when I came to take my seat. I would like her to come up and take the seat beside me. I also let her know that as long as I am at this church, she will have something to do during church service every Sunday. When I walked away from Minister Anderson, a young man approached me and shook my hand. He introduced himself and said, "My name is Henry Coleman, president of the usher ministry here at Saint Matthew's missionary. Is there anything you would like the ushers to do on Sunday?"

I said, "No, Sir, the ushers did a wonderful job on the 1st Sunday."

He said, "Pastor D, if there is anything you need the ushers to do, here's my phone number. Call me and let me know, and I will ensure it happens for you."

Henry Coleman made me feel so important on that Bible study night. I did not know what to say because no church member had ever treated me with that respect. I would see other preachers when they came to a church to do a service or if I were visiting a church. They would have church staff around them doing different things for the preacher. I always dreamt that one day, that pastor or preacher could be me. I would say to myself wake up, Bennie, it is just a dream that could never be you if I could just feel that one time here. I am at Saint Matthew's Missionary Baptist Church, and Harry Coleman allowed me to feel a love I never felt in my whole Christian walk. On this Wednesday night after Bible study, Henry Coleman allowed me to feel a certain love that I never felt in my life that was merely a dream, but now it is a reality because of Henry Coleman.

At this time, my mind was made up: I was going to become the pastor of this church. I was never surrounded by people with as much love, compassion, and the desire to succeed. It just blew my mind that this man said, "Pastor D, I had a good time tonight in Bible study." Deacon Dennis let me know that he enjoyed Bible study and was looking forward to service on Sunday morning. I got all my materials together and then got my belongings. Deacon Timothy came and spoke to me to let me know that he enjoyed Bible study. He asked me what you are doing after church service on Sunday.

I said, "Deacon Timothy, right now, I do not have anything planned."

He said, "We will talk on Sunday, Pastor D, and I will bring some guests to church on Sunday."

I walked towards the church door to go out, and someone shouted, "Pastor D., I will see you Sunday!"

I said, "Bring some people with you!" The young lady said, "I will have some guests with me, Pastor D. I will see you Sunday."

Petro was walking with me and said, "These people really love you, Pastor D."

I replied, "I also really love this church family."

As I got in the car, someone was driving out of the parking lot and said, "I will see you Sunday, Pastor D, and I am going to bring my family and friends."

I said, "Also, come to Sunday school."

After putting my things in the car, Deacon Timothy approached me and said, "On Sunday, I would like for you to teach the Sunday school lesson and do the morning service."

I said, "Deacon Timothy, it would be an honor to teach Sunday school. I had a wonderful time tonight, and thank you and the Deacon ministry and the church family for how you all made me feel like a part of the Saint Matthew Missionary Baptist Church family."

When we got on the highway, Petro called me and said that Bible study was wonderful tonight and that I did a great job. I asked Petro if he had anything to do on Sunday after church because Deacon

Timothy would like him and me to go to eat with him. Petro said, "I do not have anything to do but go out to eat on Sunday."

Petro pulled over so I could get in the truck with him, so my sister also pulled over. I got in the truck with Petro. We got back on the road, and we went to Marion so that we could go by the Huddle House to get something to eat. As we ate, Petro said, "Pastor D, on Sunday, you must stand out because Saint Matthews will be voting at the end of December. If everyone that said they will bring a guest does, it will be a nice crowd at Sunday morning worship service."

I said, "Petro, if they get the people in the house of the Lord, the Spirit of the Lord has given me a word for that house. Each person will be touched and delivered. There is no way that they will not come back to Saint Matthew's Missionary Baptist Church. I will invite all of them to Wednesday night Bible study because God will open their spiritual eye." After Petro and I finished eating, he took me home. On the way to the house, I told him that I must start working on my sermon for Sunday.

When I went into the house, I told my mother what happened in Bible study, and then I went to my room and started working on my sermon for Sunday. I had no time to waste because Sunday would come so fast, and I was expecting people to come from all over to Saint Matthew's Missionary Baptist Church. I was reading the Bible when my phone started ringing, and Deacon Timothy called me to give me the Sunday school lesson. I thanked him for calling me because I would call him tomorrow as I felt it was too late to call tonight. I reminded myself that some things come through fasting and praying as I continued my studies. I planned to fast and pray the rest of the week because this is one of those times to do it. I want Sunday to be anointed during the Sunday school lesson and morning service.

I went back to working on my sermon and Sunday school lesson. The time was passing by so fast. It was the night before the biggest day of my life. My last sermon at Saint Matthew's Missionary Baptist Church before the church voted on a pastor, I could not sleep much that night. My eyes remained open. I sat up and reviewed the Sunday school lesson several times before the sun came up. Petro called me to make sure that I was up and going over my work and that he would pick me up early. He wanted to be in the parking lot, waiting for the doors to open.

After I hung up the phone with Petro, I reviewed my Sunday school and sermon again. I got up and prepared myself for church. By the time I finished, Petro was outside my house. My phone started ringing; sure enough, it was Petro. I asked him to give me 10 minutes, and I would be out. Shortly after, I walked out the door overly excited about attending Saint Matthew's Missionary Baptist Church.

Petro said, "I thought I had to call you again, boss man."

I said, "I am far from sleep and from being late for church today."

As I got in the truck, Petro said let's go get something to eat, then head to the church. Petro ordered his food and asked me what I wanted, as it was on him that day. I told him I was too nervous to eat now but would get something after church. Petro got his food and said Saint Matthews Missionary Baptist Church is our next stop.

I do not know what was happening, but it did not take long for us to get to Saint Matthew's Missionary Baptist Church. Petro drove into the parking lot, and no one was there yet. There were no cars in the parking lot; we were the first ones at the church. Petro said, "Pastor D., just sit there and go over your Sunday school lesson and your sermon."

He never said anything else to me, and because of that, I was able to focus so much on the job that was at hand for me. About 15 minutes later, cars started driving into the parking lot. As the people walked by the vehicle, they said, "Good morning, Pastor D," as they went to the church. Some waived their hand at me.

Petro said, "Pastor D, it is about time to go into the church." Right then, I just started praying and asking God to use me in Sunday school and in morning service. "Allow someone, if not everyone, to be encouraged and come to Christ. Amen." As soon as I finished, Petro got out of the truck and opened the door for me, and he also took my briefcase. When Petro picked me up from my house, he did not get out of his truck to help me in, but when he got to the house of the Lord, he did. I said to myself, I better sit back and enjoy because this will not be happening all the time.

Petro and I entered the church. Petro led me to the front pew, and he stood there until I was seated. He put my briefcase beside me and went to the back of the class so that he could see everyone in the class. Someone started Sunday school, and then I, Dr. Bennie T. Davis, was introduced to the Sunday school class as the teacher for the day. There were more people in Sunday school than on the first Sunday in November. The class was responding to the questions I gave them, and at the end of Sunday school, to make sure that everybody was paying attention, I planned to ask a question.

Everyone participated by raising their hands and asking questions, so I knew they paid attention. The class and I enjoyed ourselves so much that time went by quickly, and Superintendent Deacon Terry Williams stopped the class. The people in the class were still asking questions, and I was answering the questions. I ended Sunday school as I was asked. I told everyone to stretch, get some water, or go to the restroom.

I went to the office. Petro grabbed my briefcase and carried it to my office. Petro said, "Pastor D, Sunday school was great. The class loved you because I was there to see each of them."

He said, "Let me go so I can hear what is being said about you."

On his way out the door, he said, "Pastor D, you must preach this sermon like you never preached before because there are no do-overs. This is your last Sunday. Let them see what they would be missing if you do not become their pastor."

Before Petro could close the door, I reviewed my sermon one last time.

About 20 to 25 minutes later, a knock came to the door. I said to the person to come in. It was Cindy. She said, "Pastor D, it is time for you to come up front." I asked her to give me a minute, and she pulled the door together. I opened the door to walk out, and Cindy was standing there. I told her, "I just do not want to be Pastor D but the pastor of St. Matthews Missionary Baptist Church." But she never said a word about what I said. She said, "Pastor D, follow me," and smiled. Cindy led me into the sanctuary, and after I took my seat, Minister Anderson came up and took her seat. I told her that I needed her to do the prayer. Before she could take her seat, another Minister came up that was a guest. I asked him to read the scripture. I looked at the congregation, and about forty to forty-five people were in the church service that morning.

I called the church to worship. The scripture and the prayer were powerful. The Saint Matthews Missionary Baptist Church choir sang a song suitable for preaching. My subject was 'Overcoming Public Opinion.'

Throughout the service, the congregation talked back to me by clapping their hands and stomping their feet; some were speaking in unknown tongues and shouting amen. I told Saint Matthew's Missionary Baptist Church, "Why are you still asking for a pastor when God has already answered your prayer by sending you a pastor, me, Pastor D, and I am standing right before you."

I told the church family and guests to praise the Lord for whatever they need the Lord to do for them right now.

"Praise him like you lost your mind."

I called an altar call, and the people came from all over the sanctuary. The altar was filled with people. I had each one to hold someone's hand on the right and left of them. I said to them tell the person next to you that one hand is for you, and the other hand is to help someone else. After the prayer, I said Amen. I told the people to find someone and tell them whatever they had just been praising God for, it has just been answered, and the answer is it is already done. Right then, some of the people started throwing up their hands, praising God and giving him thanks. I dismissed the service by telling them to go to three people, telling them I had overcome public opinion.

Now point your finger at someone and say I command you to overcome public opinion. Saint Matthews Missionary Baptist Church, consider yourself dismissed. I walked down the altar steps onto the sanctuary floor, and people surrounded me, shaking my hand, hugging me, and saying how much they enjoyed the service. I told the people the only way I could come back was to be the pastor. Some said you are coming back because you will be the pastor. I proceeded to walk into the back of the office.

As I was going, different ones still came to shake my hand. Most of them told me how much they enjoyed the service and how the Word of God touched them. I went into the office, pulled the door together, and started thanking God for the opportunity to be one of the two candidates to become pastor of this wonderful church family.

By the time I sat down, a knock came at the door. I said enter, and the deacons walked into the office.

Deacon Timothy said, "On behalf of the Deacon ministry, Dr. Bennie Davis, we really enjoyed service today."

He proceeded to tell me that the deacons came together and decided that they would like for me to do Bible study for December. He said,

"Dr. Davis, because of the turnout of people that have been coming, they are still excited about coming to our Bible study, but they would love for you to be the teacher."

I informed Deacon Timothy and the other deacons that it would be a pleasure and an honor for me to come to teach Bible study in December. I asked how about the preacher that is coming in December. Deacon Timothy said he would only preach 1st and 3rd Sunday.

The preacher has already been here for some time. He did Bible study, but more people are coming out now to Bible study than we have had since he has been teaching.

He said, "Dr. Bennie Davis, for you to come in December to do Bible study, how much money do we need to pay you."

I said, "Just give me $25 for gas, and I will be here, Deacon Timothy."

Deacon Dennis said his wife asked him, "Is Dr. Davis a good teacher? Is the former pastor as good as Dr. Davis?"

Deacon Dennis told her we never had anyone to try out to be pastor at Saint Matthew's Missionary Baptist Church that could teach or preach like him. Our former Pastor cannot touch Dr. Davis. I said to him I am looking for your vote. Deacon Terry Williams said to me that he enjoyed Bible study and the number of people coming out to it.

After we agreed that I would do Bible study for December, Deacon Timothy said, "Pastor D, would you like to go out to eat today?"

I said, "Look at my size! I love to eat, so yes, sir! I want to go out and eat today."

Deacon Timothy said, "My wife, Carrie Gerald, will be going to dinner with us."

I said, "Deacon Timothy, are we going to the same restaurant, and he said not today; I am not making a mortgage payment. We are going to an all-you-can-eat buffet."

I told Deacon Timothy, "I see you are my kind of Deacon."

He said, "I will be waiting for you in the parking lot."

As the deacons walked out the door and as soon as the door was pulled together, I threw my hands in the air, opened my mouth, and screamed in my mind, 'Thank you, God, thank you, God, for all you did for me here at Saint Matthew's Missionary Baptist Church.'

Shortly after that, I got my briefcase and my coat. I opened the door to walk out of the office, and Petro was standing at the door. He was about to knock. He grabbed my briefcase from me, and we went out the door and walked towards the truck. I told him we were going out to eat, but we had to follow Deacon Timothy and his wife to the restaurant. Deacon Timothy said that we were going to eat buffet.

We got into the truck, and Petro followed Deacon Timothy as we headed to Myrtle Beach. As we were pulling into the parking lot, I saw that it was Bennett's Seafood restaurant. Petro dropped me off at the door of the restaurant.

It was a long wait before they found a park and were back at the doorway. I was waiting for everyone. We walked into the restaurant all together. It was incredibly beautiful inside the restaurant, and food was everywhere—over 200 different foods.

I busted some crab legs. I did put a dent in the food. Deacon Timothy's wife, Carrie, laughed at me so much. Carrie said, "Pastor D, you can really eat."

I was enjoying myself, and the time just went by so fast. I said to myself, now, Deacon Timothy is courting me, but he does not have to court me anymore because the job to become the pastor of Saint Matthews Missionary Baptist Church has been filled. Petro put some eating down also. I told him, "Today, you do not have to worry about anyone asking you if you want something. Today, you can get anything you want to eat, but I need not say anything because you are doing a great job by yourself."

After we left the restaurant and were on our way home, I told Petro how wonderful service was but then fell asleep. When Petro woke me up, I was home, and he said, "Get your briefcase and get out of my truck."

I said, "Petro, do as you do for me at Saint Matthew's Missionary Baptist Church."

He looked at me and said, "Get out of my truck. I am not getting anything."

So, as I was getting out, I said, "Petro, I am going to see Mayor Bobby Davis tomorrow. I am going to go to ask him about my car. I hope he will let me get the car back because it would be good if I had my car so that I would not have to depend on you or my sister to get back to Saint Matthew's Missionary Baptist Church."

That Monday morning, I got up with my mind made up that I was not going to call because I wanted the element of surprise. The Mayor had a walk-in policy. Anytime anyone had to see him, his doors were open, so on that Monday, I made sure I went to City Hall.

The secretary asked, "Who would you like to see, Pastor D?"

I said, "I would like to see Mayor Bobby Davis."

She said, "Give me a moment," and then she pointed me toward the Mayor's office. I was going towards his office, and out of nowhere, Mayor Bobby Davis came from around the corner. As soon as I saw the Mayor, I approached him, and he only said, "Bennie, I am not able to talk with you. The city attorney has advised me not to talk with you for any reason."

What got me about that is out of everybody living in the city of Marion, why would a city attorney say to the Mayor not to communicate with Bennie Davis? The city attorney was out of Columbia, SC, so why would they say that to the Mayor? This is when I started thinking about when my mother's restaurant was busted for those handbags. That happened only because of Mayor Bobby Davis because about a week and a half before SLED came and busted the restaurant, the Mayor came to the restaurant and looked in it from the window but never came inside. Mama asked, "Why is the Mayor looking through the window?"

I said to my mother I did not know why because we were not doing anything illegal; he was looking at the sneakers that were on the rack. I did not say anything to him. I walked out because he would not listen to me. The Mayor would not allow me to say anything at all; that was all that I could think about while I was walking out of the City Hall building. This Mayor had me busted. I knew then I had to devise something else to get my car back. I got a phone call from my attorney, Thurmond Brooker, to inform me that I had to be in court soon.

I set up an appointment for my mother and me to visit his office. A few days later, we went to his office, and our attorney told us we still had to go to court about the young boy, "But Bennie, I need you to apply for pre-trial intervention (PTI)."

I said to him, "I have a site for this program. People do their community service with me." My attorney said you should be able to get into this program. Just a short time ago, Marion County had a big bust for illegal gambling machines, and not one person made any time but just got a slap on the hand with PTI. My attorney said, "Because of what you have been charged with, Bennie, you should be able to get PTI."

My attorney said, "You must get this done as soon as possible."

I left his office and went to apply for PTI the same day because I was trying out for a church to become the pastor and needed to get this off my criminal record. I aim to have these charges dismissed by the time the general session court resumes. It was time for general session court. Because I applied for PTI and received my receipt, I was dismissed from court for that term.

A month later, my application for PTI went through. I got a phone call from an agent, and she said as of this day, you are no longer allowed to be a representative for PTI. I asked the agent, "Why not? I have been doing it all these years?"

That is when the lady said, "Get a not guilty or have the charges dropped, then come back and start doing PTI again."

I said, "Thank you so much."

Bible study was amazing; it was our last Bible study for December. I know this was it before they voted for a new pastor. I told the class that I am a lion, and you must go after whatever you want in life.

"I would love to become pastor at Saint Matthew's Missionary Baptist Church. I am Pastor D; no one came before me, or after me that is better than me. This is the attitude you must have in your life. Go after whatever you want with all your heart; do not let anyone tell you it does not belong to you."

I thanked the deacons, search committee, and members for supporting me for the months of November and December. I told them to vote for the best person for this church and not vote for friendship.

"I may not have been your first choice, but I am the greatest pastor this church will ever have, so that makes me the right choice."

I let them know that I would be praying for the church family and that if they needed me for anything, I was just a phone call away. I dismissed my final Bible study class, and I wished everyone a Merry

Christmas and a Happy New Year. It was the last Saturday night in December. At about 8:00 PM, a phone call came in; I answered the phone. I was in the restaurant sitting down, and the voice on the other end was Deacon Timothy. I said hold on, then I walked outside.

I got in my car and said, "I can hear you now."

He said, "This is Deacon Timothy Gerald, Chairman of the Deacon ministry at Saint Matthew's Missionary Baptist Church. Dr. Bennie Davis, I am calling to inform you that you are the new pastor at Saint Matthew's Missionary Baptist Church."

Tears started coming down my eyes and meeting under my chin. It was tears of joy.

I was speechless because this was the first time I had accomplished something this great. When the man said it was not going to happen, some said, "Pastor D, you are wasting your time because they will overlook you." But God won't. When I got myself together, I said, "Deacon Timothy, tell me one more time." He repeated, "Dr. Bennie Davis, you are the new Pastor at St. Matthew Missionary Baptist Church."

12. UNQUALIFIED

Throughout the Bible, God has used unqualified people in man's eyesight, but God could see that they were qualified for the task. He had set before them. Man views the worst of a person, but God sees a person's greatness. Noah was a drunk, and out of all the qualified men, God chose Noah to build the Ark for the people. Jacob was a liar, a swindler, a trickster, and someone who tricked his brother from his inheritance. He was the one who wrestled with the angel all night and said I am not going to let you go until you bless me. Moses was a killer but went to Pharaoh to release God's people and let them go. David was a womanizer and had a husband killed so he could be with his wife, but God said he is a man after my own heart. Throughout my life, people listed me as unqualified, but God qualified me to do the test before me.

Today, I know I am more than a conqueror throughout everything I tried for Saint Matthews Missionary Baptist Church (SMMBC). The officers and members of the church did not look at my outer appearance, but they saw greatness and what I could bring to the church. After I hung up the phone, I called some of my friends to tell them the good news that Deacon Timothy had just called to tell me that I was the new pastor at Saint Matthews Missionary Baptist Church in Aynor, SC.

The friends I called were church people and pastors to tell them the good news. I told a pastor I was talking to on the phone that SMMBC voted for a pastor tonight, and before I could tell the pastor the good news, he said to me, "Do not put your head down because you were not chosen to be the new pastor."

"Pastor D, you are unqualified to pastor Saint Matthews Missionary Baptist Church."

As soon as the pastor finished saying this to me, I said to him, "The chairman of the Deacon ministry called me tonight and said to me, 'Dr. Davis, we voted tonight, and you are our new pastor of Saint Matthews Missionary Baptist Church. Congratulations, Pastor D.'"

Then his phone hung up, and I heard a dial tone. I was in the restaurant, sharing with my family that I was named the new pastor of SMMBC. The preacher who was a candidate with me for the church was asked to come the first Sunday in January since they believed he would be the new Pastor. God had an unqualified man for the job. I told Deacon Timothy, "Let him come in, and I will start on the 3rd Sunday, but I will be at Bible study."

I was so excited about Bible study and prayer service because this would be the first time I have been to SMMBC as the Pastor. A few new people came to Bible study and prayer service to meet the new pastor. Before I began the prayer service, I asked if there were any prayer requests. People started standing up with their prayer requests and saying how happy they were about voting me in as pastor. At the end of Bible study and prayer service, people approached me, shaking my hand, hugging me, and congratulating me for being the new pastor. Some said that they stopped coming to church, but they heard about the wonderful time that was going on at SMMBC.

We were hoping that you would be voted as pastor, and now that it happened, you will see us on Sunday. It was only a few days before the 3rd Sunday when I would be announced as pastor of SMMBC. The excitement was so great that I accomplished something that man said would never happen. This is an opportunity of a lifetime because now I can let people see that God can use an unqualified man. The one that man gave up, God has used for him. Throughout the week, I tried to figure out what I would preach on Sunday. I needed to have something outstanding, superb. I prayed and asked God to give me something that would bless the church family.

The spirit of the Lord gave me the subject 'After.' That Sunday morning, it was an outstanding Sunday school. The morning service started, and as I looked out in the congregation, there were so many new faces. It was between 50 to 60 people in our worship service. After the church announcements, Deacon Timothy Gerald, Deacon Dennis Gerald, Deacon Terry Williams, and Deacon Van Fore walked up to the front of the church, and I was asked to stand. The chairperson of the Deacon ministry, Timothy Gerald, introduced me to the congregation. He said, "Dr. Bennie T. Davis is the new Pastor of St. Matthews Missionary Baptist Church, and as of this moment, you are a Pastor and our leader. We trust that you will take us to places that we have never been before." Deacon Timothy asked the congregation to stand up and welcome me to the church family.

All but a few clapped their hands and said thank you, Lord. All I could do was stand there. The tears just started running down my face. I looked around the church, and everyone looked happy about their new Pastor. The only thing I could say was look at God. This was an accomplishment that I thought could never happen, but God took an unqualified young man and said I have use for him at Saint Matthew Missionary Baptist Church. I knew every day, every opportunity I had. I just wanted God to use me so that this church goes higher. We had a high time in the Lord during morning service. After church, people came to me, hugged me, shook my hand, and told me how happy they were that I was the new Pastor of SMMBC.

Susan Fore hugged me, and I asked her, "Would you give me your phone number so I can call you because I need your help. Only you can do this for me." Susan wrote her phone number down on paper and handed it to me. As I walked away from Susan Fore, Deacon Timothy came to me and said, "Pastor, do not leave because the deacons and I are coming to your office to see you."

Petro and I went to my office. As we were walking, Petro said, "Today, I enjoyed service, and most of the people who were in the sanctuary also enjoyed the service."

We walked into the office, and I told Petro, "The deacons are coming to meet with me, so when they come in, I need you to excuse yourself and wait for me in the truck."

Shortly after that, a knock came to the door. Deacon Timothy and the other deacons of the church entered the office. Petro walked out and pulled the door together. I asked the deacons to have a seat and said, "I thank you for the opportunity to become the Pastor here at SMMBC. Before we go any further, I need to ask you all something. Do you want a Pastor, or do you want a Preacher? Now, the difference between a pastor and a preacher is that a pastor will make decisions to make the church greater. Changes will come to the church that you may not like at all. A preacher is going to let everything stay the same. The preacher is just going to preach, then take his or her stipend and go home. Currently, I need to know what it is you want. Either one you want for this church is the job I will do."

Deacon Timothy said this church needs a pastor, and the other Deacons agreed. I told the Deacons, "It is time for this church to have a Pastor. We must work together in unity before we make any decisions for the church body. We are going to have a meeting in this office to discuss it. Then, we will vote on whatever we discuss, and the majority wins. If it is something I would like to do, but the majority says no, that is what will be done. We will do this so when we go before the church body, we will be in unity. No one will say I am not for that because whatever the majority wants to do. All of us are going to support the idea because we come together as one. The church will get behind the idea, and it will come to pass with everyone working together. There is no plan B or C; it is only plan A. If we develop plans B and C, we will take away from plan A.

That is why Plan A will fail, so let us not take away from Plan A and give it everything we have inside of us. The last Saturday in every month, we will meet just the Pastor and Deacons."

I proceeded to ask the deacons how much the mortgage was here at the church, and Deacon Timothy said the amount. I asked, "Is it a struggle to pay the mortgage?"

Deacon Timothy said, "No, we pay on time each month, but this month, we borrowed the money because we were short $1000 from the usher ministry."

I told Deacon Timothy and the other deacons that this was the last time we would borrow the money from any ministry or person in this church. "As of this day, going forward, the church will take care of itself. My vision for this church is in five to ten years, the church will be paid off, and the mortgage will be burned up. For us to do this, we must reach our goals, and then the vision will happen. On the 1st Sunday in February, I would like to have a church meeting right after church, members only."

Deacon Dennis said that would be fine, and he will make sure that it is put on the announcements in Sunday school and Wednesday night at Bible study. I asked about the trustee's ministry. Deacon Dennis said the last Pastor did not put the trustee ministry together. So, I said to them I would be working on getting a trustee ministry at SMMBC.

"Now, deacons, I would like for all of you to give me some names, and I have a few people I would like to ask about being on this trustee's ministry. I need the names today before leaving this meeting so we can vote for the trustee ministry and the meeting on 1st Sunday."

We voted, and everyone was in unity. We ended our meeting, and I was so excited about getting started.

I believe that we all left the meeting believing that a change was coming for the better here at SMMBC. Deacon Fore and his wife were still at the church. I went to Susan Fore and told her I needed you to get me every name of everyone who left the church. Make sure you give me their phone numbers because I will call each person and ask them to come back. After all, Saint Matthews Missionary Baptist Church has a new pastor with a new vision. She said, "Dr. Bennie, I will call you; if not by Wednesday, I will have it for you at Bible study." On that Wednesday night at Bible study, we had more new people to come.

I told everyone in Bible study and prayer service that the person who invites the most people each month will get a stipend from the church. We will have an outstanding member of the month. You must invite someone to Sunday service, Sunday school, or Bible study. The month's members will get a gift card, and I will present it to them in the Sunday morning service. I also announced that we will be having our first church meeting on 1st Sunday in February. There were about 40 people at Bible study and prayer service. Susan Fore gave me all the names and phone numbers of the people who had stopped coming to church. I thanked her very much and planned to focus on getting them all back in this church.

That same night, when I arrived home, I started calling every name on the list. I introduced myself as the new pastor at St. Matthew Missionary Baptist Church. I invited them to come back because they needed them at the church. I left my name and number and requested a return call if someone did not answer their phone. The next day, Deacon Terry Williams went to work and told his coworkers that Dr. Bennie Davis had more people in Bible study than he had ever seen since he had been a member at Saint Matthew Missionary Baptist Church. He has been there since the 1970s. He said, "This man can teach and preach the Word of God. We have a pastor now, and every Sunday, we have new people coming to the church."

I was at my mother's restaurant when some ladies drove up, and I welcomed them to Becca's place. I asked for their order. One of the ladies said, "We just decided to come to Marion to see our new Pastor and to let him know that we love him. Pastor D is our Pastor, and we do not want him ever to leave SMMBC."

I started blushing and said, "I am not going any place. The church would have to vote me out from being the pastor."

Then the ladies said, "We are really enjoying church and Bible study so much."

We talked for about 20 minutes, and then they were about to return to the road. Before they left, I reminded them to invite as many people as possible to church and Bible study.

"Pastor D, almost every place we go, someone is talking about SMMBC and their new pastor, Pastor Bennie T. Davis."

Shortly after the conversation, they left.

Sunday morning, when I arrived at church, I saw some more cars, so I knew that the members at SMMBC had invited some guests for Sunday school. Sunday school was packed with our youth and guests. We had an anointed time in the Lord in Sunday school. Morning service started when I walked out of my office and entered the sanctuary; it was packed with guests and people who had stopped coming to this church but are now returning. It was between sixty-eight and seventy-six people in the sanctuary. Our guests stood and told who had invited them to our service. Everybody was so excited to see how the people were coming to service. I do not know how much money was raised before I became the pastor, but now, on Sunday mornings, $3800.00 to $4200.00 was collected. Immediately after the service, we had our church meeting.

This meeting was for me to give them the vision for SMMBC. I gave them the blueprint for us to raise no less than $150,000 for the year.

I went through every program that we were having at the church for that year. We had one program to raise $10,000 and more for our men's day program. Everyone will need to collaborate with the men to make this happen. I reminded everyone about our Black History program and asked everyone to come that Saturday before the program to help clean the church (adults only, no youth). Before I dismissed them, I encouraged everyone to study the blueprint so that the vision could come to pass by reaching our goals. I ended the meeting and went to my office. As I was walking, I overheard some of the members say, "We have a pastor who is here to help us to do great things."

Deacon Timothy came to my office. Explaining that the church family really enjoyed Sunday school because they are seeing the growth of the people that are coming, "We would like for you to teach Sunday School every Sunday. If you consent to coming, what amount to add to your budget?"

I said, "Just give me $30.00 that will get gas and breakfast." He then offered to take Petro and me to dinner. Yes, we ate at Bennett's. I did as I always do; I was still eating while everyone looked at me, wondering where I put all that food. On the way home, Petro looked at me, and I was asleep. He hit me until I got up and said no sleeping in this truck. It did not take long for him to get me home.

Wednesday night, Bible study and prayer came so fast. On this Bible study night, we had questions and answers. Whatever anyone had about the Bible, I allowed them to ask.

Once, someone asked if the deacons were over the pastor. I answered, "A church cannot hear without a deacon, but a church must have a Pastor."

Bible study ended, and I approached one of the young men named Alvin Peters and asked him if he would like to be a part of the trustee ministry here at St. Matthew Missionary Baptist Church. Alvin said,

"Pastor D, let me pray over this, and then I will get back to you in a few days?"

Later that day, Alvin walked into my office with his hands in the air, just thanking God. He came to my desk, fell on his knees, and said, "Pastor D, whatever I can do to help you, that is what I want to do, and yes, I would love to be a trustee here at St. Matthew Missionary Baptist Church."

I thanked him for accepting this responsibility. "I am looking forward to working with you." As we were talking, the deacons walked into my office. I excused him because I needed to meet with the deacons. I had a mission statement for SMMBC that I handed to one of the deacons. Deacon Timothy read the mission statement aloud to everyone. A vote was taken, and the majority voted in favor of it. Now, it will be presented to the church family on 3rd Sunday.

Deacon Dennis told me regardless of who the speaker was for Black History after that program, Saint Matthews Missionary Baptist Church family wanted to hear our Pastor D. I consented, said a prayer, and ended our meeting. Deacon Terry Williams remained and wanted me to know that he objected to the young man being a trustee here at SMMBC since he was not qualified. I asked Deacon Terry Williams why he felt that way about this young man. He began to tell me what he had done with the other pastor and what he was not doing in the church as a member.

I responded, "I do not have anything to do with what happened at SMMBC before I became the pastor. He seems to be a nice man who loves the Lord, and I get along with him. I am going to have a workshop on the job of a Trustee and Deacon ministry. I will inform everyone who becomes a trustee what I am expecting as a trustee. I gave his name to the Deacon ministry. I accepted the recommendation, and three deacons agreed that he would be a great trustee, and you are the only one who disagreed. The majority rules and this young man will be a trustee at SMMBC."

As I was leaving the church, going to my car, Minister Cross came to the car, gave me my suits, and said, "Pastor D, most of the church family along with me do love you and the job that you are doing here at Saint Matthew's Missionary Baptist Church. We must work together and get the people to join the church so when that few come up against you to vote you out as Pastor, and we will have enough support for you to remain our Pastor."

I told her, "Everything will be alright. There is not anyone that wants to get rid of me from being the pastor."

I believe that Minister Cross knew something that she did not share totally with me. "I thank you, Minister Cross, for all the help you have given me." I took the suits and put them in my car. I waited for her to get in her car; after she cranked up, I got in my car, and we both left the church. I drove out of the church parking lot, praying as I went down Hwy 319.

I just started to thank God for surrounding me with such a great church family. Thank you, God, for this opportunity to be the pastor of St. Matthews Missionary Baptist Church as their shepherd. As I was praying, I said, "God, I am not going to let myself down, and I am not going to let the church family down for choosing me to be their pastor, Amen."

I started thinking about how exciting Bible study will be next week. Attendees were hungry to hear the rich word of God and get an understanding by asking questions. Each Bible study got better and better. I arrived in my yard to thank you, Lord, for allowing me a safe journey there and back home.

The next morning, I got up believing something great would happen to me that day. I was just riding around town, and I saw a building for rent out of nowhere. I said I know they want a lot of money for that building. I prayed, "God, please give me what I can afford."

So, I wrote the phone number down, and I called about renting the building. The lady gave me a price, and I told her I needed this building. I asked her to give me 24 hours, and I will have the money. I called Billy Lou Clark and Deacon Alethea Davis and said we must meet today. We set a time for us to meet. At the meeting, I told them about the building I had found and the price.

I said, "Let me show it to you all before giving an answer. Let us look inside. I believe the church will be able to take care of itself." We agreed to get the building, and then I went and paid the money. Now, Greater Christ Temple Church of the Harvest has a new home.

I decided to go to the Marion Detention Center to get my material out of my car to do Bible study. I still did not have a car. I called one of my family friends, Rochelle Hemingway, and asked if she would take me to the Detention Center. She said give me about 15 minutes. I let her know to come to the restaurant to pick me up. She picked me up and took me to the Marion Detention Center.

When she parked the car, she asked, "Can I walk with you if you do not mind?"

I said, "Come on and go with me because someone must open the gate so I can go to my car that they impounded."

We walked into the Detention Center, and an officer working the front desk informed me that I needed to get into the gate to get my books out of the car. The officer said, "Have a seat until someone comes to assist you." Rochelle and I sat down.

I began to tell her how God had blessed me to get a building to have church in and how wonderful things were going at the church. Moments later, an officer from the Sheriff's Department approached me and asked if I was Bennie Davis. I replied yes, "I am. I just came to get some books out of my car for Bible study."

Then he asked me to stand up, which I did. Then the Sheriff said, "Bennie Davis, you are under arrest for sexual assault first degree." He read the warrant to me and said, "Detective Samantha Jackson is the officer in charge of this case, and she will be coming to speak with you. Bennie Davis, as for you leaving, you will not be going home because you are now under arrest." He had me turn around, and he put the handcuffs on me. This was done in the presence of everyone in the lobby and the other Sheriff officers. I said, "Sir, what are you talking about?!" All he said was, "You have the right to remain silent…"

I told Rochelle to go let my Momma know what happened to me. She was shouting what was going on but received no satisfaction of knowing. This was totally unbelievable. As the officer put the handcuffs around my wrist, I could hear the click as he squeezed it so tight. I began to wonder what I did to Samantha Jackson for her to hate me so badly that she was deliberately and intentionally focused on destroying my life. Samantha Jackson had already put my mother and I in jail. I am not a chaplain for the state and federal prison in South Carolina anymore. I do not work with PTI, and I am not a chaplain at the Marion County Detention Center.

Some pastors do not have any respect for me. A few parents stopped allowing me to work with their children, and I am not allowed to go to any of the schools in Marion County. I started screaming in my mind. Samantha Jackson has altered everything meaningful in my life with just a stroke of her pen. I do not have a life, and everything I have accomplished is now being destroyed because of Samantha Jackson. Rochelle said, "You will be alright, Pastor D," as she ran out of the lobby and out the door.

The Sheriff took me to the booking area, and I was not able to stop crying. I told the Sheriff, "I would never take advantage of any young lady by forcing her to have sex with me. I did not do anything like that, so what is going on? You need to tell me something."

The officer said, "Samantha Jackson will see you today, but your accuser cannot come to court, so you will not get a bond until tomorrow; you will be here overnight."

I went through the fingerprinting and mugshots. The officer could not put me in the population (with others who were locked up) because I was a chaplain for years. I was put in the holding cell. I was on my 31-day sacrifice (fast), and God had just opened the door and blessed me with a new building for the Greater Christ Temple Church family. I just became the new Pastor a SMMBC.

God was not just opening doors for me, but He was opening an extra-large door for me, and not just that, but the blessings that God was giving to me could not fit through the door. He was pouring out blessings I did not have enough room to receive. Out of all that, Satan wanted to stop Bennie because if he did not, souls would be coming asking what he must do to be saved. To hear the cell door come together, being locked, knowing I was not getting out for the night was such a hurtful thing. I walked to the window with tears rolling down my face; as I was looking out the window, I was able to see my car, which was impounded a few years ago. I walked to the bed and sat down as my head descended towards the floor. My tears started drying up. I wanted to cry, but no tears were coming out of my eyes. I did not understand why this was happening because someone had made up the biggest lie on me.

Suddenly, I decided to read the warrant. As I was reading the warrant, I noticed that this incident had happened at a clubhouse. I wondered why Samantha Jackson did not ask the owner what had happened, especially since he was a retired Sheriff of Marion County. If she would have just asked him, I would have never been in this jail cell. I continued to read the warrant, and it had been signed ever since September 30, 2014; it is now February 2015. It looked like Samantha Jackson waited intentionally to see me build myself up. By doing different things in my life, she saw that I had become the Pastor of SMMBC. Then Samantha Jackson must have said to herself let me destroy this 'so-called' Pastor D's mission that he accomplished.

Now, I am in general sessions court with three charges: two are from Samantha Jackson and one from Mayor Bobby Davis. For some unknown reason, I believe that Samantha Jackson wanted to ensure I spent a long time in prison. She was not satisfied with just putting my mother and me in jail, but on top has added a sexual assault charge against me. To be a detective, she never investigated either crime but charged me with both. As I sat in that jail cell, I asked myself how many other people in Marion County were making time in prison for a crime or crimes they did not commit. I was waiting for night to come, but it seemed like time had just stopped and day would never end. If night could just hurry up and get here so morning could come, I would be released from this Detention Center. That afternoon, a young man brought dinner to my cell, and he said, "Pastor D, please eat your food. Things will get better for you and your family if you do not give up."

Then he walked away, but I did not eat anything because I was still on my sacrifice. As I was drinking my water, I started thinking about next week's general sessions court, and now I will have three charges on me. Not only that, but I am out now on two bonds and tomorrow, the judge could provoke my bonds, and then I would have to stay in jail until my court dates. I cannot do that, but I have a God that I can call on, and He will answer me. I started calling on Jesus, telling Him all about my court cases. I have faith that somehow, He will work it out because if He does not do it, it will not be done. Amen.

Nighttime finally came. I lay down, and I just stared at the ceiling. I only got an hour of sleep that night. When the sunlight came through the window, my eyes were open, waiting for someone to get me to go to bond court. Someone finally came to my cell with breakfast. He said, "After breakfast, you can make a phone call to let your family know the time of your bond court." Samantha Jackson never came to speak to me like the officer said she would do before I went to court. A young man came to get my plate from me, but I could not eat any of the food. Then he said, "I also came to let you know to come with me to make your phone call." I got up and followed the officer to make my one phone call. I knew I was going to call my sister. It took so long for me to walk to the phone, but I made it. I called my sister and told her what time my bond hearing would be then she said, "I got to get a bondsman."

She said, "Pastor D, I am going to get Emerson Hunt."

I said, "No, do not get Emerson. Go to Dr. Henry McGill Jr. because I know he will come to get me because he did it before when I was in jail. He got me out."

I hung up the phone and was taken back to my jail cell. The officer said, "Someone will get you within the hour to take you to your bond hearing." Within 45 minutes, someone came to my cell and said it was time. I got up and followed him to the courtroom, where I sat. I looked around the courtroom, and I saw my mother, my sister, and my daughter. My mother was crying. My sister and daughter's eyes were full of tears then, slowly, the tears started rolling down their faces. I could not take it anymore; the tears started flooding down my face. I put my head down and wiped the tears away. When I looked up two rows behind my family, I noticed the twin sisters. This is when I knew that one of them was supposed to have been the victim. I wondered why those sisters wanted to lie to me because several times, they came to the restaurant to get some hog maws.

We talked on the phone, and they were supposed to be my friends, but our enemies started with the letter F, 'family' and 'friends.' Judas kissed Jesus when he betrayed Him; Jesus called Judas friend, so if Jesus called His enemy friend, so should you and me. I had to go before the judge; he had my lawyer, Thurmond Brooker, and I stand. My lawyer, Thurmond Brooker, responded to the judge then the judge said to me, "Mr. Bennie Davis, you cannot be in contact with the victim or her sister. If any of your family members contact any of the two victims, you will be put back in jail until your court date."

I responded, "I do understand your Honor."

The judge set my bond and then allowed my sister to come to me. I said to her where is Dr. Henry McGill Jr., and she said I asked Emerson to come and do her bond by this time. Emerson walked into the courtroom and walked to my sister and me. I said to Emerson let me tell you something: I do not have any money for this bond. Emerson said, "Pastor D, do not worry about it. I got you." I went back to my cell, but 15 minutes later, someone came to my cell and said, "Bennie Davis, you are free to go now." When I walked out of the detention center door and into the lobby, Emerson Hunt stood and waited for me to walk out. I walked to Emerson Hunt and said, "Thank you, man, but I do not have any money."

He said, "I told you not to worry about this bond but to take care of your situation concerning this court." I went to my family, and we got in the car.

On our way to Marion, I said to my family, "You may not believe this, but that same Samantha Jackson is the same one that arrested my Mama and I for allegedly beating the little boy. Something must be done about this arresting innocent people because she does not want to do her job investigating the cases to find out what really happened to my mother and me. Samantha Jackson does not want to find out what really happened in the case against my mother and me." I wondered and asked my sister if I should tell the members of SMMBC what happened to me since it was a lie.

My sister said, "Pastor D, you must tell them because last night when you were in jail, it was said that 300 phone calls came into the detention center, and 195 of the callers were asking if you have

Pastor D. or Bennie Davis in jail. So now you know that someone from SMMBC called or heard something about what happened to you, Pastor D." I said, "Alethea, I do not want to lose the church. I want to remain the pastor because I love those people, and they also love me. I said let me call the chairman of the Deacon Ministry." I called right then and explained to him what was happening. He said, "Pastor D, I need you to come to Saint Matthew's on Saturday at 6:00 PM so that you can have an opportunity to tell the church family what happened. Then they will vote whether the church will keep you as pastor or not, but as for me, I believe in you, Pastor D."

I called the owner of the clubhouse and asked him, "What is going on with Samantha Jackson? She never asked you what happened at the clubhouse, and you are a retired Sheriff at Marion County Sheriff's Department." He responded, "I just cannot believe this, Pastor D, but she never called me because I would have told her that had never happened at my clubhouse." My sister took me straight to my mother's. When my mother saw me, she started crying. I asked her to stop crying as I explained to her and the family everything that was going on about the case. I did not want to say anything about this case at the detention center or in the car. I just wanted to get home to explain the alleged crime that happened the same night my brother was going to look at the clubhouse to have a surprise birthday party for his special friend. They both were there that night, along with the retired Sheriff.

"So, they can testify that those twin sisters are lying to me. My attorney must be told this fact…"

Momma stopped me from talking, saying, "I prayed for you all night, Bennie. Are you okay?"

I told my mother, "Do not worry, I will be alright. I did not do what they are charging me for, and I will have my time in court. I hope I do not lose the church because of this lie. I have a meeting tomorrow at 6:00 PM at SMMBC. I am having a meeting to tell the church what happened, but at the end of the meeting, the members are going to vote to keep me or to let me go as Pastor of the church. God has blessed me with something I could love, which I did on my own through God's grace and mercy. Look at what the devil came to do now. Satan will not take all this away from me. I do not know how God is going to work this out. I believe God is going to bring me out and I am going to be satisfied because God is still able regardless of what happens with SMMBC."

I told my mother, "Before you end your day, pray that I have favor at SMMBC at the meeting tomorrow."

I told my mother, "What I do not get is how easy it is for people to follow a lie before following the truth."

I asked my sister Alethea to give me a ride home, but I asked Mama what happened at the restaurant before I left. She said, "Pastor D, you know we were building our business back, but when this happened, word got out around Marion County so fast. I could not sell any dinners yesterday when you got locked up because you were charged with sexual assault. "People were saying, 'That so-called pastor had sex with a 13-year-old young girl,' then some said, 'Didn't I tell you when he got busted with those handbags, he had DVDs of children having sex with grown people. Bennie is no kind of a pastor. He does not need to be in anyone's church. This so-called pastor needs to burn in hell for what he has done to that little girl.'"

People would ask me to encourage their children to always give their absolute best and never give up on themselves. Now, some of those same people are saying, "Pastor D needs to spend the rest of his life in prison."

Remember what the people did to Jesus when he was coming to the city? There were some that went before him and some that were following him saying Hosanna! Hosanna! Blessed is He that comes in the name of the Lord. Then, less than a week later, those same people who were praising Him are now shouting and crying. Crucify Him! Crucify Him! My situation is very similar. I saw the hurt in my mother's eyes. All I could say was, "Mama, God will work everything out somehow and in some way."

My sister was offering to take me home. As my sister and I walked to the car, I said to her, "Please look out for Mama. I will come to the house after the meeting, but I will call to let you know when to get me because I need your car. I do not want to see Mama before the meeting because I cannot take that and go to this meeting with her crying."

I did not answer my phone while I was at my mother's. I had so many missed calls and texts asking if I had done that or why I did that to that little girl. There were some who said, "I will be praying for you." Those same people still smiled in my face, and I'll let God handle that for me.

When my sister drove up to the house to put me out, some neighbors were on their porch, and people were walking down the street. They would stare at me as I entered the yard; their eyes were on me. No one ever opened their mouth. It was like they just realized a rapist was living next door and just a few houses down. The ones with daughters probably asked themselves, 'did he try anything with any of my girls?' and some said, 'I remember when he was a little baby. He grew up in this neighborhood. No one knew he would turn out to be a child molester and a rapist.' I looked at the lady with her children walking down the street, passing by my house. She put her arms around her children as she passed the house like she was saying, 'You will not get my children; I will kill you first.' I walked onto the front porch and took a long look at the door because once I got in the house, I would come back out until I went to the meeting at SMMBC. When I unlocked the door, I took it upon myself to turn to each of my neighbors and say hello to everybody. Then someone said we must be more careful about the people that are in our neighborhood.

I continued to go into the house. I shut the door and turned my phone off. I did not want to talk to anyone. I lay across my bed, then hollered and cried because as hard as I have been working to rehabilitate myself, I hear someone say that about me. I just started thinking about some of the different things I have been through in my life, but this is far worse. I am at the point of losing everything that I love.

Why didn't I die when Ricky Pee set me up with that young man to rob and kill me for my money? God brought me from death's door not at once but through time. I gave my life to God from that time on. I have been saved and living a life that I respect. The people of Marion County, who knew me as Caveman then, now most of them respected me as a saved and different man (better known as Pastor D.)

God put in my spirit to start a ministry 19 years ago. Because of this ministry, we were able to help anyone who came, called the church or the youth center. We have been able to touch the lives of all different types of people. Not just in Marion County, but we helped people anywhere that needed the church or youth center. My mother is going through so much, not because of what she did but because of false accusations due to the charges. My mother has never been in jail. She believed in doing what was right so she would not go to jail. But because of Samantha Jackson, it came to pass. My mother was in a place she never thought she would be, and she was going to jail with her oldest son. My children could not go to work because everyone in the neighborhood was saying, "Your father, Pastor D, and your grandmother beat that innocent child. He is a Pastor, a rapist, now a child molester and tricking innocent people."

In less than 24 hours, I have a meeting about my future as the Pastor of SMMBC; how will I make it? Things were looking up for me because I would have never come back to Marion. Aynor, South Carolina, was going to be my new home. I have been knocked down, but never like this before, with all this happening in my life simultaneously. I would be better off dead than alive because people would not be talking about me the way they are doing. My family and friends would not have to put their heads down and act like they did not know me.

When I go to sleep tonight, if I die, let me die because of this pain that I am going through and my family because of Samantha Jackson. It would not die with me, but my family would be free from the shame I put on them. Maybe Samantha Jackson would then tell them why she picked on me and my mother, two innocent people just doing the best we could in this place called life. As I was thinking about how I felt, the tears continued to flow down harder and harder. How can she sleep at night knowing what she did to my life and never ask me one question or take a statement from me?

She allowed an innocent mother and son to go to jail and the guilty to go free. The young man lied to my mother and I. Satan is doing everything he can to destroy me. My dream is to be the greatest Pastor that SMMBC has ever had or will ever have. I got up so that I could get some clothes out for the biggest meeting in my life. I got ready for bed. I did not talk to anyone that night but the Lord.

I started praying and meditating on the Lord because if the Lord did not do something to help me, the only thing I wanted to happen was for my life to end. At the time, I wanted to sleep, but every 10 to 20 minutes, I was waking up crying because I did not want tomorrow to come, and I lost the church, not because of what I did but because of what Samantha Jackson did to me. I cannot lose the church because that will be everything. There wouldn't be anything else for me to live for. God, I need you. I asked the Lord to give me the words to tell the church family. I did not have money, I was not selling drugs, I was not on drugs, so why was it that this detective had to see me die in prison? Was it that she looked at me as a poor Black man and she had to meet her quota? I knew I must fight for my freedom, and this is what I must tell the SMMBC family.

The easiest thing for me to do was put my head down and not go around people, but my mind was made up that the devil is a liar. I am going to fight; I am not going to give up. I will keep the church because I will stay as Pastor, and I will make sure that I fight every charge against me. I am going to win because I know that God is for me, so who can be against me? It is not going to be easy, but somehow, God is going to see me out of this storm that only came to destroy my life and keep me from preaching God's word.

Not long after that, I saw the daylight coming through the window. As I was lying down, I realized there was nothing I could do to stop time from passing, and just as time passed, the meeting would take place in a few hours. I was hoping somehow all of this would just disappear, but everything is still here. I am going too fast and pray to be mentally prepared for this meeting.

This is the meeting about my future, and my future is looking great at SMMBC. This church family has love for me, and I am in love with each one of them. I would love to be the Pastor of SMMBC for many years to come. I would love to die as Pastor and be buried in the church Cemetery in Aynor, SC. Time was just passing by so fast that I just laid in bed all day praying and telling God all about this war I was in for my life.

I looked at the time and realized it was time to get up, so I got my clothes, turned my phone on, and called my sister to ask her to take me to the meeting today. She told me to call her when I was ready for her to come get me and not forget that I needed to be on time. I told her that I would call 30 minutes before time. I hung up, knowing that I would not answer my phone for anyone except my sister.

I started preparing for the meeting. When I got ready, I called my sister to come get me. I did not answer the phone, and I did not text anyone because I was focused on what I needed God to do for me. I asked the Lord to give me the words to say to the Saint Matthews Missionary Baptist Church family so they could hear the truth. I called my sister before time and let her know that she could come pick me up. It was not long before she was outside calling me to come out so I could get on the road. Before we got on the road, we prayed, asking God to give us traveling mercy and to give me a favor at the meeting in the name of Jesus. Amen. As my sister and I were in the car, people looked at us, but today is a new day for me and my faith. My sister had me at the church within twenty minutes before the meeting started. I said to my sister I am not going into the church until the meeting is about to start.

When it was time for the meeting to start, Deacon Timothy Gerald called the meeting to order. He let everyone know why this meeting was taking place. It is because our Pastor was put in jail, and we need to hear his side. Then, we, as a church, will vote about keeping Dr. Bennie T. Davis. About 30 minutes into the meeting, Deacon Timothy Gerald asked me to come and explain my side as to what happened.

I said, "I love myself, and I love Saint Matthews Missionary Baptist Church family. I will never take sex from any young lady because I respect myself too much to do that to any lady. What got me was this warrant was signed in October 2014, several months before my arrest. I am not guilty of the crime I am being accused of (sexual assault first degree). I was at my friend's clubhouse, and he is a retired Sheriff from Marion County. Now, what Ms. Jackson has against me and my family, I do not know; I cannot answer that question; only she can answer. SMMBC family, is Samantha Jackson racist?

You, the church family, must decide with the evidence that I have presented to you. One thing I can say, I am an innocent Black man on both charges. I asked the members of SMMBC, "do you have any questions for me? I will answer them all because tonight you all must vote on keeping me as your pastor, or you can dismiss me from this job pastoring the greatest church not on the earth, but the universe". After I finished the chairman of the Deacon ministry, Timothy Gerald said, "Dr. Bennie Davis, please go to your office so that we can vote on keeping you as the Pastor here at SMMBC.

As I was walking out of the meeting, I looked back, and I saw tears rolling down a few of their faces. I went to my office, closed the door behind me, and went to my desk. I began to ask myself what was going on and why is this happening to me because I was at a high point in my life. Things finally were going my way. God has blessed me with this church. Therefore, I must help this church family become great, greater, and the greatest. I realized that Satan comes to steal, kill, and destroy. Whatever people believe the first time that is what they usually believe and will not change their mind. I said a short prayer asking God to renew their minds and asking God to give me a favor so that they could hear the words that I said. Amen.

About 20 minutes later, a knock came to the door, and I said enter. It was the chairman of the Deacon ministry, Timothy Gerald, Deacon Ralph Van Fore, Deacon Dennis Gerald Deacon, and Deacon Terry Williams. closed the door. The chairman began to tell me what happened at the meeting just before the voting took place. He said that a retired police officer said to the church family, "A man is innocent until proven guilty." All charges do not mean that a person is guilty, so let us wait until after Dr. Bennie Davis goes to court. "The votes were cast, and because of what the retired police officer said, the majority voted to let you remain as our Pastor. In my mind, I started screaming, hollering, and praising God, saying thank you, God, thank you, Lord. Lord, I thank you for this opportunity. I am going to serve you until I die. I am going to make this church family proud that I am their Pastor. I looked at the four Deacons and said, "I thank you all for agreeing and standing with the congregation. I will do the job that I was hired to do, being the greatest pastor, this church ever had and will ever have here at this church."

I asked Deacon Timothy, who stood up for me. He told me it was the young man I asked to be a trustee and was in my office when Deacon Timothy came for that meeting for the Deacon ministry. I said, "Wow, I know who you are talking about now." The Deacons were so happy, but when I looked at Deacon Terry Williams, his eyes were so cold towards me. Right then, I thought, he is not happy that I am still the Pastor of St. Matthews Missionary Baptist Church. As I continued to look at him, I was reminded this was the only Deacon to say that the young man did not qualify to be a trustee at SMMBC because of this man standing up for me, and now I will remain the Pastor of the church. Deacon Terry Williams dislikes him worse than ever now. Deacon Terry Williams looks like he was so determined to get me out of Saint Matthews Missionary Baptist Church. I just cannot figure out what he was going to do, but he was not going to stop because Satan came to kill, steal, and destroy. He was not going to stop until he got me out of the church as Pastor; then, his job would be completed.

Deacon Timothy said, "Pastor D, all the members of SMMBC did not vote for you to stay; they want us to dismiss you from being a pastor." I said to Deacon Timothy Gerald, Deacon Dennis Gerald, Deacon Terry Williams, and Deacon Ralph Van Fore, "I am not going to let myself down, I am not going to let this church family down, and I am going to be proven innocent of all charges. I am going to pastor this church so that God is well pleased with the job that I am going to do here at SMMBC."

Deacon Timothy Gerald said, "Pastor D, I need to tell you that Henry Coachman, the usher ministry president, said that he refuses ever to step foot back into this church if you are the Pastor because of the charges." I told the Deacons that the general session court would start next week and last for two weeks.

I left the church and returned home, sharing the good news with my family that I am still the Pastor at SMMBC. I thanked all my family for praying for me. It's Monday, and time to get up so my mother and I can get ready for court. At 8:00 am, my phone started ringing. It was my attorney, Thurmond Brooker. He said to me, "You and your mother will be going to court this week. We will be having a jury trial because we were not taking any plea, and he asked us to be at the courthouse at 8:30 to talk." I told him we would not be late. I thought my mother was going to take it hard, but when I told her what our attorney said, we would be having a jury trial. My mother said I am glad it will be over today. We continued to get ready for court. We arrived there at about 8:20 am. Shortly after that, our attorney, Thurmond Brooker, came into the courtroom. My mother and I followed him into a smaller room and sat down.

He began to go over the strategy that he was going to use for our defense, but at the end of the conversation, he said, "I believe that you all are innocent of these charges. I believe it is time for you and your mother to go into the courtroom so you all can answer the roll call." When we entered the courtroom, the roll call started, and the guard at the door had my mother, and I find a place to sit. As I looked around the courtroom, it was overcrowded with black and Brown people. It was so many people standing up around and against the wall.

Two people moved so that my mother and I could sit down because they could see that we could not walk or stand up. As I continued to look around, I asked myself how many black and brown people in this courtroom were innocent like me, but just because of the color of their skin and classification, 9 out of 10 will make years in prison for something they did not do. I will be in the 1% because I will not plead guilty or take a plea for crimes I did not commit.

I just sat there wondering in the courtroom and wondering how Detective Jackson could sit in this courtroom looking at innocent people going to prison. She destroys people's lives (my life being just one of many). She knows that she did not do her job investigating from start to finish. I just wonder how many people she has put into prison from 2015 to 2021 and how many lives she has destroyed, yet she still remains a detective at Marion County Sheriff's Department. I don't like pulling the race card, but that really crosses my mind. Do these allegations and sloppy investigations have anything to do with my race? I can't help but notice that the courtroom is disproportionately filled with people of color. In fact, there are no Caucasian people in court today except for the court officials. I was really wondering.

When I looked up, my attorney called for my mother and me to follow him out of the courtroom. He told my mother and me that the solicitor said we would be excused from court until Thursday morning. He told us that Thursday before our case starts, they will select the jurors for our case between now and Thursday. Pastor Davis, you and your mother need to get in touch with everyone who was in the house during the incident. I called my sister to tell her that our court case starts on Thursday, so we got to get Aunt Lent and Anisha from St. Louis, Missouri, before the court. Alethea said let me call to let them know because they got to get a flight as soon as possible because you and Mama need them to testify on your behalf. I told her that I was getting the car, then I would go back to pick Mama up outside the courtroom and meet us at Mama's house.

As we were on our way to my mother's house, an incoming call came to my phone. I was surprised it was Deacon Terry Williams. After he identified himself, he asked, "Pastor D, are you going to be free today at 3:00 pm?" He and I arranged to meet at Mother's restaurant. Deacon Terry Williams called me precisely at 3:00 and was parked outside of my mother's place. I went to his car. He said, "I would like to talk with you about that charge of sexual assault second-degree."

I said to him, "That will be fine. Let us go to Greater Christ Temple Church of the Harvest, or we could stay here because Mama does not open on Mondays." He preferred that I ride to the church with him. After we entered the church, each one of us sat on the same pew. We prayed that we were blessed because of this meeting. Deacon Terry Williams started asking me different questions. I answered all his questions with truthful answers. After about an hour and a half, I said to Deacon Terry Williams, "Would you like to go to the Marion Chief of Police, or I can call him to come to the church?" He said, "No, I do not need to talk to him."

I said, "How about I call the retired Sheriff from the clubhouse, which belonged to him, and he can tell you what happened that night."

Deacon Terry Williams said, "I want you to know that I believe that you are really telling the truth." Then the Deacon started telling me about the preacher who was at SMMBC before I got the position.

Deacon Williams said that he, the other deacons, and the members decided that the preacher who was there would be the new pastor at SMMBC.

He said, "Pastor D, it is not right that they made you the pastor when we promised the other man. He was told that he would be the pastor, and we practically gave him the keys to guarantee that he was going to be the pastor. I think that the other deacons and members that voted for pastor were wrong for their decision." I said, "Deacon Williams, I believe that they would have made him the pastor if I had not tried out, but the bottom line, I am a better preacher, better teacher, better leader, and the best man for the job to be pastor at SMMBC. More people came to Bible study, more people came to morning service, and we raised more money. Nobody must borrow any money from any other ministry or any person in the church."

I continued, "Deacon Williams, did you marry the first woman that you said I love you to?"

He said, "No, Pastor D."

I responded by saying to him, "The reason why you did not marry her was because, deacon, you found a better woman. SMMBC found a better Pastor, and therefore, I am the pastor. I am going to stay the pastor because I am going to work hard to make Saint Matthews the number one church in Kingston Lake."

Then, at the end of our meeting, Deacon Terry Williams said, "I am going to stand with you, Pastor. I have your back, and I am going to let go of the other Pastor because SMMBC got the best pastor."

I said, "Deacon Terry Williams, do you remember telling your coworkers on your job how you have never seen these many people coming to Bible study, and at Sunday morning service, more people came. You said the members love Pastor D, and we never had 75 to 80 people in the church. He just became Pastor the third Sunday in January, and it is only February now."

He said yes.

I said, "Deacon Williams, I love you. I love all the deacons and all the members, but most of all, this church family gave me the greatest opportunity of my life. I am not going to do anything to let myself down or the church family. I will not do anything to embarrass myself or this great church family."

I stretched out my hand and Deacon Williams grabbed my hand then shook it. His hand was cold, and his eyes were also cold, just like when they had the meeting to vote me out. He was still disappointed that the other man was not the pastor. I believe he still had it in his heart, 'I will get Pastor D out of Saint Matthews Missionary Baptist Church.'

As we were walking out the door, I asked, "Is there anything else you need to know? I would like to be the pastor until I take my last breath on this earth."

Deacon Terry Williams said, "I am going to stand with you. I have your back; no one is going to do anything to you. As of today, I believe in what you are doing for the church family, and I am going to do my part as a Deacon by working with you and not against you."

As I was looking and listening, I knew it was not coming from the heart; he was just saying things that sounded good and things he believed I would love to hear from him. He believed in his heart that Saint Matthew Missionary Baptist Church officers and members were wrong for voting for me over the other preacher. He is going to fight back against the pastor that God has at Saint Matthew's Missionary Baptist Church. He is not going to stop until he makes the favored preacher the Pastor of the church and gets me out. What he is saying is God cannot put the pastor in SMMBC because that is his job, and he will get it done. I am reminded of when God sent Samuel, and he was rejected, and he told God all about it, but God said, "They did not reject you, but they rejected me."

This is when I realized that Deacon Terry Williams voted against me both times when it was one-on-one between me and the other preacher; he voted for the other preacher. When the church family voted to put me out because of the sexual assault second-degree charge, Deacon Terry Williams voted to put me out as pastor and did all that he could to influence others to follow him.

All of this is going on in my life only because Samantha Jackson falsely arrested me with no proof and no investigation. She is the head detective and did not even do her job. The one thing she accomplished was an innocent black man who was arrested and rebuilt himself and was living a respectable life. Still, because of her, my life is being destroyed. It is not a good feeling to be at the point of everything, and no one in law enforcement or in the church will stand to help you.

I locked the door to the church then I went and got in the car with Deacon Williams. On our way to my house, he said, "This meeting and our conversation is between you and me because I just wanted to find out where you were coming from. Now that I know I can get behind the vision that you have for SMMBC."

Then, Deacon Terry Williams stopped in front of my house. Before I opened the door, I said to him, "Is there anything else I can do to prove to you that I love Saint Matthews Missionary Baptist Church officers, the church family, and our guests. I am going to do everything in my power to make the church better, great, greater, and greatest, but for this to happen, all of us pastors and deacons must be with one accord. We cannot have any division, and this church shall grow and will grow."

Deacon James looked me in my face and said, "Pastor D, I am in one accord."

I got out of the car then I said to Deacon Terry Williams, "I thank you for coming by today. I hope this is a new start to a great Pastor/Deacon relationship, but before you make any decisions against me, let us talk about it and see if we can reason so that the church can stay together."

This man practically promised me he would talk to me before he did anything that would be against me. I was walking towards the house, and Deacon Terry Williams blew the car horn as he traveled down the street. As I was walking determined I was not going to do anything that was out of order because if I did, Deacon Terry

Williams would have everything in his power to put me out of the church as pastor.

My mind was made up; there was no money, no woman, no one, or nobody was going to take this opportunity to pastor this great church from me. This man will have the church family against me. As soon as I walked into the house, I got a text from my sister saying to meet me at mom's house in 20 minutes. I made it to my mother's house, and as I was pulling up, my sister was behind me.

I got to the door, and we walked inside the house. We had a family get-together (a little family meeting). We all sat around the table. I learned that our aunt and her granddaughter were able to get a flight, and they will be here in time to be the witnesses to testify on behalf of my mother and court case. I shared with my family that Deacon Terry Williams had a meeting with me today when he got off work. We had a long talk, but I do not think I was able to convince him how much SMMBC means to me.

This church family gives me the opportunity to pastor the greatest people on earth. They have faith in me and trust that I can take this church family to the next level. The drive that I have in me comes from their faith and trust in my ability. Still, Deacon Terry Williams is totally against me. This man is determined to get me out as Pastor at SMMBC. Deacon Terry Williams is going to undo what God has done for this church because he feels compelled to get the preacher who was my contender.

Deacon Terry Williams must have promised that preacher he would be the next pastor of the church. He couldn't turn the members against me because he knew that they loved Pastor D. My mother cried the whole time that I was telling the family what was going on with Deacon Terry Williams.

I notified my Attorney Brooker to inform him our witnesses will be in court with my mother and me on Thursday morning. Then my attorney let me know that the state has a very weak case because Samantha Jackson does not have any evidence, no pictures, no statements, except a 12-year-old, and she never questioned you or your mother. I just do not understand why Samantha Jackson would do something like this to a wonderful family that is known for helping people.

"Dr. Bennie Davis, you are a pastor, and you also do so much in the community and in Marion County." He went on to say, "Dr. Davis, be to the courtroom at 8:30 AM with your mother and the witnesses that are going to testify so we can go over the case."

"We will be on time I told him, and I thank you for the job you are doing for my family."

After I hung up the phone with my attorney, I said to my family, "Until this court case is over, we need to fast, pray, and be with one accord."

I got me something to eat, and I asked my sister to take me home. The days went by so fast that our family members' flight made it in safely. It was the night before court.

It is sad when a person does so many things to help people, but in their time of need, there is no one. There are thousands of people, and there is no one to hear or help you. This is the place I am in now. The night before, people would only call to hear how bad I was doing. I was not able to sleep, but I prayed each time my eyes opened. The light started coming in my window, and I got up. It was not long before it was time to go to court, but the family came together, and we prayed.

On the way to court, I called Deacon Terry Williams. He answered the phone. I said, "This is Pastor D, my mother, and I must go to court today."

I said, "If I plead guilty, can I stay as Pastor at SMMBC?"

He said to me, "If you plead guilty, you are out as pastor of this church. If you are found guilty, you are out as pastor of this church; the only way you can stay pastor is to have a not guilty outcome."

13. NEVER GIVE UP

I told Deacon Terry Williams, "If that is the only way to stay Pastor at St. Matthews Missionary Baptist Church, I will have a jury trial because I would love to remain a pastor. I want to make sure that you say the only way I can stay pastor is to have a not guilty verdict." Deacon Terry Williams' response was, "It is the only way that you will remain Pastor at St. Matthews Missionary Baptist Church. Pastor D, you can tell the church family what I am saying; if you are found guilty, you need not ever step a foot back into St. Matthews Missionary Baptist Church because YOU will not be accepted back into the church as Pastor." I told Deacon Terry Williams to have a blessed day and hung up the phone.

While riding in the car, my sister told my family that Deacon Terry Williams did not care for me. That so-called deacon does not want you at that church as pastor, and he wants you to be found guilty. By this time, we had arrived at the courthouse. My sister let us all get out, and she went to find a place to park. As we were waiting for her, our attorney arrived at the same time. Attorney Thurmond Brooker told us to follow him into the courtroom. Thurmond Brooker began to explain how we were going to pick our jury for the trial. I was to be the last to testify; my mother was excused. He prepped my aunt and my cousin on questions that the state attorney would ask and advised how to answer. He stated, "Any question they ask, give them an answer because if not, the lawyer will answer it for you."

It was time for my mother and me to go into the courtroom for the roll call for everyone in General Sessions Court. After the solicitor finished the roll call, he said that everyone was dismissed but must be back at 9:00 am tomorrow. The people walked out of the courtroom, and those remaining were the people to be selected to serve as jurors. After we chose the jurors for the case, our trial began. The state started by calling their witness, and their first witness was Detective Samantha Jackson. Detective Samantha Jackson answered the questions excellently for the state. She made the jurors believe that she had investigated this case very thoroughly from beginning to end.

Without a doubt, she had arrested the right people who committed this awful act to this child. The state lawyer asked Detective Jackson to point to the person or persons who have committed this horrendous crime towards that child. Do you see them in this courtroom? She responded, "Yes," then she pointed at my mother and me. We did not react at all. We just continued to stare at her because I knew my lawyer would have an opportunity to question her. It was my lawyer, Thurmond Brooker's chance to cross-examine her. He started by asking her the question, "Before arresting my clients, did you ever question them about what happened?"

She responded, "No, I never questioned them."

Attorney Thurmond Brooker said, "The accuser, Anthony, said that one of my clients hit him fifty times with a cane and twenty times with a wet towel, a total of seventy licks. Then he said that he was dragged on the carpet and slammed to the bathroom floor. Now I know Anthony had to have been bruised badly, so do you have any pictures or a video of him because his back should not look good? The jurors, the judge, and my clients need to see how badly this young man was looking."

Samantha Jackson responded, "No, I do not have any pictures or a video of the young man on the day the incident occurred."

The attorney asked, "Do you know Pastor Dr. Bennie T. Davis?"

Samantha Jackson said, "No, I do not know him."

Attorney Thurmond Brooker said, "Today, I will prove that none of this has taken place and that you have arrested two innocent people because of the lack of your investigation."

Then he ended by asking, "What type of training do you have in investigations because you are the head detective? How much experience do you have in this field of being a detective?"

She responded by saying, "The only training I have is when I accepted the job. I did not have any experience in detective work."

"I have no more questions for the witness," said the attorney.

The following people testified: social workers from the adoption agency, social workers from the Department of Social Services, and the young man who made the allegations against my mother and me. My attorney then began calling his witnesses: my aunt, cousin, police officer, and me.

After I finished, our attorney said in his closing remarks, "There are no pictures of any bruises, but it was stated that there were bruises on his right shoulder."

Then, Attorney Brooker walked to the table that my mother and I were sitting at, got his briefcase, opened it, got out his belt, and went back up to the front of the court. He stood in front of the judge, took his hand, and swung the belt over his left shoulder about four to six times, and the belt hit him on his back and his right shoulder.

The attorney said to the judge and jury, "Therefore, out of seventy licks, only a few bruises were on his right shoulder because the young man put the bruises on himself. These two innocent people are sitting in court now because there was no investigation.

Detective Samantha Jackson has not shown anything to find my clients guilty because of the lack of investigation. This is an easy verdict to come back with, a not guilty verdict."

The trial ended when the judge told the jury they were going to the deliberation room, "You must return with a verdict of guilty or innocent."

After the jury left the courtroom, the judge said to our attorney, "You and your clients are free to go to break. Ensure that your clients are close by so the court can contact them. They will have 10 minutes to return to the courtroom."

Our attorney, Thurmond Brooker, said to Dr. Bennie Davis and Mother Davis, "I would like you to wait for me before you all leave the premises."

The judge called our attorney and asked him to approach the bench. Our attorney said, "Go down to the first floor; I will be there momentarily. The judge suggested that our attorney could get one of us to plead guilty before the verdict comes back because if not and we are found guilty, both of us will spend time in prison. If one pleads guilty, the charges should be dropped on the other, and the guilty one will get five years' probation. If they wait, the book is coming at them, so do not ask for probation. It will not be either one of them."

My mother and I sat down on the bench in the hallway on the first floor. As we talked to our family members, our attorney walked up and said, "I feel confident about a not-guilty verdict. Before we go any further, I need all of us to hold hands now, and let us pray."

He led the prayer, and I was able to feel the presence of the Lord. My mother started rocking and speaking in that unknown tongue. As I looked around, tears were coming out of my family members' eyes.

All I could say was, "Thank you, Lord," because I believed as I was holding hands, something great was about to happen up in here, "Lord, I want to thank you in advance for the not guilty verdict coming back for us."

After the prayer ended, our attorney asked that we stay in the courtroom. It should not be much longer before they reach a verdict, but "I must let you know this crucial information. Mother Davis and Dr. Bennie Davis, the judge, told me to find out if one of you would plead guilty and the other one would go free. The one who pleads guilty would get five years' probation."

My mother and I quickly answered, "No, we will wait for the jury to come back with a not-guilty verdict."

The attorney then said, "Let me tell you this: if the verdict returns guilty, you will both do time in prison."

Attorney Thurmond Brooker informed us that the Judge said he would give us one more opportunity to take a plea now. He said when the judge enters the courtroom, we will stand and then be seated when he takes his chair. The judge will call me to approach his bench. Then, I will be asked whether my client will take the plea or not, and if not, he will continue by calling the jurors back in the courtroom; then, the verdict will be noted by the judge and announced by the 'Foreman.' The judge told our attorney that he does not want to put a mother and son in jail/prison. He said if anyone does not take the plea, anyone can go to prison. I reinforced the fact that we would not be taking the plea because we were confident of the job that he did for my mother and me (by defending us). We just know a not-guilty verdict will be coming back today for us, and we will walk out of this courtroom free.

Everyone was asked to stand; the judge entered the courtroom and told everyone to be seated. Shortly after that, our attorney was called to approach the bench. The judge asked what his clients decided to do.

He responded, "My clients will not be accepting the plea. They will accept the jurors' verdict."

He shared with us that the judge knows that there will not be a plea but the verdict of the jurors. The judge had the jurors enter the courtroom and proceeded to go forward with our case. He asked if they had reached a verdict. They responded by saying "yes." then the selected foreman handed the paper with the verdict to the judge, who then opened and read it. to see the verdict with a poker face, not revealing any hint of his thoughts or feelings. I could not tell if the verdict was guilty or innocent. The judge passed the paper back to the foreman.

My mother, lawyer and I stood, and then the foreman read the verdict: "Not guilty." Tears began to roll out of my mother's eyes. As I looked around, my family members were also crying. I was so happy that I did not have to look at my mother in the courtroom as her son was going to jail.

Knowing that I had two more cases that I had to win, the pressure was slightly off my mother. The threat of her being incarcerated is gone. It is all about my outcomes now. I was hoping that something would be done to Detective Samantha Jackson because when the not-guilty verdict was announced, she was not in the courtroom. Still, there were officers from the Sheriff's Department.

I saw them walking out of the courtroom on their cell phones, calling and letting people know that the verdict was not guilty. Some of those calls, I am sure, were to Detective Samantha Jackson to inform her of the "not guilty" verdict on Bennie and his mother. I can imagine that Samantha was thinking that I still have two more charges (assault second-degree and custom handbags). I would be found guilty for one, if not both, offenses.

I started thinking, could this woman be out there arresting another innocent person? She should not be the lead detective for the Marion County Sheriff's Department because the racial disparities were noticeably clear in the courtroom today.

What Deacon Terry Williams had said to me was running through my mind, "If it is a guilty verdict, you will not stay Pastor at St. Matthews Missionary Baptist Church."

I knew I was not going to tell anyone until Sunday during our Black History program. When God is on your side, I know that God will be the juror, the Judge, the lawyer, and the prosecutor. I learned that when God is for you, God is more than the whole court that is against you. The judge told the jury, thank you for a wonderful job. Now you are free to go back to your life back at home. Now, that was the greatest news. My mom and I were free from the charges of beating a child. The news traveled when my mother and I were arrested for these charges, yet the guilty verdict was hardly mentioned. People want to hear bad news, but they want to keep positive news on the down-low.

The Davis family had all smiles and laughter again. As my mother and I were walking out of the courtroom with our attorney, family and friends were coming up, hugging us, and saying, "Look at God."

As I was looking around in the courtroom, people put their heads down because they were sure the whole time we were going to prison. Innocent people saw justice served, and we will not be imprisoned. Mother was still crying, but they were tears of joy. We went to the courthouse's first floor; that was the first time I felt free. I suggested that we eat at the Chinese restaurant to celebrate. Our lawyer had to see another client who was in court that afternoon. So, we went to Florence, and we all pigged out. The family had a wonderful time. This was a long time coming. This part of my mother's life and my life has come to an end, and we will begin a new chapter.

While I was eating, my attorney called to let me know that I would be on standby for court. I would not have to report to court next week because I would not be taking a plea. As I was sitting there eating, I suggested that we would not tell anyone that we were found not guilty. I wanted to see if anyone would let the members of SMMB Church know that it was a not-guilty verdict. I started looking forward to Sunday coming for the Black History program because I would love to let them know what happened in court on Sunday morning. Also, this same Sunday, the church will vote on the mission statement that the spirit of God put in my heart for the church.

As we finished eating on our way back to Marion, my mother just started crying out to God, telling him thank you for making a way for my son and me. When I looked around in the car, everyone was saying thank you, Lord. The next day, I had to go to the clerk of the court office to get a printout of what happened in court about my trial. Showing written documentation that the jury of my peers produced a not-guilty verdict. After I read over the papers to make sure the information was not guilty for my mother and me, I was so excited about taking this paperwork to the church with me on Sunday for everyone to know of my innocence.

I could only imagine the response on the people's faces from the church, especially Deacon Terry Williams. He said, "If it is not a not guilty verdict, you will no longer be Pastor of St. Matthews Missionary Baptist Church." In 40 hours, I will not have to imagine anymore because it will be a reality. The church family will know that I am free and allow me to pastor how the Spirit of God put it in my heart.

I knew I had to go to the church on Saturday because the adults would clean the church for the youth. Sunday morning was our Black History Month program, and what better way to celebrate Black history than a black man and his mother being found not guilty. I did not tell anybody my plans because I did not want anything to go wrong. Saturday morning, I went to the church to help clean up, but somehow, I got with Reverend Norman Pee, and he went with me. On the way to the church, I told him how excited I was about what I believed God would do for the church family and how happy I was about him seeing the church. I told him things that I wanted to do as Pastor and how much respect the members have shown me. I want to do things to make the church family proud to say that 'Bennie Davis is our pastor.'

I turned on my signal light and pulled up in the church parking lot. I had to find a place to park; it was like a Sunday morning service (That is how many people were there). I was so proud of the members. While pulling up in the church parking lot, I noticed that someone had cut the grass. I looked over at Reverend Pee, and he was so surprised at how the building and yard were looking. Reverend Pee said to Pastor D, "God has blessed you, and I am so proud of you, and you are going to do a great job." That made me feel so good to hear someone say such wonderful words to me.

When I walked into the church, Deacon Dennis Gerald came up to me, saying, "Pastor D, you are late. You missed all the fun."

I wanted to know what fun did I miss?

He said, "You missed Deacon Dennis, cleaning the church," then started laughing. I went to the Fellowship Hall. Deacon Terry Williams, along with a few of the young people, were buffing the floor, and they had that floor shining. I introduced Reverend Pee to the Deacons and the church family that was there. I said to the church family how proud I was of the work they had done. I said there are so many people here I thought we had service on a Saturday. Then someone said that it was 'clean the church day'. Pastor D asked us to come to clean the church; that is why we are here because we love Pastor D.

I said to the church family, "I am not just proud of the work everyone did, but words cannot express how I feel about you all right now."

I turned around and pinched myself because I could not believe that these people had so much respect for me. As I looked around, I realized that they were finished, so all I did was walk around smiling and giving Reverend Pee a tour of the church. I took him into my office, and I let him know that I had to decorate the office to make it good-looking like me, the pastor. We started laughing, and then shortly after that, I let the church family know I was going back to Marion. I expressed to them how proud I was of their job. Tomorrow, I have something for all our youth and the youth with the best grades. As I was walking out of the door, one of the members said, "Saint Matthews church family loves you, Pastor D."

I said to them, "I love you all more."

When Reverend Pee and I got in the car, he said, "Those people love you. God has given you a family that you can love as their Pastor. You are great for them, and they are great for you."

As we were headed back to Marion, I received a phone call from Pastor James P. Gause. He said, "I just heard that you were the new Pastor at Saint Matthew's Missionary Baptist Church. I am calling to say "Congratulations to you on your big accomplishment. You will bring so much good to the church, and the church will be good for you. The church that I pastor is a few miles down from Saint Matthews Missionary Baptist Church. We can start a fellowship together."

Pastor James P. Gause did not know how much confidence that conversation meant to me. It encouraged me in so many ways because this man has been preaching for many years. This was my first church, and to hear that from a seasoned pastor was great. When I got off the phone with Pastor James P. Gause, I was coming into the City of Marion. I took Reverend Pee home, and I told him to be on time for church on Sunday.

As I was going home, I called our speaker to confirm that he would be at the church on Sunday for our Black History program. I began to thank God for Pastor James P. Gause's phone call because it came when I needed to hear someone say that they believed in the work I was doing at the church. The call encouraged me in so many ways, knowing that Deacon Terry Williams's sole purpose is to get rid of me from being a pastor. As I was getting out of the car to go into the house, my phone started ringing again, and I answered. It was the speaker for our Black History program.

He was calling to confirm that he would be in attendance tomorrow. He also asked for the physical address to put in his GPS. I told him I was about to call him because I was excited about hearing the Dr. Martin Luther King Jr. speech. People have spoken so much about how wonderfully he performed that speech. I told him that the youth at the church and the members were so excited about having him tomorrow to hear his speech.

Debra Fling said, "You make it sound like it is coming directly out of the mouth of Dr. Martin Luther King Jr. I am looking forward to hearing this outstanding speech because I have already been bragging about it. This will be my first program as Pastor, and I need it to be a success."

The pastor responded that he was looking forward to having an awesome time tomorrow. I shared with the pastor that I would be doing a mini-sermon after the speech to conclude our Black History program. I said, "I will see you tomorrow, Pastor. Enjoy the rest of your day."

After the phone call ended, I went into the house. My hands went up in the air with victory because everything was working for my good.

Sunday morning arrived quickly, and I was so excited. Petro called me to let me know that he would be outside my house in 30 minutes. When he picked me up, I was outside waiting for him. On our way to the church, Petro said, "Pastor D, I believe this will be a blessed day for the youth. They will love the plaque, and the ones with the highest grades get a $25 gift card from Walmart. I can see the love in your face for this church family, and they also love you."

Now we had arrived at the church. Sunday school was out of this world, and before it was over, our speaker came in and had a good time participating by answering and asking questions. At the end of Sunday school, I took the speaker into my office during the devotional service. The usher ministry had me spoiled. Cindy Brown always came to the door and led me to the sanctuary. This Sunday was so incredibly special to me because now, not only me but the speaker and I would be led to the sanctuary.

As we were sitting in the office, we prayed. After the prayer, there came a knock on the door, and I knew it was Cindy Brown. The door opened, and with that great smile, it was Cindy Brown announcing that she would be waiting for us today, and then she closed the door. Within minutes, the speaker and I walked out of the door and were escorted to the sanctuary. As we were following her, she let us know if we needed anything to call for her, and she would be more than happy to see about our needs.

As we entered the sanctuary, the congregation stood on their feet and clapped their hands. It was great to see the church youth occupying the first three rows of the pews. As I was going to sit down, I had the opportunity to tell Cindy Brown that I thanked her for the wonderful job that she was doing and that I was so proud of her. Our Black history program had begun. It was time to speak from the Pastor's pew. I asked for all the youth to stand to receive a plaque because of their school achievement. Kayla Shanice Gerald had the highest grade point average in the church, so she received a $25 gift card along with the plaque.

Kayla Shanice Gerald graduated from Aynor High School in the top percentile of her class. She is attending Presbyterian College, and for the last three straight years, she has made the president's list. Kayla Shanice Gerald is the proud daughter of Deacon Dennis Gerald and Sheila Gerald. I had all the youth stand up across the front of the church, and the congregation stood up and celebrated our youth for the magnificent work each of them was doing in school.

Everyone was so proud of our youth, and they were so excited about what they had accomplished. Deacon Ralph Van Fore stood up at the end and said, "Out of all the years being a church member, the youth never looked as good as they do right now."

Weeks earlier, the church family voted on the mission statement, and the church family recited the mission statement for the very first time in our Black History program.

I called for the Deacon ministry. Deacon Timothy Gerald, the chairman, came to the front, and I handed him a letter.

"I would like for you to read this letter to the church family. But before you start, let me address something to the church. On Thursday of last week, I called Deacon Terry Williams on my way to court, and I asked him if I pled guilty can, I stay as pastor of the church. Deacon Terry Williams told me that there was no way I would remain Pastor."

I then said to the church family, "My mother and I had a jury trial; I need Deacon Timothy Gerald to read the letter to the church family."

He read the letter to the congregation. By the time he got to the end, he said, "Bennie T. Davis and Bobbie J. Davis were found not guilty."

The congregation went up in praise, thanking God that it was a not-guilty verdict. Deacon Terry Williams started looking around at the people in the church, and then he started looking down. He was not happy at all about that not guilty verdict because now I can remain Pastor. It took a lifetime for me to get here. Everyone in the church could feel God's Spirit all over the sanctuary. The congregation started crying out to God, thanking Him for bringing their pastor and his mother out with a not-guilty verdict.

I asked everybody to start praising God, "Praise Him like you need God to release a not guilty verdict on whatever you are going through in your life right now."

We had an amazing time in the Lord. Our speaker eloquently delivered the Dr. Martin Luther King Jr. speech, and I did the mini-sermon. After the conclusion, the members, guests, and the guest speaker were invited to have dinner at Golden Corral. It was an enriched type of day. So many members called to tell me how much they enjoyed our Black History program.

We had our first-morning program, and it was a success. Our next program will be the birthday ministry, and that's in just a few short weeks. Everyone with a birthday between January and March had to pay $100; everyone else paid $50. This program took place on the first Sunday in March. Our guest speaker was Reverend Curtis Campbell, Pastor of Mount Ararat of Mullins, SC. After paying out the expenses, the church was blessed financially with over $1300 on the first program. The members at Saint Matthew's Missionary Baptist Church were excited about what we accomplished in under 90 days under the leadership of Pastor D. It was not enough to change the heart of Deacon Terry Williams toward Pastor D.

Almost every church family we invited came out to the program. The sanctuary was packed with different denominations, but we had a high time in the Lord. The women's ministry of Saint Matthews Missionary Baptist Church contributed over $400 from a fundraiser on that Saturday, the day before the program. Everyone was on one accord, wanting success to come to St. Matthews Missionary Baptist Church. For March, we raised over $9000 between the two Sundays and the first program.

New guests continued to come to the church services. Members that stopped coming started coming back to church. We had a meeting scheduled because I wanted Saint Matthews Missionary Baptist Church to start having a service every Sunday. After all, it is time for the church sanction. I announced to the birthday ministry program that we had a church meeting coming up, and we needed every one in attendance.

We are moving into the next level in this ministry; the church went up in praise because they were excited about what we were doing and going to do. Before Reverend Curtis Campbell dismissed the service, he let the church know that anytime Saint Matthews Missionary Baptist Church needed him that, Mount Ararat would come fellowship, just let him know.

I was in my office when a knock came on the door, and I asked them to enter. A young person came in and was terribly upset. I suggested to the young person that everything would be okay.

"What is wrong? Tell me."

Then the young person said to me, "Pastor, I do not want you to go because we never had a pastor as good as you. I am going to tell you, Pastor D, you are the best Pastor we ever had. People never were coming to church like this before, and now people are coming back because of the work you are doing here at Saint Matthew's Missionary Baptist Church. I do not want you to go. I would love for you to stay as our Pastor here at St. Matthews. Still, Deacon Terry Williams is not for you because he has convinced over 90% of the members that you are bad and will bring the church down and destroy this ministry. Pastor D, when this meeting occurs, Deacon Terry Williams wants the members to vote you out as Pastor. You will be able to do nothing to help yourself because he turned the members against you."

I responded by saying to the young person, "Do not worry about it because what I am doing is right. All I have is love for this church family. I will do my job if I am at this church."

I said, "Let us pray."

I said a prayer and said, "Everything would be all right if it were meant for me to stay here as Pastor. I would do so, but if not, the people will believe a lie."

On that third Sunday morning, we had such a high time in the Lord. There were new faces in the church service. I reminded everyone, "At the end of service, please attend the church meeting because we will be making some important decisions. The meeting is at 6:00 pm on Wednesday before Bible study, and prayer service will start at 7:00."

Wednesday came quickly. I was ready because I was fasting and praying all week long. After the meeting started, I shared with them that I wanted to start a Facebook page and a website for the church.

I let the members know that it was not going to cost the church anything. I had my sister and my daughter, Ashley Davis, working for a whole two weeks to show the members how it would look. It would attract people and tourists to the church that is vacationing in Myrtle Beach during the summertime. Myrtle Beach was not just a place to come to during the summer, but people now come all year long. I knew over a million people would be on the beach during the 4th of July.

I encouraged them that Facebook and the website would be an attraction for them to visit the church service. The ones that moved to Myrtle Beach or in the area would invite them to Saint Matthew's Missionary Baptist Church, knowing that they have become members of the greatest church in Kingston Lake. I gave the members all the advantages of why Facebook and the website would work for this ministry. With over seventy people in church every first and 3rd Sunday and the offering averaging $3900, let's start having church service every Sunday. I also shared with them that we would record the service and put it on our church's Facebook page so everyone could see the service. This would encourage people to visit the church. Still, by this time, Deacon Terry Williams had turned the church family against me.

This was when my mind went back to the young person who came to my office and said that Deacon Terry Williams had changed people's minds, so I said, "Let's do three Sundays and see how that goes. Then we could go represent the church because people are on the beach all the time."

In 2015, the members voted down the Facebook page and the website. They never got the Facebook page until 2020 and started doing it live. Because of what Deacon Terry Williams did to SMMBC, they are now five years behind. He influenced the members to go against the vision that God gave to me. God gave me the vision. It reminds me of how ten spies stopped millions of people from going to the promised land. Now, one man, Deacon Terry Williams, stopped the whole church from getting the promises of God. Just because he did not like me, St. Matthews Missionary Baptist Church suffered and suffered.

The members voted on having church on three Sundays. When the votes were counted, it was a tie. Deacon Dennis Gerald broke the tie in favor of having services three Sundays a month. At the end of the meeting, someone that Deacon Terry Williams invited to the meeting stood up and asked what we must do to vote on getting rid of our pastor. The person who asked the question does not attend the church, but Deacon Terry Williams went out and got dead people. Dead people are the members who stopped coming to church services. He also had old members who stopped attending after Samantha Jackson arrested me for sexual assault.

The chairman of the Deacon ministry, Deacon Timothy Gerald, said that someone must write a letter stating why a vote needs to occur for Dr. Bennie T. Davis to be replaced as pastor here at Saint Matthew's Missionary Baptist Church. The meeting went over the time. I canceled Bible study and let everyone know that we would have Bible study next week. After the meeting, a few other members came to me and said, "Pastor, you have not done anything but a great job. I will do everything possible to keep you as the pastor here at Saint Matthew's Missionary Baptist Church."

I let them know everything would be all right and to keep God first, then I walked out of the church and went to my car to go home. As I was walking, my eyes got full of water, and tears started rolling down my face. I was so hurt that people came to the meeting hoping to vote me out as Pastor at SMMBC.

I can live with them not doing Facebook or the website right now because I will continue to bring it up until the members see the benefits of having it.

On my way home, I called my aunt to tell her what went on at the meeting. She encouraged me by just saying, "Stay focused, keep on doing what you are doing, and leave it in God's hands."

I got home so fast on this night. I walked into the house, went to my room, fell across the bed, put my head on my pillow, and cried myself to sleep.

The next day, I stayed around the house and prepared for Sunday. The Lord laid something on my heart. Before long, Sunday was here. The service was at Greater Christ Temple Church of the Harvest in Marion. A new guest came to the Sunday morning service. At the end of the service, I informed the church family that I would be introducing the new Pastor here at Greater Christ Temple within the next three to four weeks. I let the church family know that I had to be totally focused on Saint Matthews Missionary Baptist Church. We had a wonderful time. People praised God and were delivered during the morning service.

Even with all that was going on at SMMBC, many people still came out to Bible study. Bible study was wonderful. Everyone took part by asking questions. The other members said, "Go deep, Pastor D." Deacon Terry Williams was in attendance as if nothing was going on because he also participated.

Not long after Bible study was dismissed, Deacon Terry Williams secretly passed out a criminal record on Pastor D. He had a friend of his go on the internet and printed copies off so every member could have their copy. Deacon Terry Williams let everyone know to meet him in the church parking lot at his car. This was the start of Pastor D's demise. They went out in a small group to his car and waited for him to come out of the church. Deacon Terry Williams announced that he had Pastor D's criminal records, and there were crimes that the church family had not been told. He said he also had a petition they each needed to sign. He had a copy of Pastor D's criminal record for each of them to keep as he was passing out the copies of the criminal record, and they signed the petition.

Now that the members were doing this, he was happy because the meeting would vote Pastor D out of the church. One of the members came back to the church and let me know what was going on. When I walked out to my car, Deacon Terry Williams and a few members were still talking. He had no idea that I had a copy of the criminal record he had passed out to the members.

On my way home, I knew that this meeting would take place, but I had no idea when. Now, he has a petition that the members signed to take to the meeting to vote Pastor D out as pastor. When I made it home, I started looking over this so-called copy of my criminal record that Deacon Terry Williams passed out to the church members. I could not find anything to help me, but I went straight to the kitchen table as soon as I got in the house.

As I looked over the criminal report, I saw a few crimes that I did not commit. Out of nowhere, as I was looking over this crime, the birth date of March 13, 1988, stood out to me. This was not my charge because, in 1988, I was in my first year of college when this person was born. Deacon Terry Williams never looked at the birth date because all he was looking at was the added so-called charges. He had the members believing that Pastor D lied to them about my criminal record. I could not call any of the members because I did not know who was for me or against me.

Now, the members who were for me are pretending. I cannot fight the church war when the people who are invisible are against me. I was praying and hoping that I would have an opportunity to show Deacon Terry Williams and the members that these crimes were not committed by Pastor D but by someone else. Now, the crimes that I have done, I am not ashamed to accept, but please do not find me guilty of crimes someone else did and is accusing me of.

I do not know when I went to sleep, but I got up from the table. I prepared myself for bed, and I just looked up at the ceiling with tears rolling from my eyes and down my face. I was waking up throughout the night, praying and asking God to work this situation out in my favor. As I was praying, I asked God to show me a sign to let me know that He is with me. I was looking around in the room. All the lights were off, and the door was closed. I could not see anything, not even my hand, but something happened shortly before I went back to sleep.

As I looked around the room, a shadow of my arm and hand appeared on the wall out of nowhere. This was how God reminded me no matter how dark it is in my life, and I am right here with you because there is no light, but on the wall is your shadow. The Lord was letting me know that God is my light. That is the reason the shadow came during my darkness. I just started thanking God for being by my side. I fell asleep praising the Lord during that long night.

The rest of the week went by so quickly. Sunday is here. It is time to go to St. Matthews Missionary Baptist Church to do my job be the pastor. The enemies would love me to fuss about what was going on, but I did my job. More people were in Sunday school this Sunday, and there were more new faces in the morning service. The church family was blessed spiritually and financially. Sunday school was also wonderful; everyone seemed to enjoy the class because they asked questions. Deacon Terry Williams came to Sunday school and stayed for morning services. The sanctuary was over halfway full of church family and guests.

It was between 75 to 82 people in the service when the service transitioned into my hands. I said to myself, "I must preach this thing." The subject was 'I Shall Recover It All In 2015'. From start to finish, people praised God throughout the service. After service, people came up to me, saying how much they enjoyed the service during the meet and greet. I went to my office.

While I was in the office, the door opened. Deacon Timothy Gerald walked into my office and closed the door behind him, "Pastor D, you need to know that some members worked together to write a letter to vote you out as pastor here at St. Matthews Missionary Baptist Church. If they produce this letter, there will be a meeting with you and the deacons. See if you can come up with something not to have the meeting with the church to vote you out as pastor of the church."

I said, "Deacon Timothy Gerald, that is fair enough because I will stay here at St. Matthews Missionary Baptist Church."

Then Deacon Timothy Gerald looked at me and said, "You would be a great pastor, and I want you to stay as pastor here at the church."

I stood up and said, "I will see you on Wednesday night at Bible study."

When I shook his hand, I told him to give me a call and let me know the finances for today.

Petro and I were halfway to his mother's house when I received a call. It was Deacon Timothy Gerald calling to let me know the earnings from Sunday service. I told Deacon Timothy Gerald that God had blessed the church with more than enough finances to pay all our bills for the month.

In the next ten years, "I will have SMMBC debt-free."

Petro and I had dinner at his mother's house, and what a meal she had waiting for us. After we left, I remembered walking to Petro's truck and getting in, but within 10 minutes, I was asleep. The next thing I knew, I heard Petro saying, "Pastor D." We were in front of my house. That food put me out. I went into the house and got into bed.

Deacon Timothy Gerald called me on Tuesday night to let me know that there will be no Bible study on Wednesday night. He expressed that the deacons wanted to meet with me because someone gave him a letter on why the church wanted to vote me out as pastor. He then stated now the deacons must address the letter with me.

He said, "Hopefully, we can clear this up. If we can come up with something, we will move from meeting with the church family about voting you out as Pastor."

I said, "Deacon Timothy Gerald, I will be at the church on Wednesday at 7:00 pm to meet with you and the other deacons."

I was confident that we would not have a meeting with the church family because when I first became pastor, I said to the deacons no matter what we were going through, whatever the situation was, the majority rules. We have four deacons and one Pastor. This church is governed under congregational by-laws that the majority rules.

So, when we vote for whatever the majority we must support. Now, we must come out in unity in front of the church family. So that the Pastor, Deacons, and church family can all work together.

I went to sleep with confidence that everything would be alright because it was going to be a meeting with the Deacons and myself. Before I knew it, I was on the road going to the church. I wanted to be on time for the meeting and arrived at 6:45 pm. When I drove up into the church's parking lot, the Deacons were already in the church waiting for me. Before I got out of my car, I prayed and asked God to "open my eyes to give me understanding. Let me know what is going on and see who is for me and who is against me."

I know God is going to work it out because I fasted all day about this meeting. When I entered the sanctuary, the lights were on, and the deacons were in the Bible study room. As I got closer to the door of the Bible study room, Deacon Timothy Gerald stepped out of the room and said, "Pastor D, we are in here waiting on you."

I entered the room, and all the deacons were sitting down. After I sat down, the chairman, Deacon Timothy Gerald, opened the meeting with prayer. After praying, he let me know that he received a letter from a member of Saint Matthews Missionary Baptist Church, and other members signed the letter.

He said, "Many of the members supported the accusations brought up about you. Tonight, I hope that we can settle this so that the church can continue to move on with you as pastor here at Saint Matthew's Missionary Baptist Church. Pastor D, if we cannot settle this, we will have the meeting on Wednesday after the second Sunday. At this meeting, the Saint Matthews Missionary Baptist Church family will vote to keep you as pastor or to remove you as pastor here at the church."

Deacon Timothy Gerald proceeded by reading the letter so that the deacons and I could hear how the members felt about Dr. Bennie T. Davis. At the end of the letters, Deacon Timothy Gerald lets everyone in the room know who wrote the letter by saying signed, Terry Williams.

I asked, "Who is Terry Williams? Is he a member who came back to the church after I became Pastor here at the church?"

Deacon Timothy Gerald said, "No, Pastor D, I do not know why he signed 'Terry Williams' because it is Deacon Terry Williams."

I was so surprised that the only thing I could do was look behind me at Deacon Terry Williams.

I said, "This cannot be true because this man came to Greater Christ

Temple Church in Marion, and he sat with me for over 2 hours asking all kinds of questions."

I explained everything he asked me. He said to me before our meeting was over, "I am for you, Pastor D. I will stay with you, and now, Deacon Terry Williams, you mean to tell me that you wrote this letter. Judas betrayed Jesus now Deacon Terry Williams betrayed me. Just as Jesus called Judas friend over 2000 years ago today, Jesus wants us to know that it will be our friend who takes us down in life. I thought Deacon Williams was a friend because of what he said to me at our meeting in Marion."

Deacon Timothy Gerald also had a copy of the criminal records. He said, "Pastor D, there are crimes that you had never told us about when you became the Pastor here. Deacon Williams believes that you will bring more shame to this church because you will be incarcerated for those crimes for which you went to court. Deacon Williams believes that you will be found guilty and will do years in prison. Before the church goes through the embarrassment, Deacon Terry Williams would like to have the meeting to vote you out as Pastor here at SMMBC."

I knew once I got an opportunity to explain what was going on, three of the deacons. I would be able to have four against one, and the majority rules and this meeting should not take place. I would let them know that the deacons and I decided to allow Pastor D to stay at St. Matthews Missionary Baptist Church. We were able to work everything out, but Deacon Terry Williams had another plan. It was not working out for the majority.

Deacon Timothy said, "Deacon Williams, at this time, you can speak about why we should have this meeting. Then, Pastor D, you would have the opportunity to explain this situation, and then we would take a vote if we should have the meeting two weeks from today."

Deacon Timothy Gerald said, "Deacon Williams, the floor is yours, and please present your case on why Dr. Bennie T. Davis should not pastor this church any longer."

Deacon Terry Williams said, "I do not want Dr. Bennie T. Davis to remain as Pastor at SMMBC because of his criminal record. I have a sheet with all the crimes that he committed in Marion County. He never told us about the crimes he committed. He lied to everyone to become the pastor of this church. Dr. Bennie T. Davis got over because he saw that older people were members here at this beautiful church. He will bring shame to this church family. I am not going to rest until Dr. Bennie T. Davis is out of this church. I want this man out of SMMBC tonight and to give up his keys. I want to take Dr. Bennie T. Davis before the church body to vote on keeping him as Pastor or not. The church family has already decided they wanted him out because there is an extensive list of several members' signatures on the letter to have the meeting. The members and I feel that Dr. Bennie T. Davis must not remain Pastor here at SMMBC. Dr. Bennie T. Davis is the only pastor in this church's history that we cannot allow to be with any of the young ladies because of the sexual assault charges. I should have voted him out that night. Enough is enough. I refuse to let this church go down because of Dr. Bennie Davis. It would be wrong if we do not take him before the church and vote him out unless he resigns from being the Pastor here at St. Matthews Missionary Baptist Church tonight."

"Deacon Terry Williams, let us say Dr. Bennie Davis did everything you said, but God sent him to St. Matthews Missionary Baptist Church. Since he has been pastoring, he has not made any of those accusations, but his life is better now. Our pastor has everyone working together as a church family, and some of the other people who left the church have started coming back to this church. Dr.

Bennie Davis is the greatest teacher and pastor that we ever had since I have been here, and that has been years because I am over 90 years old. I believe God wants us to keep Dr. Bennie Davis as pastor."

Terry Williams responded by saying, "I do not care if God sent him here. He will not stay as pastor at St. Matthews Missionary Baptist Church. Dr. Bennie Davis will be found guilty, and he will spend many years in prison. I believe, along with the members, that he did have $125,000 worth of custom handbags and sexual assault on a young lady. We are going to have this meeting in two weeks to vote him out as pastor. I would like to thank each of you for listening to the members' concerns and myself about our pastor." Then he took his seat.

Deacon Timothy Gerald said, "Dr. Bennie Davis, now it is your opportunity to respond to the accusations that Deacon Terry Williams made about you."

I stated, "I want to thank the Deacon ministry for allowing me to respond to the accusations Deacon Terry Williams and church members have brought against me. Deacon Terry Williams has passed out a criminal record on me. The majority of the members at Saint Matthew's Missionary Baptist Church had an opportunity to look over my criminal record. Whoever Deacon Terry Williams got this record from just typed in Bennie Davis from Marion, and every Bennie Davis with a criminal record came up on the computer. They printed out every criminal listing with the name Bennie Davis and never looked at the address or the year they were born. Yes, there were many crimes, some I knew and some I did not know about. There is more than one Bennie Davis in Marion. The person who gave Deacon Terry Williams my criminal records for the SMMBC members to review never looked at the birth date or the address. I would like for everyone to turn to the second sheet. Bennie T. Davis was born in 1988 and lived in Mullins, SC. If the crimes he did were me, I would have been 24 years old at the time. These crimes were two and three years ago, and each of you know, I may look 24, but I am older than 24 years old. So, that means that the accusation could not be validated. Now, the handbags are me. Remember, before I became pastor here, I let each of you know in our meeting about the three charges that I was facing in general sessions court. I also told each of you about my past crimes. There was not one of you that I did not tell, but I will not say that I am guilty of crimes that I did not commit. There were three charges. I was found not guilty of beating a child, and my mother was also found not guilty."

"The sexual assault first-degree and handbag charges I am waiting to go to court for. I know that there was not $125,000 worth of custom handbags; therefore, I have the handbag charges against me. I would love to run for Mayor of the City of Marion. Our Mayor is responsible for me going to court for that charge. He thought it would stop me from running for Mayor, but I will not let anyone or anything stop me. If I am proven guilty of any one of the two charges, you would have to get another pastor because I would be in prison for many years. Deacon Terry Williams is telling the members that I will make time in prison. He believes that now, because of the things he has said about me, I am guilty. That is not true. I will be found not guilty on all charges. Let us not have the meeting and wait for me to go to court, and if the verdict is not guilty, I stay as pastor, but if I am found guilty, then let the church get a new pastor. I am innocent until proven guilty. Deacon Terry Williams, let us wait because God is doing some great things here at the church. Since there were sexual assault charges, Deacon Terry Williams called me and asked me if he could come to Marion to meet with me. I told him I would love for him to come, so he said, can I come when I get off. I said, call me when you get into Marion, and I look forward to hearing from you. When he came, I took him to Greater Christ Temple Church of the Harvest to meet. The meeting lasted over 2 hours. At the end of our meeting, Deacon

Terry Williams made me believe that he was, for me, being Pastor at SMMBC. Therefore, I am so surprised that Deacon Williams wrote this letter. That is why he signed the letter Terry Williams and not Deacon Terry Williams. Now, Deacon Williams, you believe I should not be Pastor here at St. Matthews Missionary Baptist Church any longer because of what you heard about me and the criminal record that came off the computer. You went to the Mayor and the police station of Marion, and they said to you the best thing for the church and yourself to do is to get rid of Bennie as pastor. He is no pastor; all he will ever be is Caveman, the drug dealer. The only thing he will do is bring that church down and destroy any good thing about the church. Deacon Terry Williams was using my past reputation to get me voted out as Pastor. Now, why should you be a Deacon at St. Matthews Missionary Baptist Church? Let me tell you, Deacon Williams, why do people not see you as being this great or good deacon? They do not look to you as a deacon."

I proceeded to tell him about what was happening in the church. When I told him what was said, I could see the guilt was all over his face. Deacon Terry Williams was surprised because he assumed no one would tell what he was doing. I said to him, "You still are Deacon Terry Williams." There was no comment. Everyone was surprised in the meeting. The last words that I said were, "Let us not have this meeting. Wait until I go to court," and then I took my seat.

The chairman, Deacon Timothy Gerald, came to the front and said, "Let us vote with a show of hands if the meeting is going to happen or not. The ones in favor of the meeting, raise your hand."

There was only one who raised his hand (Deacon Terry Williams). Deacon Dennis Gerald and Deacon Ralph, Van Fore raised their hands in favor of not having the meeting and waiting to see what happened in court. I felt so good because the majority rules, but Deacon Terry Williams was upset with me and the other deacons, and he displayed it.

Deacon Terry Williams said, "Not just me, but the members wanted this meeting."

Deacon Timothy Gerald said, "Yes, but what you said and showed us is false information. Dr. Bennie Davis has proven that those other crimes were not his. Why are we having this meeting on charges that we know Dr. Bennie Davis did not do?"

All I could think was, this is not happening. When I look back now, this reminds me of the 2020 election, how our former president had a sizable percentage of the Republican party believing a lie.

In April 2015, Deacon Terry Williams persuaded and influenced most of the church family to believe a lie. In two more weeks, a meeting will hold up God's work because one deacon wants it his way. The meeting ended with prayer. As I walked out, Deacon Williams was so happy that he started calling the members and telling them there would be a meeting in two weeks. I got in my car and drove about 15 minutes from Marion when I received a phone call. I answered the phone, and to my astonishment, it was Deacon Terry Williams who said, "Pastor, if you tell me who gave you the information about me, I will let you remain pastor, and I will call off the meeting."

14.　AFTER

I had to catch my breath because this is a man who does no wrong. I responded to Deacon Terry Williams by saying, so if I tell you who told me your secret that you are hiding from the church family now, will you get those same members of St. Matthews Missionary Baptist Church that you have been lying to about me to let me stay as pastor? In other words, you have done just what you said to me. But in the meeting, you would not own up to it in the presence of the deacons. Now, Deacon Williams, as much as I would love to stay as pastor at St. Matthews Missionary Baptist Church, I cannot allow you to have that kind of power over me to dictate what I can and cannot do. You would put me out as Pastor when you get upset about someone. I want to work within the ministry, but I cannot do that. You are saying you could convince the other people to allow me to stay until I go to court. If I tell you who told me your secret, what I know you did is the only way you will call the members on me to stay pastor here at St. Matthews Missionary Baptist Church. I cannot tell you who told me because I do not know what would happen to them because they do not like what you are doing to this church family." Then I said, "There is nothing else we must discuss. I will see you on Wednesday night in Bible study. Have a good night."

When our conversation ended, I called the person who told me Deacon Terry Williams' secret that he did not want anyone to know.

I let the person know that Deacon Williams asked me to tell him his secret that he needs to stay on the down-low. He said if I gave him the person's name, he would influence the members not to vote me out as pastor and keep me until the court was over and wait for the outcome of my court trial. The person said, "Pastor D, you should have told him. Call Deacon Williams and tell him who I am. Please stay our pastor because we have never had a pastor as good as you and all the great things you brought to this ministry. St. Matthews Missionary Baptist Church never had or never will have a pastor like you because you make everyone believe in themselves and make us better people not just at church but at our home with our families."

When I ended my conversation, I walked into the house, and I shared with my family what Deacon Williams was doing to stop me. Because of the hate and the determination to get me voted out as a pastor and prevent the church's growth, this one decided to tell a lie about me. The only good thing I see out of this is that he cannot stop church services. I have one more Bible study on Wednesday night, and on Sunday, I will preach one more sermon before the church meeting. I pray that God opens the members' eyes before this man destroys the most significant opportunity for St. Matthews Missionary Baptist Church, the most remarkable church in Kingston Lake. My sister said to me, "I hope you remain the pastor of the church, but if not, you are still the pastor at Greater Christ Temple Church of the Harvest here in Marion, South Carolina. Pastor D, wait before you make that young man the new pastor of Greater Christ Temple Church of the Harvest." I said I would wait before announcing a new pastor. I am going to start preparing myself for Bible study for next week. The members of St. Matthews Missionary Baptist Church are always excited about learning more about the Bible. The members were still hungry to learn, and it is my job regardless of how the people may feel about me. The days just started going by so fast. The night before Bible study. I was unable to sleep, so I continued to go over the Bible study lesson.

About an hour before it was time for me to get on the road, I went over the task for the last time. When I drove up in the parking lot, there were not as many cars at Bible study. The only thing I was thinking about was this could be the last Bible study here at St. Matthews Missionary Baptist Church as their pastor.

Because it was only a few cars, I said to myself, this must have gotten to the church members and convinced them not to come to Bible study. When I walked into the classroom, it was about ten people attending Bible study. Every time I started Bible study for the last ninety days, this man always participated. Deacon Timothy Gerald opened the Bible study class and then turned the class into my hands. I started Bible study by thanking the members for allowing me to be their pastor. Then I said, "Before I go over the Bible study lesson tonight, I would like to take 15 minutes to go over this criminal record.

On the sheet of crimes, that was passed out to St. Matthews Missionary Baptist Church members is supposed to be my criminal record. There are two different Bennie T. Davis' on this so-called criminal record. Tonight, I will show each of you what Bennie T. Davis Sr.'s crimes are and what the other Bennie T. Davis Jr. crimes are because all of them do not belong to me. I must tell this class the truth so that every one of you can make a reasonable decision on Wednesday at the church meeting when it is time to vote to keep me as pastor or not." A young man stood up out of nowhere and said, "Dr. Bennie Davis, if you do not stop going over that criminal record and start Bible study, my family and I will walk out of this church now. We came here for Bible study only, not to hear about your criminal record." So, I showed everyone several of the crimes committed by Bennie Davis Jr., who resides in Marion County, but was born on March 13, 1988. The church family did not know that this was Bennie Davis, Jr., my son, but no one wanted to listen. Their mind was blinded because of the lies that were told about me by Deacon Terry Williams. The members would not accept the truth because after I let the class know who the other Bennie Davis was, Minister Cross got up out of their seats and walked out of the Bible study class. Minister Cross is the same person who told me after one of our Bible studies classes that Deacon Williams is doing all he can to get me voted out as pastor.

"Pastor D, we cannot let this happen because you are a great pastor, and we cannot let you go, but now this minister is working with Deacon Williams to put you out as pastor of St. Matthews Missionary Baptist Church." Deacon Williams was outside in the parking lot waiting for the members to come out of Bible Study so that he could continue to convince them to vote me out as pastor next Wednesday night at the church meeting. Everyone who walked out of Bible study went outside in the parking lot, where Deacon Williams continued to lie about Pastor D. He told them that he wanted everyone to boycott church on Sunday morning service. "I will have the sheriff here at the church waiting for Pastor D in the parking lot. So, he will go to jail if he does not get back in his car and go back to Marion. I will make sure Pastor D is arrested if he steps foot out of his car." Deacon Williams convinced everybody to listen to him that this was the best way for the church to go because Pastor D was bringing so much shame to St. Matthews Missionary Baptist Church.

About seven people were still in Bible study, and we had about thirty minutes left in class. I poured out of my heart, and I gave them the best that I had, just as I always did, but as I looked around the room as I ended Bible Study, I was able to see different ones' eyes get full of water and tears started running down their faces. I said to them, "We must leave it in the hands of the Lord. Let God fight this battle because the battle does not belong to me. It belongs to the Lord." Everyone who had a testimony and a prayer request gave it to the class. I led the class in prayer, and just like always, the Holy Spirit fell into the building, and the people cried out to the Lord. After the dismissal of Bible study, as we were leaving the church, Deacon Williams was still outside in the parking lot, standing up, waiting to stop the members that he could convince to come to his side. The few people who left out of Bible study early were still outside with him. He wanted me and anyone who believed in me to see he had more on his side than was for me to stay as pastor at St. Matthews Missionary Baptist Church. I continued to ask myself what this man have over these people that they have to obey and do as he tells them. Because I know that these were some intelligent people, but for them to follow a lie, the members had no desire to hear the truth. This man had power over these great people. As I passed him in the parking lot, he had a smirk on his face like it was not long. He made me feel as though he was saying I will accomplish my job. Pastor D will be gone. I will get the pastor that I want, the one that the deacons and members of St. Matthews Missionary Baptist Church promised would be the pastor, but we ended up with Pastor D. This man is going to do whatever he has to do to make this happen. He did not even want to consider that God had better for him and the church family. He reminded me of Sarah in the bible. She got to help God because He was moving too slowly. So, I went straight to my car and got into it and went home. As I was on my way home, I began to pray, asking God to give me a sermon for Sunday. I need God's word to go from heart to heart and mind to mind. Many sermons started coming to me, but none of them stuck to my heart. When I made it home, I did not stay up to talk with anyone. I just wanted to be alone to talk to the Lord. I prayed, and I waited to hear from the Lord. Not one word I heard from the Lord. So, Thursday morning, I got up early to get my haircut. I was outside of the barbershop waiting for Minister Travis Smith to open so I could be the first person to get my haircut. For some reason, it was not a lot of people waiting for a haircut. I was the first one in the barber's chair. As Minister Travis Smith was cutting my hair, I started telling him what was going on at St. Matthews Missionary Baptist Church. I said to him, "I hope you are still thinking about becoming the new Pastor at Greater Christ Temple Church of the Harvest. Before any of that can happen, I have a meeting on Wednesday night. This man does not want me to be the pastor any longer, so he turned most of the church family against me." I said to Minister Travis Smith, "I must come up with a sermon because this could be my last Sunday as pastor." Minister Smith said, "Pastor D, I have a subject for you. God put this in my spirit, but I believe this is for you." Then he said, "A Pocket Full of Rocks." I said to Minister Smith, "What is a pocket full of rocks?" He said, "When they caught the woman in adultery, God was on her side despite her adultery." As I was getting my haircut, I said that I would start working on my sermon for Sunday today. I went home and began working on my sermon. It was in my spirit when I finished it was late in the afternoon. I said to myself that I could get closer to God. I need God to move in the service on Sunday Morning. Before I knew it, the weekend was here and hours before Sunday morning service. Saturday night, I was up preaching the sermon to myself again all night. I loved the subject, "A Pocket Full of Rocks."

Someone from St. Matthews Missionary Baptist Church called me at about 6:00 a.m. "Pastor D," the person said to me, "Do not worry about Deacon Williams having a sheriff waiting on you at St. Matthews Missionary Baptist Church. The Sheriff cannot put you in jail. They told Deacon Williams the only way the sheriff does anything to Dr. Bennie Davis, the chairman of the deacon ministry or the pastor of St. Matthews Missionary Baptist Church, must call and ask for assistance from the sheriff's department. Deacon Timothy Gerald loved Pastor D, and Pastor D would not call the sheriff on himself to put himself in jail. Because of the information he received from the Sheriff's Department, Deacon Williams is not even considering having the sheriff out to the church on Sunday." I said to the caller, "Thank you. But do not worry. I will be at the church for Sunday School and morning service. I am looking forward to you being at the service. I am looking to have a high time in the Lord because I can give God praise in a time like this. Let me go so I can be on time for service because Petro is picking me up." After getting off the phone, I got up and started preparing myself for service. When I finished getting ready for church, I started going over Sunday School and my sermon. Petro called me to let me know that he would pick me up in fifteen minutes.

On our way to St. Matthews Missionary, Baptist Church, Petro encouraged me so much by telling me that I have done a wonderful job as a pastor and that not any of the members could ask for any more than the work I have done at the church. "Pastor D, the meeting is Wednesday, but let us not focus on that because you need to give everything you have in today's service. However, God put it in your spirit and give it to the congregation." Petro reminded me that Deacon Williams boycotted the service today. He is doing all he can for all the members to stay home today. Deacon Williams did everything humanly possible to take all your hope out of you. So that you will give up and not show up for the meeting because not everyone showed up for Sunday morning services, Pastor D, do whatever God placed in your heart, and everything else will fall in place." I said, "Thank you, Petro, for the words of encouragement."

By this time, we were in the parking lot of St. Matthews Missionary Baptist Church. There were only a few cars in the parking lot. But when I noticed that the members were not at church for Sunday school, my head got heavy, and tears were coming down my face. I reminded myself when God is for me, who can stop what God has for me? No one, not even Deacon Williams. All the tears started drying up. I had to get myself together to walk into the church as Dr. Bennie T. Davis. When I walked into the sanctuary, there were only five people. I used to have between twenty-five and thirty-five people in Sunday school. At that time, I knew that the St. Matthews Missionary Baptist Church members believed what Deacon

Williams said about me. I'm sure this man was pleased with his boycott because the members did not show up for Sunday school. I still hoped that more people would overcome the lie and show up for the morning service. I carried on Sunday School just as it was any other Sunday school.

Our Sunday school was very spiritual, and the members who came felt the presence of God. They asked questions, and I also asked them some questions. All the questions were answered. I knew the class had studied the Sunday school lesson because they could answer the questions. At the end of Sunday school, different ones told the class how the study impacted their lives and how it gave them so much hope. God can still work it out after that. I dismissed Sunday school. I was hyped because of the great times as a pastor here at St. Matthews Missionary Baptist Church. Then, I went to my office to prepare myself for the morning service. As I was meditating, a knock came on the door and I entered. When I opened my eyes, Deacon Dennis Gerald walked into my office. He said, "Pastor D, do not worry. Everything will be alright, but I do not want to lie to you. I love you for all the good things you brought to this ministry. Thank you for sharing your Bible knowledge in Bible study, Sunday school, and Sunday morning worship service. There has not been a pastor or anyone to try out for St. Matthews Missionary Baptist Church that gives us the experience and knowledge you shared. When God sends St. Matthews Missionary Baptist Church a real pastor, the church family asked what will we do to keep them or let them get away. You are the real pastor, Pastor D, but 90% of the church family members will vote you out on Wednesday night at the church meeting. St. Matthews Missionary Baptist Church instead believed a lie rather than the truth. What does Deacon Williams have holding over this church family's head so that they will not go against him?" I told the deacon, "I believe everything will be alright on Wednesday night. Many members may not be coming to morning service, but I will preach to the few anyway. God has been good to Pastor D. I thank you and the other deacons and members of St. Matthews Missionary Baptist Church for giving me this opportunity to become the pastor of this church. Regardless of who turned against me, I knew this was the most significant accomplishment since being saved by becoming the Pastor here at St. Matthews Missionary Baptist Church. This only happened because 90% voted for me to become the pastor, and I gave this church everything in me. Suppose they remember that they cannot vote me out, but they will vote if they follow Deacon Williams. I see that he had boycotted Sunday morning service. God cannot be pleased with Deacon Williams." I thanked Deacon Dennis Gerald and everyone else for coming today. I told Deacon Dennis Gerald to get the morning service started, and I will be out shortly.

The ushers did not even come for service this morning, but it is alright. I am so happy that the Lord is in this house. Regardless of who did not come to church, the Lord will never leave this house. As soon as Deacon Dennis Gerald walked out of my office and closed the door, I went into prayer, "God, give me the strength and ability to move in this service like never before and bless each person in some way today. Let the ones who did not come because of the boycott let them know that I still love them. Lord, I give you thanks right now in Jesus' name. Amen."

I went over my sermon again, and by this time, someone came to the door and said, "Pastor D, we are waiting for you to go to the sanctuary." I said to the person I was on my way. I went out of the office, and to my surprise, an usher was on the other side of the door waiting on me, Carrie Gerald. I began walking after her, but I said to myself, Lord, lead and guide me. When I open my mouth, please give me the words to say that somebody may ask what I must do to be saved. Then, I entered the sanctuary with my hands raised high, giving thanks to the Lord. After I went to my seat, I sat down slowly. My eyes went around the sanctuary. There were only a few people in the sanctuary for service. It was a lot of empty seats, but that is where the spirit of the Lord is. Someone was giving the Lord praise for his goodness. I do not know what will happen on Wednesday night at the meeting. I will enjoy this day by preaching to the most outstanding members, not just in the world but in the universe. My eyes got full of water. I felt the tears roll down my face. Quickly, I put my head down, took my towel, and wiped the tears away so no one would see me crying. I knew this could be my last Sunday as pastor at St. Matthews Missionary Baptist Church. I was not thinking about the different things I did as pastor here, but I thought about the happiness that this church family brought to my life. The respect and confidence they gave me out of all the churches, this was the only church family with the guts to encourage me. They made me a pastor, knowing I was autistic, epileptic, and a former drug dealer. A man who was facing three charges in general sessions court for selling counterfeit items, sexual assault, intent to commit criminal sexual conduct first degree, and assault and battery second degree. With all that, every Sunday, every Wednesday night at Bible study, and every time anyone from the church family saw me, they said, this is our new Pastor, or they would say this is my Pastor D. What joy all the members brought to my life. I was so caught up in thinking about what happened to me because of the wonderful St. Matthews Missionary Baptist Church members.

Out of nowhere, I heard someone saying, "Pastor D," then someone shook me, and I said I am alright, I am okay, and she said the service is in your hand. I went through the service order before long. It was time for me to bring the Good News. I began to look out into the sanctuary. About five people were in service. The spirit of the Lord was in the service. As I was looking around, I said, "Our subject today is, 'A Pocket Full of Rocks.'" I started preaching the word of God. I could see the tears flowing down Deacon Timothy Gerald's face, and Deacon Dennis Gerald's eyes were full of water. Carrie Gerald was clapping her hands and giving thanks to the Lord. I was able to see tears in Carrie Gerald's eyes. Susan Ford stood up, waving her hand and crying out to the Lord. Deacon Ralph Van Fore was waving his hand as he was smiling as if he was saying, everything will be alright. I continued to preach what the spirit of God put in my heart.

I believe that everyone who attended the service knew that this was my last Sunday as pastor here at St. Matthews Missionary Baptist Church. They were enjoying the word of God because the move of God was throughout the sanctuary.

At the end of the service, I informed everyone how much I loved them, how much I enjoyed being a pastor here, and how I was looking forward to continuing to be the pastor. When I dismissed service, every member came to me, shook my hand, or hugged me, and some were crying. I said, "I did not do anything wrong to shame this church family." It is great to love your pastor's cry because all of you have someone to cry to... Jesus Christ. My heart was so heavy when I walked to the office, tears rolling down my face and flowing out of my eyes. I went to my office as fast as possible so no one could see me crying because I had to be strong for the church family.

As I was in my office, a knock came on the door, and I said, "Give me a moment." I took my handkerchief and wiped the tears from my face. Then I said, "Enter." Deacon Timothy Gerald came walking through the door. He said, "Pastor D, a few people walked into service after you started preaching, but I also have a donation for you." Deacon Timothy Gerald gave me half because many people were not in church service. Deacon Timothy Gerald said, "Pastor D, the money that was raised surprised me. Many people who did not come to service sent their tithes and offerings. I told him, give me half, and if you have anything else, let it go back to the church from Pastor D." Deacon Timothy Gerald was in my office, but he never said anything or mentioned Wednesday night's meeting. He never said anything about how the congregation felt about me, but what got me was that he never mentioned Deacon William's name, who was the cause of the meeting.

As I was preparing myself to leave my office, I began to look around and noticed that I had never even had an opportunity to decorate my office. Deacon Timothy Gerald and I walked out together. When I entered the sanctuary on my way to the parking lot, almost every person in the morning service sat there waiting for me. Each one of them came and said something different to encourage me. Susan Ford said, "Pastor D, I will do everything in my power to make sure you stay a pastor here at St. Matthews Missionary Baptist Church." I responded by saying, "Thank you so much, and know that regardless of what happens on Wednesday night, Susan Ford, I love you and this church family." Then, I proceeded to go out the door. Susan Ford was the last person I greeted.

I went straight to Petro's truck. Petro said, "Do not put your head down, Pastor D, because you did as God gave it to you. Pastor D, don't be ashamed because they had the number one best pastor in Kingston Lake." Petro opened the door for me to get into the truck, and after I got in, he shut the door. Petro got in on the driver's side and said, "Pastor D, let's get out of here and go to Marion." As we went down Hwy 319, Petro saw the tears going down my face, meeting under my chin. Petro said, "Today's sermon was touching because almost everyone in the church was crying." "Petro, the only thing we can do is pray." I said to him, "First, I must leave it in the hands of the Lord. If God does not do it, Petro, it will not be done. Thank you for supporting me and ensuring that I was always at the church on Sunday on time."

Before long, Petro was pulling up to my house. As I got out of the truck, Petro said, "Pastor D, stop crying. Everything will be alright; do not get sick and worry about Deacon Williams. He has a goal to stop you from being a pastor by telling lies. Don't worry about those members that want to follow him and the lies he is telling you." I told Petro I was not, and I proceeded to go into the house.

I was home alone, so I had quiet time with the Lord. All I could do was start praying, thanking the Lord for just being good to me. "Thank you, Lord, for opening doors that man said would never open, and closing doors that had to be closed to make it in this walk of life. So many times, when I believed it was over, you and you only made a way out of no way for me. God, I need your help because this man has destroyed my character for no reason. Because I desired to work with a man he despised in the church. He is now determined to get the preacher I beat out to become Pastor at St. Matthews Missionary Baptist Church. God, I need your hedge around me and renew my mind. Look over me, protect me from my enemies. Open the church members' minds to make the right decisions and stop believing the enemy's lies. Just so he can get the man he wants as pastor and vote me out, I will give you all the praises, Lord right now in the name of Jesus. Amen."

After reading some of the Bible, my eyes started getting heavy, then they closed, and I went to sleep. At about 3:00 a.m., I woke up, went to the bathroom, and prepared myself for bed. I went back to sleep throughout the rest of the night. The next morning, when my eyes came open, I was hoping that I was waking up from a dream and that none of this was true. I was not about to be voted out of St. Matthews Missionary Baptist Church as pastor. I lay there looking up at the ceiling, realizing that it was not a dream. My heart knew the truth because the pillow on the bed was wet from all the crying I had done last night. In a few more days, my future as pastor will be in the hands of the St. Matthews Missionary Baptist Church members. If the members believed the lies that Deacon Williams said about me, I would be relieved of my pastoral duties. I wanted time to stop so that Wednesday would not come and the meeting would not happen. If I had my way, I would go back to when I first became pastor, and everyone was happy with Dr. Bennie T. Davis Sr. No matter how much I wanted it to happen, I had to face this enemy by praying, knowing God knows what is best for me.

By this time, I had to get up to start my Monday. Doing my normal running around to gather up supplies for the restaurant, besides being the pastor at St. Matthews Missionary Baptist Church, I was also a volunteer and Chaplain at the Carolina Hospital System of Marion. Every Monday, I would volunteer from 8:00 a.m. to 12:00 p.m.. I thanked Yolanda Moore so much for not firing me for being a volunteer and Chaplin at the hospital because she was the supervisor over all volunteers. Everybody else I was working with separated themselves from me because of the court cases against me. All three cases were serious charges that I could serve many years in prison if found guilty. She allowed me to stay on the volunteer list at the Carolina Hospital System of Marion. That meant so much to me. I had something to look forward to doing every Monday, and at any time during the day or night, someone may need a Chaplain. The person who would be working would be called Pastor D. Someone still believed that I was a good person. I was not pretending to be something that I was not, and that was a man of God.

This Monday, I did my volunteer hours, then went and got the supplies for the restaurant. I went to the restaurant to put everything up, and by the time I finished, my day was over. I went straight home because I was tired, and I did not care to see anyone. I knew what I was facing in just a couple of days. I read the Bible for some time, and then my sister came by the house with my dinner and made sure I was okay. After eating dinner, I made some time to cry out to the Lord. I asked the Lord to renew my mind and give me peace of mind. My mind was still on this Wednesday's meeting with the church family.

Deacon Terry Williams and St. Matthews Missionary Baptist Church members are still participating in the Pastoral election process. As I continued to pray, I heard a voice say peace comes now. Expeditiously, peace came to me. On this day, I don't know when I fell asleep. That was my best night of sleep in a long time. What woke me up was I heard a banging on the door and someone saying Pastor D, Pastor D. I went to the door, and to my surprise, it was my sister. I opened the door. As I was walking away, she came in. I asked her whether my mother was in the car. She said, "No, I am on my way to work, but Mama wants you to come get her about 8:30 a.m. She wants to be at the restaurant by 9:00 a.m. because some people ordered dinner. They will be there for the orders at 11:30 a.m. You know how she is about having the dinners ready."

"Pastor D, I got to get out of here because I have a meeting this morning, so I will call you on my way to work. How are you doing? Pastor D, Mama is so worried about this meeting tomorrow about you staying as Pastor." I told my sister I would tell mama not to worry because everything would be alright with me. By this time, my sister was walking to her truck. She said, "Don't forget to get mama."

As she drove off, I went back into the house and got dressed. Shortly after that, I went to pick my mother up and proceeded to go to the restaurant. As soon as she got into the restaurant, she started cooking, and I made the drinks. Time began to pass, and before long, it was 11 a.m., so we started fixing the dinners ordered for pickup. I was taking the trash out when a car pulled up as I left the trash dumpster. I had never seen this car before, but as I was walking, someone from the car said, "Pastor D, when you get some free time, will you come here because I need to see you about something." I went to the car, and a group of ladies were sitting in the car waiting for me. I didn't know who they were, but I informed them to give me about thirty minutes before the restaurant opened.

One of the ladies said, "We are not here to get any food, but we came to see our Pastor D. We are members of St. Matthews Missionary Baptist Church. We were hoping you could stay our pastor because you are doing a great job." One of them said, "We know that it's all because Deacon Williams persuaded most church members to vote you out as pastor. Pastor D has dead people coming to vote. Dead people are the people who have not been coming to church or paying tithes. Many members want you to stay as pastor, but they know that Deacon Williams will get back at them when they vote for you." Then someone said, "Pastor D, you are my Pastor regardless of tomorrow's outcome." "Pastor D, everyone in this car will do whatever we can to help you stay as pastor." "Pastor D, we vote to keep you because you have not done anything to the St. Matthews Missionary Baptist Church family. If anything, we are doing it to ourselves. If the members vote you out, they will vote out the best pastor and preacher we ever had at St. Matthews Missionary Baptist Church. I have been a member of this church for some years now." I said to the ladies, "I would like to thank each of you ladies for the wonderful things you said about me today. Each of you encouraged me in so many ways. I know it will be because of the jealousy and hate that Deacon Williams has towards me if I do not win. The vote isn't about me not doing my work because everything I could humanly possibly do to improve St. Matthews Missionary Baptist Church is what I did for the church family. My goal is to have St. Matthews Missionary Baptist Church better after me than before. I do not believe many people are coming to this meeting because they are tired. Every time they turn around, Deacon Williams has a problem with something I'm doing at the church. He has done this several times, but this is the only time it came before the church members. Satan doesn't stop until he believes that God has stopped the vision for St. Matthews Missionary Baptist Church."

One of the ladies said, "Pastor D, most of the people coming to the meeting will support Deacon Williams. Pastor D, we will get on the road to go back home to get on the phone and call some people to come to the meeting to vote for Pastor D. One of us will call you tonight to let you know how things went when we call the members." Then, one of the ladies in the car said, "Let me look at my pastor one more time before we get back on the road." I asked if the ladies would like to have dinner to take with them back home. One of the ladies said, "Pastor D, we didn't come to get food. We just came to let our pastor know how we feel about you being our pastor." As I was standing up, I waved my hands, saying bye simultaneously. As they were backing up slowly, I watched them go down the highway until they were out of sight. What got me was I had to hold back the tears because each one of the ladies' eyes was full of water. I saw the tears flowing down their face. I had to hold back my tears to be strong and let the ladies know that everything would be alright.

I went back into the restaurant, and shortly after that, someone came to pick up the orders. Almost every person who came into the restaurant asked the same question. "How are you doing at St. Matthews Missionary Baptist Church in Aynor, SC?" My response to all of them was the same thing. "I love being the pastor to all the members at St. Matthews Missionary Baptist Church. I am also looking forward to working harder for the vision to pass at St. Matthews Missionary Baptist Church."

At about 5:30 p.m., Dr. Henry McGill walked into the restaurant, and after he took his seat, I went and sat with him and started telling him what was going on at St. Matthews Missionary Baptist Church.

I told him that Deacon Williams hated me so much he got the church members to believe a lie, and tomorrow night, there would be a meeting to vote me out as pastor of St. Matthews Missionary Baptist Church. I told him that Deacon Williams had persuaded most members that I was no good for the church and that I would bring shame and bring the church down as pastor. Dr. Henry McGill said, "Pastor D, you did no wrong. You love being the pastor of St. Matthews Missionary Baptist Church." I said, "Dr. Henry McGill, I need you to pray that I may stay pastor at Saint Matthew Missionary Baptist Church." He said, "I will keep you in my prayers. When I speak with the chairman of the Deacon Ministry, I will let him know that they could not have been getting a better man than Dr. Bennie T. Davis Sr. I can stand on that today if they allow Deacon Terry Williams to influence them to vote you out as pastor mark this down, Pastor D. They will regret listening to him because the truth shall come out, Pastor D. You are not guilty." I said, "Dr. Henry McGill, I trust that God will fight this battle, and that same God will also fight for those members who Deacon Williams is fooling."

My sister said, "Pastor D. and Dr. Henry McGill, the restaurant is now closed. Mama and I are about to walk up out of here. Now, are you leaving now or later?" I said, "Hold up. We are walking behind you." I looked at Dr. Henry McGill and said thank you. I needed to have this conversation because the big meeting would occur in the next twenty hours. Dr. Henry McGill replied and said, "Pastor D, don't you forget the Lord is with you. The Lord is for you. Don't allow this situation to make you believe that the Lord cannot work it out for you." I said, "Dr. Henry McGill, you are right, but it's simply hard. I know that Deacon Williams is the cause of this meeting tomorrow night." As Dr. Henry McGill got in his truck, he said, "Pastor D., I will have you in my prayers because God can go from heart to heart and mind to mind. What they are going to do, God can reverse it and give you favor. I believe the Lord is going to work it out."

I got in the car and had my sister take me home. I wasn't getting on the phone to talk to anyone when I got home. I fasted, and throughout the day, I prayed because some things come through fasting and prayer. When I walked into the house, I got my Bible and started reading it and praying. I asked God for a little more faith so I could make it through the night. I thought about what I would do. There was nothing else I could do to change anything. I believe that God will work this thing out in some way and somehow. I prepared myself for it, and before 9:00 p.m., I was in bed looking at the ceiling. I was not able to go to sleep. I was reading, praying, and crying because, in my heart, I wanted to stay pastor at St. Matthews Missionary Baptist Church until I took my last breath, and now, I could be out of the church because of a lie. God allowed this in my life because I am human. I started thinking about what people would say about me to humiliate me and make me feel guilty for something that I did not do, but this is how so-called church people talk about each other and do not pray for each other.

As I read the Bible, tears were still rolling down my face. Sometime throughout the night, my eyes finally came together. I continued to wake up, looking for daylight through the window. All I could do was think about the meeting, but sometime before daylight began to break through the sky, I was in a deep sleep, and when my eyes opened, it was 10:00 a.m. the Wednesday morning, just a few hours before the meeting. The first thing I did was pray, reminding myself that A.M. means asking God for 'a miracle'. I asked God for the miracle to do what was best for me. Before my feet ever touched the floor, I went into prayer, thanking God for just another day. I asked the Lord to give me the strength. "Lord, please don't leave me by myself. God, when I take one step, don't take two because you will leave me behind two to my one God. So, God, when I step, You step; when I stop, you stop, but today, as I go on my journey to

Saint Matthew Missionary Baptist Church for this meeting tonight, I don't need You to be the spare tire. God, I need You to be my steering wheel. When I go into the meeting and open my mouth, God speak through me. God, give me the words to say, and I will give You the praise in Jesus' name. Amen."

I called my sister to tell her that I would not come out today. The only time I am leaving the house today is to go to the meeting tonight. I do not want to be around anyone today, nor do I want to talk to anyone on the phone. I decided to lay in bed until it was time to get up, and then I started preparing myself for the meeting at St. Matthews Missionary Baptist Church. Throughout the day, I prayed and cried out to the Lord. Several of my family members and friends called me and a few of the Saint Matthew Missionary Baptist Church members called, but I did not answer the phone. I didn't want to explain how I was feeling, and I didn't want to hear them say, 'Don't put your head down because everything will be alright.' Some would have said, 'Pastor D, you did a great job,' But all I know is I won't stay pastor at St. Matthews Missionary Baptist Church. I did not want to be voted out because of my opportunity with the members. I knew I might never get this opportunity that I had with the members again. I would have loved to give up, but I just wanted to work in the community and to have our younger adults self-sufficient. Ensure every one of our students in school graduates from school and help them make the honor roll. If not, they would be average students, but there would not be one student below average.

DR. BENNIE T. DAVIS

15. FEAR OR WORRY WILL NEVER STOP ME

It's so easy to say God doesn't give us the spirit of fear. Fear has been around since the beginning of time. Yes, fear is a bad boy, but death isn't scared of fear. So, fear doesn't stop death, but fear does stop living. There are so many visons, dreams, ambitions, accomplishments, and goals that have been stopped due to fear. Worrying is something else that has stopped living. The reason worrying hangs around the living is because the person will be worrying about what is going to happen tomorrow. Worrying takes away a person's happiness, peace, joy, dreams, and goals from today.

I asked Deacon Timothy Gerald now, before the vote took place, "Should I go to my office?" He responded, "Pastor D., stay in your seat as we take this vote." Then, Deacon Timothy Gerald proceeded to call the meeting to order. He explained, "Your vote counts, but the majority rules. If most of the votes are to remove Pastor D. as pastor at St. Matthews Missionary Baptist Church, the church will start accepting applications immediately. If the majority of votes are to keep Pastor D as pastor at St. Matthews Missionary Baptist Church, we will never have another meeting to remove Pastor D. because of his past. If the vote ends up in a tie, the chairman of the Deacon Ministry will make the final vote to break the deadlock. Anyone here that has any questions ask now before we proceed. I encourage everyone to vote to keep Pastor D. and not to vote to remove him. If any of you don't vote, that is a vote to help Pastor D. be removed as pastor. Tonight, make sure your voice is heard by voting. There will be no paper ballot, but you can only vote for one by raising your hand as I ask the two questions. With the showing of hands all in favor of removing Dr. Bennie T. Davis, Sr. as pastor here at St. Matthews Missionary Baptist Church at this time, raise your hand so your vote can be counted." After counting the hands that were in favor of removing Dr. Bennie T Davis Sr., now with the show of hands to keep him. "All in favor of Dr. Bennie T. Davis as pastor here at St. Matthews Missionary Baptist Church at this time. Raise your hand so your vote can be counted." After counting the votes, chairman Deacon Timothy Gerald said, "I would like to announce the results of this election. To keep Dr. Bennie T Davis Sr as pastor or release him as pastor here at St. Matthews Missionary Baptist Church." My heart sped up and started racing. Then I heard Deacon Timothy Gerald speak. "I had a hand-raising vote so that Dr. Bennie T. Davis Sr., officers and members of St. Matthews Missionary Baptist Church could see who was for Dr. Bennie T. Davis Sr. as pastor and those against him staying as pastor. The number in favor of Dr. Bennie T. Davis Sr. to stay as pastor was 14, and the number for removing Dr. Bennie T. Davis Sr. was 17." Some members of the meeting did not vote; brothers, husbands, wives, children, and friends voted against each other.

Tears started falling from my eyes, running down my face. I got myself together before anyone could see my tears. I asked Deacon Timothy Gerald if I could ask the officers and members a question, and he told me to proceed with my question. I said, "Because I have been voted out as pastor, the church is obligated to pay me for the next three months. The church must come up with a search committee and start taking applications. I want to remain pastor for the next three months because we have programs coming up within those three months. Church family, you can take your time and get a pastor. There is no need to pay the different preachers and me to come in on Sunday. Save the money, and with the programs, we could pay six months to a year of mortgage payments. We have our women's week and banquet. Out of a hundred tickets, women sold over eighty tickets. We have our annual revival meeting coming up and our father's day $10,000 program. The men's ministry had already raised over $8500 of the $10,000 we had two or more months before the program. We have put in too much time with flyers, letters, and money. This is too much to leave on the table. It is time to get over this hate about Pastor D. and make the best decision to help this church family. By allowing me to stay here at St. Matthews Missionary Baptist Church for the next ninety days, I will walk away, but the church will be in a better place." Deacon Timothy Gerald said we would take this to a vote, but Minister Cross stood up while he was still talking. She began to talk. "I sent everyone their check and money back that brought the tickets from me for the women's banquet in May. I also collected money for the men's $10,000 day. They also got their money back as well. It is not fair to this church family to allow Pastor D. to remain here after being voted out as pastor." Then Deacon Timothy Gerald said, "Let's take this to a vote. Remember majority rules. So, who is in favor of Pastor D staying here at St. Matthews Missionary Baptist Church? Raise your hand if you are in favor of Pastor D. staying here for the next ninety days?" There were eighteen that voted to keep Pastor D. "Now raise your hands if you are in favor of Pastor D leaving tonight as pastor and cancel all upcoming programs here at St. Matthews Missionary Baptist Church. There were twenty-three that voted Pastor D must go tonight."

Out of all the time that I was pastor at St. Matthews Missionary Baptist Church, the words that Deacon Timothy Gerald said to me were the most hurtful, cruel words that were said to me when he looked over at me and said, "Pastor D, as of this night, you are no longer pastor here at St. Matthews Missionary Baptist Church. I would like you to take this time to clean out the pastor's office and give me the keys to the church." Before I could say anything, Deacon Terry Williams stood up. He said, "St. Matthews Missionary Baptist Church is not obligated to pay you anything; it is not in the church bylaws. Pastor D. will not get any money from this church." Deacon Timothy Gerald said, "Pastor D, you are allowed to respond to the church family. As I stood up, I refused to allow my eyes to fill up with tears out of all the hurt I was going through. I refused to allow Deacon Terry Williams to believe he had victory over me. I don't need to get anything out of the office. The only thing that I need to remove from the pastor's office is the robe that Minister Cross gave to me about three weeks ago. Then, I walked to Deacon Timothy Gerald and gave him the keys to the church.

I never expected this to happen because I wanted to die as pastor of St. Matthews Missionary Baptist Church. As I started to walk to the door to go to the parking lot, some people started coming to me. Some were crying. Some just said, "I am sorry about what happened and how they voted you out as pastor." One of them stood out to me. First, he voted for me to be removed as pastor at St. Matthews Missionary Baptist Church. Michael Winders said, "Pastor D, I would like to say something about your leadership. Pastor D, you have excellent leadership skills. This church was never motivated like this until you became pastor here at St. Matthews Missionary Baptist Church. In less than ninety days of your leadership, you achieved more than our previous pastor did in five years." I responded by saying, "Michael Winders, I am innocent for everything Deacon Terry Williams said I did. The only thing that is not good about this church family is, that they voted me out as pastor on a lie. Deacon Williams has no proof, and out of the wonderful things you said about my leadership when it was time to vote, not one word you said, but you did vote against me and not for me. So, you also believe the lie and not the truth." Then, I shook Michael Winders' hand and said, "I will be praying for this church family that God give this church a pastor that would love the church family. Because this church family showed me love and respect, and I will never forget what this church brought to my life." As I continued walking out of the church, I could not hold back the tears any longer.

When I got to the door to take me into the vestibule, I stopped and turned around. The person I saw was Deacon Terry Williams walking around, shaking hands and thanking the people who supported him in removing Pastor D as pastor. The one thing that came to my mind was how Moses sent twelve spies to spy out the Canaan land. When they returned to give their report to Moses and the children of Israel, Caleb and Joshua said let's go up at once and possess the land that God gave us. But ten spies said we are like grasshoppers, and they are like giants. We cannot possess the land of Canaan. Now, ten spies stopped over a million people from going to the promised land. I looked at Deacon Williams, one man who persuaded a loving, God-fearing church family to let go of their promise pastor that God sent to St. Matthews Missionary Baptist Church.

I walked into the vestibule and never looked back anymore. All I wanted to do was get in my car as fast as I could because I could not allow Deacon Williams and the ones who supported him to see the disappointment, hurt, and tears coming down my face. I opened the door to my car and just sat there because I could not turn the key to crank the car. I started asking myself what happened just a few weeks ago. Everyone was so happy about the vision, the future of the church, and most of all, the growth of knowledge. Deacon Williams never saw me as a man because he was looking at my past. He was looking at me and never took the time to listen to my story, but he heard my story. If he had listened to my story, he would have heard and noticed how my experience developed me to become a better man of God. He always viewed me as a threat and not some help to him and the church family. My tears started drying up as I reminded myself what a man sows that he shall also reap. Tonight, Deacon Williams sowed a seed of hate and destroyed a man's life. It may not happen tonight, but this seed, he shall weep because of what he did to stop St. Matthews Missionary Baptist Church from growing and how Deacon Williams deliberately destroyed my life.

He didn't like the changes that I was doing to make the church better.

As I was leaving the church parking lot, waiting for the cars to pass, I said to myself, 'They say, they tell me, and I heard you beware of the white man, but it's our own kind that's doing the killing to our blacks. It was not a white man but our kind, not just blacks, who voted me out as a pastor and my Mason brothers. We all say we love each other, but why do we not do for each other in a time of need?'

I was driving down Hwy 319, looking in my rearview mirror at St. Matthews Missionary Baptist Church. A few years ago, I dreamed that I would be voted in as pastor of a church one day. Suddenly, I found out the church was without a pastor, and I applied, hoping and praying that this would be the opportunity I have been waiting for years. God opened this door for me and gave me the vision for this church. The dream came to reality, but Satan didn't like it because it was all about God. The conflict was when Satan started working through Deacon Williams to stop the vision and divide the church and the church family. I believed it was not over yet. My dream was in my rearview mirror.

So, I looked in front of me. The spirit of God reminded me I don't judge your future by your past because there is a greater future that is before you, Pastor D. I turned off the radio, everything was quiet. My mind started speaking to me, and then I started listening to the negativity in my head. "Pastor D, you will always be recognized as Caveman, the drug dealer. You will spend your life in prison because of the negative things you have done. Now you want to be called a pastor, and all you brought to the church was the ill will and shame to the church and yourself." The Mayor in Marion said, "Get Bennie out of the church because all he will do is bring the church down. Deacon Terry Williams was correct by getting Pastor D voted out as pastor." Then, different spirits came over me because I reacted by listening to my mind. The following spirits came over me:

depression, low self-esteem, stress, guilt, and anger. My confidence was shallow because I was relieved of pastoral duties. No one loves me, and I can't help anyone. The greatest thing I had ever accomplished since my new birth was when I became pastor at St. Matthews Missionary Baptist Church, and now, I was out as pastor because of who I was, no good for myself or anyone else. I lacked confidence about who I was, and I could not be a pastor because I was not happy with who I was. The only thing I could do was sell drugs. No one loved me, and I could not help anyone better themselves. I was not able to help myself get better. Deacon Williams was right to get me out of Saint Matthews Missionary Church before I went to prison for life.

When I looked around, I was coming up on the Galivants Ferry bridge. A suicidal spirit came over me because something said, "Drive your car into the river. You will be better off dead than alive because you would be helping yourself and so many people. Kill yourself, Pastor D. You don't have anything to live for. Your father rejected you because you are a bastard child. Your father's family didn't accept your mother because she quit school, and you are an autistic child with epilepsy, illiterate, sexual assault charges, custom handbag charges, you and your mother's alleged beating of a child, to name a few charges.

Pastor D, you should have been in prison years ago, but now it's time for you to go to prison for the rest of your life. You are no pastor or no Pastor D. because you are not the pastor at St. Matthews Missionary Baptist Church as of tonight. Pastor D., stop blaming detective Samantha Jackson for doing her job for putting a criminal like you in jail for sexual assault on that young lady and you and your mother beating that child. Stop blaming solicitor Ed Clemons because he doesn't see an innocent man. Stop blaming Deacon Terry Williams because you would have destroyed the church. Stop blaming the pastors for not allowing you into their pulpit because you disgrace all pastors and churches. Now, Pastor D, you are committing crimes as a pastor, so the best thing you can ever do for yourself, and everyone else, is to kill yourself."

The suicidal ideations continued to speak to me in my mind, saying, "You are victimized by being shot, not any of Marion's sheriff, or Marion police would investigate the shooting because everyone believed you would be better dead than alive." The suicidal ideations continued to say, "Kill yourself. Pastor D, kill yourself, turn into that river and end your life so everyone will be happy that your life is over."

As I approached the bridge, my hands were on the steering wheel because I was ready to die. At this time, I was right at the bridge. All I had to do was turn the steering wheel. I turned the steering wheel, not knowing I was at my turning point. I started encouraging myself and stopped listening to those negative thoughts, replacing them with positive ones. The thought that was coming to me was, "Pastor D. is more than a conqueror. There is no weapon formed against Pastor D., shall prosper God is for Pastor D., who can be against me. Now unto the God that can do exceedingly, abundantly, and above all Pastor D. could ever ask God was through that worketh within me. If David had never fought Goliath, he would have never been king. Pastor D, this is your Goliath. If you are to be great, you must destroy Goliath. I must live and not die. Goliath must die by Pastor D because I can do all things through Christ Jesus. I made it through my past, but my past wasn't through with me. As of this day, I will not allow my past to destroy my future." As I continued to encourage myself, I looked around, and to my surprise, I was passing the sign that said welcome to the City of Marion. What got me excited was the spirit that was encouraging him by saying he had no worth, "It's better to kill yourself by driving into the river and end your life by committing suicide. No one loves you because all they have for you is hate." When I saw that I was in the City of

Marion, I realized it was not a dream but a reality. I said to myself with a loud voice, "Suicide could not win because God is for Pastor D, and that is more than the whole world against me."

I went to Greater Christ Temple Church of the Harvest before I went home. I had to say a prayer at the altar because God had been good to Pastor D. I could have committed suicide, but God. I unlocked the door to the church and went straight to the altar. I got down on my knees, and I started thanking God for keeping me in my right mind. As I was praying, I asked God to help me keep this building so that we could continue to have service, but Satan came to stop our finances by getting me voted out as pastor. "God, I believe that you can supply the needs for this ministry," I asked God to go from heart to heart and mind to mind for man to give finances. "God, so that these doors to your house can stay and remain open. God, whatever they make happen in your house, it will happen in their own house. Lord, put a hedge around me and protect me. I will give you all the praises and the thanks in the name of Jesus. Amen." When I got up off my knees, I started looking around the church to see how good God has been to Greater Christ Temple Church of the Harvest. Then, that negative spirit started speaking to me again, reminding me that the rent was due in two weeks.

I was using the money from St. Matthews Missionary Baptist Church to pay the bills at Greater Christ Temple Church of the Harvest. Now that I had been voted out and fired as pastor and Deacon Williams refused to let the church pay me for the three months, I was struggling to find the means to support myself and the church. In my mind, I was hearing, "Pastor D., wait for it. After all, next, you will lose your building because you have no income to maintain the bills." I started saying, "I don't believe God has brought me this far to leave me. Some way or somehow, God will supply finances for the ministry. I praise God for doing it for this church before the battle was over."

After leaving the church, I went straight to my mother's house to inform my family about what had happened at the meeting.

When I walked into the house, all eyes were on me. Mama said, "What happened? Are you alright, son?" I told my mother and the other family members, "Don't be disappointed, but tonight I was voted out as pastor, but starting tonight, I must focus on Greater Christ Temple Church of the Harvest. God knows what is best because if I had been installed as a pastor, I would have been in a lot of trouble." Then my mother asked, "How will you pay the lawyer and the rent for the new building." I told my mom, "God will put people in our pathway to bless the ministry financially so that the bills will be paid, and as far as the lawyer, he will also be paid."

Shortly after that, I prepared myself for bed. No one else asked any more questions about the bills or the church. However, they continued to ask me if I was alright because they knew how hard I worked. If anyone at that church knew anything about me, all they could say was, "Pastor D. is one hard-working pastor, so don't you be ashamed. Don't look down because you have done so many wonderful things at St. Matthews Missionary Baptist Church." I told my family that I thank each of them for just being my family, praying with me and for me.

For some reason, it did not take long for daybreak to come because I slept throughout the night. Sometime the next day, I received a call from my lawyer. He let me know that I had to appear in court. After all, there was no way that I could get pre-trial intervention (PTI). I had to stand before the judge because someone in a high place wanted to see me make time in prison just because I didn't support him in the election.

Someone else was allegedly accused of selling custom handbags, but she never went to general session court because she was assigned pre-trial intervention. The only reason why I knew this was because they did their community service hours under my program—every time, I had to report to the general session court about these custom handbags, but she didn't. The only thing I could think of was why I was going to court, and I knew I was not treated fairly. Less than twenty-four hours ago, I was relieved of pastoral duties at St. Matthews Missionary Baptist Church for something I didn't do just because of hate. Now, I must report back to court, and this solicitor knew that this should have been over, but because of a higher power, they were holding my life. Just because I was a black man, they had it out for me.

They believed I would take time or prove my innocence regardless; it was one of the two. I had to move my eyes out of the way because my eyes showed me what was, but my vision showed me what could be if I just walked by faith and not by sight. My sight became my enemy because of the atmosphere of negative spirits that I was hearing and seeing. As long as I was going by the view, I could only see the prison. It didn't take any effort for me to go to jail. Just take the plea that the solicitor offered; that was the easy way.

In my vision, I saw myself faced with no prison time. I had the motivation and drive not to give up. Because this is what I will overcome, so I encouraged myself. These two weeks didn't take long to pass because it was time for the general session court to start. This particular day, it was raining, and everyone attending court who had a case in general sessions had to stand up outside the courthouse in the rain. The solicitor had the power to let everyone outside come into the courtroom, but the solicitor chose to let us stand out in the rain. He refused to allow us to go into the courtroom. I, along with others, got soaked and wet waiting to get inside the courtroom. We stayed outside the courthouse for over an hour. Although, all the lawyers and anyone else working with the solicitor, the judge, and the bondsman could go inside the courtroom, but he had us stand out and wouldn't allow us to come inside the courtroom. This treatment made me feel like we were like no good dogs waiting to go to prison. It was like they thought that our lives didn't mean enough. *Let them stay in the rain because they are going to prison anyway. Let them get used to being treated like an inmate.* What got me was in May of 2015, 97% of black and brown people who were inmates.

When they allowed us to go inside the courtroom within minutes, our Solicitor, Ed Clements, came out. He called the roll a little time after my lawyer came in. Attorney Thurmond Brooker called me outside. He said to me the solicitor put you on standby. He told me, "Pastor D., you won't have to report back unless you are going before the judge for the custom handbags or sexual assault case."

After I left the courtroom that afternoon, the rain stopped, and I went to Dollar General, and to my surprise, I saw the Pastor's Aid president, Willena Frink. She was an exceptional partner at Greater Christ Temple Church of the Harvest. She has been very sick for some time. However, I was happy to see her out of the house. As soon as she saw me, she said, "Pastor D, I miss coming to church service because of my sickness. I had to stop work, but they called me last week to come back." I asked her if she was able to go back to work. She said, "Pastor D, I am not able, but I would love to go back to work." I told her, "No one is getting your pastor anything to drink after he finishes preaching, Willena. I need you back at the church because no one loves me as you do." I told her that we have a new building to have church services and I would love for her to come and see our new meeting place. Then I asked her daughter to follow me to the church, so her mother could walk inside to see the work we did for our new church. The daughter said, "Pastor D., let me go pick up a few things for mama, then I will follow you to the church." Willena's daughter said, "Now, Mama, you have been dying to see your Pastor D, so you better enjoy him." Willena said to her daughter, "Hurry up so I can go to our new church!" Her daughter came out of the store and said, "Pastor D., let's go. I will follow you to the church." I slammed the car in park, jumped out, went to Willena, and opened her door. I said, "Willena, you are walking in the church with your pastor." When she walked into the sanctuary, she looked around and said, "Pastor D, it's a beautiful church." I showed her where she would be sitting when service was going on, so I could get my drinks from her.

To my surprise, her daughter walked into the church, and she brought me two drinks. "Pastor D., Mama said, get my Pastor two drinks, one for now and one for Sunday." Willena laughed and talked so much, but she got me when she said, "Pastor D, I love you." I kissed her on her jaw and said, "I love you much more." I shared with Willena how things were going at the new church in Aynor. I told her, "About three weeks ago, I was voted out as pastor at St. Matthews Missionary Baptist Church. The prayer that I have before God now is to open a financial door to continue to pay the rent for this new building. The money that I was getting from the church I was using to pay the rent here at Greater Christ Temple Church of the Harvest and any other place the church came up short with the other bills." What touched my heart was her response. She said, "Pastor D., I will have another coin program like last time. I was able to raise over $1200, but this time, let's reach $2000 or more." She said, "Pastor D., I have an offering for the church. God never let us down before, and I know God will not let us down now." Then, I asked her if I could pray for God to heal her from the pain that was traveling throughout her body. She told me, "Pastor D., I won't be leaving until you pray for me." Then, I asked for everyone to hold someone's hand, and I started to pray. I did not know that this would be the last time I would ever see Willena Frink.

A few weeks later, in June 2015, I got a call about her passing. This was the third person who passed away was a partner at Greater Christ Temple Church of the Harvest. Willena's daughter said, "Pastor D., my sister and I would like you to do the eulogy." That touched me so much because the other two deaths before Willena passed away, their families believed that I wasn't good enough to pay their tribute.

Within a week, the funeral took place. The spirit of the Lord put in my spirit the subject 'Just A Step.' After the funeral, both of her daughters came to me and said, "Thank you, Pastor D., for a well-done job. We, along with the family, could not have had anyone to do a better job. Our mother loved her some, Pastor D., and we also know that Pastor D. loved our mother." I responded by saying, "I thank both of you for trusting in me to do your mother's eulogy. If the church family or I can do anything to help either of you, we are just a phone call away." We departed, and to this day, we still communicate.

A few days later, a preacher came to me saying a church was taking applications. He said, "Pastor D, I believe you will be a good candidate for this church. Here is the information to apply for the church." The invitation to apply for the pastorship confirmed my theory. I always believed that preachers are killing other preachers. This preacher was out to finish and destroy me because if a person is out to kill someone and doesn't tell anyone, then that person doesn't know how to protect themselves. However, when a person knows that someone is out to kill them, they will know how to protect themselves. This preacher knew that I was still in court for those custom handbags and sexual assault charges. I told him that I was released from pastoral duties at St. Matthews Missionary Baptist Church. The preacher knew if I turned in my application, they would do a criminal background check. No church would allow a preacher to come in and become a pastor knowing they have a sexual assault charge.

A few months had passed by, and I saw that preacher again. He said, "Pastor D., have you heard anything from the church?" "No, I never sent my application in because I was not going to embarrass myself.

The search committee would request my criminal record, and then they would see that I have an active sexual assault case, and I still must go to court to be found not guilty." He looked at me strangely and never said a word because I did not make a fool of myself.

It was rent time for the new church. We had several programs, but we weren't able to raise the money to pay all the bills at the church. One day, I was at my mother's restaurant in the backroom, and someone walked in and asked for Pastor D. My mother called me and said, "Someone would like to see you, Pastor D." I told her that I was coming. When I came to the front, the young man and I sat down. He said, "I want to be a blessing." He gave me an envelope. Then he said, "I hope this will help you, Pastor D." I said, "Thank you. sir." I opened the envelope, and when I saw the check, the joy of the Lord came over me because I was able to pay three months of rent. I started thanking the Lord in my mind. "Look at what the Lord did for Greater Christ Temple Church of the Harvest." I shook the man's hand. He said, "I must go because I have a lot to do today." As soon as the door shut, I started telling Mama how God blessed the church financially, the rent, and the bills paid for the next three months. As I was talking, the door came open at the restaurant, it was Billie Lou Clark. I told her what happened and how God blessed the church financially. Mama, Billy Lou Clark, and I went up in worship and praises.

During this time, the church finances were very low, but I spoke to a preacher named Penny Smith. She shared with me that God told her to start a new ministry, but the building she was looking at was so expensive. I knew her, and I also remembered what God put in my spirit when I started the ministry. No one would help me. So many times, I wanted to give up, but I believed that things must get better. I won't be defeated because God is for me. I said to her, "How would you like to have an early morning service at Greater Christ Temple? Just give me this amount to help with the bills. That will take care of everything. You can have Bible study or revivals at any time as long as I do not have anything." Pastor Penny Smith was so excited. So was I because God put me in a position to help her, and she was going to be able to start the ministry the spirit of God put in her heart. After a few days, she called me and said, "Yes, Pastor D., I would love to have an early morning service."

The following Sunday, Pastor Penny Smith started the ministry Glory Belongs to God Ministry. Word got out about the new ministry in the City of Marion. A nice group of people did come out to the first service. After service, when I saw Pastor Penny, the joy and glow that covered her face, a person could see her love for the Lord. We shared the facility until God opened a new door for her. Pastor Penny Smith said, "Pastor D, I am moving to a new building."

My heart, for just that moment, felt like it had stopped. The first thing that I thought about was what I was going to do. I thought, "How will I replace the finance that 'Glory Belongs to God' was sowing into Greater Christ Temple Church of the Harvest?" I started complaining about what I didn't have and what I lost because 'Glory Belongs to God' was moving into a new building. I had more faith in what *they* say, than in what the Lord said about supplying the church needs. The Lord immediately reminded me how He sent manna and quail down to the children of Israel so that they would have food to eat. One day, someone said that something might happen, and no manna or quail may not come down. Let me put some food up for tomorrow, but by the time he went to get the food, the food wasn't any good to eat.

Maggots were all over the food. Failure to preserve the food lets a man know that God will supply if he trusts in the Lord. Now, I must trust in the Lord. When we come short, the Lord will give us the idea to make up for the shortcoming. Greater Christ Temple Church of the Harvest will have the finances to pay all the bills at the church. From that day to this day, I can say that I never allowed any other ministry to come into the church. We were never behind in our rent, lights, or water bill. God supplied more than enough finance.

The last scheduled 2016 general sessions in court were in progress. The alleged charge for the custom handbags continued for three years, and the sexual assault continued for two years. My Attorney, Thurmond Brooker, went to the Solicitor who was over my case. Attorney Thurmond Brooker asked, "Why you haven't tried my client? Because he will not take a plea. So, if charges are not being dropped, I would like a jury trial. Dr. Bennie T. Davis Sr. has been in court since 2014. Now, we are at the end of another year and another general session court. Dr. Bennie T. Davis, Sr., would be in this court for three years when the next general sessions court starts. Now, if the charge for the custom handbags does not drop, I would like a jury trial to prove my client's innocence. Officer Tony Flowers and his informant will be called or subpoenaed to testify in my client's jury trial. I also know that Dr. Bennie T. Davis Sr. wasn't the only one arrested for custom handbags. Not one of them has been in general sessions court except Dr. Bennie T. Davis Sr, and it is coming on three years. I know that my client, Dr. Bennie T. Davis, Sr., supervised someone who was arrested for custom handbags. The same solicitor's office denied my client pre-trial intervention (PTI) but awarded someone else with the same crime, PTI." My lawyer said, "Get it together or drop the charges on my client. Taking a plea is not an option." "We will be having a jury trial then." The court dismissed me for the rest of that day because it was a jury trial. The solicitor said to my attorney and me, "This trial will last about three to four days. Mr. Bennie T. Davis Sr, you are to report back in court after trial. Your attorney will let you know when you need to report back to court."

I got a call from my attorney Thurmond Brooker. He informed me that I had to be in court the next morning. The young man who was having the jury trial decided to take the plea. "Pastor D., you must be in the courtroom at 9 a.m. Please don't be late and miss the roll call because a bench warrant for your arrest will be issued. So be on time, so this won't happen to you." When I got home, my sister was not home from work. When she did get home, I asked her if she would drop me off at the courthouse in the morning. I had to be there at 9:00 a.m. She said, "Pastor D., I have to be in Columbia at 9:00 a.m., so I have to be there at 8:45 a.m. so that I won't be late. What I can do, Pastor D., is to drop you off at the courthouse at about 6:45 a.m., or you can get one of your friends to come to take you to the courthouse." "No, I am going to let you take me on your way to Columbia to your meeting." My sister got me at 5:30 a.m. She had me at the courthouse at 6:40 a.m. As I got out of the car, my sister said, "Pastor D., will you be alright until someone else gets here?" I told her, "I would be fine because daylight was cracking through the sky." She waited until I sat down on the steps of the courthouse. As she was driving off, I started praying to thank God for just being good to me. I said, "God, I need You to end these court cases because I am innocent. Man would like to see me in prison, but I need You to free me. I need your favor today in this courtroom like never before. I'll give You all the praises in Jesus' name, Amen."

It was like time stopped, and as I looked around, there were only a few cars. At times, no cars were going down Main St. After looking around as I was sitting on the step, I put my head down between my legs; slowly, I closed my eyes and began to meditate on the word of the Lord. It was 8:00 a.m. A young lady walked up the steps, and she had keys in her hand and garbage bags. She unlocked the courtroom door and started cleaning inside the courtroom. Not long after that, people started coming to the courthouse, other defendants, officers of the Marion County Sheriff's Department, lawyers, and solicitors.

I was sitting on the steps because I wasn't able to stand up for a long time. By this time, I had been at the courthouse for a little over two hours. Different people were entering the courthouse. I moved as close as possible to the rail to give more room for the people to walk up the steps comfortably. Then, one of the solicitors entered the courthouse. When he started up the steps, instantly, he stopped and looked down at me. He said, "Mr. Bennie Davis, if you don't get up off the steps, I will have an officer to arrest you." I looked up and said, "Sir. I can't stand up for a long time." My legs just would not let me, but I got up and leaned on the rail, and then the solicitor entered the courthouse. After the solicitor entered the courthouse, an officer of the Sheriff's Department walked up to me. The officer said, "Pastor D., if you would not have gotten up, believe me, I would not have arrested you for sitting down." After this incident, an officer came to the door and said all the defendants could come inside. It was time for the court to start, but our solicitor had to do a roll call first.

As I was in the courtroom, I started praying that my cases come up to get this part of my life behind me. The solicitor said all the defendants need to see their attorney about their case or cases at the end of the roll call. My attorney walked out from the backroom in the courtroom and asked me to follow him outside the courtroom. Solicitor Todd was over my case. Not long after, my attorney and I walked out of the courtroom, and so did Solicitor Todd. My attorney told me to follow Solicitor Todd, and I did as he said to me. Solicitor Todd walked over by this big window in the hallway, and then he introduced himself to me. Then he said to my attorney and me, "Mr. Bennie T. Davis never approached the SLED agent or anyone else about purchasing any handbags. Now, after looking over everything, we have no reason to continue this case. So, as of now, the charges for custom handbags have been dropped." "Why has my car been impounded for a few years?" I asked. Solicitor Todd said he would do the paperwork to release my car. I was so happy this ordeal was over, and I only had one more case. I asked my attorney why they dropped the charges on me. Attorney Thurmond Brooker said, "Pastor D., they dropped the charges because they would have had to bring out the informant. Lieutenant Tony Flowers would have had to give the name of his informant. They didn't want to expose the informant in court because it was best to keep the person undercover." Then my attorney said, "Pastor D, you won't be getting your car back today. The solicitor filed the paperwork, but Pastor D., you don't have to return to the general sessions court." My attorney said, "I'll see you the next court turn," and then I shook his hand.

As I walked out of the courtroom, I was so happy I called my sister to tell her what happened to me. I called her three times, and then I heard a "Hello, hello?" I said. "Alethea, I know you are in your meeting, but the judge dismissed my handbag case today, and I am getting my car back in a few weeks!" Alethea said, "I am happy to hear that, but let me go back to my meeting. I will call you when I get on the road to come home."

I was walking down Main Street, giving God the praise. Praising God removed the burden from me. Someone saw me walking. They pulled over and said to me, "Would you like a ride Pastor D.?" I said, "Yes, I do." As I got in the car, I said, "God is good to me," to the young lady that knew me. I told her what happened in the courtroom. She said, "Won't He do it, won't He do it, won't God do it, Pastor D. God isn't finished with you yet because God is going to finish this war, Pastor D." As the young lady was giving me a ride to my mother's house, the excitement was building up inside of me. I said to the young lady, "There is one more charge, that's the sexual assault charge. I need my lawyer to get this behind me so I can look forward to my great future. In the next general sessions court, I will have my lawyer ask for a jury trial. A jury trial will force Angela Allen, the alleged victim, and her sister, Ashley Allen, to perjure themselves. Remember, Detective Samantha Jackson did not investigate the accusation. Detective Samantha Jackson is not right. I believe she has something against black people or me because she had two cases against me. I won the first one in a jury trial. In the second case, the young man told Samantha Jackson, my mother and I hit him seventy times with a wet towel and my mother's walking stick. There were no bruises on his back, and the detective took no pictures to show in the court of the child's back. After I beat this sexual assault charge, the only thing that should happen to Samantha Jackson is the sheriff of Marion County should fire her for destroying the life of a mother and son." "Don't forget you are black, and Samantha Jackson is white. The sheriff or no one else is going to do anything to her," said the young lady driving the car. By this time, she was pulling up in my mother's yard.

As I got out of the car, I asked her how much gas money she wanted from me. Before she could say anything, I put $10 in her hand, and then the young lady said, "Keep me in your prayers." I responded, "I will and thanked you very much." I pulled the car door closed and then ran into the house to tell the great news of what happened to me in court. I was not able to run to the house, but I went as fast as my legs could take me. I walked in, calling for my mother. I told her the wonderful news that happened to me.

"God was in the courtroom on my behalf. Sit down, Mama. The charges for the custom handbags have been dropped. Now, when they finish the paperwork, I will be getting my car back." About this time, my mother went up in praise. She was crying. Mama was so happy to hear that her son had won the case. She said, "Now, Pastor D, you only have that sexual assault. I believe God will also have that same solicitor to drop that charge." I said, "Mother Davis, I receive that because I am innocent of that charge." Shortly after that, my sister walked into the house smiling and said, "God did it for my brother, Pastor D." I responded by saying, "Yes, He did because God specialized in doing the impossible." Then my sister asked if there was anything I would like to do to celebrate, and I said, "Yes, I would like to go out and eat some buffet Chinese food in Florence." My sister said, "For what God did for you today, Pastor D., get ready." Then she said to everyone else, "Let's all go and do this as a family." As we were on our way to Florence, I shared with the family that I was at the point of losing my mind at one time, but God gave me a vision of how to help others.

I asked God to give me an idea so I could be a blessing to other people. God put the idea to start a Bible college, but the devil was determined to stop the Bible college. I called a preacher friend to ask if I could start a Bible college under his leadership because of his experience, and I would not have to start from ground zero. The pastor said to me, "Pastor D, get yourself together because you will make time in prison. You have done some bad things to the young lady. Stop worrying about starting a Bible college and get things right before you go to prison." What blew my mind about this pastor was that we both are black, we both living for God, we both were encouraging people that God will save us, and we both let people know that God can be a lawyer in the courtroom, but I would not give up because I was determined to start a Bible college.

Two days later, I called Dr. Wayne Miller, Founder and President of All Nations Bible College and Seminary. Now, this was a white man who I contacted about starting a Bible college. I said to him, "I would love to start a Bible college in Marion." He said, "It would be great to have a new Bible college. I will have someone call you back, Dr. Bennie T. Davis Sr." In a few days, Dr. Linda Stowe, Academic Dean of All Nations Bible College and Seminary, called me to start Greater Christ Temple Bible Institute. She let me know everything I had to do, and in the summer of 2016, college started. This past summer, the college got started with about six students. The spirit of God put in my heart to call Evangelist Harriet Wilson. It had been over five years since the last time I saw her. I called Pastor Penny Smith to ask her for Evangelist Harriet Wilson's phone number. I called Evangelist Harriet Wilson to tell her about Greater Christ Temple Bible Institute. I shared with her how the spirit of God put in my heart to contact her about attending Greater Christ Temple Bible Institute. I said to Evangelist Harriet Wilson, "I would like to invite you to come to class starting Monday, and you will be able to see if this is the college for you to learn more about the bible." She said, "Dr. Bennie Davis, I will come to class on Monday because it has been in my spirit to start college." "Evangelist Harriet Wilson, look at God because this is the college that will give you the knowledge you seek. I believe you will be a student at Greater Christ Temple Bible Institute."

Because this college, along with those six students, allowed me to work with them, this is why I did not lose my mind. Most of all, I would have given up, but they gave me a reason to forget. Mama said, "Let's go into the restaurant. We can't eat outside." When I walked into that Chinese restaurant, the food looked delicious and hot, and I had four to five plates and desserts. My nephew, Elijah, had to help me out from the restaurant to the car to go home. As my sister Alethea was driving back to Marion, she said, "Pastor D., I don't know what you are going to do when you win that sexual assault case. Don't go back to this restaurant because those people don't want you to come back. You ate a lot of food tonight." She said, "Pastor D, I don't know how you will get up in the morning." I told her, "Alethea, I'm not getting up in the morning. I am going to stay in bed and rest." She dropped me off at the house. She waited for me to go into the house before she drove off to go home. After walking into the house, I went straight to my bed and lay across it for a few minutes. The few minutes ended up being the next day after 1:00 p.m. So, after I got up, I started working on my sermon for the Sunday morning service.

Sunday came so fast but seemed so long away. I was so excited about sharing my testimony with the church family. We had a high time in the Lord that Sunday morning service. I did not tell anyone until I got to church because the spirit of God was over the sanctuary. The majority of the church went up in praise when I said the judge dropped the charges for the custom handbags. They must return my car after over two years. I will have my car to drive, to go and come as I need to. It was all over Marion County about my arrest, but no one said a word when they dismissed the charges.

All week, Monday through Saturday, some so-called church people were out telling terrible news about other people. Then, on Sunday, they spoke in tongues, testified, sang, and didn't have any love for their brothers or sisters. That Monday, I got my car, so I called Bishop Eugene Park, who is known as the dancing man. When I got to the jail, Bishop Eugene Park met me there to get the car. The holidays came and went so fast that it was already time for New Year's Eve watch night service. People went to the service believing that God would do something supernatural in this service. Just as God had my car released now, God is about to release whatever you asked him for, starting the last night in 2016. "Church, I'm going to go ahead and put praise on God for dropping those sexual assault charges in 2017."

A few weeks passed, it was time for the general session court to start. I was expecting a phone call from my attorney, Thurmond Brooker. I was on standby during the last court, but the court did not call me to appear. My attorney called to say he asked the solicitor to drop the sexual assault charges, "Pastor D, I will do everything to close this case because I am asking for a jury trial. I will put Angela Allen and Ashley Allen, those twin sisters, up on the witness stand to testify. I will eat them up because they must stop making false statements and destroying people's lives on a lie. Pastor D., you need to be in court a week from Monday."

The general session started Monday, but this time, I was not able to get on standby. After reporting to court each day, my lawyer would say, "You are free to go after roll call, Pastor D., but report back in the morning." Time was ending for any candidates who would like to run for Mayor of Marion to file their application. They had to sign up before noon on Friday to be a candidate eligible to run for Mayor. Wednesday night, I was at the point of making up my mind to run for Mayor of the City of Marion. I wished my friend, the late Dr. Henry McGill, was still here. It has been a little over a year now since he passed. As I was lying in bed, I was thinking about the night of his wake. I sat right by Gusand Weeks. She got the attention of Poiette McGill Bromell. She said, "Pastor D. is here. Let him say something about your father and their friendship." Not long after I walked into the church, Poiette McGill Bromell said, "At this time, my classmate, Dr. Bennie T. Davis, Sr., is going to come for a few minutes to share an experience or two with my father."

"I have had many wonderful moments with Dr. Henry McGill. Tonight, I would like to share two of the moments with his family and friends. Dr. Henry McGill loved going hunting, but one night, he asked me to go along with him. It was at nightfall when Dr. Henry McGill came and picked me up to go hunting. When I walked out to get in the truck, he asked me to drive because he couldn't see at night. I said to him, no problem, show me where to go because I need to kill a coon." I said, "Dr. Henry McGill, I need a gun, so where is my gun?" He said, "Dr. Bennie, you cannot walk now. How can you carry a gun and walk at the same time?" He said, "Dr. Bennie, you may fall, and the gun might go off. The bullet may hit me, and I could get killed. No, it won't happen like that. My life is not going to end like that because you cannot walk and then fall with that gun." When I got to the place to go into the woods, Dr. Henry McGill said, "Stop, I will drive from this point on, Dr. Bennie." We went deeper into the woods.

The further we went, the darker it got in the woods. I said to Dr. McGill, "Let's see the Mayor about getting some light poles down here so I can see." Then, all of a sudden, Dr. McGill just stopped the truck. I slowly started moving my head. I said, "Wow, it is dark. I am not able to see my hands, and I have them in front of my face." I didn't want to speak loudly, so I said, "Rev. Rev, what is going on now? What am I to do?" I was looking out the window on the passenger side. So, I took my left arm and stretched it to make sure Dr. McGill was still with me. "Rev. Rev, I can't see anything." I started to feel for him, and no one was there. I felt the steering wheel, but the hands of Dr. McGill weren't any place to be found. I took my hand without turning my head to see if I could feel him in the driver's seat. I did not feel his body because the seat was empty. Sweat started rolling down my face, coming from everywhere. "What am I to do now? Rev is gone." My mind went to the scripture that two would be in the field, and one would be left. 'Yes, we are in the field, but we are sitting in the truck, and tonight is not the night. My heart can't take this, and I can't see anything.' I was the one that was left by myself this time. I was getting my mind ready to start screaming as my mind was about to scream for help, I felt for Dr. McGill one more time. Now, if I don't feel him this time, everything in these woods will be running. After I react to the fear of being in the woods alone because of my running and jumping, the state will deny my SSI benefits.

By this time, I felt for Dr. McGill, and he was there. I told him, "If you don't want a new seat in this truck, I would advise you, Dr. McGill, to let me know the next time you get out of this truck when I am with you." I was sweating, and I said, "It's time, so let's get out of here now. I have been in these woods too long, and I will not be back." From that night to this day, I haven't been hunting or in anyone's woods anymore.

The last thing I would like to share with you was one Sunday afternoon, Dr. Henry McGill asked me to drive him to Sunny Acres Nursing Home. A few of Mount Pisgah Missionary Baptist Church's family members were at the nursing home. I would love to visit them today and say a prayer with each of them. At this time, Dr. Henry McGill wasn't in perfect health, but he was still concerned about the church members. "I would take you to the nursing home, but you will have to give me directions." After we got to the nursing home, Dr. Henry McGill said, "I would like you to come in with me to see the members." It was only about two to three members in the nursing home, but most of the patients at the nursing home knew Dr. Henry McGill. Every room we entered was members except for a few rooms. Dr. McGill prayed with them.

In the last two rooms, he had me pray, and in one of them was a man named Mr. Reed. God healed this man from his sickness, and he went home. He is now a partner at Greater Christ Temple Church of the Harvest, and I am the Pastor. As Dr. Henry McGill and I walked out of the nursing home, he said, "Go every Sunday to visit the members in the nursing home. If you can't make it, make sure a Deacon goes in your place." When we got into the truck, I asked Dr. Henry McGill, "How do we get back to Marion?" The sun was going down, and it was getting dark. I had no idea how to get back. All we were passing was woods. It was getting darker and darker. I wasn't able to get a signal on my phone, and then my phone went dead. I drove so much I didn't know where I was, so I stopped on the road.

I looked up in the air and saw a big South of the Border sign high up in the air. Dr. McGill and I were someplace in North Carolina. I told him gas was running low. He said, "Pastor D., don't worry, we can make it back to Marion." I didn't stop until I got back in Dillon, and then I went straight to Marion. I loved my friend, and I will miss Dr. Henry McGill. Then tears started running down my face as I was walking back to my seat at the wake.

I knew I would be running for Mayor of the City of Marion when I got up the next day before I went to court. I went to the voter's registration office to become a candidate for Mayor of the City of Marion. Then, I went to court to answer the roll call. I was in court for about an hour, and then my attorney, Thurmond Brooker, entered the courtroom and called for me to come to him. He had me follow him outside in the hallway. He said, "Pastor D., this sexual assault must go before the jury, or it must be dropped this court term. You never asked anyone to purchase the custom handbags, but SLED said that if the Thomas lady had not stopped him and asked if you would like to purchase an MK handbag for your wife, you would have never been in this courtroom. They dropped the charge of selling custom handbags because they did not have sufficient evidence against you." I told him, "Don't forget that Ms. Thomas is friends with the Mayor, and they are members of the same church. Yes, that is right because the Mayor, Bobby Davis, told me the City Attorney told him not to say anything to me. Out of everyone in the City of Marion, why would the City Attorney call my name only if the Mayor had nothing to do with me being in court for those handbags?"

Thurmond Brooker replied, "Pastor D., that is behind you. Now it is time to put Angela and Ashley Allen behind you, also. But you are on standby, and I will call you if your case comes up. I am going to the solicitor and let him know that they need to get in touch with Angela and Ashley Allen. We will be calling the retired Sheriff to testify on your behalf since the incident occurred at his establishment." I will tell him, "My client would like to have a jury trial. We will not forget that Detective Samantha Jackson." Then, I walked away from my attorney to go home.

On Saturday morning at about 10:00 am, my attorney Thurmond Brooker called, "Pastor D, I came into my office today. While I was here, I checked my fax machine, and I had a fax from the solicitor's office, to my surprise. Pastor D., the fax let me know that my client Bennie T. Davis Sr. need not come back to general session court because the court dropped the sexual assault charges." I said to Mr. Brooker, "You mean to tell me not one person from the Marion County Sheriff's office or the Solicitor's office was man enough or woman enough to tell me that they wasted two years of my life and almost destroyed my life, and who I am as a person? This is why I must become Mayor of the City of Marion to stop innocent black and brown men and women from going to prison for crimes that they did not do. I am running for Mayor for the City of Marion."

He said, "Pastor D., I would love for you to be the next Mayor of the City of Marion. Inconsistent investigations must stop, and with Bennie T. Davis Sr as Mayor, it will stop.

16. THE STORY BEHIND MY LAUGH

There was so much wrongdoing against me by the Marion County Sheriff's Department, Marion City Police Department, and the Mayor of Marion. The law says innocent until proven guilty. Except for the intervention of God on my behalf, the law did not apply to me. Each of them was determined to destroy my life just because they had the power and authority. The only way I could help stop innocent people from being falsely arrested, going to prison, and having their lives destroyed was to become the next Mayor of the city of Marion. The Mayor of Marion snatched my dream away from me. I was the new Pastor of St. Matthews Missionary Baptist Church, and the Mayor was not satisfied until my pastorship ended. The only thing I ever wanted in life was an opportunity. St. Matthews Missionary Baptist Church gave me the opportunity when the members voted me in as pastor. But the Mayor of Marion, Marion County Sheriff's Department, and City of Marion Police Department took it from me. The only reason it could be was that I was a drug dealer before and now I have a positive life. I am a black man seeking greater in my life.

Since the dropping of the alleged charges, I was beginning to focus on my campaign. Mayor Bobby Davis will not serve two terms as Mayor. I promised myself that Mayor Bobby Davis would not win the election. If I don't, then another candidate will be Mayor. I started my campaign by telling the voters the truth on Facebook live. I let the people know the Mayor set me up with his friend. The city lawyer told Mayor Bobby Davis not to say anything to me. Now, out of everyone in Marion, how was my name the only name?

Wait, just over four years ago, just before the Mayoral election, Mayor Bobby Gerald passed away. Rodney Berry then ran as a write-in candidate. He decided that he wanted to be Mayor of Marion. There was a woman republican that ran against Rodney Berry for Mayor of the City of Marion. At this time, Barack Obama was President of the United States, but that woman didn't believe he should be president because he was not born in America. Mayor Bobby Davis supported this republican, but in the last election, Mayor Bobby Davis supported Rodney Berry when running against Mayor Bobby Gerald. Now, he was voting for a republican dressed in democrat clothes. Solicitor Ed Clements was running for solicitor against a republican attorney, Parham. Now, our Mayor, Bobby Davis, supported the republican attorney, Parham, so he was also a Republican dressed in democrat clothing. His time is up as Mayor of the City of Marion.

For over three years, solicitor Ed Clements knew that those charges against me wouldn't hold up in court. I voted for Ed Clements, but Mayor Bobby Davis loves Republicans. I let the people know I would not be paying anyone to work for me, and I explained to them when anyone pays someone to get votes, and they win when you go to them for help, they will let you know that they paid you for your service, and I don't owe anyone anything. With me not getting any money now, if I won, I would be able to work for everyone in the City of Marion for the next four years.

One more person was running for Mayor, Ashley Brady. I started asking who Ashley Brady was because I thought he was a lady, so I said we have our first woman running for Mayor of Marion. I found out later that Ashley Brady has his own business selling insurance, houses, and buildings. Ashley had a billboard of himself sitting on his front porch. I let him know he needed to stay right there on his front porch selling insurance, houses, and buildings and let me become Mayor of Marion. I let the people know I'm not the only one that Mayor Bobby Davis disliked. He also disliked Emerson Hunt. City Councilman Emerson Hunt had a deal for his District to build forty to forty-five apartments, but Mayor Bobby Davis blocked the apartments because of his dislike for Hunt. I promised the people of the City of Marion, "If Bennie T. Davis Sr. becomes Mayor, the first thing I would do is get rid of that block and allow for the construction of the apartments in District 3. If the constituents of Marion do not elect me as Mayor, Ashley Brady would also allow the construction of the apartments in the City of Marion."

I encouraged the citizens of the City of Marion to go to our Mayor Bobby Davis and ask him if he voted republican or did he stop the building of the forty to forty-five apartments from coming to the City of Marion because he disliked the City Councilman Emerson Hunt. There was a lawyer who came to me in general sessions court. He said, "When they drop the charge of sexual assault before the ink is dried good, Pastor D contact me to pursue a lawsuit against the Marion County Sheriff's Department because it is not right what detective Samantha Jackson did to you. Ms. Jackson's supervisor and the sheriff of Marion sat back and allowed this to happen to an innocent black man. Pastor D, this would have never happened to a white man. If this were a black sheriff's office, he would have been relieved of his duties before it would have gone this far in court." I did not just call. I went to him so we could meet face-to-face.

By this time, two years later, someone must have gotten to the lawyer because he said to me, "I can't help you, Pastor D. There is no case to pursue a lawsuit." I said, "Sir, how did I have a case in the beginning? And now I have the truth to back me. These charges were done to me only because I am a black man doing the right thing. Staying out of trouble and helping other young people make better decisions with their lives." I shared this on my campaign about how bad sheriffs and police officers had to go. No one will ever represent the City of Marion, who arrests anyone black, white, rich, or poor without doing a fair investigation and having his life destroyed because of a rush to justice. The police officer who fails to conduct a proper investigation will find himself fired on the spot.

That night, I had a basketball game with my little players. I was so excited because this was the last game of the year. I was looking forward to sharing with the New Breed Basketball team that I was running for Mayor of the City of Marion. On our first day of basketball practice, I told them they were champions because they were New Breed players. We must find a way to have victory over any and everything we do in life. I will let the team know what happened a few years ago with my other New Breed team and how they went undefeated. I was named the All-Star coach for the first time. We had an All-Star game in Marion. The gym that was designated to host the game was too small. The game was hosted at the Marion High school gym.

Billy Thomas hosted the game. People loved to see New Breed play, and they loved to see coach Bennie T. Davis Sr. walk in the gym with one of many of his suits on, looking oh so fly. Sometime during that day, someone would come to me and say, "Pastor D., there is a warrant for your arrest for breach of trust, and you must pay a fine over $1100 or go to jail for thirty days." I was warned not to go to the basketball game because the Marion City Police were under orders to arrest me in front of the New Breed Basketball team and the citizens of Marion. I began to think about my joy when coaching these young people, so I asked my sister to coach the team. I reminded her that she was the assistant coach and this was her job. Usually, there was never a police officer in the gym. On this particular afternoon, there were a few police officers in the gym, and some were standing by the exit, so if I came in or out, they would have arrested me.

When they saw my sister, they knew I was somewhere in that gym or on my way to the gym for the basketball game. Ten minutes after my sister's arrival at the gym, the police officers started walking around looking for me. Four or five police cars surrounded the gym, waiting for me to drive up to or come out of the gym. After some time, they knew I was not in the gym or coming to the game, and slowly, each police officer started leaving the gym. Just before the game started, my sister got the team together. She told them, "This is the last game, and Coach Bennie cannot come to the game. The police have a warrant for his arrest, and they are looking for him to come to the game to arrest him and put him in jail. Coach Bennie loves this team too much to allow that to happen." When she finished speaking, one of the player's mothers asked her, "Will Pastor D be at the game?" Alethea said no, then explained what was going on with me. The mother replied and said, "My son loves his coach. He believes that Pastor D. is the best coach out of all the coaches. Not just him, but all the children love Pastor D. so much." Then she said, "Let Pastor D know that I will be praying for him."

I stayed in the house the entire weekend because I had to hide out. The church service was affected because of the police's warrant on me. My sister went to the police station on Monday morning to see why the arrest warrant was issued. The secretary told my sister, "Yes, there is a warrant for Bennie T. Davis Sr. for breach of trust. He must pay the fine, or he will be arrested and stay in jail for thirty days." It was not a surprise to Alethea, so she gave the secretary $1200, and the secretary gave her a receipt back with just a few dollars. The secretary never told Alethea who signed the warrant on Bennie T. Davis Sr. because it was not anyone. They produced this charge just because Bennie T. Davis Sr. was running for Mayor of the City of Marion.

The night of the debate, Mayor Bobby Davis, Ashley Brady, and Bennie T. Davis Sr. were all together waiting on the debate. The debate was the greatest time of my life because I am a young man with many problems. I was diagnosed with epilepsy and autism.

Statistically, I would never graduate from high school. As a drug dealer, I overcame a fatal attack on my life because the drug deal had gone bad. My mother and I were alleged to have beaten a child, and I had a sexual assault with an attempted rape charge. Still, tonight, I was in a debate to become the Mayor of the City of Marion. I was sitting between a black man and a white man. Both of them were high in society, and people looked up to them. As I looked out over the audience, the only thing that was going through my mind was I was in a position that I had been dreaming about for years. I dreamt about running for Mayor of the City of Marion. Society said it would never happen, but look at God. I know for myself that God does specialize in doing the impossible. Will God do it? Yes, He will!! Do not let anyone stop you from going after your dreams because those are your dreams and not society's. Do not go after some of your dreams, but all your dreams.

Each one of the candidates introduced himself to the voters of the City of Marion. I introduced myself by saying, "My name is Dr. Bennie T. Davis Sr., and I am a graduate of Marion High School, Voorhees College, and Cathedral Bible College. I am at the bottom of the mountain. The other two candidates are at the top of the mountain. The only people they can help are the ones that are at the top with them. The other 96% of us will never get any help from either one of the candidates. For the last four years, Mayor Bobby Davis could not do anything for the 96% of you and I. Now, everyone on the top of the mountain with him is the only reason they can vote for him. I am the best choice for the job to become the next Mayor of Marion. It is time for the City of Marion to have a Mayor who will work for four years for the majority of our people." The faces of the audience were so surprised to hear the truth about the treatment we received. Ashley Brady asked questions about Mayor Bobby Davis, but this one question stood out to me. Ashley Brady asked, "What did you, Mayor Bobby Davis, do with the $1,000,000?" Mayor Bobby Davis responded by saying, "It is in the bank." Ashley Brady continued talking, and he said, "If I became the next Mayor, I would help the people of the City of Marion." Ashley went on to say, "Mayor Bobby Davis, the City of Marion, needs more than two and sometimes three police officers patrolling the City of Marion. If I am elected Mayor, I will have between five to seven working each shift."

Now, it was my turn to talk. I said, "The only thing our Mayor Bobby Davis could remind the citizens of the City of Marion is that he did not do anything to help the 96% of the people of Marion. He said I don't care who works to help me to become Mayor. Don't look for any favors. He said if my wife gets a speeding ticket, she will pay her fine to each of you who worked for me to become Mayor, and I hope you are not looking for any favors. Mayor Bobby Davis will not be giving any help to anyone. To the 96% of these citizens, the black ones or the white ones, especially our black ones. The first black Mayor did not help us in the last four years, and if we give him four more years, the same thing will happen, so on April 11, 2017, let's vote out the enemies; this is what vote means. I am the only candidate who lives in the same area now as you, the 96% to have more. It is time to vote for someone in 96%, and that is Dr. Bennie T. Davis Sr. As I make things better for me, life will get better for 96% of each one of you because it is only three to four police officers working only in the white part of the City of Marion. Our police are not looking over the black neighborhoods because on Mondays City Court, 97 to 99% are black and brown standing before the judge, but Dr. Bennie T. Davis Sr. As Mayor, the city police will patrol the black and white neighborhoods. I promise if I become Mayor, the crime rate on our black and brown people will go down, and I will have programs in place of jail or prisons."

After the debate, our local news interviewed each of the candidates. No one told me where to go for my interview, so I left without being interviewed. They knew I was coming with everything I had in me. People mistreated me because they believed I did not belong on stage with the other two candidates. I thought to myself, I will not be defeated, and it is not over until I become Mayor of the City of Marion. Other people's opinions of you do not have to become your reality. I don't care what people say about me because I know greatness is inside of me. People saw my laugh but did not know my story. Every day, I continued to go on Facebook Live, three to four times daily, telling the people why they should vote for Dr. Bennie T. Davis Sr., the next Mayor of Marion. I reminded the people about the past four years, and things did not get better. I said, "The only way things will change is if Dr. Bennie T. Davis Sr. replaces Mayor Bobby Davis. If not, your life will get worse for the 96% of you and me, so this coming Tuesday, April 11, 2017, you need to vote Bennie T. Davis Sr. for the next Mayor of Marion. Allow Ashley Brady to continue to work in his family business selling insurance, houses, buildings, and sitting on the front porch. Whatever you do, don't reelect Mayor Bobby Davis for another four years. We cannot make it like that, so if you don't vote for Bennie T. Davis, Sr, then vote for Ashley Brady." Mayor Bobby Davis would not have another debate not because of Ashley Brady, but because Bennie T. Davis Sr.

Tuesday, April 11, 2017, came so fast. Here it was, Election Day in the City of Marion. A lot of people came out to vote after the polls closed. Everyone was on the edge of his seat. It was possible that an ex-drug dealer, a man accused of all types of crimes, a young man who overcame epilepsy and autism, could be Mayor. If I became Mayor from day one until the last day I was in the Mayor seat, I would make things happen for the people of Marion, not just for the 4% but all 100% of the people in the City of Marion. Then, the election results started coming out. The first thing I heard about the election was that Mayor Bobby Davis was not reelected. Could it be Bennie T. Davis Sr, the new Mayor of Marion? Not long after the news came out, the announcement came that Ashley Brady was the new Mayor of the City of Marion. The one thing I knew was if it were not for me, Dr. Bennie T. Davis Sr., Ashley Brady would never have won this election. One of the first things Mayor Ashley Brady did was unblock whatever former Mayor Bobby Davis did to stop the apartments. Within a year, I could let everyone know that the apartments are in the City of Marion. Yes, those apartments are in the Mayor pro-tem, City Council Emerson Hunt's district.

About two months later, I sent my resume to a church in North Carolina that was looking for a pastor. I received a letter from the church giving me a date to interview for the church's pastor. So, I called Brenda Turner and explained to her the opportunity presented to me. I had to go to North Carolina for this interview to become pastor of this church, but I did not have any money. I asked Brenda Turner for money. She said, "Pastor D, whatever you need, go to my store, BP." By the time I got to BP, Brenda Turner had called the cashier and told her to give me whatever he needed. I got something to eat, and I filled my car up with gas, and I still do. She never asked for any money in return. If it were not for Brenda Turner, I would not have been able to go to the interview, but God will put people in your life to bless you. Sometimes, Brenda Turner would see me, and call me her pastor. From time to time, she comes to church. Now, she is a sponsor and partner of the ministry that the Lord started in Marion, SC. I did make it to the interview. It was wonderful. The search committee loved my laugh, and sometimes they laughed with me. I gave the best interview, and I had the most credentials. The search committee believed that I was the Pastor that they needed for the church. The rest was great, but because of the sexual assault charge with attempted rape. Yes, the charges are dropped, but this is still on my records. It is essential to have one's record deleted, so I encourage white, rich, poor, especially black and brown people, not to get in trouble because your record will still follow you even when proven innocent. I refused to give up because there was a better life.

I will not stop until I win because I am so close to my breakthrough. I don't believe in 'trying' because that is another word for failure. That is why I 'do.'

For over twenty years, I did volunteer coaching for Marion Recreation Center. I also coached basketball, football, and baseball. I was the head coach's assistant coach because I love making young people better and believing in themselves. Most of all, I told them that greatness is in each of them and success belongs to them. I let them know that if you work hard to make yourself better in basketball, you will work just as hard in life. There will not be anything to stop you in life but yourself because each of you is a champion. The sky is not your limit because there are planets beyond the sky. How can I encourage young men and women to work hard and go after their dreams if I don't dream of becoming a head coach or assistant coach for Marion High School for any sport one day? As long as I could work with our young men and women to make them better in sports and life. I decided to become a Marion High School basketball head coach or assistant coach.

It was the summer of 2017, and I started my quest to become a Marion High School coach. I knew the only way that I couldn't get into the school to coach was if the principal of Marion High School would not allow me to come into the school. The first thing I did was make an appointment to meet with the principal, Dr. Michelle Wright, about two weeks before school started. I made it to the meeting about fifteen minutes before the meeting started. Within about ten minutes after I got there, someone came and asked, "Are you Dr. Bennie T Davis Sr." I responded, "Yes, I am." She said, "Follow me." Then she escorted me to the Principal's office. We introduced ourselves to each other. She said, "Have a seat, Dr. Bennie T Davis Sr. Now, how can I help you?" I told her, "Five or six years ago, I asked Coach Towns about being his assistant coach because he would get sick and did not have anyone to coach for him.

The varsity coach would help, but his heart wasn't in it because he was coaching varsity. I asked the varsity coach several times to allow me to be Coach Towns' assistant coach. He would always come up with some reason to say no. I remember letting the varsity coach know that Coach Towns said I could assist him because he didn't have anyone to help him when he was out sick. Because of how another coach did me about coaching." I don't think he wanted me to become a coach for Marion High School. "Before I called for this meeting, Dr. Wright, I would like you to know that I have called Coach Towns about being his assistant coach, and he said as long as Dr. Wright approves it, I could be a coach." I shared with her the negative parts of my life and how I can help our young men of Marion High School today.

"They would be able to take the things they learned from me and apply them to their life. As they are successful in basketball, they will also be successful in school. I will give my best each day we have basketball practice to look for the same from them. Dr. Wright, I respect myself, and I won't let you or Marion High School down. Most of all, it will be zero tolerance and discipline in each of the player's life. We will have practice every day like we play our basketball games, hard." Dr. Wright said, "If Coach Towns says yes, the school district must give its approval. Dr. Bennie T Davis, Sr., I went to the school district and asked for Mr. Leon Stuckey. He is the district athletic director, and he will be able to tell you everything you need to do to submit the application." At the end of the meeting, I thanked Dr. Wright for the opportunity to become an assistant coach at Marion High School. As I shook her hand, I said to her, "I would love to give you this CD of my testimony. When you have time, I would like for you to hear what God has done for me throughout my life." She said, "Thank you, Dr. Bennie T Davis, Sr., and I said, "Call me Pastor D.

As soon as I got in the car, I called the district office, but Leon

Stuckey was not available. Still, the secretary said, "Would you like to leave a message on his answering machine." I said, "Yes, please transfer me to his answering machine." On the answering machine, I said, "Mr. Leon Stuckey, this is Dr. Bennie T Davis, Sr., and I am calling about becoming an assistant coach for the JV basketball team at Marion High School. I need to know how to submit my application for the job. The secretary has my cell number, so at any time, feel free to call me. Thank you in advance. Dr. Bennie T. Davis Sr." The next day, Mr. Leon Stuckey returned my phone call at about 6:00 PM. I said, "Mr. Leon Stuckey, I would like to become an assistant coach, but I don't know how to put my application into the computer." He explained how to put the application in the computer system, and he told me to call him after I put it in the system and give him a week, and he would get back to me and let me know if I could be a coach or not.

Over three weeks passed, and I didn't hear anything from Mr. Leon Stuckey after submitting my application. I did let him know everything was completed. One Sunday after church, while speaking with Mayor pro-tem/City Councilman Emerson Hunt about becoming a coach for Marion High School. Mayor pro-tem/City Councilman Emerson Hunt looked at me and said, "Pastor D, I am tired of people just walking over you." I asked Emerson what to say about the people in the Marion School District, and he said, "Pastor D, it is not just them, but it is anyone in Marion. Because you come to do good for all our young men and young women, but the people who can help you are the ones that are stopping you." He went on to say, "Pastor D, Leon Stuckey could have already called you and given the answer about becoming a coach for Marion High School. You will work hard with those young men to make them believe that they are champions. You became the conference champion in 11th grade. You've worked hard in everything you accomplished in life. Now, Pastor D, you will bring it to Marion High School because you will be the best assistant coach in all of Marion High School before and anyone after you. With your work ethic, I believe that Pastor D will be a head coach one day. Now, Dr. Wright could have gotten in touch with Coach Towns or Mr. Leon Stuckey to let him know if she could allow you to become a JV basketball coach at Marion High School. But all of them black balled you in anything you do to help black, brown, and young white men. Don't forget the young women at Marion High School."

"Mr. Hunt, all that you said I could say is right, but this is my faith on trial. I'm going to win this war because I will become the first assistant coach for JV basketball at Marion High School." Emerson Hunt said, "Pastor D, if this is what you will do, I will stand with you, but I don't want to see these people hurt you anymore or make you look like you are begging them to be a coach. So tomorrow, call Mr. Leon Stuckey and tell him that you don't want to be the JV assistant coach and get this over." I decided I wouldn't call, but I would go to the Marion school district tomorrow because phone calls aren't working. Then, someone called Mr. Hunt to come to the Marion County Detention Center to get their son out of jail on bond. He said, "Pastor D, money's calling. I must do my job and free this young man from jail. Now, if you find out anything tomorrow, do call me. Let me know how things go after the meeting. I will be praying for my Pastor D that things work out some way for you."

My family and a few church partners came out to the church to go to their cars, and within twenty minutes, everyone was gone, including my family and me.

Sunday night, I was in bed early, praying that God opened people's eyes and let them see that He was with me. "God let the people see that you still specialize in doing the impossible. Most of all, I remember God is the same yesterday, today, and always. God, I know you are for me, and you will go from heart to heart and mind to mind. Allow the no to become yes. Put your favor and grace upon me in Jesus' name, Amen." After finishing my prayer, I had peace of mind. My confidence was up. It was not long after that I went into a relaxing sleep. When my eyes opened, I saw the light outside my window. It was about 9:00 a.m.

I woke up knowing I was going to the Marion School District Office to find out about my application. I knew I had to see Mr. Leon Stuckey because nothing could happen with my application without him. Before I got up, I said my morning prayer. As I was praying, the spirit of the Lord put in my heart not to go to the Marion School District Office but to call the school district, set up a meeting with the Superintendent, and let the Superintendent know who Dr. Bennie T. Davis Sr. was. At about 10:00 a.m., I called the school district and asked to be connected to the office of the Superintendent. The operator connected me to the Superintendent's secretary, and I set up the meeting with Superintendent Dr. Kandace Bethea. I scheduled the meeting for that Wednesday at 2 p.m.

After I hung up the phone, I made up my mind that I was not telling anyone about this meeting. Right then, I started thanking God for giving me the knowledge to set up this meeting with Dr. Kandace Bethea. Thank you, Lord, thank you, Lord Amen.

Monday, in Bible College class, I told the class to go after their dream and don't let anyone stop them. I want the class to know that I can't tell you to do something, and I will not go after my own dreams. During this time, the Bible College only had one student, Evangelist Harriet Wilson. The other students quit. I gave my all because I believed God would multiply the Greater Christ Temple Bible Institute students one day. Evangelist Harriet Wilson never forgot her purpose. She said, "Even if I go alone, because one day, I will have my Doctoral degree in the Theology of Ministry." Because of her determination, she had to learn God's word to have more knowledge and graduate from not any college but Greater Christ Temple Bible Institute. That made me more determined to become the greatest instructor ever at any Bible College. Not just the world but also the universe. It was going to happen.

The conversation was the night before my big meeting with the Superintendent of the Marion County School District. I knew if I presented myself as Dr. Bennie T Davis, Sr., If I could get the opportunity to be part of the family of coaches of the greatest High School around Marion High School, it would be a dream. I made sure that I was going to wear my best suit. I was not able to go to sleep. I was so excited because this was Becca's son, the ex-drug dealer.

I am the man shot because of a drug deal gone bad, the man jailed for beating a foster child, the man jailed for sexual assault with a rape attempt. Dr. Kandace Bethea would know about all the negative things that happened in my life and how I overcame each of them. I will never stop fighting for a greater life for myself. I will fight even harder for our young men and young women at Marion High School. The youth doesn't have a father in the home or in his life and doesn't have discipline. I will help him set a standard because if he is going to represent Marion High School. We are going to be proud of them so much as they will be proud of themselves. With all this excitement going through my mind sometime in the night, I fell asleep. I was sleeping so well that it was sometime after 10:00 a.m. when my eyes came open.

After I had done my morning prayer, I was more excited than the night before sleeping. My heart felt like it would stop because the joy going through my body was so fast. Before I knew it, I had to get ready for my big meeting with Dr. Kandace Bethea.

As I was driving up in the parking lot of the school district office, sweat started coming down my face. After parking the car, I said a short prayer thanking God for this opportunity and asking Him to give me favor with Dr. Kandace Bethea. I entered the building through the main entrance. The secretary asked, "How may I help you, Sir?" I responded to her, "I have a meeting with Superintendent Dr. Kandace Bethea at 2:00 PM. My name is Dr. Bennie T. Davis Sr." The secretary said, "Have a seat. Dr. Bennie T. Davis, Sr., I will escort you to Dr. Kandace Bethea's office when the meeting is ready." A few minutes later, the secretary said, "Dr. Bennie T. Davis Sr., follow me to Dr. Kandace Bethea's office for the meeting." I walked into the office looking for an older Superintendent, but to my surprise, she was a young Superintendent. We introduced ourselves to each other, and then Dr. Kandace Bethea said, "Dr. Bennie T. Davis Sr., have a seat."

The meeting started with me telling Dr. Kandace Bethea, "I applied to become a community basketball coach, but if any other coach or coaches needed any help, I would love to work with them. About five years ago, I asked Coach Towns to be his assistant coach, and he said yes. Coach Towns said, 'I never had anyone to help me. If I got sick, there was no one to keep up with regular basketball practice.' Dr. Kandace Bethea, someone in the school system, would always stop me from becoming a coach at Marion High School. It was always starting with the Marion High School basketball coach or coaches. I am not in the buddy, buddy club because they look down on me. I live in the same community where over 97% of the black athletes at Marion High school live. Dr. Kandace Bethea, at one time in my life, I was a drug dealer. While indulging in negative behavior, I was shot several times because of a drug deal gone bad. I have done many negative things, but today, I am a new man in Jesus Christ. Today, I have come to see who I am now and not who I was yesterday. When people come to you, Dr. Kandace Bethea, and speak about me, they will talk about the negative things I did in my life. But I would like for you to see who I am now. If you look at my background, Dr. Kandace Bethea, I will never be a coach at my school in this district; you will be able to assess better who I am today because of this meeting. Now, you can see the passion that I have for our children. As I work with them, the greater they will become because they believe in themselves."

At the end of the meeting, Dr. Bethea's words touched me. She said, "Dr. Bennie, I believe you would do a wonderful job with our children." I said to her, "I must inform you of a few more things about me. When I am allowed to become a coach for Marion's High School basketball team, Dr. Kandace Bethea, you will be the only Superintendent in history to allow a person of my character to have a second chance to have a productive lifestyle. A second chance of an opportunity is what will happen when I become a coach at Marion High School. Giving me an opportunity will separate you from all other superintendents in any place in the world. Dr. Kandace Bethea, I will never let myself down, and with this opportunity to become assistant coach, I will never let Coach Towns, Dr. Wright, or you, Dr. Bethea, down. All of you played a part in bringing one of my many dreams to come to pass, which is to be an assistant coach for this upcoming basketball season." Our meeting ended with me giving Dr. Kandace Bethea a CD of my testimony and a handshake, thanking her for just meeting with me.

As I was on my way, walking down the hallway just before I got to the door to go out of the district office, to my shock, I saw Mr. Leon Stuckey. So, I walked up to him and shook his hand. I said, "Hello to Mr. Leon Stuckey. Have you heard anything yet about me becoming a coach at Marion High School?" Mr. Leon Stuckey stated that he is still waiting for an answer about my becoming a coach. I said, "I remember years ago when you were not working in the school system when you were working for Housing Authority, and you said if I ever get a chance to get into the school system, I would like to be a basketball coach at Marion High School.' God gave you that opportunity, and you won the only state championship for basketball at Marion High school. Now, I'm asking for that same opportunity. One day, if I become a head coach for varsity boys or varsity girls basketball or track, I will bring a state championship to Marion High School for years to come. I am a champion and believe I can make them champions." Then I said to him, "And I look forward to hearing from you soon."

As I walked out of the district office, I was confident that I had the support of the Superintendent, Dr. Kandace Bethea, and the principal of the High School, Dr. Wright. "God, I need you to finish this prayer request." When I got in the car, I made a joyful scream, giving God thanks in advance because God would bring this request to pass. Tears of joy were rolling down my face, and my hands went up in praise. A few days later, I got a phone call, and low and behold, it was Mr. Leon Stuckey. He asked me, "Dr. Bennie T. Davis, whatever happened with the drug charge." I told him that my sentence was two years' probation because I took the plea. My sister went free with nothing on her record. That was the only reason I took the plea. Then, after I got off probation, I went to Columbia and got a pardon from the governor of South Carolina.

Mr. Stucky said that I needed a letter, some type of proof that this pardon happened to put into my file. That is the only way to finish the application process because I could not go any further without it. I asked him to give me by the end of the week to get the information he needed. He said, "Dr. Bennie T. Davis, bring it to my office and call before coming because it needs to be placed in my hand." I said, "OK, I will get on this today. Have a good day because, Mr. Leon Stuckey, my day just got great." I hung up the phone and started working on getting him the information that he needed.

As soon as I hung the phone up, I started looking for probation and parole in Columbia, South Carolina. I knew I had to get in touch with them to get a copy of my pardon. Without the pardon papers, my application could not be processed. I called my sister to ask her to get on the computer to get the necessary information to get a copy of my pardon, but she was in a meeting at about 5:00 p.m. I was going to my mother's house. I was going by the probation and parole office in Marion, SC. When I got down the road, I remembered that it was where I did my probation. So, it should be something in my files showing when I received my pardon. As soon as I turned around to go to the probation and parole office to find out if I could get a copy of the pardon, they were closed by the time I made it to the office.

I told myself I would be back tomorrow morning so I could get the information I needed for this job. What got me excited was knowing that I could be the first assistant JV coach in Marion's High School history with a criminal record, different disabilities, and sickness.

That night, I went to bed early because I was so excited about going to the probation and parole office. Not long after I went to bed, my eyes came together. I went into a wonderful, deep sleep. It did not seem long, but as soon as my dream started, I was coaching a basketball game with a coach from Marion High School. My alarm clock came on, my eyes opened, and I was smiling. I said, "Lord, bring this dream to reality because only you can bring this to pass. When my feet hit the floor, I believed that this would be the greatest day of my life. Today, I will receive the news that I will be a Marion High School assistant basketball coach."

At 9:30 a.m., I was on my way to the probation and parole office. Shortly after, I signed in to see an officer. Someone came out and called my name to follow him. He took me into his office and then asked, "Are you here to start your probation or parole." I quickly said, "No, I was on probation from 1996 through 1998. Mr. Tron Grant was my probation officer. I was here some time ago because I got a pardon from the governor of South Carolina." I asked him,

"Sir, how could I get in touch with the state probation and parole office to obtain a copy of my pardon." Then he said, "What is your name so I can access it from my office." After giving him my name, he pulled up my information, then printed a copy of my pardon and gave it to me. I said to him, "Thank you so much because this will help me become a Marion High School assistant basketball coach. Sir, now that you have helped me, if you have community service or are looking for a job, I am the man you need to call because I am the director of a youth center named 'I'm Not That Way Any More Youth-Adult Center Incorporated' I help young people become self-sufficient."

I gave him my card, and he said, "Call me anytime because I will help any way I can." We built a wonderful relationship because I was able to help everyone, he sent to me. I wanted to run out of the probation office, but my mind told me, Bennie, you cannot run, but as fast as I could move my legs, I was moving my legs.

When I got to my car, I was so excited I called the school district and asked for Mr. Leon Stuckey. The secretary connected me to his office, and to my surprise, Mr. Leon Stuckey answered the phone. I let him know that I had the information that he requested. He said, Dr. Bennie, come now if you are free because I will be in my office today." I told Mr. Leon Stuckey, "I would be in his office in fifteen minutes." I thanked him, and I could not crank the car fast enough. In less than fifteen minutes, I was pulling up in the school district parking lot. Before the car stopped, I was trying to open the car door. I told myself, slow down because you don't need to fall in this parking lot in front of these people as they pass by the parking lot.

I entered the building through the main entrance. There was no one in the window or sitting in the lobby. I went straight to the window where the secretary was and gave her my name, and I told her that I was here to see Mr. Leon Stuckey as he was expecting me. The secretary said, "I would get in touch with him. Will you please have a seat?" While I was waiting, I started patting my feet and humming to myself because I was so nervous with anticipation. The secretary said, "Dr. Bennie T. Davis, Mr. Leon Stuckey will be with you shortly." While she was speaking to me, the door from the hallway came open. It was Mr. Leon Stuckey. He said, "Dr. Bennie T. Davis Sr., come with me." As Mr. Leon Stuckey and I walked towards his office, he turned and said, "Dr. Bennie T. Davis Sr, let's go into this room. The school board will have their meeting here."

After we entered the room, he said, "Dr. Bennie T. Davis Sr., do you have the copy of your pardon?" I said, "Yes, sir, I have it." Then I handed it to him, and as soon as he saw that it was my pardon, he said, "Dr. Bennie T. Davis Sr., I would like to take this time to welcome you to our family of coaches here at Marion County School District. You have met all our qualifications to become a community coach for Marion High School basketball."

There was a joy and a feeling I had never felt before in my life. I have now accomplished something that society, family members, and friends said would never happen because of my criminal record. Mr. Leon Stuckey proceeded to say, "There are two more things, Dr. Bennie T. Davis Sr. You must pay $30 so that a SLED background nationwide check can be completed on you. Once the background check comes back and is clear, you must wait on a phone call from the head principal of Marion High School." I asked Mr. Leon Stuckey, "Why did you wait until now to get this SLED check on me?" He said, "Dr. Bennie T Davis Sr., the reason anyone, not just you, must get a SLED check at the end of the application is that if something had come up in your application, you would not have made it because of something that happened in your past. Then you would have been out of $30, but now the only thing that can stop you from becoming a coach for our school district is if, for some reason, Coach Towns or Dr. Wright changed their mind. As I stated earlier, the principal, Dr. Wright, will be calling you to come be on the Marion High School coaching staff. You will be allowed to start coaching alongside Coach Towns. Dr. Bennie T. Davis Sr., remember that you are to help the head coach, and you are the assistant coach. Whatever he needs you to do, you need to do just that, and there will be no problems." Then he said, "Dr. Bennie T. Davis Sr., you are going to do a respectable job. If I didn't believe that this meeting with you would not have happened." I responded, "I am not going to do a respectable job but the greatest job. There will never be any other assistant coach to work as hard as Pastor D to make our young men greater than they have ever been in their life in sports and their personal life." Mr. Leon Stuckey stretched his hand towards me and, shook my hand, and said, "Whatever happens, you can now apply to coach at any school in the school district." I said, "Thank you so much." Then we walked out of the room. He went towards his office, and I went to my car.

As soon as I got outside, my hands went in the air, and I started praising God in the school district parking lot because I knew God's favor and victory were on my side. All I could do was to start thanking God for what he did for Pastor D. After I got into my car, I sat there for a moment thinking about the words that I heard coming out of the mouth of Mr. Leon Stuckey. No one ever said anything like that to me before this day. Usually, the words that come out of someone's mouth about Bennie Davis are always negative. But Bennie T. Davis Sr.'s ears have never heard positive words come from a man with the power that Mr. Leon Stuckey has in the school district. Only one thing was going through my mind, 'ears had not heard,' and the tears started coming down my face. They were not tears of sorrow but tears of joy. I didn't get on my phone to call anyone. All I wanted to do was give God the glory because of what God had done for me.

Two or three days passed, and no one called from Marion High School. Still, I kept the faith. One afternoon, between 4:00 and 5:00

p.m., I got a phone call from an unknown number. Usually, I don't answer these calls, but this particular time, something said to answer this call. I answered the phone, and the other end said, "May I speak with Dr. Bennie T Davis Sr?" I responded by saying, "This is him. How may I help you?" The person said this is "Dr. Wight, the principal of Marion High School. I am calling you to let you know that your SLED background check has cleared. I am calling to let you know you are now officially the assistant coach for JV basketball at Marion High School. Dr. Bennie T Davis Sr, you will be working with head JV Coach Towns. As of today, Dr. Bennie T Davis Sr, you can start going to basketball practice. You need to contact the head coach on what time their basketball practice will be starting today. If there is anything else I can do for you, feel free to call me at my office anytime." I told her, "Thanks for this opportunity to coach at Marion High School. What is so great about this school is that I am a 1987 alumnus. Thank you so very much. You have a wonderful day, but I must go now because I am about to pull over to park my car." I started thanking God for working through the hearts of people to be able to help me. "God, it happened for me, God, it happened for me, and You have all the glory. You did it for me. What first happened to me should encourage people with epilepsy, autism, and criminal records not to let anything stop you from going after your dream."

By this time, I was on the road for about thirty to forty minutes. After getting myself together, I pulled off the road and then called Coach Towns. He told me that basketball practice would be tomorrow at 5:30 p.m. He said, "Dr. Bennie, I do have basketball practice today and tryouts. I have to get started at 5:30 p.m. today." I responded, "Coach, give me about thirty minutes, and I will be at Marion High School gym." I could not hold it back anymore, so I told my sister the great news. As I was going home to get dressed for basketball practice, I called my friend Emerson Hunt to share the great news. "I am a Marion High School new assistant JV basketball coach!"

I was overexcited because now I could work with these young kings and champions to believe in themselves. As I was walking, I was still on the phone with Emerson Hunt. He said, "I'm so proud of you because you did not give up on your dream of being a coach at Marion High. I encouraged you to call the school district to let Mr. Leon Stuckey know that you didn't want to be a coach anymore because I didn't want my pastor to be embarrassed, but that never stopped you. Now I hear you say that today is your first day at basketball practice to be introduced as the new JV basketball assistant coach for Marion High School. Pastor D, when those young men believe in your system, they will be champions and winners."

I said, "Emerson, I got to go now because I just pulled up to the high school. Let me go to this gym for basketball practice so Coach Towns can introduce me as the new assistant coach to the basketball team." "That sounds so wonderful. Bennie T. Davis is a Marion High School assistant coach." I told Emerson Hunt I would call him tonight because I would love to help with the team. After all, tryouts are going on this week. When I got out of my car, I looked at the Marion High School building for the first time in my life. I was not looking at the school but a goal that I accomplished through Christ Jesus. I am in a position to help our young men become responsible young men. I held back the tears of joy and continued to move towards my goal as fast as possible.

When I walked into the gym, I was looking around at the young men trying out for the basketball team. I said to myself, look at my God. I have the opportunity to help each of the young men shine brighter than they are right now. By the time I made it to basketball tryouts, I had sat on the bleachers, and not long after I was in the gym, Coach Towns asked me to come to the center of the basketball court. When walking to the center of the court, I felt nervous. Sweat was rolling down my face because I was so happy, and everyone who was able to look at me saw the love and the excitement all over me. By the time I made it to the center of the court, the basketball team varsity and junior varsity had gathered in a circle. Then he said to the players, "I would like to take this time to introduce Pastor D, the new assistant coach for junior varsity basketball. Pastor D and I will be working side by side with each other to make this team better." Then he introduced me to another Coach. "He is the new varsity head coach. I want everyone to give our new assistant, Coach Bennie T. Davis, a handclap and show him some love." As soon as practice was over, Coach had a meeting with all the basketball coaches. He allowed me to voice my opinion. The meeting was about the rules and regulations he would put forth for the varsity and junior varsity basketball teams. I asked Coach Towns when the cut would take place for the basketball team. He said there would not be any cuts because this is not basketball tryouts. Tryouts hadn't started yet. It was not time for basketball tryouts, but this was volunteer conditioning. Conditioning allows us to look at young men's skills. When basketball tryouts start, we should choose the most talented players at Marion High School. The coach said to me, "Call me 'Coach Towns.' I said, "Call me 'Pastor D.' Our meeting ended with the Coach telling us about our next practice.

When I was walking out of the gym, a few of the young men who were conditioning asked me if I could get a ride home. I said to them, get in the car. I will drop you off at home. Before I went home, I had to go to my mother's house. As I walked into the house, I started telling my family that I had a wonderful day at my first basketball practice. I told them, "All of the coaches made me feel like a part of the basketball coaching family. Before conditioning practice started, Coach Towns said to me, standing in front of the team, 'Pastor D, if you get to the place that you cannot walk across the basketball court, grab hold of me, and I will help you get to the other side. If coach Bennie Davis needs a chair at any time, I am asking the managers or players to find a chair so he can sit down.' The managers and players said, 'Coach Bennie, just let us know if you need us to do anything to make your life better.' When practice started, Coach Towns said, Pastor D, I would like you to do the conditioning for the next forty-five minutes. I had them doing drills that were conditioning to get them in shape. When the players finished practice, everyone jogged to the center of the court. The players said to each other, and now today, we had a great workout."

Each one of the coaches was able to say something to the basketball team. When it was my time, I said to the young men. "Each day you come to practice, give your best because how you practice, I will be how you will play in the basketball games. Give your best every time you come to basketball practice. Yes, it will be hard, but I am asking all of you to do something I must do each day of my life. I was walking differently from you because I had been shot in my right leg some years ago. The doctor found gangrene, and the only way he could let me keep my right leg was to cut it out of my leg and leave a hole in my leg. To this day, you can still see the bone in my right leg. The only thing the doctor could do was graft skin and cover the hole in my right leg." Then I showed the team my leg and said, "I give you my all. That is why each of you will bring it every day to basketball practice. It is no bad day, but every day is a wonderful day of hard work. If you are not able to bring your best, this team is not for you. It is no choice. The expectation is that you will bring your best every day. You are a champion!" Along with the coaches, the team started clapping their hands and shouting, "I am a champion," over and over. Coach Smith said, "Coach Bennie Davis, starting tomorrow, we will have varsity and junior varsity. You are the coach over conditioning." That sounded so wonderful because my hard work is paying off.

As soon as I walked out of the gym, I called my friend Emerson Hunt. I had to let him know the great news that happened to me. When I got him on the phone, I told him that Coach Smith had promoted me to conditioning coach for both teams. Emerson said, "There is not anyone better than you, Pastor D. Those young men will be able to play the whole game and not be tired because they will be in condition." Emerson and I were disconnected as I was pulling up to my mother's house. I went into the house and shared the greatest news I had ever gotten since being an assistant coach at Marion High School.

Everything was looking up for me. I was a basketball coach; new people started the Bible College, and I tried out for St. Matthews Missionary Baptist Church. The church was without a pastor because the members voted the pastor out a few weeks ago. I contacted chairman Deacon Timothy Gerald about applying to become Pastor at St. Matthews Missionary Baptist Church again. Deacon Timothy Gerald said, "Yes, you could turn in a resume but include the papers from the court stating that the sexual assault and the custom handbags charges were dropped and a not guilty verdict for beating the child. I will get in touch with you, Pastor D, after receiving the information I asked from you." Deacon Timothy Gerald said, "I will call you to tell you the month that you will come to teach Sunday school and Bible study." I said, "I will mail you everything within the week." I had a lot of confidence because now, what was against me was the false charges. Now that my criminal record has been updated, my opportunity to try out for the church is more favorable. The members now know that I was innocent and telling the truth about why this was done to me by the County and City of Marion law enforcement. I was able to get all the information together and to Deacon Timothy Gerald within the week.

The day before basketball practice started, I told Coach Towns what was going on because he is a preacher. I asked him to keep me in prayer. I told him I was trying out for a church that I was the pastor of at one time. Coach Towns said, "I will put you in my prayers, but Pastor D., you have basketball practice for now." I said, "Yes, sir."

It was about two weeks before junior varsity basketball season started. We could not have basketball practice at Marion High School, so we had it at the National Guard Armory. I called Coach Towns to tell him that some of the players were in the car with me. "When I drop them off, I will go back to the school to get the other players." I got out of the car and was walking to the gym. Coach Towns stopped me. He said, "Pastor D, until you meet with Dr. Wright and Coach Smith, you cannot contact any basketball players or attend any High School basketball practice." I asked Coach Towns what I did because I hadn't done anything. I worked too hard to lose this opportunity. "Coach, do you know what is going on." Coach Towns said, "Pastor D, and I don't know what is going on. You will hear something before this week is out so that you won't miss a game." Coach Towns said, "Pastor D varsity season starts before JV season starts. You are also an assistant coach for varsity basketball. I am the head assistant coach, so if you don't hear from anyone, you are still good because we have about two weeks before the season starts."

As I was walking back to my car, a few players were coming towards me. They all said together, "Coach, we're going to basketball practice, and we are ready for you today." I told them I could not come back to practice until the principal called me. "Coach Towns said I did something, but he didn't know anything about what was going on." One of the players responded, "Pastor D, everyone is mad because we will be the best basketball team at Marion High School. Yes, Pastor D., your conditioning is hard, but now that we are in shape, we know the purpose of winning. The whole team must be able to run up and down the court the whole game. As you said, Pastor D, we play as we practice, and we practice hard every day." By that time, I was not able to take it anymore. The tears were about to start coming out of my eyes. So, I said, "Young champions, get on in the gym, so Coach Towns will not have you all running extra laps and sprints." As soon as I got to my car, tears were running down my face. To hear those young men say, 'Pastor D, we are happy that you are our coach.'

I got myself together, and then I called the school. I asked Coach Smith what was going on and why I couldn't go to the basketball practice anymore. He said, "Pastor D, I don't know. All I do know is I have a meeting with you, Dr. Wright, and Coach Towns." I said, "So, you cannot tell me what I did that now, and I may not be an assistant coach this year." He said, "Pastor D, let's find out what is going on because you are doing an excellent job with helping me and Coach Towns." So, I said, "I will wait for the principal to call about the meeting."

A few days past and I received a phone call from Dr. Wright. She said, "This is the principal of Marion High School. I am calling you because I would like to meet with you in my office tomorrow at 4:00 p.m." I asked, "Can you tell me what I have done for this to be happening to me?" She replied, "Coach Bennie, I will go over everything with you at the meeting." That night, I went to bed early, hoping that morning would hurry up and come.

I was so ready for this meeting to come and learn what I had done that was so bad. I can't get fired before the season starts. I do this free because I love working with young people to let them know they are so much greater than what people believe. I was not able to sleep throughout the night. My eyes would just come open, and I would stare at the ceiling, asking myself what I had done. Not one person knows what happened or refused to tell me. It is something to be in a fight and not know who you are fighting. It's like, who am I fighting? They were invisible, but tomorrow, they would come out of hiding. I drifted off to sleep for the last time. When my eyes came open, I was able to see the light from the sun coming through my window.

I got up because I could not stay in bed any longer. Today was the day for the big meeting. So, what is going on with the three people? No one was man or woman enough to tell me what I did that was so bad. Now, I must go to the principal's office to keep a job I do for free to help other young men. Throughout the day, I prayed and fasted that whatever they set out to do to me, God would bring me out. When I pulled up in the Marion High School parking lot prior to getting out of the car, I went into prayer, asking God to allow me to be quick to listen and slow to speak, whatever is right.

I walked into the school with my head up. I went to the head office and asked for Principal Dr. Wright. The secretary knew I had a meeting with her today. She said, "Dr. Bennie T. Davis Sr., sit over there, and I will come for you when Dr. Wright is ready." Within ten to fifteen minutes, the secretary said, "Follow me to the office." When I got to the office, the only ones in there were Dr. Wright and Coach Smith. After I spoke to both of them, I sat down. Coach Towns came walking into the office. I said hello to everyone in the office. As I looked around, I asked myself which one of the three was the reason for this meeting. I know one of them could have told me why they called the meeting. What got me was all of them are grown professional people in their field of employment. Why couldn't they treat me as a professional man and not like a child? Why do I have to guess what is going on and who is the cause of this meeting? With any meeting that any of them call or go to, they know the nature of the meeting.

Each of us followed Dr. Wright to the other side of the office. She asked for everyone to be seated around the table. The meeting started with Dr. Wright informing Coach Towns that we were here today because of Coach Smith and myself. The only thing that ran through my mind was, what have I done to this Coach? Nothing! Then Dr. Wright proceeded to say, "Coach Bennie, Coach Smith said you did not follow protocol. He stated that one day during basketball practice, you came to him to ask about the diamond defense." I put my eyes directly on Coach Smith as soon as he looked across the table. When he saw I was looking at him, Coach Smith put his head down. He was not able to look at me. If you had any questions about junior varsity basketball, Coach Smith said to go to the Coach you are working with. I responded to her. I said yes, "Dr. Wright. That same day, we had basketball practice before varsity practice. Coach Smith said we must run the diamond defense, so we did, but we disagreed. So, after practice, Coach Smith came into the gym. I asked him because this was the defense that he gave us to run. I told him what I said by explaining what went on in practice. Coach Smith said, Coach Bennie, you are right. That is the way the diamond defense is supposed to run. Then he said, Coach Bennie, go out there and do conditions for varsity basketball." Dr. Wright said, "If Coach Towns is wrong, let him be wrong. Don't you ever say a word? Do it wrong with him. If you come back to my office because you did anything to get him right, you won't be a coach here at Marion High School." I put a laugh on my face and said, "Yes, ma'am, I understand. Dr. Wright, you don't want me to say anything, but I have one question: what purpose am I here for if not to help Coach Towns." She said, "Do as I say if you want to stay an assistant coach." I knew then that Coach Towns was not a part of what Coach Smith was doing to me. Coach Towns asked to be dismissed from the meeting because he had basketball practice.

After Coach Towns walked out, she asked Coach Smith if he had anything to say to Coach Bennie. He said, "The only thing I have to say is to follow protocol and do as the principal asks you to do as of this day." I laughed in my mind, and I said, "Yes, sir." Then, the meeting ended. She looked at me and said, "Coach Bennie, you can return to basketball practice today." I said I would never correct Coach Towns anymore. Whatever he says is right.

At the end of the week, we were at our last practice before junior varsity basketball season when it was announced to be at practice thirty minutes early because there would be a coaches meeting. I made sure that I was there on time. I went into Coach Smith's office as soon as I got to Marion High School. He was in the office waiting for the coaches to come to the meeting. Not long after I was sitting in the office, Coach Towns entered the office. Coach Smith got started with the meeting, and to my surprise, Coach Smith pulled out some boxes and said, "The Marion High School coaches' shirts and jackets were back before the season started." I had to pay for my shirt and my jacket before Coach Smith would take my order. None of the other coaches paid for any of their shirts or jackets. They were getting their shirts free with some modern designs from Marion High's name and symbol. The shirts looked exceptionally good, but I had to hold back my tears because I was overlooked. Just because they could do this to me and not one person in leadership would support me to be treated fairly. I kept to myself because I just had a love to work with our young men. I wasn't going to tell anyone about what happened to me because I didn't want to lose this basketball coaching opportunity.

A few days after the season started and at the end of practice, Coach Towns said that the next day at 4:00 p.m., we would take our annual basketball pictures for the school yearbook. He said to me, "Pastor D, please be on time and dress appropriately." I said, "Coach Towns, I will have on my best suit because I will be looking like a head coach at Marion High School." The next day, I was at Marion High at about 3:45 p.m., and when I got out of my car, all eyes were on Pastor D. As I walked into the gym. The basketball players said, "Pastor D, you are looking great today." Coach Smith called me to the office. On my way to his office, he was coming to the gym. When he saw me, he called for me to come to him. Coach Smith said, "Besides you, Pastor D, who else has on a suit." I said, "No one but me, Coach Smith." Now, Coach Towns knew what I was going to have on today. Then I was told that I could not take pictures with the basketball team today. They said, "Pastor D, you can go home for today, and you won't be here when the team takes pictures." I walked out the door but never put my head down, and not one tear came down my face, but I was so hurt.

I went to practice and walked in laughing, but the players did not know my story. The players started saying, "Here comes Pastor D., he is back," The players said, one to another, "We better get serious and practice like we're going to play because Pastor D. is only looking for five players who want to play basketball." It was not long before the season started. We were winning back-to-back games. It was our first home game. I walked on the floor of Marion High School's basketball court, not as a student, not as a basketball player, not as a fan, not as a player, but as a coach for the mighty, mighty Marion High Swamp Foxes. This dream was true once in my life; I was the star. I was laughing, but knowing one did not know my story to walk out with these great Marion High basketball players. During the season, Coach Towns got sick and could not be at the game or basketball practice. Coach Towns said to me, "Pastor D, I will be out for a few games. We have a winning record. Now, Pastor D., I hope we still have a great record when I come back."

He missed five games and two and a half weeks of basketball practice. What made me feel so good was that junior varsity was the only team that had practice. I was not just over the basketball team but the whole school because no one was there. Here is a man society said would be in prison or lying in his grave, but look at God. They said that I would never be a coach for any school. I am a coach for Marion High School. We went undefeated out of the five games Coach Towns missed. One game stood out: Marion versus Mullins. Mr. Brown was the coach for Mullins. Mullins was the first team that came against Pastor D's defense. Marion blew Mullins out, over twenty points. Mullins had no answer for Pastor D's defense. One of the players' fathers said, "I have never seen my son dunk in a game."

I promised him it would happen today. You will see your son dunk in this game tonight. Mike-Mike did have his first dunk in a regular-season game against Mullins. I remembered another game we were playing, the Pastor D defense. The game was against Carvers Bay, and it was close. I believe out of spite, Coach Smith went live so Coach Towns could see the game, not for good, but so he could comment about how I was coaching. Shortly after the live started, Coach Smith came down and said, "Coach Towns said to stop playing that defense. Coach Towns is on the phone. He has something to tell you." Coach Towns said, "Go to a zone or man-to-man defense, but get out of that Pastor D defense or let Coach Smith take your place." So, I went to the zone defense, and it was not working. Then I went to man-to-man defense, and it still was not working. Then I said forget it, and I went back to Pastor D's defense, and we won the game.

At the end of the practice, each player was allowed to address the coaches and the team. A few other players asked Coach Towns whether we could do the Pastor D press defense. We got one hundred points in a game-best one running and doing the Pastor D press defense. "We can run the Pastor D press defense all four quarters." We went 5-0 with me as the coach. The team knew whatever I did worked because we had not lost a game. One of the players said, "Pastor D, what will happen if someone on the starting lineup is late for practice?" I told them, "I remember coaching New Breed basketball some years ago. Yvonne brought her son JJ to practice, and he was late. When JJ got out of the car, he told his mother that Pastor D would give him extra running because he was late for basketball practice. Yvonne said, let me get out of this car and go into that gym because Pastor D will not have you doing any extra running. I am going to tell Pastor D off today. JJ won't be playing basketball anymore. JJ said, Mama, last year I quit because you took me off the team. This year, I'm not getting off the team because I am not a quitter but a New Breed, a champion, and a winner. Pastor D taught us he doesn't treat us equally, but he treats us fairly. Then Yvonne said, JJ, I will be back to pick you up from practice in an hour. Son, I know you are a champion, a winner, and not a quitter because you are Yvonne Durant's son. I then said, I don't care who you are, but you will do extra running if anyone comes late for practice. Now, the same rules that I had years ago are the same rules today."

After practice, on my way home, I received a phone call. It was Deacon Timothy Gerald. He said, "I am calling to find out if you can be at St. Matthews Missionary Baptist Church next month. Dr. Bennie T Davis Sr., you will preach, do Sunday school, Bible study, and Prayer service." I said, "Deacon Timothy Gerald, I would be able to come next month. I will see you and the church family on Sunday."

I was ready to start back working with pre-trial intervention (PTI) through the solicitor's office. They had to let me go because of the false charges. Now that the court cases are over and I have been proven innocent of all charges, I could return and continue to be a site for pretrial intervention in the City of Marion. I have the best site in that area. I had a 10:00 a.m. meeting with the director over PTI. When I spoke with a representative over the phone, the representative desired to have more sites because they had more people in the system than sites to do the community services. When I got their director, I had a 10:00 a.m. appointment to see him. During the time I was standing at the window a white man walked out of the office. The secretary said, "Dr. Bennie T. Davis Sr. is here for an appointment at 10:00 a.m. with you." He said, give me ten minutes, then send him to my office. During the time I was waiting, one of the agents saw me. She recognized who I was, and then she came to me. She said, "Pastor D, I hope you come back because you are missed so much. There are not enough sites around, but it was so good when you had your site. Anyone we sent to your site, you would always find work for all of them. Now, some sites won't take some people with certain crimes. I hope our director allows your site to come back because we need more sites." The secretary said, "Dr. Bennie T. Davis Sr., your meeting is in the first office on the right. Our director is waiting on you now." As I walked towards the office, the same agent saw me and said, "I have five people. I will send them to your site tomorrow, but I will get in touch with them today. My office is right beside the office you are going to for your meeting." My confidence was up because of what was said to me.

I went in and introduced myself to the director of PTI. I was asked to have a seat. He said, "Dr. Bennie T. Davis Sr., now you would like to become a site for community service." I said, "Yes, sir, but I had a site for over ten years. Three years ago, I was in general session court for several crimes that I did not commit. Over two years, one by one, the charges were dropped. The sad thing about this is that the Sheriff's and the Solicitor's office knew about my charges but didn't want Detective Samantha Jackson to look bad, so they decided to destroy my life. The one thing that I enjoyed was working with young people. Showing them it is a better life than prison or death. I have a Bible College, so when someone has community service, I will have them read and record the books on tape. I will also have someone type the work for me. I will have the young men and women work in the yards for the older people in the community."

When I finished telling the director about the different things that I have the workers doing for community service, the director looked at me and said, "Dr. Bennie T. Davis Sr., at this time, we have too many sites. We don't need any more in Marion County. If I need a site, I will call you. I want to thank you for taking the time out to come over to meet with me." I said, "Sir, someone is lying because someone who worked with me in the past said there were not enough sites on my way to your office today. Someone told me five people would be coming to me tomorrow to start work. So, is it someone from the solicitor's office who doesn't want me because of what I did to them in court? Now, when everyone was thinking I was going to take a plea, all was great." The director never said that I was lying. I would not allow myself to start looking down, but I was looking at him in his face. He started looking around and acting like he was reading something. I knew this meeting was over before it started. I stood up, knowing I would never be a part of this family anymore. "Black, brown, and white when I am a black man that had been found not guilty. But now you treat me like I was guilty of all three charges. I now know who it is you want to help. I know this myself because the solicitor's office has blackballed me. Just because I am a black man who decided prison is not my home. I have a desire to help make people see that they have a life of freedom. On the completion of the PTI, the charges would be taken off my criminal record. But now, I will never be able to help anyone else because of how this office feels about me." Then, I walked out of the office.

A few days later, I got the news that I was Chaplin for all the prisons in South Carolina.

TELL ALL I AM NOT THAT WAY ANYMORE

17. TOMORROW

I was so excited because now I was able to go back to the prisons. I was now able to give the inmates hope because I made it out of the streets. Yes, I had on the same shoes of failure but today I have on the shoes of success. Each one of you can do the same thing, but that is all up to you. I was not able to wait anymore because three years had gone by, and I was not going to let another day go by me. I called a prison, and within two weeks, my prison ministry had started back up. Things started to look good for me. It had been a long time coming. This coming Sunday was the return of Pastor D at Saint Matthew's Missionary Baptist Church.

I went around asking most of my friends to come and support me on Sunday morning worship service. Most of them said they would be in the house on Sunday morning worship service. Now, two days before, I returned home to the church that opened their doors and hearts to give me the opportunity to be their pastor. This was something that other churches that I applied for did not have the heart, guts, or courage to do. They were scared about what other people would say about having a pastor not to look up to, but he was an ex-con. It would make the church look bad. I believe that now that all the charges had been dropped, I had run for Mayor of the city of Marion. I was an assistant coach at Marion High School and it should not be any problems with my becoming the pastor at Saint Matthew's Missionary Baptist Church. The members now know that this officer hates Pastor D and that he did everything in his power to get him voted out as pastor. He did achieve his goal. Pastor D was out as the pastor. So now, the only one that could stop this from happening was the officer of the church.

It was just hours away, but invitations were sent out to churches. I personally went out and invited people that I believed would accept the invitation and support me. Sunday morning came fast. It is a true saying that time does not wait on anyone. Deacon Alethea, Billie Lou Clark, and the Greater Christ Temple Church family all supported Pastor D. After Sunday school, I went to the pastor's study. I stayed in the office until the usher came for me. The usher said, "Pastor D., It's time for worship service. Follow me." When I was seated, I looked around, and my eyes got full of water because, on the pulpit, there was Evangelist Harriet Wilson, Minister Travis Smith, and Pastor Penny Smith. That brought me so much confidence because they took the time out of their busy schedule to come support Pastor D.

Then, after I was seated, I looked out into the congregation and saw Mayor pro-tem Emerson Hunt, Marion Police Chief Dewayne Tennant, Attorney Robert E. Lee, Lorie Bellamy, Joe Payton, Joyce Moody, Chris Davis, Alice Brunson Legette, Olentha Davis, Lorie Strickland, Gusand Weeks and Precious Weeks, it was between fifty to sixty people. The majority were guests that I invited to support me. It was black, brown, and white people across the sanctuary. There were members of Saint Matthews Missionary Baptist Church who did not attend service. We had a high spiritual time in the Lord. After church, different people came to me, saying how wonderful it was and that they enjoyed the service. They were so happy to see Pastor D., but most of all, to know Pastor D was proven not guilty.

The following Wednesday was here, and it was time for me to get on the road for Bible study. I put together a Bible study that I believed would help the church family. When I pulled up to the church, there were not a lot of cars in the parking lot. Once I got Bible study started, I gave them my absolute best, and everyone who was at Bible study was incredibly happy about the class. As soon as

I dismissed Bible study, I went to my Facebook page. A member of Saint Matthews Missionary Baptist Church created a Facebook page under a false name. They sent me a message saying, "Pastor D, you are a great pastor, but Pastor D, you have too much baggage. All you are going to do is destroy our church's great name. It was great when you came to visit our church, but now, we don't want you as pastor a second time here at Saint Matthew's Missionary Baptist Church. The crime you committed; all you did was pay the lady off not to come to court. Pastor D said that attorney Thurmond Brooker was a paid attorney who knew how to get over into the system. You should be in some prison and not a candidate to be pastor here at Saint Matthew's Missionary Baptist Church." Several of the members came to me immediately and said, "We know who made that Facebook page. The person is not brave enough to call you, Pastor D., or to speak to you face to face. They will not put their real name on the page because they know what they are doing is wrong. Pastor D., this is not right, but we love you."

I did the remaining of my time at Saint Matthew's Missionary Baptist Church. There was a beautiful turnout on Sunday morning worship service and Bible study. There was still a percentage of the members of Saint Matthews Missionary Baptist Church that believed Pastor D did all the crimes he was accused of doing. When it was time to vote for the new pastor of Saint Matthews Missionary Baptist Church, the deacons narrowed it down to two candidates. This was when I knew it was a setup and Deacon Terry Williams used his influence to persuade the other deacons and search committee.

The same minister that I went against the first time and beat out to become the pastor of Saint Matthew's Missionary Baptist Church, Deacon Terry Williams, got this preacher to become one of the two finalists. Knowing one of them would be the new pastor and Pastor D would not be in the running. He made sure that he was going to make him pastor this time. It was wrong how the members did him the first time by looking over him and voting Pastor D as a pastor, but that won't happen this time. I knew my preaching was so much better than his, but he was not able to beat Pastor D. Then, there is no way he would have beat Pastor D now because the members knew that he lied about Pastor D. Just as Deacon Terry Williams told me he also told the Saint Matthews Missionary Baptist Church family it was wrong how this church family used this man to help us for months and made him believe he was going to be the pastor but when it was time to vote the majority voted for Pastor D but not this time. This is why the congregation government was the worst kind of church government.

The night of the vote, Deacon Terry Williams did it this time. His man became the new pastor. From that day to now, he remains as pastor of Saint Matthew's Missionary Baptist Church. The same thing that happened to Pastor D in 2015 has also happened in 2020. During our presidential election, 70% of the Republicans believed what our former president said about the presidential election. The election was fixed and stolen from me. Now, they knew this was a lie, but they still followed him, believing what Deacon Terry Williams said about Pastor D that all of it was a lie. The majority of the members of Saint Matthews Missionary Baptist Church still voted a second time not to allow Pastor D to become their pastor. Deacon Terry Williams made sure Pastor D was not one of the last two candidates because Deacon Terry Williams made sure his preacher went against someone who wasn't in any competition to guarantee that he would become the pastor of Saint Matthews Missionary Baptist Church.

In my first year as assistant coach, the team record was 12-2. What a great season we had! Track season had started, and I had submitted my application to be the head track coach. The principal of Marion High School, Dr. Michelle Wright, hired a teacher at Marion High

School because she did not want anyone who wasn't at Marion High School to be the coach. Once upon a time, to be a coach for any school in Marion, especially Marion High it, would only be the best one for the job. But now, a person must be employed by the school so they can add something to their stipend. I was not looking for any pay; I was just looking for the opportunity to make champions out of our young people. Our young people today don't have the love or heart because it starts from the head coach and goes down.

I asked to be one of the assistant coaches, but I had to complete an application once again. About two weeks later, I received a call, and I was told the great news: I was a Marion High assistant track coach. I was so happy because I went to Voorhees College and received MVP my first year running. In 1986 and 1987, I ran track for Marion High School, and in 1986, I was a conference champion in the two miles. We won the conference and the state in 1986 and 1987, so I know what to do to be a state champion.

By this time, I was a volunteer softball coach for the Marion Recreation Center. I was a volunteer softball coach and then a volunteer track coach at Marion High School. I would leave track practice and go to softball practice because I was in love with making our young people champions in sports and in schoolwork. After that first week of track practice, the track team knew that Pastor D. was a coach who loved to win. I had a new workout each day, but one day after practice, Mr. Jimmy Howard came to me about his daughter Yazmie Howard, who was on the track team. He said, "As of today, my daughter will no longer be running track because of a coach." I was so upset to hear the news about his daughter, so I asked what the coach did to her because he may need to go to Dr. Michelle Wright. Mr. Jimmy Howard responded, "Pastor D, I don't have to see Dr. Michelle Wright because it was my daughter's decision to quit running track to become the scorekeeper for the track team." I said, "Mr. Howard, I cannot understand, a coach did something to your daughter, and you are not going to the principal, and you are not going to speak to the head coach. This is your daughter, and you are just going to allow her to make this decision." He said, "Pastor D., I can accept her decision because she came to me as a responsible young lady. It is not that the coach did something out of order to my daughter, but this time, the coach is actually doing his job." I said, Mr. Howard, don't understand Yazmie Howard has been running track since she was at Johnakin Middle School." Her father said, "As of today, she is no longer running track."

This is something she loved, being a part of Marion High School's track team. "Pastor D, Yazmie said to me the reason she was not running track anymore is because of you. She has been a part of this track team for years, but she never had a coach like you. Yazmie said you expect everyone to bring their best every day to practice because before you became a track coach at Marion High School, the coaches would tell them what to do for practice and then walk some other place whether they did or not run hard or just jog it out. The coach would not know, and most of all, they never asked. But Pastor D would go to the finish line and wait for each of us to cross the line. He never had a stopwatch, but if we didn't run hard, he would have us do it over as a team. He made us believe that we had to give our best to become region and state champions. Anything less, we could not become champions. Now, Pastor D, why did you desire them to do their best every day at practice?" "The way they run at practice, that is how they will run at track meets," I said to her father. "I have a leg and a half, and I can't stand up. Each day, a manager has to bring a chair for me to sit. Some days, I came to practice, and both my legs were hurting, but I brought my best. So, when I asked the team to bring their best questions, they brought their best." Mr. Jimmy said, "Therefore, I am not mad because I can live with how she feels about not running track because she said, 'daddy, I can't bring it every day and Pastor D. is not going for anything less than my best.'" I was not able to go to any of the track meets because, on the days of the meets, I had a basketball game to coach. I just love going to track practice and leave right from track practice and go to basketball practice. Just to have the opportunity to work with young people and be a part of making them greater meant so much to me.

I was so excited. This was just my first year coaching basketball, track, and baseball. Seeing how much the young people enjoyed learning the fundamentals, that excitement that covered their faces motivated me to go deep into my spirit to give each person the best I could give to them. Track season was going along fine. That was not for me. I was not able to go to any track meets during the season because I had baseball practice and games.

One day after baseball practice, I got a phone call from the City Hall of Marion. When I answered the phone, the voice on the other end said, "This is the city of Marion administrator, Mr. Allen Ammons. I would like to speak to Pastor D." I answered back, "This is him. What can I do for you?" He said, "I am calling on behalf of Mayor Ashley Brady and City Council Emerson Hunt. They would like to start a basketball program for adults seventeen years old and older. Mayor pro-tem Emerson Hunt recommended to the Mayor that you would be the best person to be over this program. I would like to set up a meeting tomorrow at 2:00 p.m. Will you be able to be there?" I said, "Yes, I will be to your office. I will see you at 2:00 p.m. tomorrow, Mr. Allen Ammons," And I hung up the phone.

When I made it home, I was not able to keep it to myself. I walked into my mother's house, and as soon as I put my eyes on her, I told her about the wonderful phone call that I received from Mr. Allen Ammons, our City Administrator. "He said to me that I was recommended by Mayor pro-tem Emerson Hunt to be over a new basketball program for only adults seventeen years old and older. I have a meeting tomorrow at 2:00 p.m. Mother and I would like for you to fast and pray with me until the meeting is over tomorrow. This job belongs to me."

I met with the city administrator, and it was a very productive meeting. Mr. Allen Ammons, the city administrator, asked me, "Would you manage the new program adult basketball 17 years old and older?" He went on to say, "The City of Marion would not be responsible for paying you to open the gym. The gym was open two nights a week, but if you managed the gym right within 90 days, the gym would be open three days a week. I also wanted you to start an adult basketball league that would travel throughout South Carolina. Now, the only money that you would receive would be the money you charge to come in the gym to play basketball. Know that if no one came, you wouldn't get any money." I said to him, "I would take this job and make it work." He said, "Pastor D, you can start this week, and here is your key to the city of Marion Gym." "Mr. Ammons, I thank you for this opportunity, I will not let myself down, Mayor Ashley Brady, Mayor pro-tem Emerson Hunt, and most of all you, Mr. Allen Ammons." Then he responded by saying, "Pastor D, if you managed this adult basketball like you did your club Stitches, there would be no problems." Then I shook his hand and walked out of his office happy and excited because now I had been appointed to manage an adult basketball league, coach Marion High School basketball, coach Marion High School track team, and coach Marion Recreation Center Department baseball.

At the end of the baseball season, I had an appreciation service for the baseball team. Every player got an award and the parents. The Marion County Sheriff Brian Wallace was a part of this day for our youth. He gave each player something from himself and let them know how proud he was of each one of them for not getting in trouble but representing themselves, their parents, and the county and city of Marion. The players were so happy to meet Marion County Sheriff Brian Wallace and city of Marion pro-tem Emerson

Hunt. The players were so happy because this day was set aside to honor the New Breed baseball team. The players aged from five to eight years old, but I was just as happy as they were on their day. I started looking forward to the next year because I believed with hard work, we would bring a state championship for track, and baseball for Marion High School, and Marion Recreation Department Center.

During the summer, Coach Towns and I discussed different things to make the team better for our upcoming basketball season. He said, "Pastor D., next season, I will be giving you more responsibility, not just with helping me. Coach Smith will be named the conditioning coach for junior varsity and varsity basketball because of the great work you did this basketball season. Our junior varsity was in so much better shape than varsity basketball or any other sports at Marion High School. Anytime a basketball team does a full-court press all four quarters that team is in excellent shape, and Pastor D., because of your determination, those young men were in the best shape of their life. This is why you will be over all conditioning and that Pastor D defense." Throughout the offseason, I went to different prisons in South Carolina. I encouraged and reminded the inmates that they could still accomplish their dreams. "When you get out of prison and off parole, I encourage each of you to get a pardon to clean your criminal record. The reason I know that you can is because I got a pardon from the state of South Carolina. I did this without a lawyer but with God on my side. Each one of you could do the same thing because I will help you get this started, get out of prison first, then let's get to work on yourself." To see the faces of these young men and the excitement that was over each of them. I said to them, "I believe in each one of you, yes, you could and would be successful in life." This did not just help them, but it also helped me because the next day, I was on the phone calling the solicitor's office about me becoming a site for PTI.

The man that was over this program continued to lie to me to say they had enough sites, but not knowing I was sending people over there giving them sites because they were coming to my Youth Center for help. I was telling them how to recommend a site to do their community service. Over time, I learned that a lot of them that were doing community service were making up names and were not doing any community service. They were just signing the papers. The people were responsible for sending people out to do community service. So, there were many people that were not doing any community service hours. They would fill out the paperwork like they completed the hours of work. The officers that assigned the clients to the place to do their community service at were not doing any follow-ups by calling before they started and after they completed the assignment.

They took the word of the clients and dismissed the truth, obviously. They are not doing their job but who cares because they just needed the paperwork with the hours of the community service. The supervisor just gave me the runaround by not allowing me to be a site anymore. I really believed when I was found not guilty and the other charges were dropped because after three years, I walked out the courtroom a free man but lost everything but my life. The solicitor decided against me, not to allow me to ever be a site for pretrial intervention again because I was not found guilty in the courtroom. This is my punishment from the solicitor to remind me that I am just a black man. They had to remind me that I did not get away. I was still praying that Greater Christ Temple Bible Institution would get more students because at this time it was only one student, Evangelist Harriet Wilson for about a year and a half.

One day, I was in the church doing some work, and the door opened, and someone walked in the sanctuary. When I looked up, it was Bishop Lorenzo Washington. He said, "Pastor D., the Lord put in my spirit to enroll in the Bible College that you started here in Marion. I am not coming by myself, but I am going to get some other people to come. I am going to work and get my doctoral degree from this college. I will start with my associates degree. I am not coming alone because my wife, Pastor Annie Washington, will also be attending Bible College. I gave him all the information he needed to start college and let him know the classes would be every Monday 4:00 p.m. to 7:00 p.m. and that I would see him and his wife on Monday. God started adding to Greater Christ Temple Bible Institution. Bishop Lorenzo Washington and his wife became students at the Bible College.

My second season of being a basketball coach for Marion High School had started. The excitement just built even greater than my first-year coaching because last year, our record was 12-2 but this year, we went undefeated. I had the confidence. Together, this could and would happen having a greater season than last year. As soon as I walked in the gym, Coach Smith said, "Pastor D., for the next forty-five minutes, your job is to do condition drills. Today, you will be working with varsity and junior varsity basketball teams." Anyone that desired to come to this conditioning workout was free to come so the coaches could have a better look at the players. Because a person would come to volunteer conditioning doesn't necessarily mean they would make the basketball team. It was a great turnout of players and all of them gave their best.

I put in an application to become the varsity head coach at Mullins High School. I also put in an application to be the head coach for junior varsity basketball at Mullins High School. I got a phone call from Mullins High School about an interview to be head coach for varsity basketball. I was just as good as any of the other candidates. I beat the candidate most would win by twenty-two points.

Coach Towns was sick and was out for over a week. He had faith in me that I could have the team ready to play and beat any high school with that Pastor D press defense. One of the many questions that was asked during the interview was, "Why do you believe that you will be the best person to be the next head coach for the Mullins High School varsity basketball team?" I said, "I will be the best person to become the new head coach because I will bring a new voice to the team, new ideas, new energy, and a fight they never had in their life.

"The fight is to win on a basketball court and in their personal life. This team will bring a regional championship, lower state championship, and a state championship. I would not lie to them if they cannot play on the level that I am expecting them to play on. I would tell them you must be one of the best fifteen players here at Mullins High school. If you are any number higher than fifteen, there is no way you can make this basketball team. I will let everyone know this team is one level from college, two levels from NBA.

My coaching philosophy is to prepare this team for the next level of basketball. The players would be disciplined on this basketball team but most of all, this team will compete all four quarters until the last horn is blown."

At the end of the interview, the principal and the athletic director of Mullins High School stood up and said, "Thank you for coming out today. Someone will call you about the job here at Mullins High School in a few days." I thanked each of them for this interview. I said, "I hope that the person selected to be the next coach at Mullins High School will be the best one and not one because of a promise. Let it be the best coach, and that will be me. If I don't do the best job, you won't need to fire me because I would quit Mullins High School." I shook each of their hands and then walked out of the office. As I was walking down the hallway going to my car, I said to myself, 'I thank all for the interview but now as I look over it, this was just what they did so they could say they interviewed a few candidates for the head coaching job for Mullins High School varsity basketball.' They would have to give the job to the Junior Varsity Coach only because he has been working with Mullins High

School basketball team for a few years. Because he does his job filling in for the varsity basketball head coach, that does not make him the best coach. It just shows a buddy, buddy thing, and not the best person gets the job.

By this time, I was back in Marion, and it was time for me to get ready to go to Marion High School for junior varsity and varsity volunteer conditioning practice. Emerson Hunt called me to find out what was going on. I told him that I had an interview today for a varsity head coaching job at Mullins High School. He said to me, "Pastor D., are you going to walk away from Coach Towns?" "I will only stay here at Marion High School if I don't become the new head coach at Mullins High School," I said to Emerson. "Last year, I coached five games because Coach Towns was out sick, and we went undefeated. When he came back, the team's record was better than before he left. I have more opportunities here at Marion High School than acting as an assistant coach at Mullins High School. Emerson, if I don't become head coach, I would not be leaving Coach Towns as his assistant. I will talk to you later today, but it's time for basketball practice right now." Before practice started, Coach Towns went into Coach Smith's office and stayed there until it was time to go into the gym. I told Coach Towns about the interview at Mullins High School to become the new head coach for varsity basketball. I believed with all my heart that I was a better coach than the junior varsity Coach. If I didn't get the varsity coaching job, and if Eric Troy got the job, he was not the best coach. The only thing is he was so faithfully working toward becoming the head coach for varsity basketball. He is the head coach of junior varsity basketball, a graduate from Mullins High School. Out of all of that, it still does not make him the best man for the job.

Within a few days, Mullins High School did what most people had an idea would happen; Eric Troy was named the new head coach of varsity basketball. Immediately, I applied to be the head coach for junior varsity basketball at Mullins High School. I knew they would do the same thing with Eric Troy's varsity basketball. They are going to keep giving it to a coach in the family. This coach would be a part of the Mullins High School history and would have been an assistant coach at Mullins High School. I am not a part of any of that, but I am the best coach for this junior varsity basketball team at Mullins High School. The only thing that got my attention when I walked into the interview was the three people conducting the interview; the principal of Mullins High School, the athletic director, and the new varsity head coach, Eric Troy. How could he be fair when one of the two people was his former assistant coach? At the same time, knowing I was the best coach for the job because head-to-head, I whipped him by twenty-two points, so already, he had a personal vendetta against me. So how could he recommend Pastor D to be the next new head coach for junior varsity basketball for Mullins High School? The interview was not long. I was able to answer all the questions very professionally. I was going against the odds, but I had faith in my ability to make this junior varsity basketball team the greatest in Mullins High School's history.

A few days after the interview, they named Eric Troy successor, the new head coach of Mullins High School junior varsity basketball. The only hope I have is there will be a tomorrow for Pastor D because things must get better. So, I decided to work extremely hard with the young men at Marion High School basketball. Junior varsity basketball will have another winning season by the leadership of Coach Towns and me. My tomorrow must first start in me before anyone else can see how the Lord is turning things around for my good.

After the enrollment, Bishop Lorenzo Washington and his wife started going around in the Fellowship of Ministry, encouraging and inviting pastors, members, and people throughout the community and cities to come to the most incredible bible college in the world and universe to come to get more knowledge about the Word of God. Because of the work of Bishop Lorenzo Washington, men and women were able to see the growth spiritually. Because of Bishop Washington's influence, Pastor George Williams, Minister Heyward Addison Jr, Annette D. Addison, Minister Betty Wells, Evangelist Birdie Mae Rouse, and Herbert Rouse enrolled in Greater Christ Temple Bible Institute. None of them was from Marion. The students were coming from all over the state of South Carolina.

Greater Christ Temple Church of the Harvest celebrated its Church's 20th anniversary. Mr. James Woods is a sponsor of this ministry. He donated a car to give to some beautiful person. God blessed the Church to raise the money to put on the most exquisite banquet in our 20th year of being in existence. At our 20th church anniversary banquet, Pastor D announced the first three people receiving an honorary doctorate in Divinity. The honorees were Mildred Riggins, Jeanette Waiters, and Deacon Timothy Gerald. Each of them was so surprised, but I informed everyone that his/her support of the ministry had earned them the recognition to receive the degree. The church anniversary celebration was a great success, and people had a great time. Greater Christ Temple Church of the Harvest evolved from 'I'm Not That Way Anymore Youth/ Adult Center Inc.' This ministry assisted hundreds of people in finding jobs, receiving their high school diplomas, helping people avoid going to prison, helping people find housing, and Greater Christ Temple Bible Institute was birthed from this ministry. But most of all, people came to Christ to be saved. There is nothing better to see than people becoming self-sufficient and learning the knowledge of the word of God. The people stood up and clapped because of their accomplishments in this ministry.

For the churches that are just starting with only a few members, don't stop; don't give up because this ministry today has less than ten members but look at God's work. I never stopped believing that there was a tomorrow for me. Mr. James Woods and Mayor pro-tem Emerson Hunt put the icing on the cake. For this church anniversary sponsoring the giveaway, they gave me what I could not afford, but at a price I could afford. The first prize was a car, the second prize money, and the third prize was a gift card. My mother, better known as Pocahontas, put together a wonderful dinner with all types of different foods. At the end of the banquet, I gave thanks to all the sponsors: Barberholics of Marion, Robert E. Lee attorney at law of Marion, Wood/Emerson Bonding Company of Marion, Sanders Automotive and Paint of Marion, Turners BP of Marion, Extreme Medical Transport of Marion, Swamp Fox Reality and Appraisals of Marion, Doc's Furniture-Bedding-Appliances of Marion & Columbia SC, and Auto Money Title Loans of Marion SC. After the banquet, the people left excited about how this small group of partners at Greater Christ Temple Church of the Harvest worked together. They pulled off an outstanding program. For a few days, that was the talk around Marion.

Basketball season was in full gear. We were winning more games than we were losing, but the season was greater because of the discipline. Each player had a thirst for learning and getting better. We were halfway through the fall and mid-way point of the halfway point. We had a home game, and after the game, the players were in the locker room. Coach Towns and I came in to speak to the team about what we must work on to get better before the next game. I let the players know they were imposing on tonight's game. Now I was hoping you could bring that same energy to practice tomorrow because anyone who doesn't start can take someone else's starting position. You must work hard because someone else can and will replace you if not at any time. This game was great because we worked as a team.

As I was walking out of the locker room, a player asked for a ride home, and I said, "Yes, boss man, I will be waiting outside in the car." So, I waited for about fifteen minutes before David came out to get in the car. As I was driving him home, he said, "Pastor D, I need to tell you something. He said tonight something happened in the locker room. After the game, the team and I dressed in the locker room; I checked for my wallet, but all my money was gone. Coach someone got me, and it had to be a teammate. I started going around asking about my money and looking at the ones that had money tonight but other game nights they had little money or no money at all to buy anything." He let me know he informed the Sheriff Officer and Dr. Michelle Wright, the Principal at Marion High School. He said, "Someone in his family was paid off, and they came by the school today to give him some money. He is lying to his family, and the principal will not do anything."

That is when he told me what the young man's name was. I told myself I do know his people, so I told him, "Let's find out, let me call someone." I called while he was in the car with me. I knew one thing; someone could have been killed and put in jail for life. As a coach, I must do something now before he gets out of my car. So, I called and let the young man hear me because no one has a life to give or a life to take. I called the cell phone; the person did pick up and said, "Yes, Pastor D." I proceeded to tell her my reason for calling. "It is about some money someone took out of a player's wallet tonight. Now your family member had money, did he have any money tonight?" She asked his grandmother, "Do you know anything about him having any money." I told her that some of his people got hurt money because a case was closed, and they did bring him some money to the school. The young basketball player heard that the young man did get some money, and I said, "Now don't do anything to be put off the basketball team. This team needs you as a basketball player and not one that would never play to represent Marion High School anymore." Before he got out of the car, I said, "Don't call or go by this young man's house because someone may get killed." He said, "I believe what I heard tonight from his family member, and I will not be calling or going out anymore tonight." I waited outside of David's house until someone opened the door, and he walked into the house. Not long after he walked into the house, his mother said, "Pastor D., Pastor D., wait, I need to talk to you." She came to the car and said, "Pastor D., and I want to thank you for making sure my son made it home. He told me what had happened with his money, and he was upset. God put you in place to help my son and the young men on the Marion High School basketball team."

I let her know that I had called someone in the young man's family to verify his money at the game. "Now your son isn't going out anymore tonight." She said, "Thank you so much for all you did for my son. Pastor D., my son, loved him some you, and he would do whatever you asked him to do."

The money issue happened on Friday, but on Monday, as I entered the school to go to the gym for basketball practice, Coach Smith stopped me from going into the gym. He said, "Pastor D, the principal said that as of that day, you were not allowed to attend basketball practice until you met with her today at 4:00 p.m. She was looking to meet with you today." I asked Coach Smith, "Do you have any idea why she wants to meet with me?" He said, "Pastor D., the only thing she said to me was to have Pastor D come to my office on Monday at 4:00 p.m." I took my time walking to her office. I was at a standstill of disbelief. So, when I got to Dr. Wright's office for the meeting, I was asked to have a seat and that someone would come to take me back to the office for the meeting in a few minutes. Then someone came to me and said to follow them to Dr. Wright's office. To my surprise, when I walked into the office, the first face I saw was Coach Smith waiting for me. Dr. Michelle Wright had me take a seat and said, "Coach Davis, I asked you to come today because of what happened on Friday night. You had no reason to call anyone about the money stolen from David in the locker room.

The right thing to do was to contact me, Coach Smith, or Coach Towns before you started calling around." I told Dr. Wright, "I did not have your phone number. Coach Smith got upset with me, and his cell phone number was changed. He gave his new number to all the head basketball coaches, boys and girls, and all the assistant coaches, boys and girls, but not to me. Coach Towns, I called him, but he never called or texted me back. So, because I did not reach anyone, a decision had to be made, and that is what I did. I decided not to just sit back and allow a young man to be killed or brutally beaten about something he did or could not have done after the basketball game. I live in the same neighborhood as most of the basketball players, so at this point, I chose to save two lives because of the phone call, we found out that this basketball player was accused of stealing money from David, a player on the team, but wasn't the person taking the money." Dr. Michelle Wright said, "Coach Davis, you had no business calling anyone about this situation regardless of who." So, I asked Dr. Wright, "You would rather for me to walk away and allow someone, if not all, both of them to get hurt or killed?" Her answer was, "Yes, you should have walked away." Coach Smith supported everything she said to me. "Pastor D, why did you insert yourself in this situation?" "I cannot believe that both of you are agreeing with each other. I was wrong for saving a life, saving a person from going to prison for life for murder with premeditation?" These two young men would have never received their high school diploma. So, if I had to do it again, I would respond the same way as a responsible coach of Marion High School, who loves human life.

Then Dr. Wright reminded me, "If coach Towns is wrong, keep your mouth shut, as I said before. Don't re-direct; let him be wrong about anything else, about money, or anything that goes on with this basketball team. If you get involved, you will never coach at this school or any other school in Marion County again. Do I make myself clear to you? Coach Bennie T. Davis Sr., you are an assistant coach. Coach Smith and Coach Towns deal with what's going on with the team, not you." Dr. Wright did not say anything else because human lives do not matter. Because the protocol is more important, but from this day, she is my boss, and I respect what she told me to do, but lives matter to me. She said, "You can return to basketball practice as of today. Just be an assistant coach to the head coach." Before I walked out of the door, I said to Dr. Wright, "Am I not to say anything else because human life does not matter in our schools anymore because the protocol is more important. From this day forward, I respect what you said to me, but living matters to me if they play basketball or not. Their lives matter to me." I said, "I thank you for allowing me to stay on as a coach because I look at them as family. I love working with the coaches and the players. I can share my basketball knowledge and the real world with the players after high school. With this opportunity, I can put as much love and hope as they have room for in their lives." Then I got out of my seat and shook her hand and the two Coaches as well. I said to both of them, "I would only be the assistant who works alongside Coach Towns, and when this basketball season is over, each of you will be proud of the work I have done to make this team proud and Marion High School. Coach Smith, I will see you at basketball practice, so let me get to my job." I walked out of the office.

As I was walking down the hallway, my mind went back to a few weeks ago as I was approaching the school to come to basketball practice, and there was a football coach using profanity towards each player that was going to the weight room. As the players were approaching the coach to enter the building, the coach cursed each player by calling them out of their name. He said something different to each of the players but not anything to help them but to bring them down. There were about three players together, and he said, "I see why you all are together because not one of you will have anything in life. If your life is anything like you're playing football, your life never will be anything because you will lose at everything you go out to do in life." One young man was walking up with a young lady, and he said to her if you would like to have someone good in your life that what you are walking with is no good for himself and no good for you. "He can't play football, and he won't be anything in your life so let that no-good boy go today."

That young man put his head down. I will never forget when he said this to a player. "Why your parents allowed you to play football because they know when you asked you were never going to play in any games because you are just downright sorry, and they wasted their money on you. You are not playing in any more games this year, and if you quit today, I will not be mad, but if you do, you will never play another sport at Marion High School." I hope you understand that coach took the life out of that young man.

He then said to another young man, "Why are you going to the weight room? Don't get dressed, go home because you won't be playing Friday night; I will see that it happens." Some other coaches and instructors worked at Marion High School; not one person said anything to this man. Tears came to my eyes, and I said this is why white parents don't allow their children to play football. This coach did not know how to motivate black players even though he was black.

By this time, I was walking into the gym; here I am, saving a life and about to get fired. Everyone loves him from the principal on down; this man is in our school system working with our children. Not any young man or young lady can say Coach Davis/Pastor D ever called anyone out of their name or talked down to them at any time, but not all coaches at Marion High can say the same thing. When I walked into the gym, Coach Towns never said anything, but he had me start working with them on defense. The first half of the basketball ended, and we were out for the Christmas holidays.

On Christmas eve, December 24, 2019, there was a bad fire in the city of Mullins. Every one of the people was burnt alive, it was said only two or three were at the point of death. I said, I would keep the families in prayer. Sometime after 5:00 p.m., I received a phone call from my baby daughter Antoinette Davis. I was so happy to hear from her because it was the day before Christmas. So right then, I said, "Now, what is it that she could not get for Messiah. His papa must make it happen so Christmas can be in her house." I always said, "I miss you, my love, and that son that big Papa loves, little Bennie III." But when I heard her voice, it was one I had never heard from her in my life. I could not feel that joy of energy and excitement about Christmas coming the next day. But this call was one of crying, tears, fear, and sorrow.

"Daddy, I have something to tell you; listen to me, my mother was just in a house fire." I said, "Baby, she will be all right because she loved life, and most of all, she is a fighter." Then she shouted with a loud voice, "Daddy, Mama was in that fire today that everyone was burnt alive. Mama and someone else are still alive, but they said that the way things are looking, I don't think she will make it out of this in her condition. They have her wrapped up, but daddy, I could smell her flesh burning. When they got there somehow, she made it out, but the fire was burning her, and her flesh was falling on the ground. What is going to happen to my mother? What am I going to do without my mother? I have no other mother; I need my mother. I love my mother, daddy. I got to get out of here. Daddy, I am leaving this hospital. I need you. I am going home." Then the phone went out. There was no voice on the other end of the phone. By this time, I was walking out the door as fast as possible because the only thing I could do was make it to my daughter's house because she needed her daddy. By the time I got to my daughter's house, her car was in her yard. I got out of my car and went straight into her house. I had to put my eyes on my daughter to let her know her daddy is here for anything you need from me. I walked into the house, and she was still crying. Family and friends were there sitting around her, but now daddy is here. I got right beside her and said, "I love you so much. Just let me know what I can do for you." "I am good. Mama is in Augusta, GA. They have a specialist that knows what to do if she is to make it out of this and live her life. This is the only way she will survive those awful burns she has covering her body. Daddy, I got to get my clothes together because I am going to my mother. My son will stay with my aunt because I am leaving for Augusta. I am taking off from work, so I can be with my mother. Daddy, I love her so much, and I am leaving tonight. I can't wait anymore. Mama needs me." She did go and was with her mother for three days.

Later, on Thursday, December 27, 2018, in Augusta, GA. Her mother, Sharon M Davis departed this life. A few days later, I got a phone call, and I was asked to do the eulogy on Wednesday, January 2, 2019, at 11:00 a.m. I said yes, I will because Sharon was a wonderful person. The day of her homegoing celebration came so fast, but her family and friends showed up, and what a great time we had looking back over parts of her extraordinary life. It was great to see her children Crystal Howe, Antoinette Davis, Jonathan Davis, Jamesha Davis, Donnie Davis, and Tyshanna Davis to know that all six of them graduated from high school and have the foundation to live to be successful. Sharon made sure all of them were in an environment for success, but I let them all know anytime any of them needed me, I was only a call or text away. I am here as a father anytime, day or night, and I love each of you.

It was a great homegoing service. Tomorrow is a day that may never come, so make it happen today. Do everything you can do today, so if there is no tomorrow, you would have accomplished everything you could have. I let the people know the only thing you can change about yesterday or today is us. After the homegoing service, different ones came from the family, and Sharon's friends came up to me, saying how much they loved the service.

Next season should be more excellent because everyone would be back on the team. It was time for a Greater Christ Temple Bible Institute graduation coming up in May. It was just days away. I was so happy about this graduation. It was now the day of graduation, and everything got started, as I was looking around in the auditorium, I was just so proud of what each student accomplished through their hard work. We had our first three people to receive their honorary doctoral degree. Mildred Riggins, Deacon Timothy Gerald, and Jeanette Waiters were the ones who received their honorary Postgraduate degrees. Bishop Lorenzo Washington, Pastor Annie Mae Washington received their Associate degree, and Harriet Wilson and Marilyn Rogers received their Bachelor of Science degree.

I was at basketball practice, Greater Christ Temple Bible Institute, and going to the different prisons during all of this. The basketball season ended, and we had an excellent record because every game, each young man on the team gave all they had at practice first, so they would play as they practiced. Throughout the summer, Coach Towns and I stayed in touch with each other talking about the upcoming basketball season. Coach Towns said, "You will be over conditioning and running the Pastor D press defense this coming season." He shared his vision with me, and I said to him, "I am here to help your vision for this basketball team to come to pass. We will walk together as Coach Towns and Assistant Coach Pastor D. This can happen."

Summer went by so fast, and I had summer class at Greater Christ Temple Bible Institute, summer adult basketball, and summer programs at the Church. It was time for volunteer conditioning for basketball. I was so excited and ready because Coach Towns had already let me know what my job would be. During the summer, Coach Towns let me know his expectations of me and his vision. He let me know he was with one accord. I could not sleep because the closer it got, the more excited I became to see all the old players and the new ones that would make the team. Working with young people is a love I have because we are not our future, but they are ours.

They must be taught now so we can have a future. A few days before basketball started, a call came from Coach Towns. I was so happy to hear from him. As our conversation continued, I asked Coach Towns when will conditioning start. I was so excited about this upcoming basketball season, and I was looking forward to making my mark. As a great assistant coach, that would become a greater head basketball coach for high school or college. Coach Towns voice changed, and he said, "Pastor D, Coach Smith would like to go in a new direction. So now I have the job to inform you that you are no longer a part of the junior varsity basketball coaching staff. Coach Smith has brought in new coaches, and there is no room for your way of coaching." When I heard this, I was speechless for several minutes and my heart was crushed. The oxygen was just sucked out of my body. Here is something that I was looking forward to, working with our young men. I was so hurt to hear those words come out of his mouth. Here is a black man telling another black man you are not good enough and replacing him not with a black man but a white man.

Now it hurt my last track season. I would not be working with the track team because I didn't have a good relationship with the students at Marion High School. I was fulfilling a dream to become a basketball coach at my alumni, and now it has just stopped. I believed that I could see one day. This was my time, but now to hear that I was fired expeditiously, my eyes filled with water, tears began to roll down both sides of my face. I couldn't believe what I had just heard. My head dropped down, and the spirit of failure came upon me. Saying, 'Pastor D will never amount to anything.' I pulled myself together. "When can I meet with you and Coach Smith to find out what is it about me not coaching this year?" Coach Towns said, "Pastor D, that won't be happening, Coach Smith don't want you to be a part of this coaching team. So, there isn't anything to discuss. You won't be a part of this team anymore. There's nothing else to talk about and thank you for your service."

Those were the most hurtful words. I was doing this coaching for free, volunteering my time giving back to the community, but my best wasn't good enough for Coach Towns and Coach Smith, but out of all, I still love those young men on the basketball team of Marion High School. I was going to walk away from it all, but as days passed, I called Emerson Hunt to tell him how Coach Towns and Coach Smith did me and how much it hurt me. Coach Towns said, "Pastor D, Coach Smith said as of this day, your services are no longer needed for this basketball season." The words that came out of our Mayor pro-tem City Council Emerson Hunt's mouth were, "Pastor D; you have done a wonderful job with those young men on the basketball team. The young men on the basketball team love and respect you because some don't have a father in their lives, but you put discipline and love in all their lives. Most of all, Pastor D, because of you now, they have a father figure in each of their lives on the basketball court, and they can call you anytime. The team loves the system, making them better basketball players and young men. Because of your love for each of them, the other so-called coaches see the hunger you have to make each player better, and neither one has that in them."

At the last home game, I told the other coaches and people at the district office, "The best coach out of varsity or junior varsity was Pastor D." Now, before I say to you that I gave up, I found a way to become a coach for Marion High School, so whatever I did before, do the same thing today. I called to talk to someone in the district office, and I was advised to do whatever I did to get the job, now do the same thing to keep the job. But when I hung up the phone, I said, "No, what I will do is a Facebook live as the Thorn." My job is to tell everything about the coaches at Marion High School on Facebook live. I will put it on my Facebook page tonight at 7:00 p.m. I will tell how God gave Coach Smith a new start at Marion High School. Telling what went on between Coach Towns and me. This live will be at the men's basketball for seventeen years and up on tonight. All day, people were calling and texting. I will be looking for your live tonight and fighting for you to get your job back, Pastor D.

As the players were playing basketball just before I was about to begin my live and as I went to hit the start button, a knock was at the door. I opened the door thinking it was someone to play basketball but the door opened. The person on the other side was not someone that came to play, but as he continued to push the door open, to my surprise, it was Coach Smith. He said, "I have something to say to you before you do your live." The former players from Marion High basketball team started looking at the coach and me. Coach Smith asked me, "Why are you doing this live, Pastor D?" I told him, "I would keep my job as a coach at Marion High School. Coach Towns let me know that you fired me and because of you, I don't have a job." Coach Smith then told me, "Coach Towns is a liar because he said, 'I don't care to have Pastor D as my Assistant Coach anymore.' Coach Towns also said that Pastor D couldn't coach. I desire to go in a different direction, and Pastor D won't be a part of this team anymore." About ten times or more, Coach Smith called Coach Towns cell phone while he was with me, but not one time did he answer the phone. Coach Smith said to me, "I am the head varsity coach, and I am over coach Towns, so as of right now, Pastor D, you will be working with Coach Towns, and tomorrow, I will show you that he is nothing but a liar because I never said that to anyone. He can have more than one assistant coach. I will do this at basketball practice to show you." I said, "No, because I want my job back to work with our young men to make them better men now and after finishing high school." I shook Coach

Smith's hand, and as he proceeded to walk towards the door to exit, a few of his former basketball players said hello to him. He stopped, and some of the players came to him, and about three were coming into the gym. Coach Smith spoke with them for just a few minutes then walked out the door. Most of everyone knew why he was talking to Pastor D because of his Facebook live that was about to air. I let my Facebook family and friends know that I would not do a live-on tonight. Coach Smith and I just had a meeting about what was said about my job, but Coach Smith offered me my job back. I accepted it, so now there is no need to do it live. I want to thank each of you for whatever you did to help this come to pass. I will be back at basketball practice tomorrow.

DR. BENNIE T. DAVIS

GRADUATES OF 2019
GREATER CHRIST TEMPLE BIBLE INSTITUTE

The first three people to receive the honorary doctoral degree in divinity at greater christ temple bible institute.

FORMER DRUG DEALER; DR. BENNIE T. DAVIS SR. RUNNING FOR MAYOR-2017

VOTE Bennie Davis VOTE
Want Better for the Citizens of the City of Marion!
"VOTE THE ENEMIES OUT"
Tuesday, April 11
2017
VOTE
Bennie Davis
Mayor Of Marion

A VISIT WITH THE FIRST AND ONLY FEMALE AFRICAN AMERICAN VICE PRESIDENT OF THE UNITED STATES!

18. SURVIVING THE THREE H'S BECAUSE OF THE FORTH ("H: HATERS, HINDERER, HELLRAISER... HELPER-JESUS!")

Shortly after Coach Smith left the gym, the young men came up to me and said, "Pastor D, we were glad that you were back helping with Marion High School basketball." The majority, if not all of the former basketball players of Marion High School, said to me, "Pastor D, you had impacted our lives, and we knew that you would be a great help to Coach Smith and Coach Towns. Pastor D, you loved working with young men, to help develop us in this real world." Then all of them shook my hand and said, "Thank you so much, Pastor D." Those words meant so much to me because they came out of the mouth and from the heart of each one of them. Tears filled my eyes to hear the words that were so powerful. This is why I had to fight, so I could continue to help other young men. This was and still is the most incredible night of adult basketball, and that was over three years ago.

The next day, there was a basketball practice. I was so excited that I had another opportunity to coach at Marion High School. I entered the gym, and everyone could see that I was so happy to be back on the basketball court doing what I loved. As I looked around, there were new faces that I had never seen before. They were standing around the basketball court with Coach Smith and Coach Towns. Coach Smith called me over to introduce me to the new faces. Then he said, "These are the new staff of assistant coaches from Florence, South Carolina." The one that was going to replace me was a white man. A few minutes after being introduced to everyone, Dr.

Michelle Wright walked into the gym. She called for Coach Smith to come to her, but no one could hear what she said to him. As he was coming back, he was running slowly. As he made it back to us, Coach Smith looked straight at me and said, "Pastor D," and in my mind, I was thinking 'not again, I just got back. What have I done to deserve what is about to happen to me?' He went on to say, "Pastor D., I was told that you must leave the gym now because you are not allowed to coach here at Marion High School." The first thing that crossed my mind was who set me up to embarrass and belittle me in front of the basketball players and the parents. No tears, not this time. I am going to fight this one. I am not going down. Then I started walking towards the gym door to go home and the Principal, Dr. Wright said, "Coach Bennie, stop, don't go out that door. It is not *you* that can't coach; I told those new coaches they must leave the gym. Coach Bennie Davis, you stay to do your job."

Beside the time she called me to welcome me into the family of coaches at Marion High School; this was the most significant thing she ever said to me. "Coach Bennie Davis, you are the only one qualified." My heart was filled with joy I had never felt in my life. I was accepted regardless of how other people felt about me.

Coach Smith said, "Pastor D, for the next forty-five minutes, run all the basketball players." I said, "Yes sir, I will do as you asked me to do and also, I would like to say thank you very much. For once in my life, I held my head up high and was not ashamed or embarrassed." Coach Smith then said, "Pastor D, for the next forty-five minutes, is conditioning for varsity and junior varsity, get them in basketball shape." I would get the job done before the first game. What a fantastic day this was for me. I wish every man, woman, boy, and girl could share an experience like this, accomplishing something society said would never happen, but God. I was given responsibility, and Marion High School's principal stood up for my rights and feelings. What a day because this day will stay in my heart forever. That never happened to me before, where someone with power would speak up for me. She could have said many bad things about me because so many times, I was put down and treated lower than trash like society has always done to me, but she showed me respect. It was the second volunteer basketball practice. Coach Smith informed both teams that I would be conditioning for both teams.

The next day sometime before 11 a.m., the word was on the streets that Coach Smith was resigning from coaching basketball at Marion High School. I couldn't believe this because new students transferred from other schools to play for Coach Smith and now, he was no longer coaching. At that time, Marion High School varsity boys' basketball was ranked the top three in the state. Coach Smith had to resign because of issues that happened in the army. So many people called and were upset about him leaving the team.

A news reporter came out and televised as Coach Smith entered the courtroom with his head down in shame. Whatever alleged crime coach was charged with; all types of different news reporters were standing in and outside the courtroom. The newspaper took pictures of him standing before the judge for his arraignment. Touch not my anointed, Coach Smith is a Christian, and I am a Christian. God will fight the battle for his children, and we need not say anything.

Basketball practice was still on as scheduled, and Coach Johnson was named the new interim head coach for Marion High School's varsity basketball system. Our young basketball players had difficulty adapting to a new coach's basketball system. Most of the players refused to adapt to the new coach and his system because they had the former coach's attitude. A few days later, the basketball season started for junior varsity basketball. When I walked into the gym, the big picture of the varsity basketball team hung over one of the exit doors in the gym. The picture had Coach Smith and Coach

Towns with all the other assistant coaches.

Someone in the school system walked up to me and said, "Pastor D, you should be so happy about this day." I asked him, "Why should I be happy about the picture being removed?' He said, "Dr. Wright had the picture removed because Coach Smith and Coach Towns did you so wrong. As long as you are at Marion High School and Dr. Wright is the principal, she will never let anything like this happen to you or anyone else at this school." That made me feel so good about the work that I was doing to make our children so much better.

I found out all that this man said about his friend was a bold-faced lie. He was looking for a fool, but he knew I was not anyone's fool. The picture was removed because of what Coach Smith was charged with; it happened within Marion High School. Whatever it was, it brought so much shame to Marion High School. I wondered whether Dr. Wright could have known what was going on before it came out but was covering herself, and if that was the real reason he resigned, before the press put it out.

The season has started great. Coach Towns said this is an up and down year. From the start of tryouts, a young man named Darren James came to all our practices. Darren James' son also made the basketball team. Not knowing his goal and desire was to be an assistant coach. All the basketball coaching jobs were filled. Dr. Wright never asked him to leave the gym like the other coaches that were brought in to become assistant coaches. Dr. Wright created a position for Darren James and named him a mentor for junior varsity basketball. He was never asked to do an application nor a background check from SLED. He became a mentor for Marion High School's junior varsity basketball team. He could sit on the bench during the basketball games, come to the locker room during halftime, and after the games. He addressed the basketball players just as Coach Towns and I did. So, in short, he was an undercover coach but was named a mentor by Dr. Wright.

Why did she do this special favor for only this one man but put everyone else out of the gym, and there are no more volunteers? I was not paying any of this attention because I only saw to help Coach Towns win ball games.

We were midway through the basketball season, having an up and down year. It wasn't our greatest, yet it wasn't our worst year. We had eight games left. Coach Towns' job was on the line to turn this season around. Coach Towns decided to better the basketball team. He said Pastor D, for the remainder of the basketball season, I am putting you in charge of the rotation of the basketball players. I would also like you to initiate the Pastor D full-court press, whatever it takes to win. To everyone's surprise, out of the eight games, we went seven to one; we finished the season winning it and looking to take the momentum into our next basketball season. What made me feel great was that Coach Towns and the team mentor Darren James said, "What a great defense the Pastor D full-court press was for the team." Darren James said, "Pastor D, this summer, when the youth basketball starts, I am an assistant coach for one of the teams. I will get with the head coach and ask him to train the Pastor D full-court press team because this defense wins games if played right." I told him to call me because I love working with our youth. I said, "Boss man, I look forward to hearing from you this summer."

I was told that I wouldn't work with the Marion High School track team this upcoming season. No one could explain why I couldn't work with the track team anymore. Then out of nowhere, someone came up with, "Pastor D don't get along with the students on the team." Now they knew that was a lie, but that was the best excuse they could offer. It wasn't money because I did it for free. I love track, and I received an athletic scholarship to run track; that was how I went to college. I couldn't be their friend; I was their coach, and my only job was to coach, teach, and show them how to become a winner and a champion.

Track is a sport. It's all on the person running the race. A person must have been a winner and a champion to teach someone else to become a winner and champion. I, qualify because I have accomplished both in my time on this earth.

After Coach Towns finished the track season, he and I had a lack of communication. He called and told me about the upcoming basketball season. Coach Johnson was hired as the new varsity head coach. He will make Pastor D the conditioning coach for varsity and junior varsity basketball teams. Coach Johnson said, "I was able to see the wonderful job Pastor D did for you this year." Out of nowhere, Coach Towns proceeded to tell me I am so proud of all the things you accomplished this year with basketball. "Pastor D, you have improved. Thank you for always stepping in when I was absent, making sure the basketball team never missed basketball practice because of my sickness or other situations. I can say I have learned to depend on you, taking over and looking out for the team's best interest." I said, "Thank you, Coach Towns." Now I wonder why Coach Smith would make this man look like this hateful hinderer and hell-raiser of a man. Then we hung up the phone.

I applied for different jobs in the Marion School District for different head coaching positions throughout the summer. As it got closer to school starting, I expected to get a call for an interview. If not an interview for all the jobs, at least some of the jobs. I did not receive one call from any of the jobs. There were over four job openings in our school district. One of the vacancies was varsity basketball at Marion High School. I knew that this job would belong to me if I could get an interview.

School started in Marion, but a coach wasn't named for varsity basketball. I still had hope that my phone call was coming for my interview for the job. Now that Coach Johnson had a winning basketball season, Marion High School basketball team was the conference champions. This will help Coach Johnson become the new head basketball coach. Johnakin Junior High School had a first-year coach. He had a winning basketball season, and they won the championship. The new coach named for Marion High School varsity basketball team was Coach Page. Coach Johnson didn't get the job even though he had an outstanding season. He brought discipline back to the players. Anyone could sit on the bench any given night. The so-called great players didn't play some games because of their attitudes and disrespect to the coaches. A person can lose a job or position if he lacked discipline or respect. Coach Page was the coach of J-3, Squirt, and Jamarous who were all in the eighth grade.

I begged Coach Towns to pull these young men up to junior varsity basketball. It is only two types of players, now or the future. The now you play, the future, you sit on the bench. All three of these players would have been the now, who would have started. J-3 will be the best all-around basketball player at Marion High School. I reminded Coach Towns the reason we must do this. The last time varsity or junior varsity didn't move, the young man was the number one pick in the NBA draft in 2019. His name was Zion Williamson. Coach Towns wouldn't do anything, so I put the word out, and my parents were mad. They knew if this happened, their child would not be starting, and some wouldn't play. The parents started calling the school district office. Then I got a call from someone out of the school district, and he told me to take down the flyer on Facebook about those three basketball players. If you don't know, "Pastor D, you will never coach for Marion High School or any school in Marion School District." Just because I had the vision to make them better basketball players here, it is now three years later that Coach Page and Coach Towns are bringing players up from junior high school to playing high school basketball.

The school has now started back. It was the third week of October, and I had not received one call about volunteer conditioning for basketball from Coach Towns or Coach Page. That Saturday, I picked food up from Canaan Land Revival Temple in Marion, SC. A young lady was helping to put food into my car, and after she had put the food into my car, she came to my window and said, "Coach Davis." Right away, I knew then she had to be a freshman at Marion High School. She proceeded to say, "Coach Davis, I am ready for you because I have been running, and I am in shape. I am excited about trying out for junior varsity or varsity basketball, but I will make one of the teams. I would be looking for you on Wednesday at tryouts." Before the conversation with this student, there had been no mention of basketball tryouts at Marion High School. I told the young lady I would be looking to see you next week. So, as I was leaving the food bank, I told myself I was going to wait until Monday, and if Coach Towns didn't call me by Monday afternoon, I would call him to see what was going on about tryouts. The only phone call I received was from Darren James. He asked me how to put in an application to become a volunteer coach at Marion High School. I told him how to put an application in at the Marion County School District. He said, "Pastor D, I will be doing my application so that it would be in on Monday." After I hung up the phone, I started thinking about who needed an assistant coach because it was said no more than one assistant coach for either basketball team at Marion High School. I was the junior varsity assistant coach, and Darren James was the mentor for the junior varsity basketball team. I told myself, "Let me call back and ask him if basketball tryouts start on Wednesday of next week." I called, and asked him about the tryouts, but he said he didn't know anything about tryouts being next week. I wondered why this man would be applying for a coaching job as a varsity basketball assistant coach. Coach Towns had his assistant coach, me. The weekend passed, and not one call or text from Coach Towns the whole weekend about basketball tryouts. So, I called Coach Towns on Monday afternoon before he got off work.

I asked him whether tryouts start on Wednesday at 6:00 PM. Someone told me on Saturday that they were going out for the girls' basketball team. Coach Towns said, "Pastor D, I don't know when tryouts are because the new coach Darren James has not told me anything about when tryouts start." So, I asked him how about the girls' basketball team. Coach Towns said that he didn't know anything about their tryouts. When I put the phone down, something didn't sound right; he didn't know anything about tryouts for the boys or the girls. I didn't understand why Coach Towns was the head coach for junior varsity basketball and didn't know when tryouts occurred. So, I told myself the best thing I could do was go and see the Athletic Director, Larry Addison on Tuesday. There will be no more calling from this day on; it will be face to face.

I could not sleep throughout the night. My eyes kept opening. The last time I woke up, I stayed up until the sunlight came through the window. I got up and began praying and telling God how I felt. I knew time wasn't going to wait, and I would be at Marion High School. I would be in the face of the Athletic Director Larry Addison because I must find out what is going on about me coaching basketball. I made sure that things were right for once in my life. I wanted to see what I did so that I could work with our young men at Marion High School. I was on my way to the school by 10:00am, but I called to ensure that the athletic director was on the school's premises. When I called, the secretary said, that he was at the school in his office. When I made it to Marion High School, the car wasn't in the parking lot, and I was getting out of the car. I had to calm down to get myself together because I knew I was getting upset. Instinct felt like I was getting played, but I didn't know who the players were in the game against me. I walked into the school determined to identify who the players were against me. I had to go into the main office as fast as possible. As I entered the office, a secretary said, "How may I help you, Pastor D?" I asked to see the athletic director, the secretary called his office. After she put down the phone, she said, "Go out that door and have a seat, and the athletic director will join you within 5 minutes, Pastor D."

Shortly after I sat down, the Athletic Director, Larry Addison, approached me. I stood up and stretched out my hand, and we shook hands, and at the same time, we both said, "Good Morning." The athletic director said, "You need to see me about something? The secretary said you were here to see me." I said, "Yes, I need to know what is going on about basketball this year. I would like to know when basketball tryouts start." He said, "Tomorrow, the girls start right after school and the boys are after the girls' tryouts about 5:00 PM. The junior varsity girls and varsity girls' basketball and the junior varsity boys will have tryouts together." I told the coach I had not been given information about tryouts. "Do you know why?" Coach Addison said, "You must not have done your CPR class because you have your two-year card. You must not have made your application, and it's not active by now. It would help if you got it active."

I told Coach Addison, "My application is active because the head athletic director over all the schools, Leon Stuckey, reactivated my application and told me how to reactivate my application." Then Coach Larry Addison said, "No, Pastor D., now they have paper applications." I said, "No. Coach Addison, how can they make paper applications when the Marion County School District is closed to the public because of COVID-19. Now please tell me how we can get a paper application when no one can go inside the school district office but the employees in the district building." He stated, "The coaches' meetings are held virtually on Zoom and via telephone. There aren't any more in-person meetings except for with the people that worked in the school district building." I never said anything to Coach Addison about Darren James calling me to ask about the process of submitting an application to become a community coach. I knew if this man doesn't have the CPR class, the application isn't in, the SLED background check would take a week to two weeks to come back. A person can't pay the money until then. Dr. Wright was the only one who could appoint a person to become a community coach. I could not walk on the Marion High School basketball court until everything came back, and she then called to welcome me to the family of basketball coaches at Marion High.

I thought to myself that Darren James could not actively be on Marion High School basketball floor coaching by tomorrow afternoon at 5:00 p.m. What got me was this white man lied to me just like the black man, Coach Towns. Both lied to me, one on the phone and the other one in my face. When Coach Addison looked at my face, he knew that he was lying, so he told me to call our new head coach of varsity basketball, Coach Sam Page. He put in some new rules and changed many things. He may not need any more coaches with him at Marion Intermediate School.

The first time at Marion High School, someone looked and reminded me of a hinderer. A person who did things to stop you by putting out all kinds of traps and ditches to make a person turn around. But I was not that man to give up because I was a fighter and a winner. I had to ask him who I must see about my coaching this year. He said, "Pastor D., get in touch with Coach Sam Page because tryouts started tomorrow. If he says that you can come, that would be fine." I told him that Coach Towns said that he didn't know when tryouts started, so he didn't have any say about his assistant coach. He responded by saying, "Yes, he did because he had to be able to work with that person, and Coach Towns will be at tryouts. Here are the announcements about junior varsity and varsity basketball tryouts." Coach Sam Page wouldn't have put this out if Coach Towns didn't know anything about when tryouts started. "Pastor D, I don't know why Coach Towns would tell you something like that when he knows and will be at tryouts." When our meeting ended, I thanked him for his time, and he gave me the information about basketball tryouts. I shook his hand and walked away. As I was walking away, I knew Coach Addison was passing the blame because he knew just what was going on, and he could have told me about my coaching career at Marion High School.

As I was getting in my car, I said I would be calling Coach Sam Page but let me find a place to park because I would know something today. I parked my car at Emerson Barber Shop, then I called Marion Intermediate School. The secretary answered the phone. I asked to speak to Coach Page, the new varsity basketball coach. The secretary said, "Just one minute, and I will connect you to him and you can leave a message." Coach Page answered the phone. I introduced myself as Dr. Bennie T Davis Sr, but most people call me Pastor D. "The reason I am calling is about basketball tryouts that started tomorrow." He said, "Yes, tomorrow tryouts started for all the basketball teams at Marion High School, male and female." I asked him, "Was Coach Towns informed about the starting date for tryouts?" He said, "Yes, he was." I said, "Dr. Bennie Davis Sr. is the head coach of the boys' junior varsity basketball at Marion High School, Coach Sam Page, somebody lied to you or Coach Towns because yesterday, Coach Towns said to me that he doesn't know when basketball tryouts start." Coach Page said, "Dr. Davis, I have no reason to lie about something I said to Coach Towns." I told Coach Page, "I have been Coach Towns' assistant coach for the last three years. Each year, something would happen with Coach Towns, he would miss basketball practices and games, but I made sure everything kept going just like he was there. This year, Coach Towns said something about going in a different direction with the basketball team." I said to myself, this is the same thing Coach Towns said to Coach Smith last year. I know Coach Smith and Coach Page weren't coaching friends, so how would both say the same thing if Coach Towns didn't say that to both of them. I told Coach Page, "The only direction I go in is to win basketball games."

Last year, we were having an up and down basketball season. Coach Towns put me over the lineup, the substitute, and the Pastor D full-court press defense. We were 7-1 in the last eight games. Coach Page knew that I wasn't getting off the phone because I would find out who was not for me coaching this upcoming basketball season. I told him that the athletic director Larry Addison said that you put in some new rules and changed a lot about anyone coming to coach at Marion High School, so tell me what I must do to be a coach for Marion High School. He said, "Dr. Davis." And I said, "Call me Pastor D." "I haven't made any new rules, and I didn't change anything. Pastor D, let me call you back. A young lady just walked into my room; I will call you back." Within five minutes, my phone began to ring. I answered the phone without looking at who it was calling.

To my surprise, it was Coach Towns on the other end of the call. I asked Coach Towns what was going on. "Did Coach Page say anything about tryouts? I don't understand. I said there are basketball tryouts tomorrow, and if so, I am good because I don't have COVID-19, and I will take the test. I have everything in to be a volunteer coach at Marion High School." Coach Towns said, "Pastor D, no one said to me when tryouts start, I would love for you to work with me this year. I will call and see what is going on about this basketball." Now, does Coach Towns think I am a fool? Coach Page just got off the phone with me, and he works at the same school as Coach Towns. He was the one that had Coach Towns call me to tell me what was going on with his coaching, but Coach Towns still said he doesn't have any idea about basketball tryouts.

Look at all 3 H's hater, hinder, and hell-raiser. All three of them knew what was going on but didn't want to tell me. I decided, I am going on Facebook live after discovering who is in charge of doing this to me. They were out to embarrass me, bring me down, and bring shame to my name. They treated me like I didn't even exist as a person or a man. They are throwing the rock and hiding their hand. Not long after Coach Towns phone call ended, a text came from his phone. Coach Towns would never talk to me on the phone because I asked too many questions, and I'd be looking for answers. I will put the original text in this book so you, the readers, can see Pastor D isn't lying. The text from Coach Towns said: "Coach, you will not be with me this year. If you have any questions, talk to Page or Dr. Wright. I apologize for this decision. They will try to give me James." I responded to Coach Towns, saying, "No one called me to say I was relieved of duties because I loved working with the young people. I never did anything to embarrass myself, the coaching staff, or the school. Thank you for the opportunity you gave me to be a basketball coach for Marion High School. That was something man said would never happen, but God." Coach Towns never texted me back or called me.

To lose this position was the only time I said it would have been better for someone to shoot me all over than to be fired because it hurt me so badly. I would never be able to work at Marion High School anymore because it looks like it is coming down from the top. Why did Coach Towns, Coach Page, and Dr. Wright do this to me? The only thing I am guilty of is giving each player my absolute best, and I wasn't going to accept anything less from each player. Anyone could see the improvement in each player from the start to the end of the basketball season. All I did was my job, and I loved doing it because I was able to see great improvement in each of the players. I had a conversation with three coaches, and they lied about what was going on with me and my future as a Coach at Marion High School.

When I got out of the car, I couldn't stop the tears from flowing down my face. When I walked into the house, my mother asked me, Pastor D, what happened to you crying like that? Who did something to you? She was in the living room, so I couldn't enter the house without her seeing me. I said, "Mama, Coach Towns texted me to let me know the principal fired me at Marion High School and they hired a new varsity basketball coach. All of them were lying because none of them was man or woman enough to call me or tell me in my face. Coach Towns was on the phone with me but said he didn't know what was going on, but about 12 something, here is a text that came to me saying Marion High School no longer needed my services. I will call Marion High School because everything must end today." I called Marion High School for Dr. Michelle Wright, but the secretary said she was out of her office and to leave my name and number, and she would have her call me. When I said my name, she said, "Pastor D., I will also send you to her voicemail so you can leave your message so she will call your phone." The secretary said, "Pastor D, and I will tell her that you need her to call, and she'll have a voicemail with your phone number."

Dr. Michelle Wright never called me back. I called Coach Page while waiting. I asked, "What happened to you calling me back yesterday." Now Coach Towns said that Dr. Wright doesn't want me to coach anymore. He said, "Pastor D, I don't know anything about your coaching, so how can I say anything about your coaching or your position? Pastor D, I didn't have anything to do with you not coaching." I told him, "Coach Towns said he doesn't know anything about tomorrow's basketball tryouts." He told me, "Coach Towns would be at tryouts, and his assistant coach would be with him." That cannot happen because after Dr. Michelle Wright gave me the go-ahead, it was about three weeks before I could come and coach a basketball practice. Now, Darren James would like to be an assistant coach, but as of a few days ago, his application wasn't in, and I told him how to submit his application. He must do a SLED background check, and he must have his CPR certificate for two years before walking onto the court. I asked Coach Page, "What am I doing so badly in our community that the Principal would say I bring shame to Marion High School? Blacks would say that we can't get in the school in high positions like principal, superintendent, and head coaches back in the day, and today blacks are in all of these positions. It's not the whites killing our blacks, but it's our kind. Dr. Michelle Wright is black, the head basketball coaches are black, our Superintendent is black, and two are black women. You may say you didn't fire me, but Coach Towns said he didn't fire me. Dr. Wright will not call me back. Each name and position I called was a black woman or black man. Have all the black people have decided that Pastor D would not be coaching at Marion High School this year and the white man put it on the black people. So, you and your friends need to be happy because today, each of you has destroyed black people at Marion High School. You all have done your job destroying this black man named Pastor D., Dr. Bennie T. Davis Sr, but I will fight, and when I come back, I hope to be coaching a high school team. I will come back and show you black people that I am the best coach, and whoever you get, they aren't a better coach than Pastor D." I asked whether I could come to the tryouts, and Coach Page said, "Not at this time because of COVID-19."

On that next day, basketball tryouts were at Marion High School, just as Coach Page said, Coach Towns was at tryouts with his new assistant coach Darren James. Now, this man is good, but I had to go by rules, so should he. The policy is what put the fire back in me to run for Mayor of the city of Marion. I grew up in the same neighborhood as most of the basketball players on the team from Marion High School. What's so good about that I was able to see them four to five days out the week. I would always remind them that they represented themselves and Marion High School during basketball season and when it was over. I don't want them to forget that they are young men in school and out here in society. Let them have people say positive things about each of them because when they saw me, no matter what they were doing, someone would say, 'Look, Pastor D just walked up.' Their representation was so good for Marion High School because they had a coach in the community right where they lived. But now it is all over. Why did Coach Towns pretend not to know about tryouts and about me being relieved of my duties? One day a young man wanted to know what happened to me, but he knew what happened. He said, "Pastor D, don't put your head down. Pick your head up and be happy because you did an outstanding job." He was a student whom I would see from time to time. I encouraged him because he wasn't going to play basketball, but one day, I saw him in the neighborhood, and I encouraged him why he should try out for basketball but most of all what he would bring to the team. The same young man reminds me of who I am and showed me so much, love. By him sharing his love with me during a low point in my life; he was able to lift my spirit and put a smile on my face when I was feeling like my world was crashing down around me.

I am a pastor of this church with only a few partners. We averaged about four to eight members on Sunday services, and eight would be many people, including me. One afternoon, I got a call from Larissa Barr, the daughter of a woman who was the backbone of the church from the start of this ministry for over twenty years. I was so happy to hear from her. I asked her how the great Larissa was doing on this fantastic day. "Pastor Davis, I am calling to let you and the church family know that Mama just passed." I was hoping that something was wrong with my phone. So, I said, "Who Larissa?" My heart felt like it had just stopped beating by this time. I said, "No, not Mrs. Billy Lou Clark." She said, "Yes, Pastor Davis Mama passed away today." The tears started flowing down my face, and immediately my breath got short, and it was hard to breathe. It was like a large hole that came out of nowhere was created in my heart. I just talked to her last night, and nothing was wrong with her. She said "Pastor Davis, I don't know. Let me call you back." I said, "Wait, Larissa, where are you? Are you still at the hospital in Marion?" She said, "Let me go. I will call you back, Pastor Davis." My mother said, "Pastor D, what happened? Why are you crying?"

I said, "Mama, Mama, Mrs. Billie Lou Clark has passed away. What am I to do because there is no more Mrs. Billie Lou Clark?" Mama started crying because they were more than a church family; they were friends from school and cousins.

After telling my mother and my family the news, I called the few partners, starting with our chairperson, Deacon Alethea Davis. Then I called the rest of the church family to inform them that our dear Mrs. Billie Lou Clark had passed away. All of them were in shock about the news. Mrs. Billie Lou Clark was always on the go. She had so much life and vision regarding her Pastor D. Her vision of life was to always make up our minds and get everything out of life as much as possible. She would always say rule your day by always being around positive people because if you are around negative people, that is the day someone else is ruling your day.

What am I to do with no backbone at the church? The person that gave everyone at the church encouragement to move forward and get whatever we wanted in life. Sometime later that afternoon, I received a phone call from Larissa. I answered by saying, "Hello, this is Pastor D. Is there anything that the church can do for you." She said, "Mama isn't dead! The emergency room doctor worked on her, and they brought her back to life, she is about to be flown to MUSC in Charleston." I asked her if she needed me to come or if there was anything the church family could do for her or the Clark family. She said, "No, Pastor, but I will call you myself and tell you how she does if anything comes up. "When I got off the phone, I called Mayor Pro-tem Emerson Hunt to tell him about Mrs. Billie Lou Clark. He was in disbelief about hearing about her passing. He said, "Pastor D, if the church needs anything, let me know, and I will see that our church family has whatever the Clark and Barr family needs." "Thank you so much for helping the church, but I will call you when I hear something." Larissa's call was coming in during that call, and I saw the name, and I knew the call was from someone in Mrs. Billy Lou Clark's family. I said, "Bossman, let me call you back because this is news about Mrs. Billie Lou Clark." So, I went to the other phone line and said, "Hello, is everything OK with Mrs. Billie Lou Clark." She said, "Pastor D, all is going fine for now, but this call is to let you know we made it to MUSC, and if anything changes for the better or worse, someone from the family will call you."

So, when I got off the phone, I told Mama and my family that was in the house that Mrs. Billy Lou Clark made it to MUSC, and she is still alive. Then I had to call the church family and a few friends who knew Mrs. Billie Lou Clark to share the great news. I made calls throughout the night about how good she was doing, but she wasn't out of danger. She was still alive.

After some time had passed, I received a call from Larissa, but I heard disappointment and stress in her voice this time. She said, "Pastor D., Mama didn't make it. She passed away about thirty minutes ago. After getting everything right about who was getting her body, my family and I will come home." Before I could get off the phone, the tears started coming down my face, and I couldn't hold back the tears because I found myself thanking God for putting a woman with so much respect for herself and others in my life. She brought so much love to the church family and taught each of us many things to make us better men and women of God. Mrs. Billie Lou Clark could have walked out so many times, and no one could have gotten mad, but she never walked out the door. She was a partner for over twenty years. She was a part of us, and we were a part of her. I just went into one of the rooms and lay on the bed crying, still saying, what will I do without Mrs. Billy Lou Clark?

That next night, I went to her oldest son's house for the setting up. I let him know if there was anything I could do as her Pastor or the church family could do; let me know because his mother was the rock at Greater Christ Temple Church of the Harvest.

The homegoing service for Mrs. Billie Lou Clark came so fast. No one asked the church or me to do anything from the Clark or Barr family. The night before the funeral, I called Mrs. Billie Lou Clark's oldest son, he let me know I was over the homegoing service. He had someone else do the Eulogy. "Pastor D, we have you doing the remarks about her church life." Yes, that cut me deep, but I said a few minutes I had. Mrs. Billie Lou Clark, Pastor didn't let himself down or the church family. I said to her son, "Yes, sir, I would love to say a few words about your mother." Here it is a family that looked over me because only a few people came to the church that I pastored. If I didn't do anything else at this homegoing, each person in the church would know that Mrs. Billie Lou Clark was loved and will always be loved. Time didn't wait. Before I knew it, everything was held the next day.

I was walking into the church crying. Because this would be the last time I would see the woman who brought so much to our church family. When it was my time to give the remarks, I said, 'Lord, I surrender it all to you, my mighty God. Have your way in my life right now. Give me the words to describe this woman who represented many great qualities.' When I got to the microphone, the words started coming out of my mouth. People started standing up all across the sanctuary. One of her daughters hated me, so she walked out of the sanctuary so that she wouldn't hear me. She never said why she felt the way she did about me. She didn't return to the sanctuary until I finished whatever I had to say about her mother. But what stayed in my heart was Mrs. Billie Lou Clark knew something about the five-point star.

About a year later, I was relieved of my duties as coaching basketball, something I loved, and not one person would tell me who fired me, but one thing I knew was all of them agreed that I had to go. Dr. Wright, I called her repeatedly, and to this day, she never called me back. I left messages with her secretary to have her call

TELL ALL I AM NOT THAT WAY ANYMORE

me, but she never returned not one of the messages I left on her answering machine or gave to her secretary. This year I went to a game, and she wouldn't look at me, not one hello, because she knew I would ask her why she fired me. Coach Page never said anything to me face-to-face. Coach Towns texted me to get to the recreational center gym so he could practice, but I'm not good enough to coach. I'm not good enough to sit at practice for an hour and a half to look at their practice.

He still doesn't answer my phone calls. He will text before talking to me. There were three blacks and one white now, and it wasn't the white man. They say we don't fear the black man, but the three blacks said the black man must go. They say, they tell me, and I heard, to beware of the white man, but our kind is doing all the killing today. Let's not forget Marion High School athletic director Larry Addison. He lied about it and put it all on Coach Page. I believe that he felt like I wouldn't go to Sam Page. I have worked many years to become a coach at any school, but Marion High School is my heart. I am not just going to walk away without finding out what happened for everyone to turn against me.

At this time in my life, I could see myself going higher, but here came my so-called friends who had a part in pulling the rug from under me. The hurt I felt was worse than when someone shot me because now, I could help the young men better themselves, and now, I cannot help any of our young men anymore. All of this comes from jealousy and hate. I need one high school to give me a head coaching job for boys' basketball. I would take either team, junior varsity or varsity, to let them see that I am the best coach. Anytime I notice a coaching vacancy at any of the local high schools, I would always ask Pastor Penny Smith to apply to each school seeking a coach for any of the following coaching jobs: basketball, football, and track. Up to this day, the only school that gave me an interview was Creek Bridge High School and Mullins High School, but

Marion High School never gave me a chance.

I believe if the person who gave the interview had opened his heart, the job would belong to me, Pastor D. I did find out that Dr. Michelle Wright, Athletic Director Larry Addison, and Coach Towns were involved in deciding to let me go. Coach Page may have learned after the plan was already in place that Dr. Michelle Wright had her plan in action about firing me from the start of last year.

Coach Towns needed an assistant coach, so now I understand why she let Darren James become a mentor for junior varsity basketball. The bad thing was I didn't believe it was for a basketball coach, not knowing about Dr. Michelle Wright's plan for him to move Pastor D. and replace him with Darren James. On the first day of tryouts, Coach Towns and his new Assistant Coach, Darren James, were at the tryouts. Now, how could Dr. Wright let him be in the gym working without all of his paperwork in order? I had all of my paperwork in, and I had to wait two weeks for my SLED background check to come back. That was good for me. Why wasn't it good for him? Now, he was a member of the biggest church family in Marion County. Yes, this pastor had a lot of support from everyone in the Marion County school system: the school board superintendent, principal, assistant principal, and coaches of Marion High School. I also believe Anthony Lester was never part of the streets like I was in the streets, and most of all, he never was in jail or court, so he had a better criminal record. I had one, but his criminal record was clean. I don't care who it was. I was the best coach out of anyone else from Merion High School or any other high school or college. I knew what it takes to be a champion. How do I know because I have been a champion all my life?

A champion heart will never stop going after greatness. After coach Anthony Lester got the job and not one phone call to say, 'Thanks, Pastor D, for telling me how to put my application in so that I could take your job.' That man said, you would never have, but God made way for Pastor D. This is the only time I cried, and other times I cried.

It is now two years later, and I am still crying because I don't have the opportunity to work with our young men. I don't know how or when, but God will one day open a new door bigger than the door that Dr. Doris Gore, Coach Felix, Coach Bostick, Athletic Director Brian Hennessy, and Anthony Lester, closed in my face because they had the power. I pray that they will become the woman or the man who will tell a person face to face that they are relieved of positions and why because lying isn't good enough. Because they did me the way they did, I will never know the truth. They lied to me, and Dr. Doris Gore never returned my phone calls. She heard my messages on her answering machine, and her secretary gave her the messages that Pastor D had called several times. It was the one thing that gave me hope. It made me believe. The enemies came to take it from me, and it felt like the one thing I had great in my life, out of nowhere, came crashing down on me. Things must get better for me because it just can't get worse.

About a week and a half later, I worked on this book one night. I had to get five thousand friends because the book launch would be on Facebook. The more people, the larger your audience, the more the word got out on social media about the book release. I was about a hundred and fifty to two hundred friends away from having five thousand friends on Facebook. I sent out friend requests to people that I might have known from the area who should have known me, and I should have known them. So, at night, I sent out over three hundred friend requests, and throughout the night, someone accepted me as their friend for a few hours. No one accepted me, but at about 5:34 a.m., I still worked on my book. Someone accepted my friend requests. So, I sent them a picture of a hand waving and said hello. I hoped to hear back from them to get their email address so I could send a chapter out of my book. About two hours later, a text came to my messenger on Facebook. The message said, "hey," so I sent a text back saying hello, I hope your day looked great, so have a greater day. At 9:18 a.m., a text came to me asking if I was still a pastor, but I couldn't text because I had to go out and do something. I walked into the clerk's door of the court office, and my sister called right after her call. My daughters Ashley and Antoinette called me. As I walked out of the door, looking at the warrants I put in the book, my sister called me back to back after making it to the car. I called her back. My sister said, "Pastor D, what's going on? People are on Facebook saying that you texted a 12-year-old girl, and word is out that Pastor D is stalking little girls, and he is a child molester and has been found guilty of rape. Pastor D, the people are also saying that you should be registered as a sex offender all over social media." My daughter Antoinette was so upset because I had the picture of her daughter on my Facebook page. They shared it on people's pages so they could see or meet a Pastor but a child molester. I told my sister, Alethea, "I didn't do anything to anyone, and I never texted a little girl. Someone lied about me." I went to my Facebook page to see what was going on, and it was about the person who became my friend at five-something that morning. I didn't say anything out of the way to no little girl. I thought this happened because it was time to run for Mayor of the city of Marion. To that day, I believe someone got this young lady to do this to stop Pastor D from running for Mayor of the city of Marion in 2021. Someone paid this lady or promised her something. So many different people gave their opinions about what was going on. Some were so-called friends of Pastor D. Some knew the mother or the little girl, and most of them knew Pastor D or followed me on Facebook. Many things that were said about me were so heartbreaking that they brought me to tears. People called, texted, and some came to the church saying many negative things about me. This so-called pastor was selling drugs and paying little girls to have sex for underage movies. When they busted him for custom handbags, Pastor D or this Caveman had movies of underage girls having sex with grown men. He needed to stay the rest of his perverted life in prison. As I read different messages on Facebook, tears rolled down my face.

I looked at people in the church with me, in the gym working out with me, and at my Bible College on Facebook. Some of the people called me and texted me. Now I read about how the people felt and thought about Pastor D. This was a low point for me, and just before I went into a depression blaming myself, a call came through to me from Facebook, and when I saw the name, it was my Aunt Mildred. I answered the phone, and before I could say hello, she said, "Bennie, what's going on about you and that little girl." I told my aunt Mildred that this was a lie because I never said anything out of the way to anyone, especially a 12-year-old little girl. I will do this. I am sending you the only text I sent. Read it because I just sent it to you. Then Aunt Mildred read the text, which read, "Hello. I hope your day looks great, so have a greater day." Then my aunt Mildred said, "Bennie, is this all you texted?" and I replied to my aunt Mildred, "That is all that I texted." My aunt Mildred then said, "Why are the people on social media saying all those awful things about you." My aunt Mildred said, "Let me go, Bennie, so I can make some calls and send your text out so people can see what you text the girl." I didn't think it was a little girl who lied to her mother because the person was her. These actions reminded me of what the former Mayor Bobby Davis did to me. My car was impounded because I was allegedly charged with counterfeit handbags.

About a month later, I decided to go to City Hall in Marion to speak with Mayor Bobby Davis. I went there without him expecting me to come to visit him about getting my car out of impound. The secretary permitted me to go to Mayor Bobby Davis's office. As I walked to his office, Mayor Bobby Davis walked down the hallway towards me. He was so surprised to see Pastor D in City Hall. He couldn't go into anyone's office because there was no one to go into, and he couldn't turn around to go back to his office. As soon as I put my eyes on him, I said, "Mayor Bobby Davis, I would like to speak with you about something." The first thing that came out of Mayor Bobby Davis's mouth was, "The city of Marion's attorney advised me not to have any conversations or dealings with you at all for any reason." Now it surprised me to hear that from our first black Mayor of the city of Marion. What got me was, out of all the citizens in the city of Marion, why would the city attorney pick me for our Mayor not to have any contact with? At that time, I knew Mayor Bobby Davis was the center of all my troubles with those counterfeit handbags. Until that point, I was assuming, but because of his response, I knew then that this was the man who set me up, hoping that I would go to prison for only one reason: I would not be able to run for the Mayor of the city of Marion. I proved Mayor Bobby Davis wrong, and now I would prove this mother and her daughter to be liars. Aunt Mildred said, "Bennie, be careful because you don't know what that mother or father might try and do to you because of what this woman put out on Facebook and social media. That mother is out to destroy your life and your reputation. Do not go any place by yourself, at any time, day or night. Always have someone with you so they can be a witness and give an account of the place you are at day or night." After my aunt and I had gotten off the phone, Gusand Weeks called and came through. Before I could say hello, she said, "Pastor D, what's going on about some 12-year-old girl?" I told her someone was out to stop me from running for Mayor. I had never said anything to any 12-year-old girl in all my life. Gusand, I had never heard so many horrible things about me, not from strangers but from people I knew." But the one that stood out was the one Miko Pickett had sent out to Lee Queens and Sherita Sanders. It hadn't been that long since she had been running for office and looking for blacks to come out and vote for her. She loved to say, 'black lives matter,' but after reading what she had said, the only thing I could come up with was some black lives matter, but not any that voted for the other person. Let's read Miko Pickett's text: "Lee Queens, I saw this, and it made me incredibly sad and upset. I had words I wanted to use, but decorum restrained me. Now, I would say BIG UPs to Miss Sharita Sanders. It took so much courage to do what you had done to protect your child." The people were texting so much about how they felt about Pastor D until it almost went viral. Someone texted, "That so-called Pastor D. I was waiting for something, anything, and now he would be stopped."

Today, I went to Senator Kent Williams, Sheriff Brian Wall, Interim Chief Marilyn Rogers, and Bobby Crawford. Ashley Brady had just hired Bobby Crawford as the city of Marion's new chief of police, but Bobby Crawford was waiting his two weeks from the Sheriff's Department. Whoever wrote this text had promised the little girl's mother that 'the cross-eyed, red ass, so-called no-good pastor would be in jail for the shit he did to your 12-year-old daughter.' I had had some days when things weren't working out for my good. Accusations against me made me feel this was the worst day of my life because I believed a day like this was behind me. It was like deja vu when detective Samantha Jackson had me arrested for sexual assault and never investigated. Everyone who sent out a text voiced their opinion by saying, "Pastor D is guilty and needs to be in jail." It was a saying that went like this: if you put a $1,000,000 check in a book and don't tell anyone, no one would ever get it because people just won't read. People texted from all over social media but never took the time to read the text. The content of the text only said, "Hello. I hope your day looks great, so have a greater day." The mother and the other person who promised that I would be in jail by the end of the day, went to law enforcement and our elected officials. Each one said to them, "We cannot bring him in for questioning just for that text. Not one thing in this text led us to believe he was out to have sex or do anything out of order towards your daughter." This mother obviously had hundreds of people texting when she never read the content. All people were made to look like fools because all they did was get paid. Here is Miko Pickett. How can she be anyone's leader or representative when she found a black man guilty before reading the text or seeing the evidence against the man.

It's not the white man doing all the killing, but our blacks did the killing to each other. I was more determined than ever before to run for Mayor of the city of Marion. For real changes and opportunities to come for all people, Dr. Bennie T Davis Sr. had to become Mayor of the city of Marion. I decided not to tell anyone because there wasn't anyone on the side of right for the people but Pastor D.

A person's ending to anything they did in life was much greater than their beginning. Because of that, I encouraged myself to run for Mayor. I believed that I was going to run for Mayor of the city of Marion. When I started telling a few people who were close to me, they looked at me like I was crazy, that is when I said they saw greatness in me. There was only one person who believed that I could run for Mayor for the city of Marion and win. That one person was Pastor D, himself. In anything a person initiated, they would be the only person that believed it could be accomplished. I waited until the last week, the day before the last day anyone could sign up to run for Mayor. I knew the word was traveling throughout the city and county of Marion that Pastor D was running for Mayor. I believed this because I received a call from Mayor Pro-tem Emerson Hunt.

The first thing he said before saying hello Pastor D., was, "Why didn't you tell me that you were running for Mayor of the city of Marion." I responded by saying I will keep running for Mayor until I become Mayor of the city of Marion. I knew at that point that I had to start doing my Facebook live campaigning. I must come out serious so the voters of the city Marion could see for the last four years they had been played by our Mayor. The citizens of the city of Marion deserved to have much more and better than what they were getting from our previous Mayor. I reminded them how our former Mayor, Bobby Davis, didn't accomplish the things that he said he would do in four years. He stopped the development of new apartments from being built in the city limits of Marion. You, the voters, put him in to do a job and former Mayor Bobby Davis failed at the job so we, the people, voted him out of office. Now, great people of the city of Marion, it's time to do the same thing to Mayor Ashley Brady because he also failed you, the people of the city of Marion. Four years ago, we had a rehearsal and what we did at that rehearsal, we must now do it all over by voting Ashley Brady out of office. Let's send him home so he can sell houses, buildings and etc. Mayor Ashley Brady must go because he's not doing anything for the 96% of the people in the city of Marion.

Sometime before the election, our chief of police resigned and walked out on the Mayor and the great citizens of the city of Marion, to pursue his dreams. Now, this was his second time leaving and it should be his last time ever working for the city of Marion Police Department. There had never been a black man or woman resigning then come back to this Police Department and get their job back, same position along with the same pay, but this man did that and some. If you can't do that for everyone, then don't do one color. Society was still putting a knee on our necks in the workplace. We needed to stand up but some of us still thought what's right was for us to bend over so people could sit on us.

Not long after our Chief Tony Flowers resigned, Mayor Ashley Brady hired a new chief. The new chief was only on the job for about 45 to 60 days and now the City of Marion was looking for a new chief. About 60 days under the leadership of Mayor Ashley Brady there had been two chiefs of police and two interim chiefs of police. Then, Mayor Ashley Brady appointed Lieutenant Marilyn Rogers over 20 years of loyalty to the Marion City Police Department. She would have been the first black woman chief of police. Everyone I saw said this was a power move. Mayor Ashley Brady got the attention of everyone in the City of Marion, that he was moving in the right direction but during my campaign, I revealed to the citizens that our Mayor Ashley Brady was more concerned about his reelection as Mayor of the city of Marion. He did not give the most qualified person the job. If he would have gone outside of Marion County that would have been great, but Mayor Ashley Brady stayed in the county of Marion to hire the police chief. Not everyone that had been working on one job over twenty years had the experience and respect from her peers. Lieutenant Marilyn Rogers worked under the people in the community and four different Mayors. Each of them along with the City of Marion had much respect for her. Our Mayor hired a young man based on the color of his skin and not the qualifications to be chief of the City of Marion. The young man served time in our military, a man of war. This man also worked with the Marion County Sheriff's Department for many years, but he never had any type of supervisory skills in law enforcement also he had no degree in criminal justice and most of all, he never worked for Marion City Police Department.

Coming from the Sheriff's Department to the Police Department was like a Holiness pastor going to the A.M.E to pastor. That was like going to a foreign country and speaking their language. That was impossible without training. This was what our Mayor Ashley Brady did to this young man, set him up to fail just so the blacks would vote him back as Mayor a second time. I revealed to the citizens of the City of Marion that Mayor Ashley Brady, if he was reelected that new chief of police would be fired or forced to resign before his second term was over. If I would have kept it to myself Mayor Ashley Brady would have fired him within ninety days after going back in office.

The City of Marion had the worst streets. When it rained a long time, a number of streets overflowed because the streets did not have any place for the water to go after the rain. Some people had to move their cars, so they wouldn't flood out after the rain. But with Bennie

T. Davis as Mayor $1,000,000 was put in the budget only to work on our streets in the City of Marion. I would put that back for four years and I would have $4,000,000 to invest in our streets and roads to improve all of them. Every street that needed a drainage would have it before any more work got done because all this patching the streets would be over. The City of Marion had had some killings and the killers were never found. I would put up state of the art cameras in the worst neighborhoods also in our housing complexes, where the worst killings were taking place.

Weeks before the election, I let the people know that our Mayor Ashley Brady broke the bank to get this young man to be his chief so he could win this election. We had a chief of polices with associates degree in criminal justice some even went to college for two or three years but this man with no experience and no degree received over $60,000 a year. I was looking forward to having a debate with Mayor Ashley Brady. Our local NAACP sponsored the debate about two weeks before the election. The City of Marion would always have a debate, but Mayor Ashley Brady didn't want any of Bennie T. Davis Sr. I believed that because he was Mayor, and it was a virus called COVID 19 he was able to call the one that the City of Marion always had, doing a Mayoral race.

Four years ago, when Bobby Davis was Mayor, Ashley Brady and myself was at the one the city of Marion, and Ashley Brady went off on Mayor Bobby Davis about some $1,000,000 but everyone knew I was going off on both of them. After the debate, Mayor Bobby Davis and Ashley Brady was interviewed by our local news reporter but not one of them told me about the interview because they knew I was going to go off on the job Mayor Bobby Davis didn't do and why Ashley Brady can't do the job and won't do the job. I will never forget the night of this debate that the NAACP had because when I walked in for the debate, I was stopped before I walked into the auditorium. Someone stopped me that was working on the debate panel. The lady said to me, "Pastor D, if you say anything to Mayor Ashley Brady about the job he did as Mayor, you will be escorted off the stage." What gets me is, when the black man was Mayor Bobby Davis, we were able to jump on him but when it comes to the white man, that was off limits. This wasn't a debate we had a boy scout meeting. How can it be a debate when we can't ask the current Mayor anything about the no-good job, he did by leaving 96% of us out. Ashley Brady shouldn't have a second term as Mayor of the great city of Marion. I was on Facebook live three to four times a day. Closer the election came the more and longer I stayed on Facebook live. I reminded the voters that I wasn't paying anyone to take people to the polls to vote. Because when a person pays you and when you go to them for help or a favor, they would then remind you that they paid you because of that I don't owe you anything. You have been paid by the other candidates, but I am not paying anyone now for the next four years I must work for all the citizens of the city of Marion. After each Facebook live was over, I would delete it from my Facebook page. I was forcing them to come see my campaign live, it went from forty to over two hundred people watching my Facebook live. A lot would look at the Facebook live and had the ability to not let anyone see them so they wouldn't be counted. People were so mad at me for telling the truth some of my so-called friends stopped speaking to me. One young man was going to help sponsor this book but because I told the truth about Mayor Ashley Brady, he changed his mind. From that time to this day, he had never said anything else to me.

On Monday before class, we always have had someone to start class with prayer. This Monday, I asked minister Birdie Rouse and she said, "Pastor D, I must pray for you because someone was going to kill you because I was looking at your Facebook live and you were calling people by name, white, black, rich and poor. Pastor D, if I lived in the City of Marion, I would vote for Bennie T. Davis Sr. for Mayor." When she started praying, she said, "God protect Pastor D from all danger and don't let anyone kill our instructor." That Sunday after service Michael Beaty said, "Pastor D, someone is going to kill you because of what you are saying on Facebook live. Yes, it's the truth and the people that are looking at the Facebook live also know what you are saying is not a lie. He then said to me, "Can I put insurance on you because I don't think you're going to make it to see the election." Just before the election, the Republican Party had a debate. Mayor Ashley Brady wouldn't say hello or anything else to me. The other candidate spoke to him, shook his hand, and took pictures with him. Everyone had people working for them on Election Day. It was about a week away from the election and some people were in Walmart talking about the Mayoral race that was going on in Marion. Both of them was my friend at the time but the young lady said, "Pastor D is the most ignorant pastor I ever seen in my life. I am not voting for a black person because whites do a much better job than any black person. I am going to do everything I can to make sure Pastor D don't win this Mayoral race." What got me was for years, she was my friend and attended the church I pastored.

The day of the election was now here, and the people of Marion voiced their opinions with their votes. Not one person went on Facebook live and said they were voting for Bennie T. Davis Sr. for Mayor. Not one pastor, Bishop, or minister voted for Bennie T. Davis. At the end of the election, Ashley Brady was reelected as Mayor for four more years. There were three people running for Mayor, and I came in third. I got fewer than fifty votes, but I gave it my all because I wanted to be the Mayor of the City of Marion. I am making this announcement now; I ran for Mayor, but now everyone knows Bennie T. Davis Sr., better known as Pastor D, will not be in the next Mayoral race. After the race was over, Mayor Ashley Brady said that former Mayor Bobby Davis had no business having a chief of police and an assistant chief of police for the City of Marion. But today, Mayor Ashley Brady rehired the former chief of police, Tony

Flowers, to the City of Marion Police Department. This is the chief who quit, resigned, and walked away. Now, our Mayor, in less than a month after he was hired, has made him the assistant chief of police. Our Mayor also has two captains. When Bobby Crawford was hired to be the new chief of police, he had to wait two weeks before starting his new job. Both Bobby Crawford and Tony Flowers were working at the Marion County Sheriff's Department. The black man, Bobby Crawford, had to wait two weeks before starting his job, yet the white man, Tony Flowers, started in three days. I have never seen or heard of a black man resigning and being able to go back to the same job, not once but two times, and holding onto their job. The City of Marion did it for Assistant Chief of Police Tony Flowers. Mayor Ashley Brady will make Assistant Chief Tony Flowers the chief of police of Marion City for the second time around. The citizens of the City of Marion can now see that everything I said about Mayor Ashley Brady was true, and he is now doing it, and they can see it with their own eyes.

The only reason Marion didn't have a new chief of police right after Mayor Ashley Brady won the election was that Pastor D uncovered that he just gave Bobby Crawford the job just to become Mayor. This is what I said during the election, and I still believe it to this day. Marion City Police Department has a young black lady who has been working in the police force for over twenty years, and she is the most qualified and loyal worker ever on the police force. The only problem I see is that she is black. She was the interim chief like Assistant Chief Tony Flowers was before they gave him the job. Now, the same Mayor is going to give him the job a second time. The citizens of the City of Marion should stand up straight and not bend this time. Let's get the knee off our neck this time in the City of Marion; justice must be served. The buddy-buddy thing should end now in 2022. After this Mayoral election, I have been blackballed. The Mayor Pro-tem Emerson Hunt and the City Administrator Alan Ammons appointed me to be over the adult basketball league. Because I was running for Mayor, they closed the gym for over five weeks because of one light. The 17-year-olds and younger were coming on Sundays, and they stopped that and closed it down. For over fifteen years, I was a volunteer basketball coach, and sometimes I would have two teams, but now they don't have enough coaches. Before they let me coach, they will cut the team and won't have anyone playing. The Mayor is over everything but the adult basketball. Bennie T. Davis Sr. can't and won't be able to be a part of it just because I was running for Mayor. I am going to start going after my goals, and becoming Mayor is my number one goal.

Saturday, October 17, 2021, was a day that man said would never happen, but God. In the summer of 2016, the Greater Christ Temple Bible Institution began. For about a year and a half, there was only one student, Evangelist Harriet Wilson, due to COVID-19. On that Saturday, October 17th, there was a graduation for the class of 2020 and 2021. I would like to share the class of 2020 and 2021 starting with the first honorary Doctor of Divinity in 2019 and 2020. Greater Christ Temple Bible Institution had the largest graduation class of 2020 and 2021. I would like to share all the names of the graduating class of 2020 and 2021. Doctor of Divinity-2019, Mildred Riggins, Jeanette Waiters, Timothy Gerald, and 2020 late Billie Lou Sanders Clark. Doctoral of Theology in Ministry 2021- Alethea Davis, Marilyn Elaine Rogers, Jacqueline V. Thomas, Harriet McBride Wilson, Vanessa Sansbury. Evangelist Harriet Wilson was the first student at Greater Christ Temple Bible Institute; she started with her associate's degree, and in 2021, she received her earned doctoral degree. What a wonderful accomplishment she has achieved through her hard work. Master of Christian Education 2020 and 2021-Marilyn Elaine Rogers, Alethea Davis, Jacqueline V. Thomas, Vanessa Sansbury, Harriet McBride Wilson, 2021 Birdie Mae Rouse, Denise Bethea Kennedy. Master of Theology in Ministry 2021-Michelle B. Barr, Lorenzo Washington. Bachelor of Theology in Ministry 2020 and 2021- Annette Dolford Addison, Howard Addison Jr. 2021, Michelle B. Barr 2020, Larry Mack 2021, Lorenzo Washington 2020, Annie Ruth Washington 2021, George Williams 2021. Associates of Theology in Ministry 2020 and 2021- Annette D. Addison 2020, Howard Addison Jr. 2020, Larry Mack 2020, Mattie Mack 2021, Jacqueline F. Page 2021, George Williams 2020, Betty Wells 2020. One year certificate 2020-Jacqueline F. Page, Mattie Mack.

I would love to thank all students for their determination to learn and gain more knowledge about the word of God because without knowledge, we all will perish. But with knowledge, we can live in the land that is flowing with milk and honey. What makes me so happy is seeing each one of these seeds growing and making deep roots. I was able to share my knowledge with the greatest seeds, and now they can go share their knowledge so they can live for days and years after their job is finished on this place called earth.

God is so good because when I was campaigning to become Mayor of the City of Marion, from the first day I started, I let the people know that our Mayor only made this man chief to have two terms as Mayor. I told the people that before our Mayor's term is up, he will have the chief out, either by being fired or forced to resign. He wasn't fired because Pastor D would have been on Facebook live and started my campaign that day. This is what got me; about ninety days before this man could retire making over $60,000 a year, out of nowhere Bobby Crawford, Marion Police Chief, resigned after one year. Guess who our Mayor, Ashley Brady, announced as the interim chief? The same man who resigned two times, and one of them, Tony Flowers, was the chief. This is a man who caused all the problems at our Police Department. There has never been a black man or woman to ever resign, not once, but two times and come back to the same job. This time, he will be making more money, over $60,000. This was nothing more than a set up. How much longer will the people of Marion put up with this? I hope at the next election, if they vote, we vote out the enemy and elect Dr. Bennie T. Davis Sr. as the Mayor of the wonderful City of Marion.

Both times, this Tony Flowers came back to the Marion City Police Department because our Mayor, Ashley Brady, was the only man who could do the job, but that is not true. We have a young black lady who's been with the police department for over twenty-one years. If anyone needs to be chief, it is her because she knows her job. She never resigned and worked under five different Mayors. This is why I believe this is a setup with Chief Bobby Crawford resigning. Now, most people believe that Chief Bobby Crawford did something during the time he was chief. Because most of the time, when anyone resigned, they did something or made problems to get fired from that job. To save their career so that they can continue to work. That person would resign so they wouldn't be fired.

Someone asked a question, and it was said to be a conflict of interest. I was asked by an elected officer, "So, what do you believe that former Chief Bobby Crawford did wrong in office for him to resign?" I said to the officer, "He did not do one thing because it was all done to him." The only reason he got the job was because of the election. Over 70% of the voters in the city are black. If the blacks don't vote for you, there is no other way to win. Now, the next election is a few years away, and the black man had to go. Now that the same man is coming back as the Chief of Police for the City of Marion. When Tony Flowers resigned the second time, he was the chief making $50,000, but now, it's between $61,000 to $65,000 because he has experience. Now when the Mayor goes to our Marion City Council and asks for more than $60,000, the council can't say no. Why is it that the black man with no experience as a chief or working at any Police Department for over five years made over $60,000, and now the white man can't? Someone on the City Council may ask if we are going to accept any applications for the next chief. This is Pastor D. letting the people know that the answer is no. Why? Because when the black man got the job, there were no applications, and there will not be any now for the white man. People of Marion, our City Council has been 'had'.

To each of you who made this happen, thank you from the heart of Pastor D because now the people know that I am not a liar. Pastor D is looking forward to the next Mayoral election because this time, I will not be defeated.

Greater Christ Temple Bible Institute is only a few months away from our next graduation. I would like to congratulate the following students for their commitment and hard work. Graduation will be held on Saturday, October 8, 2022. I would love to announce the following Doctoral graduate class of 2022- Annette Addison, Birdie Rouse, Michelle Barr, Larry Mack, Denise Kennedy, and Harriet Wilson (3rd doctoral), Lorenzo Washington, and Brenda Turner. Master graduate- Karleyne Joiner, Samuel Barr, Larry Mack, Annette Addison, George Williams, Mattie Mack, and Brenda Turner. Bachelor of Science- Herbert Lee Rouse, Jacqueline Page, Sarah Fulton, Clarence Singleton, and Samuel Barr. Associates degree- Clarence Singleton, Herbert Lee Rouse, and Linda Finklea.

In September 2021, the late Deacon Debra Fling's daughter, Jessica Fling, passed away. She was a part of Greater Christ Temple Church of the Harvest. I was so saddened to hear that she had passed away. She was in charge of the children's choir and the summer feeding program at Greater Christ Temple Church of the Harvest for some time. I think about her often, and it brings tears to my eyes. She will be greatly missed.

The adult basketball team has been a significant part of my life because this is the way that I am able to help so many young men. Because of this weekend basketball, every young man will always have an alibi, so if any crimes are committed, Pastor D will be able to prove the location of that person because when entering the gym, each person must sign in, and we go on Facebook live. Facebook live can't lie for anyone. It is a safe place because no guns or drugs are allowed in the gym. Our motto is to come in peace or leave with the police. I thank God for each of the young men who come out on Wednesday, Saturday, and Sunday. I have built a relationship with each of them. Some I knew from coaching them on the great New Breed basketball team, and some came to the gym that played against the New Breed basketball team. I still remember how New Breed beat them. I am looking forward to starting an adult traveling basketball league in the City of Marion.

What has me excited about the future of Greater Christ Temple Bible Institute is at the end of October, after graduation, Dr. Jacqueline V. Thomas, who started a Bible College in January 2022, named it Victorious Living Bible Institute. Dr. Jacqueline V. Thomas is a graduate of Greater Christ Temple Bible Institute, and I believe many more students will start their own college because of the knowledge I was able to instill in the students. God started with one man, and now there are over six billion people in the world today.

Throughout my life, I was mistreated because the facts were always against me and not for me. I was treated by the facts and not the person God made me. People believe facts over the power of God. Facts say what a person can and cannot do, but God specializes in doing the impossible. All my life, facts said what Bennie can't do, but God worked the impossible. So today, I would love to thank everyone for how each of you mistreated me because without each of you doing what you did, I wouldn't be the best-seller ever for a person who was diagnosed with epilepsy, autism, a drug dealer, a victim of gun violence, and falsely arrested. Don't ever give up; don't let anyone tell you what you can't do in life. The sky isn't your limit; not when there's a moon, stars, and planets above the sky. There is something greater for each of us, but a person must believe in themselves.

Make your life whatever you want it to be; don't let society dictate to you what you can and can't do. From this day forward, don't let facts stop any of you because if facts had the last word, I would have been dead at one week old. I would have never graduated from high school or college. I would have been in prison for life. I would have never run for Mayor of the city of Marion. I would have never started a Bible college. I overcame the facts because God is on my side, and that same God is on your side. Each of you can and will achieve anything in life you desire.

Anytime a person has a vision, they may be the only person to believe it can happen; keep the faith. I had a vision to write a book; no one believed it could happen but me. People said, "Bennie can't read, therefore he can't write," but God put an idea in someone to make a cell phone with voice recording, so anything a person says the recording will type it out. Because of this idea, along with God putting the right people in my life to help me. Like it is said, two people can do more than one. I thank God for putting Dr. Jacqueline V. Thomas, Pastor Penny L. Smith, Patricia Gaskins, Pastor Dr. Vanessa Sansbury, and all the students at Greater Christ Temple Bible Institute and all the partners, sponsors of Greater Christ Temple Church of the Harvest in my life. I would also like to give special thanks to Fanny Mason for all the ways she helped the families and the children in the community, including hosting programs and vocational bible school.

Because of an idea, I was inspired and have now completed my first book, "Tell All I'm Not That Way Anymore" by Dr. Bennie T. Davis Sr. To everyone who reads this book, you are someone great, and don't let anyone take that from you. Stay motivated and encouraged; never stop; get whatever you want out of this thing called life. Chase your dreams and get whatever you want out of life; it's waiting for you.

Bennie T. Davis Sr.
Facebook
You're friends on Facebook
Lives in Marion, South Carolina

5:34 AM

👋

7:06 AM

Mm hey

HELLO I HOPE YOU DAY LOOK'S LIKE YOU LOOK GREAT SO HAVE A GREATER DAY!!!!!!

The reason for the following string of Facebook messages is simply because this young lady accepted my friend request at 5:34 a.m., and I responded at 7:06 a.m. I believe someone paid this mother to pretend that she was an eleven-year-old because it was a few months before the election, and they knew I was running for Mayor.

Sherita Inman
Dec 3, 2020

Pastor better stay out of my child messenger before I make his day a living hell!!!

DR. BENNIE T. DAVIS

👍😮😢 **Patricia Green and ot...** > 👍

Jay San Tan
One thing about God he will bring it Bak like what's that to tell that lil girl 🤔 meaning you been watching her

1y   Like   Reply   3 👍

Sherita Inman
That's why he so close to kids and they parents needs to be aware of him

1y   Like   Reply   3 👍👍

Jay San Tan
Sherita Sanders indeed

1y   Like   Reply   2 👍👍

Barbara Powell
Nasty ass

1y   Like   Reply   5 👍👍😮

Vanessa Reaves-Carmichael
And I know him. Oh WOW! Y'all better be aware of these fake wanted be pastors. Just sad af

1y   Like   Reply   2 👍

   Sherita Inman Vanessa Reav...

Vanessa Reaves-Carmichael
Don't he do things with other kids like play basketball or taking them places! It's no telling what he's doing with those kids

1y   Like   Reply

Write a comment...

456

👍👤 **Patricia Green and ot...** > 👍

Israel Crystal
Y'all he been that way for a long time and I was a kid. All it took for him to look at me wrong when he had that building down that road in front of bluff road.

1y   Like   Reply   1 ❤️

Monique Knowlin
Israel Crystal but "he ain't ntg like that" u think you know a person cuz they're your family but u really don't I'm not sayin ntg none of my family won't do or not like cuz u never know a person

1y   Like   Reply   1 ❤️

Israel Crystal
Erica M Knowlin exactly you don't defend nobody who's after a child shit then I start thinking shit is that person like that too. Hell his own daughter didn't defend him all she wanted was the post took down with the baby pic up there. So if the daughter didnt defend him why are you. That's because she know her daddy.

Write a comment...

DR. BENNIE T. DAVIS

😀😀 **Patricia Green and ot...** > 👍

Miakesha Ishamina Brigmon
Sherita Sanders u should report his ass. Pedophile ass

1y   Like   Reply   1 ❤️

Sherita Inman
Oh I'm doing that now. He pick the wrong child this time

1y   Like   Reply   4 ❤️❤️

Miakesha Ishamina Brigmon
Sherita Sanders 👊👊👊

1y   Like   Reply   1 ❤️

Martina McZeke
Gabrielle Williams Grice look

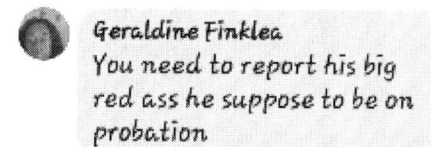

1y   Like   Reply

Geraldine Finklea
You need to report his big red ass he suppose to be on probation

1y   Like   Reply   11 ❤️❤️😮

  Brent Green Geraldine Finkle...
  Cynthia Boykin Geraldine Fin...

Cnote Paige
Make his life hell fukk that greezy motha fukka

1y   Like   Reply   8 ❤️❤️

  Sherita Inman Cnote Paige A...

Rogerstina Phillips
SMDH

Write a comment...

TELL ALL I AM NOT THAT WAY ANYMORE

Patricia Green and ot...

1y Like Reply

Jesse Dixon
Israel Crystal this my damn niece 😩😩😩😩 Ill fuck around and kick that peg leg from under his ass bout my damn neice fat bitch

1y Like Reply

Israel Crystal
Jesse Dixon girl apparently he got all of us wanting his ass. That just sickens me to my soul man for a man of God to be in a child's inbox. Adults ok but a innocent child can't defend themselves man. How would they expect for a mother to react to that. Ion blame no one from exposing someone like that. This just sad.

1y Like Reply

Israel Crystal
Then it done been so many others over the years.

1y Like Reply

Jesse Dixon
Israel Crystal 😩😩😩😩😩 tagged marion PD

1y Like Reply

Write a comment...

459

> **Monique Knowlin**
> Do WTF you got to do and say WTF you wanna say cousin Sherita Sanders

> **Pecoya Jones**
> Erica M Knowlin exactly !!

> **Monique Knowlin**
> Pecoya Jones ppl get on my nerves she got a strong family behind her and we definitely don't play about shit like this IDGAF WHO IT IS RIGHT IS RIGHT AND WRONG IS WRONG

> **Pecoya Jones**
> Erica M Knowlin cause why are you messaging a child at that time smh I wouldn't even defend something like that 😐

> **Monique Knowlin**
> Pecoya Jones definitely wouldn't then it's plenty of other ppl saying the same shit about him

> **Carolina Swampboy**
> Somebody need to knock tht eye and leg bacc straight. Shit sad is fucc, but he's not the only people like tht round the way its alot more.
>
> 1y Like Reply   10

> **Nita Reed**
> Carolina Swampboy you right he's not the only one that damn Jerome d richardson inboxed me (OUT THE BLUE) 4:51 AM about some dude wanna stripping for me. I told him not to contact me about shit. I inboxes dude and sent him the message that dude sent me ans he didnt know dude inboxed me
>
> 1y Like Reply   2

> **Tiera Finklea**
> Oh so I'm not the only one having problems wit him he blocked tho
>
> 1y Like Reply   8

> **Miakesha Ishamina Brigmon**
> Idk what kinda mother would trust him around their kids. He's fuckn disgusting and I've always thought that
>
> 1y Like Reply   9

Write a comment...

DR. BENNIE T. DAVIS

👍😊 Patricia Green and ot... > 👍

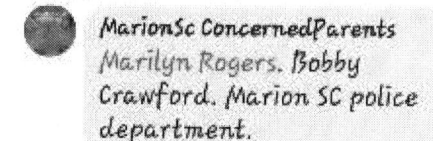

MarionSc ConcernedParents
Marilyn Rogers. Bobby Crawford. Marion SC police department.
1y   Like   Reply

MarionSc ConcernedParents
Jonathan Herring
1y   Like   Reply   1

Rinea Girlie
SICKKKKKK
1y   Like   Reply   3

Chris Rollins
Rinea Girlie that nigga gonna bust hell wide open his bitch ass
1y   Like   Reply

MarionSc ConcernedParents
Lucas Atkinson, Kent Williams
1y   Like   Reply   2

MarionSc ConcernedParents
Tammy Stella Hyatt
1y   Like   Reply   2

MikeMike LW

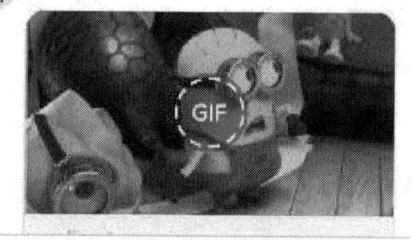

[GIF]

Write a comment...

462

> **Patricia Green and ot...**
>
> **Miko Pickett**
> Lee Oweens I saw this. Makes me incredibly sad and upset. I have words I want to use but decorum has me restrain myself. Now, I will say BIG UPS Ms. Sherita Sanders, it takes so much courage to do what you have done to protect your child. Prime example of using your Vs!
>
> 1y   Like   Reply   5
>
> **Elijah Shaw**
> Lol girl this funny as hell the pastor is pervert 😂 we been knew this
>
> 1y   Like   Reply   3
>
> **Sherita Inman**
> Elijah Shaw Right
>
> 1y   Like   Reply
>
> **Tracy McCray**
> God is pulling the cover off these nasty ass men.
>
> 1y   Like   Reply   6
>
> View 1 previous reply...
>
>   Tracy McCray Marzey Davis fir...
>   Tracy McCray Marzey Davis i k...
>   Tracy McCray Marzey Davis u...
>   Marion Sr ConcernedParents
>
> Write a comment...

👥 **Patricia Green and ot...** > 👍

place cuz I told him I'll run up in his mama house don't play with me about my child I don't blame you cuz he's behind need to be in jail for sure. 😡😡😡

1y   Like   Reply

Sherita Inman
Some men are so sad...They rather find pleasure in youngsters than with a woman.

1y   Like   Reply

Melissa Davis
You so right about that cuz, but I don't blame you protect yours to the to the fullest, even though mine's grown I still protect mines to the fullest but that's what real mother supposed to do. He need some mental help or some counseling if nobody don't F him up about their children first

1y   Like   Reply

Chris Rollins
Sherita Sanders cuz what u gonna do bout this shit

1y   Like   Reply

Chris Rollins

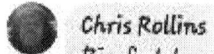

Write a comment...

Patricia Green and ot...

1y   Like   Reply

Chris Rollins
Sherita Sanders cuz what u gonna do bout this shit

1y   Like   Reply

Chris Rollins
Big fat hypocrite ass pussy!!

1y   Like   Reply

Tamara Wilson
Laquita Baldwin

1y   Like   Reply

Renzo Rollins
Sad to say nobody can be trusted

1y   Like   Reply

Devisha Calhoun
He need be lock up 😠😠

1y   Like   Reply

Write a comment...

DR. BENNIE T. DAVIS

> 🔴 Patricia Green and ot... > 👍
>
> **Cynthia Boykin**
> This should be taken to the police/mayor/judges....its bad enough that children have to watch out for strangers....but for them to have to be afraid of people who they believe that they can trust....this is horrible
> 1y Like Reply   5 👍
>
> **Diamond Hope**
> So sad
> 1y Like Reply   1 ❤
>
> **Israel Crystal**
> Sherita Sanders check your inbox
> 1y Like Reply   1 ❤
>
> **Jesse Dixon**
> Somebody tagged tonya brown
> 1y Like Reply   2 😮
>
> View 4 previous replies...
>
> 🔴 Jesse Dixon Israel Crystal 😩 ...
> 🔴 Israel Crystal Jesse Dixon ion...
> 🔴 Jesse Dixon WPDE ABC15
>
> **Cindy Washington**
> 😮😮😮😮😮😮😮😮😮😮😮😮😮😮😮
> 😮😮
> 1y Like Reply   1 ❤
>
> **MarionSc ConcernedParents**
> Marilyn Rogers. Bobby

Write a comment...

Brent Green
Sure his page didnt get hacked or can he not type complete sentences. Lol

Israel Crystal
Brent Green he didn't get hacked. This ain't his first rodeo

Sherita Inman
No it's not his 1st time doing this

Brent Green
Sherita Sanders oh boy

Carnesa Sunshine McFadden
Oh no buddy tripping

Nita Reed
You doing what's right for your child and I would do the same and more. I see he loves to copy and paste and send messages early morning. The damn 🌙 is not up that time of the damn morning

Sherita Inman Nita Reed Rig...

👍👀😮 Patricia Green and ot... > 👍

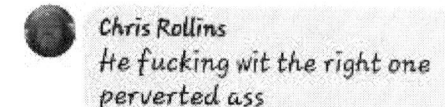

Chris Rollins
He fucking wit the right one perverted ass

1y   Like   Reply   2 👍❤️

Melissa Davis
You need to have his behind locked up, my God that's a child what is wrong with him, that down right down sick 💢 😡

1y   Like   Reply   2 👍❤️

Sherita Inman
Melissa Davis I did the report yday. They have many complaints about him. He's not even allowed at the Huddle House for sexual harassing the women there.

1y   Like   Reply   2 😮

Melissa Davis
I know a long time ago he was perverted but he messed with the wrong one, mess with my little cousin, cuz you got a lot of them out here like that cuz, even though I know Veve she 22 and she had this 50 year old man in her inbox when he used to try to talk to me I had to put him in his

Write a comment...

> **Teofilo Clark**
> I remember he use to come to the county an he would never give God credit for nothing!!! I knew he was faking
>
> 1y Like Reply   7 😀😀

> **Idella Tameka Dingle**
> Jay San Tan I'm pissyyy
>
> 1y Like Reply   1 😀

> **Tracy Green**
> Watch he try and lie and say his page was hacked? Smdh!!! Can't even trust the pastors!!!! 🙈🙈
>
> 1y Like Reply   3 😀😀

>> **Brent Green**
>> Tracy Green girl I hope it was because his typing was worst. Lol
>>
>> 1y Like Reply

>> **Tracy Green**
>> Brent Green I swear it was!!! I thought a kindergarten typed it. 😂😂😂
>>
>> 1y Like Reply   1 😀

>> **Boogal Godfrey**
>> That's his favorite line my page was hacked nope telling lies yes papa 😂😂😂😂😂

Write a comment...

Patricia Green and ot... >

Shenita Nicole Robinson
He ole nasty stank ass leg fucka

Sherita Inman
Shenita Nicole Robinson Girl my blood is boiling

Shenita Nicole Robinson
I know it is I'm grown and he sure tries me

Vanessa Reaves-Carmichael
Shenita Nicole Robinson OMG! Mr. Bennie the pastor with that mess up leg! WOW! That's fuck up

Shenita Nicole Robinson
Vanessa Reaves-Carmichael all the way fucked up

Vanessa Reaves-Carmichael
Shenita Nicole Robinson right

Casandra Jones

TELL ALL I AM NOT THAT WAY ANYMORE

> 👍❤️😂 **Patricia Green and ot...** > 👍
>
> Most relevant ⌄
>
> **Lena Mcclellan**
> You better tell it cuz!!! Oh dirty bastard,!!!
>
> 1y Like Reply   3 ❤️
>
> **Sherita Inman**
> Right!! Nothing but a pedophile!!
>
> 1y Like Reply   2 😮❤️
>
> **Lena Mcclellan**
> Sherita Sanders!!! That's all the hell he is!!! You should turn his ass in!!! 🎯🎯🎯...
>
> 1y Like Reply
>
> **Shante McClellan**
> Look at the time 🤐..ummmm
>
> 1y Like Reply   1 ❤️
>
> **Sherita Inman** Shante McClel...
>
> **Shenita Nicole Robinson**
> He ole nasty stank ass leg fucka
>
> 1y Like Reply   5 💬😮❤️
>
> View 2 previous replies...
>
>   **Vanessa Reaves-Carmichael**
>
>   **Shenita Nicole Robinson** Vane...
>
>   **Vanessa Reaves-Carmichael**
>
> **Casandra Jones**
>
> Write a comment...

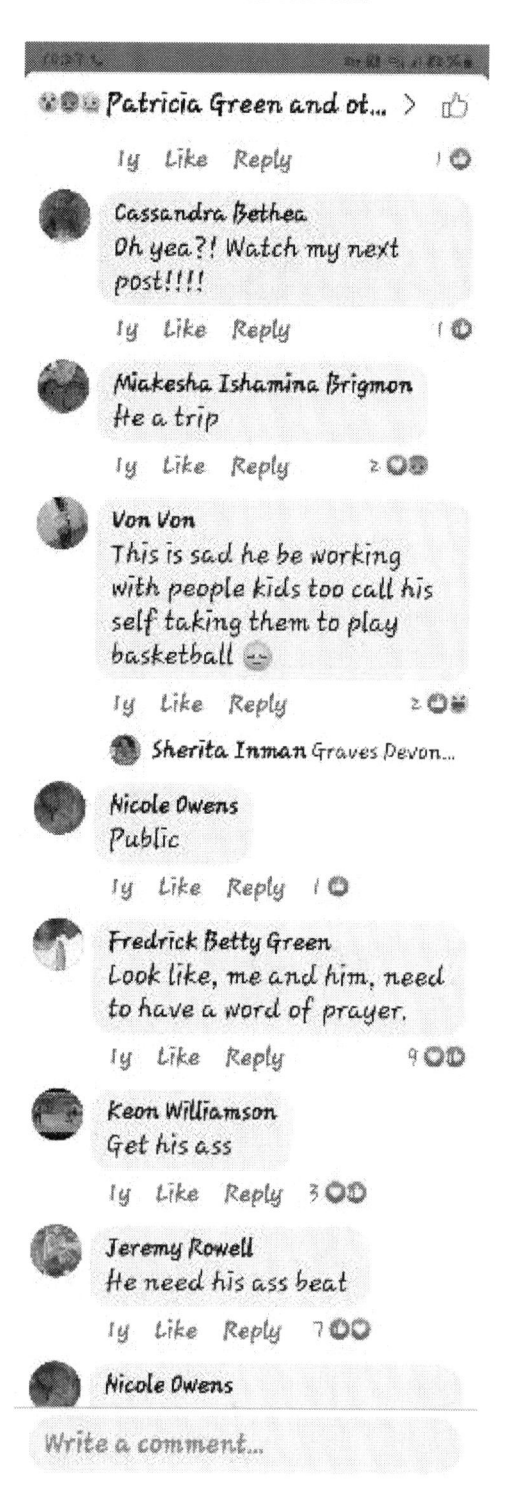

Patricia Green and ot...

1y Like Reply

Cassandra Bethea
Oh yea?! Watch my next post!!!!

1y Like Reply

Miakesha Ishamina Brigmon
He a trip

1y Like Reply

Von Von
This is sad he be working with people kids too call his self taking them to play basketball 😒

1y Like Reply

Sherita Inman Graves Devon...

Nicole Owens
Public

1y Like Reply

Fredrick Betty Green
Look like, me and him, need to have a word of prayer.

1y Like Reply

Keon Williamson
Get his ass

1y Like Reply

Jeremy Rowell
He need his ass beat

1y Like Reply

Nicole Owens

Write a comment...

👍💬😀 Patricia Green and ot... > 👍

Kimberly Paige
Israel Crystal that's sad
1y   Like   Reply

Sherita Inman
Jay San Tan 💯💯💯
Right
1y   Like   Reply   2 😊😊

Israel Crystal
Kimberly Paige very and he got away for a long time
1y   Like   Reply   1 ❤

Jay San Tan
My son played for him an I'm not a profit but you can feel when somebodies intentions ain't rite
1y   Like   Reply   2 ❤

Kimberly Paige
Israel Crystal omg 😱
1y   Like   Reply

Israel Crystal
Jay San Tan exactly bruh
1y   Like   Reply

Israel Crystal
Kimberly Paige yes he did
1y   Like   Reply

Jay San Tan

Write a comment...

DR. BENNIE T. DAVIS

Marion police chief resigns after 1 year

Kevin Accettulla   4 mins ago

Thanks to Angelo's Steak & Pasta restaurant for all that they have done in supporting this book.

Congratulations Dr. Bennie T. Davis Sr. On Your First Book

"Tell All I'm Not That Way Anymore"

Greater Christ Temple Church of the Harvest
Sunday, Worship Service 11:15 a.m.
1828 Senator Gasque Road, Marion, SC
Pastor Dr. Bennie T. Davis Sr. (843)260-7196

New Mission Community Church
Sunday, Worship Service 1:00 p.m.
Pastor Dr. Vanessa Sansbury (425) 436-6338 PIN 429864

Mt. Calvary Missionary Baptist Church
Sunday School 9:45 -10:45 a.m. Morning Worship 11 a.m.
Bible Study Wednesday 12 p.m.
714 Camden Hwy, Bishopville, SC
Pastor George Williams (803) 459-3163

St. Beulah Missionary Baptist Church
Sunday School 9:30 a.m. Morning Worship 10:30 a.m.
Bible Study Wednesday 6 p.m.
822 Beauty Spot Rd, PO Box 676, Bennettsville, SC
Pastor Victor & Dr. Denise Kennedy
"For Nothing Will Be Impossible with God" Luke 1:37
Faith Does Not Make Things Easy, It Makes Things Possible.

Deacon Dr. Timothy & Carrie Gerald & Family of Aynor SC
Love You and Great Work Pastor D.

Dr. Jeanette Waiters & Family of Darlington, SC
Success Belongs to Pastor D.

DR. BENNIE T. DAVIS

Dr. Mildred Riggins & Family of Jamaica, New York
Love You Nephew Dr. Bennie T. Davis Sr.

Glenn Brown & Family of Atlanta, GA
Voorhees University Alumni
I Love You Pastor D.

Congratulations on the success of "Tell All I'm Not That Way Anymore"
Our Love & Prayers Mr. Herbert L & Evangelist Dr. Birdie Rouse & Family of Lynchburg, SC

We Bid You God Speed, Success & In All Your Future Goals
Dr. Larry & Mattie Mack & Family of Bishopville, SC

Minister Betty Wells & Family of Bishopville
The Greatest Instructor & Book Writer Going Today

Greater Christ Temple Bible Institute
Classes on Monday 1-5 p.m. & Independent Classes
1828 Senator Gasque Road Marion, SC
Founder & President Dr. Bennie T. Davis Sr (843) 260-7196
Dean of Academic and Student Affairs: Dr. Birdie Rouse

Marion Christian Fellowship
Sunday School 10 a.m. Sunday Worship 11 a.m.
Wednesday Bible Study 7 p.m. Thursday Prayer Service 7 p.m.
1452 Old Corner Road Marion, SC
Pastor Craig Dewayne Hopkins Sr. Cell (843) 618-2198, Church (843) 433-8139

Fred's Barber Shop
Tuesday-Saturday 8 a.m.-6 p.m. Appointments
Marion Street, Marion, SC (843) 275-1440
Owner: Mr. Fred Gause

Tim's Mega Baber Shop
Monday-Saturday 8 a.m. -6 p.m. Appointments
Main Street, Mullins, SC (843) 433-1203
Owner: Timothy Johnson

Williams Landscaping & Power Wash
Marion, SC (843) 616-5022
Owner: Desmore Williams

Hughes Lawn Service
Call Day or Night (843) 616-1657
Owner: Billy Hughes

Angelo Antonucci
Angelo's Steak & Pasta
2311 S. Kings Hwy Myrtle Beach, SC (843) 626-2800
www.angelosteakandpasta.com, angelos@sc.rr.com

Thurmond Brooker
Brooker Law Firm
238 Warley Street Florence, SC (843) 679-0056
brookerlawfirm@aol.com

Turner BP
Highway 76, Marion SC
Breakfast, Lunch & Dinner Daily
Call Today (843) 423-7043

Precise Care Transport Inc.
Patent Care First
Main St. Marion, SC 843-765-3480 or 843-617-4136

Emerson's Barber Shop
Tues.-Sat. 7a.m.-7p.m. appointment and walk-ins accepted
Owner: Emerson Hunt Main St. Marion, SC 843-453-6459

Woods Investment Group
Real Estate, Surety Bonds, GPS monitoring, Stocks & Shares and Senior care investor
843-774-4184

Extreme Monitoring Concepts, LLC
2538 Highway 301 South Suite-D
P.O. Box 863 Dillion, SC 843-774-0077
Distributor: James Woods jameswoods1@att.net
extrememonitoring.org

Emerson's Bonding Company
Call Day or Night Marion, SC 843-453-6459

Sanders Automotive and Paint Mon.-Fri. 8 a.m.-6 p.m.
700 W. Liberty St. Marion, SC 843-250-4928
Owner: Terrel Sanders Sandersautoandpaint@gmail.com

Extreme Medical Transport
2019 Highway 76 Marion, SC
Call Day or Night 843-774-4117

Greater Christ Temple Bible Institute, 2426-C, 3rd Loop Road, Florence, SC, 29501
Dean of Academic and Student Affairs: Dr. Michelle Barr (843) 617-5848
Founder: Dr. Bennie T. Davis Sr (843) 260-7196

New Breed Basketball
Established Spring of 1988
At Voorhees University

Josephus Payton
Everett Hall
Darren Mazyck
Alvin Smith
Glenn Brown BKA House
Tyrone Void
Fedrick Butkus
Theron Robinson
Alonzo James
Yamod Rowell
Yamasi Buey
Chris Brunson
Eddie Washington
Dominique Vereen
Jamel Ham
Joshua Hughes
David Moore
Kobe Goodyear
Tariq Nowlin
Jamell Corish

Jordon Bell
John Brown II
Anthony Lester
Dahmir Wallace
Jaryd Jenkins
Anthony Samuels
Dy'Shaan Johnson
Marus Bryant
Roy Hayden
Kashawn Rowell
Devonte Bethea
Quinton Howard
Artavis R. Evans
D'Ante Allen
D'Vonte Allen
Reese Moe
Kyle Allen
Dwight Allen
Octavia Ortiz A.K.A. Rico

DR. BENNIE T. DAVIS

Marion Adult Basketball Program

YaQuan	Vick	Shane
Genwright (YG)	Chris	Kay Fox
Michael J	Cheese	Shemar
Old School	Boss Hog	Ronnie
Dre	Josh	Kobe
Eddie	KB	Boodie
BJ	Huey	Shone Gause
Mike	Justin	Tracy Grant
Dee	Moon	
Brandon	Charles	

Losing A Loved One Through Gun Violence

DaShamel Prince Drayton was shot and murdered at the age of twenty-three. Losing him was like having the rug snatched from under me. Life before his death was usually a daily routine of responsibilities and plans, never imagining or thinking twice about how those plans could change in a matter of seconds. I never thought much about it until the shock and horror of it happening to me and to my family.

DaShamel was here, and just like that, he was gone.... The total unbelief that my brother, my sibling, my friend had been shot and killed still causes intense sorrow and anger today. His sudden, unexpected, violent, and senseless death stabbed my heart with such horrific pain and grief. It took away my reason for hope (because he would not be coming back). His death has caused my family to try extremely hard to adjust to the world without him. I realize too that my parents lost their child which is a very different type of loss with more intensity and grief. I heard it, and I believe it: "there is no pain like the death of your child."

It has been almost five years since DaShamel's murder, and the grief and pain still linger, and the sights and sounds of that horrible time are still ever present. Occasionally, the pain is not as severe, but it is always there, and there is always something to bring back to mind that fatal day. My mother, father, and the entire family are slowly healing, but the scar of such a horrendous event will never totally leave us. His death was senseless, and his life was snatched away due to GUN VIOLENCE. My daily prayer is that all gun violence stops. We are losing young men every day, and it is the loved ones who must remain in continued grief and pain.

Raymond Christopher White III was born on November 6, 1971, and left this life on April 11, 1998, due to gun violence. He was killed when six men broke into his home and began shooting. Raymond and two of his visiting friends were murdered (one a US soldier). My brother was in his own home where this merciless and brutal murder occurred. This was my brother who was loved deeply, and just by the pull of a trigger, my brother was gone. I could have never imagined his life would have been stolen from him in such a tragic way (raging GUN VIOLENCE). The pain has never stopped. My heartache is severe because the killers evaded capture even after being positively named. There has been no Justice. No, nothing will bring him back, but to have no closure makes the hurt forever present. We (my family, community members, those that heard or read about it) do know that justice was not served fairly.

It has been twenty-four years since Raymond Christopher's death. My mother and I were at the Flea Market last week when my brother's murderer walked by us. Oh, how hurtful, fearful, unfair, and frightening that was. My mother grabbed her chest. The feeling she experienced was indescribable as it was because of that person her son no longer lives. Thoughts overflowed mother's mind, but hearing the Lord whisper softly, "The battle is the Lord's," gave us both the strength to walk and get into the car. Gun violence harms and destroys so many people. It affects the victim, and it extends to the survivors, bystanders, neighbors, and all those who love them. Gun Violence is so tragic, so devastating, and it must STOP! Please continue to pray for the healing of my family and me.

ABOUT THE AUTHOR

Reverend Dr. Bennie T. Davis Sr. is the eldest child of Bobbie J. Davis and the late Daniel Thomas Jr. He is the father of three children (Ashley Davis, Antoinette Davis, and Bennie T. Davis Jr.) and three grandchildren (JaMiyah Davis, Kehlani Fletcher, and Messiah Davis). Pastor Davis graduated from Marion High School in 1987. Upon graduation, he went on to further his education at Voorhees College. He obtained his Bachelor of Science degree in Criminal Justice in 1992. In 2000, he continued his education at Cathedral Bible College and obtained his master's degree in Christian Education. He said, "Why stop there?" In 2005, he received his doctorate degree in Christian Education. He is currently an instructor for Cathedral Bible College. He continues to further his education with Grace Tabernacle Bible College, pursuing his master's degree in theology.

In September 1997, God called him to bring the Word of God to every man, woman, boy, and girl. In November 1997, he started a youth/adult center. He started the center because of the different problems and situations that he encountered and had to endure. Dr. Davis wanted people to know that he was not the same man that he used to be. This is how he came up with the name "I'm Not That Way Anymore Youth/Adult Center Inc." The purpose of the center is to help young people find jobs, educational referrals for GED, housing, and things to help them become self-sufficient and productive citizens of Marion County. Dr. Davis believes through Christ that he would be able to help every person that came through the Center regardless of sex, crime, religion, and their status that society has put on them. Dr. Davis' theme is 'lifting and lending a helping hand'.

In 1994, Dr. Davis joined Power Outreach Cathedral of Faith Ministry where Dr. William Young Jr. is the pastor. In October 2000, he joined Pleasant Grove Missionary Baptist Church where Dr. A.C. Robinson is the pastor. In 2001, Rev. Dr. Bennie T. Davis Sr. became a licensed ordained minister.

Dr. Davis currently serves on many boards throughout Marion County. He is serving on several committees for school district 7. He is over the pretrial intervention (PTI) community service program through the solicitor's office. He is a licensed mentor for the state of South Carolina. He is an instructor of Strong Sons in which he works on developing the young men of Marion County into self-sufficient adults. He serves on the Truancy Council for Marion School Districts. He also serves as Chaplain for all the state and federal prisons of South Carolina.

In the community, he also served as a chaplain at the local detention center and at MUSC hospital in Marion County. He served as an assistant coach for Marion High School JV and Varsity Basketball team from 2017-2020. In 2016, Dr. Bennie T. Davis Sr. founded and started Greater Christ Temple Bible Institution; he is also the president and instructor. The graduation class of 2020 and 2021 Greater Christ Temple Bible Institution had the biggest class both years.

On November 12, 2022, Dr. Davis became an author of, "Tell All I'm Not That Way Anymore". He ran for Mayor of the city of Marion two times but will keep running until he becomes Mayor. Every person has success; they must make a choice to sink or swim. Dr. Bennie T. Davis Sr. all his life he always chose to swim. This is some of the things that Dr. Bennie T. Davis Sr. was able to accomplish as a below-average student. In September 2022, Dr. Bennie T Davis Sr. released his first book "Tell All I'm Not That Way Anymore". Dr. Davis also started a new social club called "Forward March". This social club is to stop gun violence, drugs, crimes, or anything that will send anyone to prison or death. Dr. Davis believes whatever effort a person used to fail in life, it takes the same effort to succeed in life. Life is like a football field. A football field is a hundred yards. If a person stands on the 50-yard line. To get to the touchdown to the left is fifty yards and touchdown to the right is fifty yards. To fail in life is fifty yards; and to succeed in life is fifty yards. Now make the decision on which way you would like to go in life. To fail or to be successful each is fifty yards. Now make the decision to fail or be successful.

To Engage Dr. Bennie T. Davis Sr. for:

Church

Organizations

Speaking

Workshops

Revivals

Please contact:

Dr. Jeanette Waiters

Email: jeanettewaiters@att.net

Phone: 843 992-3333

Or

Dr. Vanessa Sansbury

Email: vsansbury1953@gmail.com

Phone: 843 393-7952

DR. BENNIE T. DAVIS

Made in the USA
Columbia, SC
09 November 2023